D1602471

RELIGIOUS AMBIGUITY
AND
RELIGIOUS DIVERSITY

RELIGIOUS AMBIGUITY
AND
RELIGIOUS DIVERSITY

ROBERT McKIM

OXFORD
UNIVERSITY PRESS

2001

OXFORD
UNIVERSITY PRESS

Oxford   New York

Athens   Auckland   Bangkok   Bogotá   Buenos Aires   Calcutta
Cape Town   Chennai   Dar es Salaam   Delhi   Florence   Hong Kong   Istanbul
Karachi   Kuala Lumpur   Madrid   Melbourne   Mexico City   Mumbai
Nairobi   Paris   São Paulo   Shanghai   Singapore   Taipei   Tokyo   Toronto   Warsaw

and associated companies in
Berlin   Ibadan

Copyright © 2001 by Robert McKim

Published by Oxford University Press, Inc.,
198 Madison Avenue, New York, New York 10016

Oxford is a registered trademark of Oxford University Press

Library of Congress Cataloging-in-Publication Data
McKim, Robert.
Religious ambiguity and religious diversity / Robert McKim.
p.   cm.
Includes bibliographical references and index.
ISBN 0-19-512835-4
1. Religion—Philosophy.   2. Hidden God.   3. Religious pluralism.
4. Belief and doubt.   I. Title.
BL51.M226   2000
200—dc21   99-44714

1 3 5 7 9 8 6 4 2

Printed in the United States of America
on acid-free paper

To Norma

PREFACE

Once upon a time the religious traditions were distanced from each other, both geographically and mentally. The typical member of the typical tradition would learn about other traditions from travelers' tales, for example. There was us and there was them. Now they are our neighbors, and we are no longer at a distance. If they are our neighbors, and we are no longer distanced from them, then what can we do but try to find out what they think? What can we do but ask what is the appeal of their point of view?

But here is the rub. Taking other traditions as seriously as they ought to be taken may shake one's tradition to the core: in particular, it may require a different attitude toward one's own beliefs. For each tradition, by its very presence, is something of a barrier to the certainty and confidence that are expected of the adherents of the others. By its very existence, Catholicism is a difficulty for Islam, Islam is an obstacle for Hinduism, Hinduism is an inconvenience for Judaism, and so on.

Yet the religions of the world have barely begun to wrestle with the implications of the fact of religious diversity. In many countries today the traditions cooperate in various ways; they are all to some extent trying to cope with the modern world, and the attempt to cope in this as in other contexts can make for strange bedfellows. Nevertheless, among the main religions there are precious few genuine attempts to take other traditions seriously.

Predictions in this area are risky, but in our increasingly interconnected world it probably will become difficult to escape the fact that reflection in this area now has to be engaged in with an appreciation of the diversity of the world's religions. An awareness that none of the traditions may reasonably be distinguished from the others by virtue of the integrity of its adherents, or their intelligence, or their degree of virtue, will—in some contexts at least—generate a tendency to think of adherence to one's tradition as a matter of choice, perhaps as a matter of choosing the lifestyle or code of conduct or cultural ethos that goes with it, or as a matter of selecting one viewpoint when there are a number of reasonable ones. Perhaps there will emerge from an acquaintance with other worldviews some awareness that the traditions represent a number of honest attempts to grapple with something obscure, or that these attempts are equally credible or close to being equally credible, or that one should be tentative in the beliefs that one holds as a member of any particular tradition. The latter reactions are especially likely to occur if the acquaintance with other worldviews is not derived from books or documentaries, for example, but is rather based on firsthand and extensive interaction with people from other faiths. However, my aim is to make recommendations rather than predictions.

My view is that in our era other religious traditions can no longer properly be dismissed or ignored. It should no longer be respectable to accept any particular set of religious beliefs without taking note of, and taking to heart in certain respects that I will explain, the fact that there is such great diversity in religious beliefs. It seems clear that people in the religious traditions should be more bothered by the fact of diversity than they are. For diversity is a great difficulty for orthodox religion. We might think of it this way. The data with which you have to deal as a religious believer typically include both data that are internal to your tradition and data that are external to your tradition. The internal data include the teachings of your tradition, the contents of the sacred texts if there are any, and the pronouncements of recognized religious authorities if there are any. The external data include information both from the sciences and from other academic fields, as well as information about other religious traditions. The task which the traditions have to confront, and the task which one has to confront as an individual, is to try to combine all of these data. This is difficult. And there is no saying what will issue from the process. Responsible religious belief should involve dialogue, openness, exchange, open-ended exploration, and conversation with various other bodies of discourse. Anything less is parochial and unsatisfactory.

In this book I will not try to assess thoroughly the merits of any religious position, whether it be theism, atheism, agnosticism, or the set of views associated with one of the great nontheistic traditions. I assume that these are all serious options for intelligent people: they may all be held in an intellectually respectable way. There are considerations that support various religious claims, and there are considerations that count against those claims. For example, there are reasons to be a theist, a believer in God, and reasons not to be a theist. Thus the religious experiences that many people enjoy provide them with significant evidence for the beliefs that they associate with that evidence, such as the belief that God exists. Evils of various sorts, on the other hand, constitute significant evidence against the claim that God exists. While religious belief cannot reasonably be dismissed by appeal to some easy device such as the positivists' account of meaning or one or other of the naturalistic theories that purport to explain it away, such as Marxism or Freudianism, the availability of various naturalistic alternatives to religion, some of which are not altogether implausible, nevertheless constitutes something of a challenge to religious belief.

Which side is supported by the most reasons, and how one might go about deciding this issue, is another matter. There is a vast and ever-growing literature in this field, and in this book I will not make major forays into it. For example, I will not attempt to wade through the classical arguments for and against the existence of God. Actually, I am doubtful about our capacity to resolve conclusively issues such as those about which there is disagreement among the religions. For instance, it seems that the existence of God can be neither proven nor disproven. A consideration to which theists are inclined to point in support of their beliefs, such as the fact of apparent design in the world, obviously is open to interpretations that weaken its support for theism. Contemporary theistic appeals to cosmic fine-tuning are balanced by naturalistic appeals to chance and, for example, the many-universes hypothesis. It seems equally clear that it is not possible to disprove the existence of God. And as a general rule, apologetic maneuvers that can be made on behalf of one tradition can be made on behalf of the others. This includes, for example, appeals to religious experience and to the basic belief apologetic. Where does that leave us? In my view, it leaves us with the conclusion that the world is religiously ambiguous.

People who are deeply committed to the existence of God tend to think that God's existence can be proven; their opponents tend to think that it can be disproven. It is natural, and to be expected, that people on all sides should deploy arguments in attempts to buttress their positions. In fact, it seems that there is no limit to how clever and ingenious people who hold the various familiar positions can be in unearthing and concocting considerations that they can make use of. If you are really clever, after all, you probably will be able to think of some objection to almost any position and of some response to almost any objection. We seem to have a remarkable capacity to find arguments that support positions which we antecedently hold. Reason is, to a great extent, the slave of the prior commitments. Take the best known theistic philosopher and the best known atheistic philosopher you can think of. Would it not be surprising if the former were to produce a publication whose purpose is to point out the weaknesses of an argument for theism or the strengths of an argument for atheism? And would it not be surprising if the latter were to produce a publication whose purpose is to point out the weaknesses of an argument for atheism or the strengths of an argument for theism?

I find all of this unsatisfying, although not surprising. It makes me wonder about the role of systematic reflection in debates about religion: Are such debates just so many spinning wheels that do not contribute to generating new positions and to changing how people think? Surely there is something dubious about looking incessantly for arguments to buttress your own position, whatever it may be. Surely there is something to be said, too, for acknowledging and exploring the *weaknesses* of one's own position and the strengths of the opposition. Why spend one's time trying to show the superiority of one's own side over the alternatives? Why not try to understand what is to be said for the opposing view? People tend to do what they can to support their beliefs about religion: they read books that support those beliefs, and they associate with those who agree with them; would it not be prudent also to read books that support other people's beliefs? For they, too, have wrestled with the perplexing issues, have honestly tried to understand, and sometimes have even been willing to make sacrifices and to suffer for their beliefs.

The majority of people get their religious beliefs from their upbringing, and they grow up to inhabit a religious world that feels as real and solid, or almost as real and solid, as the physical world. That is, the world *is* a certain way, and that is that: and this applies to its religious dimensions as much as it does to, say, its geology. This is so for the man or woman in the pew, in the mosque, and in the temple, alike; it is also so both for laypersons and for those who lay claim to special expertise, such as clergy or theologians or other religious leaders, alike. Increased knowledge of other traditions and more interaction with members of other traditions probably tend to change this attitude. They certainly *ought* to do so. In the past the important issues confronting a member of a tradition included the questions of how deeply to go with your own tradition; how greatly to let it matter to you; and how dominant it should be in your life. Now we confront many traditions. And it is sheer parochialism to look at things in the old business-as-usual way. To fail to see this is to suffer from a failure of imagination.

If you are a serious member of a religious tradition, your own tradition *feels* right. Its beliefs and practices feel right and appropriate, whereas those of other traditions typically feel strange and alien. There is an obvious reason why this sense of what feels right is a most doubtful and unreliable indicator of what is true. Consider your own religious position, whatever it may be. Now consider what it must feel like to be a devout Iranian Shiite Muslim, or a committed Northern Irish Presbyterian, or an observant Israeli Orthodox Jew, assuming that you do not answer to one of these descriptions. Is the sense of being on the right path any less developed, the sense of inner conviction less intense, the sense that one's life experience meshes with one's life less deep, for those others? Of course not. To think otherwise is sheer parochialism. It is plain, in short, that a sense, even a deep sense, of being on the right path is not a reliable indicator that one *is* on the right path.

I approach the issues with which I deal in a very individualistic way: by this I mean that I assume that to a considerable extent each person can make up his or her own mind about what to believe concerning religious matters. Philosophy of religion typically is individualistic in this respect, and I follow suit: as I discuss in chapter 3, I assume that each of us can exercise some control over our beliefs. We certainly feel that we can do so.

I share with much contemporary explicitly theistic philosophy, and with ordinary theists in all of the theistic traditions, a realist interpretation of many religious claims. For instance, I assume that, if God exists, God is a being who in important ways resembles a person, who is omnipotent, omniscient, and benevolent, who acts, thinks, wills, and so forth, and *who is external to us*. I also share with many more traditional philosophers of religion an impatience with those who would presume to tell us, often with an arrogant dismissal of those who lack the requisite insight, what is *really going* on among those who hold religious beliefs, but whose account of what is going on differs markedly from what people in the tradition themselves believe to be going on.

On the other hand, one of the many points on which the religions, including their philosophical adherents, deserve criticism is this. In general the religions do not encourage their adherents to probe, dissect, question, and think critically, to take what they choose from the tradition and to discard the rest. Rather, each tradition typically expects its adherents to throw themselves into acceptance, to wholeheartedly embrace its practices, way of life, and outlook. Indeed, the religions often go beyond expecting this: when they can get away with it, they *demand* it.

I consider it to be obvious that the religious traditions, whether they be Christian, Jewish, Muslim, Hindu, Buddhist, or something else, typically attempt to give an account of, among other things, how it came about that there is a universe, of how it came about that there are beings like us in it, and of what sorts of beings we are. Religions attempt to describe how things are in these and in numerous other areas. Let us call this the cognitive part of religion. Now the claims of the different traditions in these and in many other areas are for the most part inconsistent. Although there are areas of agreement, and there may be some areas in which apparently incompatible claims may turn out on closer inspection to be compatible, it is generally correct to say that if, for example, the Buddhists are right, the other traditions are wrong in much of what they claim. Religions obviously include a lot more than their cognitive part. And it is wrong to put too much emphasis on beliefs and doctrines and to ignore, say, the social aspects of religion, the role that religious beliefs play in the lives of those who accept them, the entire structure of practices and institutions with which the beliefs are associated, and so forth. Yet if you disregard the cognitive part of the traditions and say that the religions are really all about something else, such as providing moral guidance, or expressing the moral aspirations of a culture, or providing hope, or providing ways of coping with grief or hardship or distress, you simply empty religion of much that is distinctive of it, and of much that its practitioners value about it.

I should also say here at the outset that I am interested in exploring a certain religious perspective: I want to explore the possibilities for involvement in a tradition in the face of the arguments contained in the following chapters. My concern in part of what follows is with the forms of religious belief that are viable, given what I take to be our circumstances. So what follows has both positive and negative parts. The negative part is critical of religious orthodoxy; and the positive part consists in an exploration of forms of religious commitment that remain viable.

I try to focus on issues that are important to ordinary people rather than on esoteric problems that are of interest only to professional scholars in the relevant fields. I have found the following two questions to be of deep interest to many people. Why are the facts in the area of religion not more obvious? For example, if God exists, why is it not more obvious that God exists? And do the competing claims of the traditions cancel each other out as far as their believability is concerned?

Religions provide people with a way to feel comfortable and at home in the universe. But the nagging fact of ambiguity and the new awareness of diversity (and the growing consciousness of its import) lead many people to feel a sense of disquiet. And so they should.

My debts are numerous. Many friends, colleagues, students, and correspondents have helped me greatly as I have tried to work out my views on the topics with which I deal here. Some have given me extensive written comments, and some have given me the benefit of their thoughts in conversation. In particular I would like to thank Philip Barnes, David Berman, Hugh Chandler, Eric Freyfogle, Frank Gourley, Jeff Jordan, Reza Lahroodi, Michael Liston, Barry Long, Mark Michaelis, Bryan Nevins, Paschal O'Gorman, Paul Saka, Bill Schoedel, Bill Schroeder, and Tim Van Laar. Comments from the reviewers for Oxford University Press, one of whom I now know to be Philip Clayton, have also been of great assistance. Special thanks to Matt Davidson for many acute and insightful suggestions.

January 2000
Urbana, Illinois

R. M.

CONTENTS

Part I: The Hiddenness of God

1   The Hiddenness of God: Introduction   3
    1.   What Does It Mean to Say that God is Hidden?   6
    2.   Two Competing Tendencies   9
    3.   Reasons for Believing That God Is Hidden from Everyone   10
    4.   The Disadvantages of God's Hiddenness   12
    5.   Unsatisfactory Responses to God's Hiddenness   14
    6.   Classifying Theistic Responses to the Hiddenness of God   16
    7.   Ambiguity   21

2   God's Hiddenness and the Possibility
    of Moral Action   26
    1.   The Importance of Being Responsible   26
    2.   Kant on the Need for God to Be Hidden If Morality
         Is to Be Possible   29
    3.   The Importance of Being Able to be Immoral: Swinburne   34
    4.   Mesle's Objections   39
    5.   Schellenberg's Objections   41
    6.   Conclusion   46

3   God's Hiddenness, Freedom to Believe, and Attitude Problems   49
    1.   God's Hiddenness and Freedom to Believe   49
    2.   Penelhum's Objection   55
    3.   Responses to Penelhum's Objection   56

   4. The Varieties of Religious Belief 58
   5. Responses to the "Varieties Objection" 60
   6. The Trouble with Cryptovolitionalism 63
   7. Attitude Problems 64
   8. The Problematic Attitudes 66
   9. Problems 69

4 Trust and Other Goods of Mystery 73
   1. Divine Hiddenness and Human Trust: Adams and Adams 73
   2. Varieties of Trust 75
   3. Some Other Alleged Goods of Mystery 80
   4. Unknown Goods of Mystery 87
   5. Implications of the Possibility of Unknown Goods of Mystery 90

5 The Hiddenness of God and Arguments for Atheism 92
   1. The Case for Epistemic Atheism 92
   2. Being Well Situated Epistemically 93
   3. Having "No Good Evidence" for p 94
   4. Schellenberg's Case for Atheism: The Central Argument 97
   5. Objections to Schellenberg's Argument 100
   6. The Possibility of a Cumulative Case 103

6 The Hiddenness of God: Implications 105
   1. The Hidden Emperor 105
   2. Implications of God's Hiddenness 108
   3. Explaining God's Hiddenness 108
   4. The Balance of Goods and the Importance of Belief 112
   5. Disaster Avoidance 116
   6. Disaster Avoidance, the Hiddenness of God, and
      the Importance of Belief 120
   7. God's Hiddenness and Tentative Theistic Belief 123

Part II: Religious Diversity

7: Religious Diversity: Introduction 127
   1. "The Other Side" 127
   2. Disagreement about Religion 128
   3. Deep and Widespread Disagreement 133
   4. Importance 137
   5. The Critical Stance: The E-Principle and the T-Principle 138
   6. Allies and Anticipations 142
   7. Examining Beliefs 146
   8. Observations on the E-Principle and on Its Implications for
      Beliefs about Religion 149

8 The Critical Stance I: Tentative Religious Belief 154
   1. Tentative Religious Belief 154
   2. But Can Religious Belief Be Tentative? 159

3. Tentative Belief and the Prospects for Commitment 166
4. Tentative Belief and Cognitive Commitment 170
5. Audi's Proposals 170
6. Tentative Belief and Tolerance 177

9 The Critical Stance II: Arguments and Objections 181
1. The Appeal to Ambiguity 181
2. The Appeal to the Integrity of Others and
    to Respect for Others 184
3. The Appeal to the Possibility of a Compromise 187
4. The Import of These Considerations 188
5. Objections 190
6. Conclusion 203

10 Religious Experience and Religious Belief 206
1. Experience and Initial Justification 208
2. The Principle of Credulity 210
3. Disagreement and Justification 212
4. Differences between the Two Cases 213
5. Some Varieties of Religious Experience 216
6. The Possibility of Indubitable Experiences 221
7. The Gap between Experience and Doctrine 225
8. The Two Sources of Religious Experience 229
9. More on the Significance of Appeals to Experience 231

11 Alston on Religious Experience 234
1. Alston's Theory 234
2. External Contradiction 238
3. The Force of Alston's Claims 240
4. Religious Diversity 243
5. Reduced Justification 245
6. Reduced Rationality 250
7. Third-Person Justification 252

Notes 255

Index 275

I

THE HIDDENNESS OF GOD

1

~•➤•◦•◄•~

THE HIDDENNESS OF GOD: INTRODUCTION

It seems, or so I shall argue at any rate, that neither the existence of God nor the nature of God is apparent or obvious. It therefore needs to be asked why, if God exists, it is not entirely clear to everyone that this is so, and why in general the facts about God are not entirely clear to everyone. By "God" I mean a being that is omnipotent, perfectly good, omnipresent, infinitely perfect, and than whom no greater being can be conceived. Theism is the view that there is such a being.

There is considerable reason to believe that it would be well within the abilities of God to let God's existence and nature be known more fully to us.[1] One wonders therefore why the existence and nature of our Heavenly Father are not as apparent as, say, the existence of our various earthly fathers. If God exists, why isn't atheism as foolish as, say, denial of the existence of other people or of the external world or of the past? In this and the following five chapters, I address such issues. I examine various attempts that theists have made to explain God's hiddenness, and I discuss the plausibility of those attempts.

There can be no doubt that, if God exists, the fact that God exists is a fact of which plenty of sane, well-balanced, honest people are thoroughly ignorant. Attempts to contend that people who claim to be ignorant of God's existence actually know that God exists in their "heart of hearts" are unconvincing, not to mention presumptuous:[2] they are about as compelling as the counterpart sweeping claim that theists know in their "heart of hearts" that God does not exist but are deceiving themselves or engaging in wishful thinking.

Of course there are plenty of facts, and plenty of dimensions of human life, of which plenty of people are ignorant. It might be objected that a widespread lack of knowledge of God is on a par with, say, a lack of knowledge of art or of some other dimension of human life, or area of human knowledge, of which large numbers of people are ignorant, and sometimes are so in virtue of some fault on their part: it might be objected that since there are many such areas, the hiddenness of God is not at all unique. As is the case with genetics, nuclear engineering, and literary criticism, for example, there are those who have the requisite background and training to understand what is going on and others who don't. That outsiders are baffled is just what you would expect.

Yet the existence of God is such a globally significant fact, one with ramifications for so many areas in human life, that ignorance of it is, on the face of it, surprising. If some people are in constant communication and interaction with God, asking things from God and sometimes receiving them, and if some are even in a position to write great tomes and sets of tomes on the nature, character, intentions, and so forth, of God, while many others are unaware even that there is such a being, this too, on the face of it, is a remarkable state of affairs—although it does not follow that it cannot be explained. It seems roughly on a par with ignorance of the fact that there are other people, or that there are such things as emotions, or that China exists, for example. One feature of ignorance in the theistic case is that unlike the cases of academic disciplines that require special training, and the areas of inquiry that are not of interest to everyone and are recognized by the cognoscenti as such, the theistic traditions themselves generally think of an awareness of God as something that is available to everyone; widespread ignorance in this area is, therefore, that much more of a puzzle.

Many theists seem not to think that our present ignorance of the facts about God is desirable or at least is altogether a good thing. This is suggested by the belief in a future state in which our ignorance will be remedied. Most theists hope for, believe in, and await a future state in which what is now hidden will be made clear. The Christian New Testament, for instance, writes that "now we see through a glass darkly; but then face to face: now I know in part; but then shall I know even as also I am known" (1 Cori. 13:12). God's hiddenness appears to be thought of by some theists, at least to some extent, as something to be remedied.

The general topic of the hiddenness of God includes a number of distinct issues. Why are the existence and nature of God not obvious to everyone? If God exists, why is it not irrational to be, say, a nontheistic Hindu or an atheist or a polytheist? Why is there room within theism for so many competing and contradictory interpretations of the nature and activities of God? Why isn't one group (e.g., Presbyterians or Hasidim or Shiite Muslims) obviously right? These are some of the questions that I propose to consider.

I will examine the plausibility of various theistic responses to the hiddenness of God. However, my arguments are intended to be equally relevant to the various forms of theism, and in particular to Judaism, Christianity, and Islam. No doubt my own orientation and background are apparent at many points, including some I do not recognize, but my aspiration is to pose a problem and to consider various putative solutions to it in terms that would at least be intelligible to members of the various theistic traditions. My arguments are also intended to be as convincing to the skeptic as they are to the theist. Indeed, if it should emerge that there is an adequate explanation of God's hiddenness, this result should lead at least some skeptics to question their skepticism. For if it should emerge that a state of affairs in which we are not aware of the existence of God, or in which our awareness is very limited, is just what you would expect if God were to exist, then the fact that we are not aware of God's existence, or have little awareness, does not provide much evidence against God's existence. In that case, to the extent that skepticism is based on the fact that we do not have much of an awareness of God's existence, it would be poorly based. But while my arguments presuppose no particular version of theism and are intended to be convincing to the nonbeliever as well as to the believer, they concern an issue that arises within theism. The fundamental question before us is this. Theism presents an account of a being in whom we are to believe and yet whose existence and character are not clear to us. Does this aspect of theism compromise its coherence?

Deployment of a generic sort of theism might be questioned. It might be objected that to talk of God is to talk of a being about whom very specific things are believed by the different traditions and that it is not altogether clear what talk of God which does not presuppose the context of some particular tradition is *about*. My response is as follows. We *could* proceed by assuming the teachings of some particular tradition about God, framing our questions in the context of its assumptions. We could examine the teachings of this tradition about the hiddenness of God and see what they amount to. But I prefer another approach. A degree of abstraction from the particular traditions is possible. Many of the same beliefs about God are shared by the theistic traditions: these include the belief that God exists, is omnipotent, thoroughly good, and thoroughly just, has created the universe, deserves to be worshiped, wishes for human beings what is best for them, wishes that human beings will worship God, and so forth. A being would not count as God unless it had such attributes as these. The question as I pose it is this. Can we give a satisfactory account of why a being of this sort would be hidden from us to the degree that God is now hidden? We can approach this question without thinking of it as a question posed within the confines of any particular tradition; yet in wrestling with it we can draw on suggestions and proposals from any of the theistic traditions. By discussing theism of a generic sort, I mean to discuss an issue that arises for all of the theistic traditions.

In characterizing the hiddenness of God, we can distinguish two dimensions to it. On the one hand, there is the fact that God's existence and nature are not obvious. If God exists, this is a fact about God. On the other hand, there are facts about the world we live in that (if God exists) tend to conceal from us the fact that God exists. (By "the world we live in" in this context I mean the observable universe, and not the totality of all states of affairs that obtain; if God exists, the fact that God exists, and whatever other facts there are about God, are of course part of that total state of affairs.) For instance, the fact that atrocities are frequently perpetrated against the innocent and defenseless, including in particular both innocent and defenseless people who have called on God for help and innocent and defenseless animals that are not in a position to call on anyone, is the sort of fact about the world that generates a certain amount of uncertainty and bewilderment about the existence and nature of God.

The former dimension (that is, the fact that God's existence and nature are not obvious) is the more fundamental one. For even if there were no suffering or other evils it might still be that the facts about God would be unclear. Again, in the face of suffering and evils of other sorts, it might be clear that God exists, and that God has a certain sort of nature. In that case, there might still be a problem of evil, but evil would have a different significance: it would be unlikely to lead people to question God's existence or nature, but it might still be a puzzle, although in such a situation people would perhaps also be in a better position to come up with an adequate and clearly correct theodicy.

However, while the distinction mentioned in the last two paragraphs is a genuine one, there are ways of thinking of the situation such that this distinction becomes unimportant: thus God's existence and nature would be clearer if there were in the world clear and obvious signs of God's presence, as would be the case if virtue were always rewarded, vice always punished, and if various signs and wonders were constantly available. That these clear and obvious signs are not currently available seems to be a fact both about God and about the world.

A brief comment on the relation between the hiddenness of God and the problem of evil. The entire problem of evil may be thought of as part of the problem of the hiddenness of God, since the presence of evil in the world is a fact that makes for the hiddenness of God. It creates uncertainty about the nature of, and even the existence of, God. But one might equally well think of the hiddenness of God as part of the problem of evil. If you consider any aspect of the world or of our human circumstances that seems difficult to reconcile with the existence of a deity who is omnipotent, omniscient, and benevolent, to be part of the problem of evil, then the hiddenness of God is part of the problem of evil.[3] Insofar as this is the case, an explanation of the hiddenness of God is of course a contribution to accounting for the existence of evil.

1. What Does It Mean to Say That God Is Hidden?

Talk of the hiddenness of God (and claims such as the claim that God is hidden) can be construed in various ways. Someone who considers it to be utterly obvious that God exists might say that God is hidden. By saying this he might, for example, mean that the purposes or will of God is concealed from us, or is not clear in some situation. Or he might mean that God is somewhat removed from our day-to-day experience, or that God acts in unexpected ways, or that God has failed to intervene in some situation, or is felt by believers to be neglecting God's people.[4] I mean something quite different by the claim that God is hidden. The central idea is just that it is not clear whether the claims that theists make about God are true; and this applies both to the claim that God exists and to numerous theistic claims about the character, purposes, will, and so forth of God.

It could be clearer than it now is that God exists. Perhaps there could be a proof of God's existence. If there were a proof, it would be irrational for anyone who has access to it not to believe that God exists. There seems not to be such a proof; at least there seems not to be a sound deductive argument with premises acceptable to someone who does not already believe that God exists. However, the significance of this fact is not altogether clear. It may be that the existence of God is not something that could be proven, either because there is nothing whose existence can be proven or because the existence of God, in particular, cannot be proven.

Whatever may be the explanation of our lack of a proof, it seems easy to think of phenomena that would render God's existence more apparent than it now is. There might be voices from on high, writing in the sky, and so on. (Suppose the sky over Teheran were lit up with the words "Allahu Akhbar" every night; or suppose that the sky over Sligo were lit up each evening with a verse from the Psalms. And suppose that in neither case were we able to see any plausible naturalistic explanation of the phenomenon.) Or it might be that we enjoy experiences of some other sort that would render the existence of God sufficiently evident that it would be irrational, or a lot less rational than it now is, not to believe that God exists. The character of the experience might be such that the best available explanation of its occurrence is that God has caused it or has contributed to its occurrence. Or the experience might involve perceiving clearly that God exists or that certain propositions that entail the proposition that God exists are true. Or it could be that when people pray to God for help, they always receive help in a clear and incontrovertible way, often including the provision of sudden and apparently miraculous cures. Or next year's astronomical discoveries could be announced to us in advance. Again, the veracity of a being with whom we are constantly interacting could be made very clear to us, and this being could tell us that it is God. So it seems clear that we could encounter phenomena that would make it somewhat, and perhaps even a lot, less rational than it now is not to believe that God exists.

Whether we could encounter phenomena that would make it as irrational not to believe in God as it now is not to believe in, say, the existence of other people or the existence of the external world and whether any such phenomena could have probative value akin to that of a proof is more questionable. It seems that any communications we received, or experiences we had, could be accounted for without appeal to an infinite, omnipotent, thoroughly good (etc.) being, but rather by appeal to a lesser being. (To labor the point, the government, or aliens, could arrange for writing in the sky.) It is a familiar point that it does not take infinite power or knowledge to provide us with what will be next year's astronomical discoveries, to heal the sick, feed the hungry, or even to raise someone from the dead; *great* power would suffice. If this is right, it seems that no such phenomena could make it irrational not to believe that God exists to the extent that a proof would make it irrational not to believe. Still, such phenomena could make it less rational not to believe than it now is. And quite apart from the issue of the existence of God, the nature, character, and purposes of God could be clearer. It could be clearer to us what God's purposes are and what God's nature is like: it could be clear, or at least clearer, to us that on all such matters one of the competing views is correct and the others incorrect. The general picture is that the facts about God might be clear, or at least clearer than they now are.

Yet some people, including both ordinary folk and some philosophers and theologians who have reflected at length on such matters, seem to find the existence of God entirely obvious; they say things like this: "How can anyone wonder whether or not God exists? Look at the trees, the birds, the flowers, see how spring comes every year. . . ." And so on. One author has referred to this as the "biblical perspective," since, as he points out, the biblical writers "accepted the existence of God as a manifestly evident fact. The rising sun, the growing wheat, the flying sparrow all made it perfectly clear, given their pre-scientific worldview, that God exists and cares. . . . . It is important to recognize that God's existence was thought to be obvious to all, not merely to a few prophets and saints."[5] People who have the biblical perspective may be willing to *say* that God is hidden, but as indicated earlier, they would mean something different from what I have in mind.

Are people who have the biblical perspective just aware of things that other people are missing? Do they see something to which others are blind? Or are they imposing a certain interpretation on what they experience? For example, have they thought of the coming of spring in a theistic way for so long, and with such depth of feeling, that when they think of spring they take it as obvious that God is responsible for it?

My response to these questions is as follows. Perhaps for some people the existence of God is obvious, and the nature of God is also obvious so that it would be irrational for them not to believe that God exists and not to believe that God has the character they believe God to have. Perhaps in virtue of their experiences some people have their faith confirmed to such an extent that it is perfectly clear to them that God exists and that God has such and such a nature. Certainly there are plenty of people from numerous traditions who will tell you that they know about God, that God is not hidden from them, and indeed that the problem of the hiddenness of God, as construed here, is not a genuine problem. I see no way to rule out, nor do I wish to rule out, the possibility that some people are in this privileged position. On the contrary, this is a possibility to which everyone should be open: we should recognize that we may be missing what others notice, that we may be oblivious to what others discern. However, I will shortly present a series of arguments in support of the claim that God is hidden from all human beings. In any case, my remarks in this and the following chapters pertain mainly to those who are not as fortunately situated as these people claim to be.

Nevertheless, it is clear that many theists are not without reasons to believe that God exists. Such reasons fall into two categories. Some, such as a sense that God is speaking to one or directing one's life, or a sense that God is involved in the ordinary events of one's life, are available solely to the theist.

Others are available to many nontheists. The considerations in this category include the fact that many people report that they have had experiences of God. This information is available to theist and nontheist alike. Many people who report on such experiences seem to be honest and not to be setting out to mislead others. Such reports provide others with some reason to believe that God exists unless, say, those others reasonably believe they have a disproof of God's existence or have every reason to believe that those who report on the experiences in question are deluded. This claim is not called into question by the fact that there is considerable disagreement among the theistic traditions about the being that, it is claimed, is being experienced. What follows from this disagreement is rather that not everyone can be right about everything they say about God. And the disagreement in question may reduce somewhat the amount of evidence provided by reports of experience of God; but there is no reason to think that it reduces it to zero.

In this category (of reasons that are available to many nontheists as well as to theists) are also, for example, design arguments, cosmological arguments, and moral arguments for God's existence: I assume that *some* support for theism is to be found in these areas (although how strong or weak it may be is of course a hotly debated issue); the fact that this is so can be recognized by theists and nontheists alike. But I take it that all of the available support falls far short of constituting a proof and falls short of rendering it irrational not to believe that God exists. The situation is, rather, that honest, intelligent, and reasonable people are nontheists, whether they be nonreligious or belong to one of the nontheistic religions, and they hold such views without compromising their rationality.

So I understand the claim that God is hidden in a rather comprehensive way. In part, as I have just indicated, it bears on the existence of God: if God exists, this is a fact that is not clear to us. And it also bears on the nature of God: if God exists, God has a nature that is not clear to us. It may be that the fact that it is not clear whether God exists is to be explained in one way, whereas the fact that God's nature is very unclear to us is to be explained in another way or in a somewhat different way; or some considerations may contribute more to the explanation in the one area, whereas others may contribute more to the explanation in the other.

Of course a being would not count as God unless it were omnipotent, omniscient, kind, just, and so forth. So we know *that* much about what God is, or would be like: that is, if God exists, God is omnipotent, kind, just, and so forth. So if God's existence were clear to us, it would be clear to us that a being with that sort of nature exists. But our knowledge of what it would take to count as God falls far short of a full understanding of the nature of God. We might know enough about a being whose existence we were sure of to know that being to be God, while remaining in the dark about many aspects and features of this being, such as many of its purposes and other thoughts, and many of its activities, including some that we are capable of understanding. It seems clear that we cannot read these off to a great degree by considering what it would be for God to be just, kind, omnipotent, and so forth. The fact that the belief that God has these properties is combined with quite different beliefs about God's purposes, activities (etc.) in the different theistic traditions provides strong evidence for this latter claim. Still, if God's existence were clear, various aspects of God's nature might then be clearer to us than they now are.

2. Two Competing Tendencies

Actually, the theistic traditions appear to manifest two competing tendencies, which in turn involve two conflicting readings of how hidden God is. As I have mentioned, some theists, or some theists some of the time, assert that God is not hidden at all, and that on the contrary the facts about God are obvious and that people who do not recognize these obvious facts are blinded by sin, or for some other reason lack the ability to recognize these obvious facts; so although the existence of God may not seem obvious to everyone, it certainly is obvious to them, perhaps in virtue of experiences they have; and it would be obvious to others too if they were not blinded by sin or some other defect. Such people believe that they can just perceive that, for example, God is forgiving us (or forgiving them) with much the same clarity that they can see that there is a tree in front of them. There is no need for hesitancy here. It is just obvious.[6]

The second tendency, which is in tension with the first, involves an acceptance that God really is hidden from everyone. As we have already seen in a preliminary way and as we will see in detail as we proceed, theists have offered various putative explanations of why this is so, including explanations that construe God's hiddenness as a consequence of God's nature and others according to which God's hiddenness has important benefits for human beings. This second tendency receives a philosophical formulation in the work of John Hick and Blaise Pascal, for instance. (Pascal goes so far as to say that "any religion that does not say that God is hidden is not true, and any religion which does not explain why does not instruct.")[7] A position of this sort seems to be implicit in the remark in the New Testament that God dwells in "the light which no man can approach unto" and that God is a being "whom no man hath seen, nor can see" (1 Tim. 6:16). Again, in the Hebrew Bible we read as follows: "And the Lord said unto Moses . . . Thou canst not see my face: for there shall no man see me, and live" (Exod. 33:20).

I expect that most theists who take this second position, and who think the facts about God not to be obvious, also think that the facts about God, at least those facts to which we are capable of having access, are at least somewhat more obvious than not. Clark H. Pinnock's position probably is fairly representative: "There will come a day I believe when God will reveal his glory in an unmistakable way and there will no longer be any room for doubt and hesitation. But that day is not yet, and in the meantime we work with reasonable probabilities which, while they do not create or compel belief, do establish the credible atmosphere in which faith can be born and can grow.[8]

Each of the tendencies I have distinguished is well represented within the orthodox forms of theism, and each is consistent with some other standard theistic beliefs and practices. For example, the former tendency fits well with the standard theistic view that an absence of belief is culpable, and with the wish of some theists to deny that their theistic views need to be supported by external evidence. The latter tendency fits well with the fact that the traditions have generally thought it necessary to evangelize and to proselytize. For evangelism typically involves trying to persuade people to adopt a certain religious position—something that would not be necessary, or would be less likely to be necessary, if that position were obviously the correct one. The enterprise of evangelism is more of a puzzle for the position represented by the first tendency, although it is not as though an explanation could not be found for it: emphasis might be placed on the need for a reorientation of character, a changed outlook and vision and a different set of priorities, or on the need to admit what you already know. Such changes as these might need to be made even if the relevant facts *were* obvious for all to see, or as obvious as they can be for beings like us. But evangelism has also typically involved an attempt to persuade people of the truth of certain claims, a fact that supports the latter tendency.

By pointing out that there are these competing tendencies, I mean merely to draw attention to something interesting about theism. I do not mean to suggest that there is no way to reconcile them or even that it is especially difficult to do so. Nor do I mean to suggest that the average theist needs to work out his or her views on such a matter as this. For it would be absurd to expect every believer to ponder every puzzle that arises for his views. Believers have other things to do. In the next section I give my reasons for endorsing the second of these tendencies and for thinking that it should be the dominant one.

3. Reasons for Believing That God Is Hidden from Everyone

My operating assumption is that God's hiddenness is at least an extensive enough phenomenon to merit an explanation. If God exists, God is hidden to a considerable degree from all human beings at all times. This is an enduring feature of human life. Here are eight reasons for thinking this to be so.

First, there are some considerations having to do with the possibility of loss of belief that are relevant. I take the fact that theists sometimes lose their belief in God as evidence that this is so: one wonders how such a belief could be shaken were it not that even for the believer God is hidden. Also, many believers of the most devout and convinced sort sometimes find themselves wondering quite sincerely whether or not God exists, perhaps when they are in circumstances of difficulty or hardship or when they find others in such circumstances, which is something one need not look hard to find. But if the existence of God were clear to them, they would not find themselves so situated. Moreover, the fact that theists generally consider it important to take steps to avoid loss of belief indicates that they think that there is a danger of losing belief and that this is a danger against which all believers should protect themselves: this would not be a danger were God not hidden even from the believer. None of this is conclusive evidence, since it is possible that there is some other explanation of how loss of belief might occur. And there are of course numerous believers who never lose their beliefs, who never find themselves wondering whether or not God exists, and who never feel that they need to take any steps to avoid loss of belief. But it is an important piece of evidence.

Second, countless millions of ordinary people claim, and appear, to have no awareness of God. Many people who appear honest and impartial, and for whose honesty and impartiality as good a case can be made as can be made for anyone else's honesty and impartiality, are not sure what to think about the existence and nature of God.

Third, believers often feel that they lack a clear and strong sense of God's presence, and they often characterize their awareness of the presence of God as sketchy and indecisive. Thus William P. Alston, in his recent sustained defense of the reliability of experience in which people understand themselves to perceive God, says that the perception of God is usually "dim, meager, and obscure."⁹ Not all putative perception of God is reported to be of this indecisive character, but it seems that much of it, at any rate, is.

Fourth, as will be clear from the rest of this chapter and from the next four chapters, theists have offered many explanations of God's hiddenness: the very abundance and variety of these explanations bespeak a widespread recognition among theists of the hiddenness of God. Since there are so many attempted explanations, there probably is something to explain.

Fifth, the preoccupation that many theists have had, and continue to have, with searching for, and formulating, arguments for God's existence, and with undermining arguments against God's existence, is relevant. Why advance the former sort of arguments, and attack the latter, if the fact of God's existence is obvious for all to see?

Sixth, it may be that the explanation of why some people find that God is hidden is that those people have the wrong attitudes or the wrong beliefs or have gone wrong in some other way. This, as I will discuss later, might be thought of as a matter of failing to seek the truth with enough of their energies, being proud instead of humble, refusing to countenance the possibility that God might exist, being utterly unwilling to think or live or respond in ways in which one thinks one ought to think or live or respond if God were to exist, or something else. Insofar as the explanation is to be found in an area such as this, one has reason to concede that God is always hidden from everyone to some extent. At least this is so provided one makes the standard theistic assumption that all people at all times suffer from such defects to some extent.

Seventh, the hiddenness of God has a *cultural* dimension. It seems obvious that the dominant Weltanschauung sometimes makes belief that God exists easier than it does at other times. To a large extent the hiddenness of God consists in the fact that belief that God exists is not a live option for many people in virtue of their cultural context. Thus many people in Buddhist countries, for instance, just do not encounter the belief that God exists as a viable option for belief. It is not among the array of possibilities that their culture delivers to them. I take the fact that cultural transmission of this belief is so important in determining whether someone accepts it, with some cultures or groups making this belief available and some failing to do so, to be a function of the fact that the belief is not obviously true.

Eighth, and last, suppose that it is proposed that it is in virtue of various religious experiences that various people enjoy that God is not hidden from them. I will discuss the relevant issues in more detail in chapters 10 and 11 but, for now, some promissory notes. Reasons to believe that God is hidden even to those who have such experiences are provided by some of the foregoing points. But there are also reasons that have to do with the character of the experiences in question. Suppose, for instance, that the experience in question takes the form of feeling guided by God in various respects in your daily life, perhaps in response to requests for divine guidance. Such an experience seems to provide support for few of the large array of beliefs about God that is accepted in virtue of being, say, a Christian or a Muslim.

The cumulative weight of these reasons is considerable. Even if only some of them are convincing, we have reason to conclude that, if God exists, God is hidden to a considerable extent from almost all human beings at almost all times.

4. The Disadvantages of God's Hiddenness

If God exists but is hidden, this is a perplexing state of affairs. One reason that it is perplexing is internal to theism and arises from the fact that the theistic traditions place such importance on belief. Typically each theistic tradition asserts that to fail to hold theistic beliefs, and especially to fail to hold its theistic beliefs, or at least what it considers to be the most important among them, is to go wrong in a very serious way whereas to adopt theistic beliefs, and especially the set of theistic beliefs associated with it, is a worthwhile and important thing to do. These traditions say, too, that one ought to regret or even feel guilty about a failure to believe. Yet if God is hidden, belief is more difficult than it would be if God were not hidden. If God exists, and if the facts about God's existence and nature were clear, belief would be ever so much easier for us. The theistic traditions are inclined to hold human beings responsible and even to blame them if they are nonbelievers or if their belief is weak. But does this make any sense?

God's hiddenness creates uncertainty and contributes to profound disagreement about the existence and nature of God. Indeed, I would suggest that it contributes more to the occurrence of nonbelief than does the presence of evil in the world (or of other evil in the world, if the hiddenness of God is understood as a type of evil). This is not to deny that there are people who are nontheists because of evils that they either encounter or are familiar with; but it seems that the explanation in most cases of how it has come about that people do not believe that God exists (whether they are atheists or agnostics or members of nontheistic religions) is not that they consider God's existence to be incompatible with various evils. Rather, it is that they have nothing that they understand as an awareness of God. They do not understand themselves to be familiar with God. Consequently, they do not even reach a point where evil is perceived as a problem. If this is correct, it is no exaggeration to say that the hiddenness of God is the main wellspring of nonbelief in God. (This is so whether or not, all things considered, the hiddenness of God is a more serious theological and philosophical problem for theism than is the [rest of the?] problem of evil. My point is a psychological one concerning the role that certain ideas actually play in people's thinking.)

Another reason that the hiddenness of God is perplexing has to do with the sort of personal relationship with God that some theists advocate. This is also a reason that is internal to theism, or at least to theism of a certain sort, especially evangelical and fundamentalist Christianity. The personal relationship in question is understood to involve trust, respect, and, above all, ongoing intimate communication. Is it not reasonable to suppose that if God were less hidden, this sort of relationship would be more widespread?

The hiddenness of God, therefore, seems to be a particularly acute problem for strands of theism that emphasize the importance of fellowship and communication with God.[10] But it is also a problem for the other major strands of theism because they all emphasize the importance and value of belief. And they declare that God cares about us; if God exists and if God cares about us, why does God leave human beings to such an extent in the dark about various religiously important facts? If God does not care about us, there is less to explain. Theism typically requires, too, that we put our trust and confidence in God: But why, then, are the facts about God not more clear? If God exists and the facts about God's existence and nature were more clear, people would be more likely to see that they ought to put their trust and confidence in God and would be more willing and more able to do so.

Another important, and related, disadvantage associated with divine hiddenness is this. If God exists, God is worthy of adoration and worship: given the good, wise, just (etc.) nature of God, and the relation between God and God's creatures, a worshipful response from human beings would be appropriate. For if God exists, God is our Creator and we owe all we have to God. But if many of us are in the dark about the existence and nature of God, then this appropriate human response is made more difficult than it otherwise would be. So part of the cost of divine hiddenness is its contribution to the large-scale failure of human beings to respond to God in ways that seem appropriate in the case of a good, just, and wise creator.

And there are further costs. The profound disagreements about God, and more broadly the profound disagreements that there are about numerous matters of religious importance, often play a role in promoting and exacerbating social conflict. If God exists and if the facts about God were as clear as they could be, there might not be as much room for disagreement, and hence such disagreements would not contribute to social conflict. The mystery surrounding God also provides opportunities for charlatans and frauds to pose as experts on the nature and activities of God, and for religious authorities in numerous traditions to acquire and exercise, and sometimes abuse, power and control over others.

To each of these apparent disadvantages, or costs, of God's hiddenness there corresponds an advantage or benefit that, it appears, would accrue if God were not hidden.

Thus if God were not hidden, and the facts about God were clear for all to see, it appears that belief would be easier for us, a personal relationship with God would be facilitated, more people would worship God, religious disagreement would be less likely to exacerbate social tensions, and there would be fewer opportunities for people to pose as experts and to acquire power and influence over others.

I will refer to the benefits of the relevant facts being clear as *goods of clarity*. I will have a lot to say about these goods, as well as about their counterparts, *goods of mystery*. Goods of mystery are goods that are available only if God is hidden. So their loss would be a cost or disadvantage of God's not being hidden. Correspondingly, as we have just seen, the loss of goods of clarity is a cost or disadvantage of God's hiddenness.

5. Unsatisfactory Responses to God's Hiddenness

There are some responses to the issue of God's hiddenness about which I will say little beyond this section of this chapter. First, there is a theistic response that I will set aside. This is the response that knowledge of God is bestowed on some people and is not bestowed on others in accordance with policies, or in pursuit of purposes, that we are completely unable to begin to understand. So it is impossible for us to understand why God is hidden to some but not to others. And that is all that is to be said. End of discussion. Perhaps it is something along these lines that Pascal has in mind when he writes that "[we] can understand nothing of God's work unless we accept the principle that he wished to blind some and enlighten others."[11] I set this response aside here, since we can make considerable progress in envisioning reasons that God is hidden. Indeed, the theistic traditions are rich in putative explanations of God's hiddenness. A retreat to saying that the whole issue is entirely baffling is therefore unnecessary.

Another response is this. Some would say that it is peculiar to consider the hiddenness of God to be a problem for religious belief, and to suppose that if theism is unable to account for it, then this indicates that there is something problematic about theism. This is peculiar—so this response goes—because the fact that God is hidden is, as it were, partly constitutive of theistic beliefs and practices. God's hiddenness is *assumed* by religion, in its beliefs and practices and institutions. To ask, or try to ask, from the outside, whether theism can account for the hiddenness of God is to impose the standards of one sort of language game on another. Philosophy should try to understand what religious people are about in their thinking and practice and not try to ask inappropriate normative questions about it. God's hiddenness—so this line of thought continues—is part of the *grammar* of theism. Theistic beliefs and practices develop and take their shape in a context in which it is assumed that God is hidden. This is so—this response might, I conjecture, continue—in spite of the fact that theists frequently ask God to reveal God's self or God's plans or purposes to them. For it might be wondered what the point of these entreaties is if God's hiddenness is taken for granted as part of the fabric of theism. But someone who advances the response under discussion might reasonably contend that the entreaties in question are offered in a context in which it is assumed that God will remain hidden to a great extent, and that the point of these entreaties is merely to ask for a slight lifting of the veil of mystery.

This response, which will be forthcoming from some of the advocates of "Wittgensteinian fideism," is salutary insofar as it serves to remind us of the importance of attending to how members of religious traditions actually think and practice. It is important to pay careful attention to the work that beliefs do, the role that they play, in people's lives. It may not be what it appears. D. Z. Phillips rightly says that "religion is not some kind of technical discourse or esoteric pursuit cut off from the ordinary problems and perplexities, hopes, and joys which most of us experience at some time or other."[12]

It is true that the fact that God is hidden is indeed frequently taken for granted in the institutions and practices of theistic religion. That this is so is manifested, for instance, in the fact that religious practice often involves a search for God; it also partially accounts for the further fact that religious people are inclined to dismiss out of hand the suggestion that God's hiddenness is a difficulty for their beliefs, or even at all puzzling. Some who so dismiss this suggestion may feel that the fact that God is hidden has already been taken account of and that there is nothing much here about which to be puzzled.

This response also usefully serves to remind us that there is some truth to the idea that religions develop in such a way that they take account of what are widely believed to be the facts about human life and about our world: typically they do not make assertions that are plainly at odds with what we encounter in the world. This last remark might be challenged on the grounds that it suggests that what people perceive to be the facts about their lives and what they believe in virtue of their association with their religious tradition are two different things. And of course they are not. But some of what we believe about ourselves and about our world, including various biological facts, seems quite independent of the religious traditions: these facts, such as the fact of human mortality, are just there, and people have to live with them. And the point is that religions typically accord with such beliefs. Hence it is no accident and not at all surprising that the theistic religions reflect the fact that if God exists, there is a great deal of mystery about God's existence and nature.

But the move under discussion can be seen to be deeply unsatisfactory once we begin to probe the justification for, and coherence of, the various beliefs that are embedded in the various practices. The mere fact that a certain belief is assumed by members of a tradition, or is reflected in its practices, hardly settles the question of whether it is a reasonable belief, and the further question of whether it coheres with the other beliefs that are held along with it. How unsatisfactory this response is may be seen by considering the analogous move in the case of the problem of evil. It is an utterly inadequate response to the problem posed for theism by the presence of evil in the world to observe that theists recognize that evils of various sorts are a permanent feature of human life, and that this recognition is woven into the fabric of theism. The mere fact that a religion has developed a recognition that evil is a permanent feature of human life does not itself contribute anything to a solution to the problem of evil. This suggestion about the grammar of religious beliefs is, in short, a magic wand with which problems for theism (or atheism, or any other set of beliefs) can be all too conveniently waved away.

Furthermore, this general line of response attempts to make a virtue of what is actually a necessity. *Since* God is hidden, theistic religious institutions have had to develop in such a way that they take account of this fact. But the question that remains to be addressed is this. Can theism give a satisfactory account of *why* the facts of the matter are as they are, so that institutions and practices have had to develop as they have? To acknowl-edge that traditions have developed in such a way that they recognize that God is hid-den is not to obviate the need to provide such an account. In fine, the particular institu-tions and practices that we are familiar with have developed as they have in response to what have been perceived to be our circumstances. It is ludicrous, therefore, to argue that some aspect of our circumstances, such as the fact that God is hidden, is accounted for by the fact that it makes possible, or is integral to, those institutions and practices.

It is also worth asking if those who make this response wish to suggest that if God were not hidden, and if the facts about God, including the facts about the nature and purposes of God, were clear, then worship and other religious practices with which we are now familiar would become impossible. It probably is true that the practices would be rather different. We may even be able to imagine some respects in which they would be different. But that is hardly an objection: Why should we be so attached to the prac-tices of mystery?

Finally, here is a response that many nontheists will be inclined to offer to the main issues under discussion: it is not that there is a hidden God, but rather that there is no God at all. An atheist may say that it is not surprising that theists have come up with nu-merous attempted explanations of God's hiddenness: they have had to do so because it is far from obvious that God exists. The numerous attempted explanations of God's hid-denness are merely the responses of intelligent theists to the fact that there is a great shortage of evidence for God's existence. In chapter 5 I discuss two versions of the claim that our lack of evidence for God's existence provides a basis for atheism. But in most of what I say on this topic I take it for granted that the nontheists are wrong, and that God exists. I also generally assume that to take theism for granted is to take for granted many standard assumptions of theism, such as the belief that it is good and important for us to worship God, and the closely related belief that it is in virtue of God's nature that it is good and important for us to worship God. The aim, in part, is to ask whether theism has the resources to account for the hiddenness of God.

6. Classifying Theistic Responses to the Hiddenness of God

Theistic attempts to explain the hiddenness of God purport to explain why the facts about God are not more clear even though this has resulted in the loss of various goods of clarity. Such putative explanations can be classified in various ways. Some of them emphasize the defective nature of humanity: they say that it is the fact that we are wicked, or ignorant, or stupid, or sinful, or defective in some other way, that explains why we do not know more about God. The relevant flaws may or may not be thought to be our own fault. The defect may be thought of as something incurable and permanent or as something curable. Thus if it was human arrogance that caused the trouble, it might be that we could be cured of this, or at least partly cured. The relevant flaws may be thought of as the *cause* of God's being hidden from us, in which case something about us renders the facts about God obscure, or the flaws in question may be thought of as the *occasion* of God's being hidden from us: for example, it might be that in re-sponse to our wickedness God chooses to be hidden.

The defect may be thought of as an individual matter. An example of this which has received some discussion of late is the Calvinist idea that while God has implanted in each of us a disposition to believe that God exists, a disposition that is activated by, for example, our observing the complexity of our world, we are individually capable of resisting the effects of this disposition. Alternatively, the defect may be thought of as something that operates at the collective level. As I said earlier, it seems obvious that some cultural contexts encourage theistic belief while others discourage it. The defect may of course be thought to involve both individual and collective components.

I refer to explanations of the hiddenness of God that focus on human defectiveness as *human defectiveness theories*. George Berkeley has a nice statement of a position of this sort, although his unique metaphysical system is presupposed by his reasons for thinking various facts, obscured for many by human cupidity, to be clear to someone who is unbiased and attentive:

> Could we but see [God] . . . say [the unthinking herd], . . . as we see a man, we should believe that he is, and believing obey his commands. But alas we need only open our eyes to see the sovereign lord of all things with a more full and clear view, than we do any one of our fellow-creatures . . . everything we see, hear, feel, or any wise perceive by sense, being a sign or effect of the power of God. . . . [Though] God conceal himself from the eyes of the *sensual* and *lazy*, who will not be at the least expense of thought; yet to an unbiased and attentive mind, nothing can be more plainly legible, than the intimate presence of an all-wise spirit, who fashions, regulates, and sustains the whole system of thought.[13]

Other attempted explanations of the hiddenness of God focus on the nature of God, and since they generally emphasize the transcendence of God, I refer to them as *divine transcendence theories*. (We could equally well call them *divine incomprehensibility theories* or *divine infinity theories*.) Such theories say that God is not the sort of being who could be understood very well by creatures like us. "'Tis only the splendour of light hideth Thee," says hymn 34 of the *Methodist Hymn Book*.[14] Some theories of this sort focus on God's complexity. Pascal advocates such a theory at one point: "If there is a God, he is infinitely beyond our comprehension, since, being indivisible and without limits, he bears no relation to us. We are therefore incapable of knowing either what he is or whether he is" (*Pensées*, from "The Wager," 150).[15] The idea is that a being that is infinite in knowledge, power, goodness, and so forth, would be far beyond our comprehension, much as geometry, for instance, is beyond the comprehension of a goldfish. Outline a geometrical proof ever so clearly and stick it right under the nose of a healthy, well-functioning goldfish, and the creature still will not grasp it. To appeal to God's transcendence in this context is not at all ad hoc: on the contrary, it fits well with our understanding of the characteristics that a being would have to have in order to be God.

So we have a distinction between human defectiveness theories and divine transcendence theories. It is to be expected that a theory of the former type should be combined with one of the latter type, or at least with some elements of a theory of the latter type. Indeed these are two sides of the same coin. For if human defectiveness is to be part of an explanation of God's hiddenness, it is likely that an appeal to divine transcendence will be a part of it too. For there must be something about God in particular that makes for God being hidden, given that there are other things whose existence is altogether apparent to us and whose nature, or much of it, is apparent to us. And God's transcendence would explain God's hiddenness only if we lack the ability to comprehend a transcendent being. So it is hardly surprising that we find these themes intertwined, as they are in these remarks from Rudolf Otto, the first of which is a quotation from Chrysostom:

> [It] is an impertinence to say that He who is beyond the apprehension of even the higher Powers can be comprehended by us earthworms, or compassed and comprised by the weak forces of our understanding.
>
> The truly "mysterious" object is beyond our apprehension and comprehension, not only because our knowledge has certain irremovable limits, but because in it we come upon something inherently "wholly other," whose kind and character are incommensurable with our own, and before which we therefore recoil in a wonder that strikes us chill and numb.[16]

Since Otto thinks of mysteriousness as a fundamental element in all strong and sincerely felt religious emotion, I assume that he would take the view that any serious form of theism requires that a great deal of hiddenness should surround God's existence and nature.

The same themes are intertwined in Joseph Butler's sermon "Upon the Ignorance of Man": "Since the constitution of nature, and the methods and designs of Providence in the government of the world, are above our comprehension, we should acquiesce in, and rest satisfied with, our ignorance; turn our thoughts from that which is above and beyond us, and apply ourselves to that which is level to our capacities, and which is our real business and concern."[17]

Divine transcendence theories and human defectiveness theories imply that God's hiddenness is a by-product of certain facts about us or about God. But some attempted explanations of God's hiddenness take a different approach. They say that the explanation is rather that there are great benefits to God's being hidden: that is, it makes available to us various goods of mystery. The implication in all such cases is that God would be harming us by revealing God's existence or character to us in a clear and unmistakable way. Thus it is argued, for example, that God's hiddenness makes possible human autonomy or a measure of control over whether to believe that God exists, or that it makes possible a choice of whether or not to have faith and trust in God. A locus classicus for the claim that faith requires that the facts about God not be clear to us is the work of Kierkegaard. Consider these remarks from *Concluding Unscientific Postscript*:

> Without risk there is no faith. Faith is precisely the contradiction between the infinite passion of the individual's inwardness and the objective uncertainty. If I am capable of grasping God objectively, I do not believe, but precisely because I cannot do this I must believe. If I wish to preserve myself in faith I must constantly be intent upon holding fast the objective uncertainty, so as to remain out upon the deep, over seventy fathoms of water, still preserving my faith.[18]

Attempted explanations that appeal to either divine transcendence or human defectiveness (or to both) and attempted explanations that appeal to one or more goods of mystery are not mutually exclusive. It would be perfectly consistent to hold both that (a) God, being infinite and perfect, is beyond the comprehension of finite human beings and that (b) certain important benefits are derived from the fact that this is so. Butler's sermon "Upon the Ignorance of Man" combines all of these themes. In addition to appealing to the themes of human defectiveness and divine transcendence, Butler says that [there] is no absurdity in supposing a veil on purpose drawn over some scenes of infinite power, wisdom and goodness, the sight of which might some way or other strike us too strongly; or that better ends are designed and served by their being concealed, than could be by their being exposed to our knowledge. The Almighty may cast clouds and darkness around about him, for reasons and purposes of which we have not the least glimpse or conception.[19]

In spite of what he says in the last sentence, Butler does not think that we are hopelessly in the dark about the divine purposes that are served by God's hiddenness. Elsewhere in the same sermon he says that our current conditions facilitate our being tested and tried in important ways. It is appropriate, he says, that we "should be placed in a state of discipline and improvement, where [our] patience and submission is to be tried by afflictions, where temptations are to be resisted, and difficulties gone through in the discharge of our duty" (235). His idea is that doing our duty when the evidence for God's existence is scarce implies "a better character" than doing our duty when there is an abundance of evidence. Consequently, our current conditions are very beneficial to us. (I return to the idea that God's hiddenness might be morally beneficial in chapter 2.)

Alleged goods of mystery come in various shapes and sizes. Here is one respect in which they vary. To say that God must be hidden if a good such as moral autonomy is to be achieved is of course to imply that if God were not hidden, this good would not be achieved. Instead, we would suffer from the cost or disadvantage of clarity that is involved in the loss of this good. But sometimes the good seems to consist in avoiding one or more evils. For instance, as I discuss in chapter 4, Immanuel Kant and Hilary Putnam contend that it is very important that God should be hidden so that the evil of religious fanaticism may be avoided; they believe that this evil would be a concomitant of the facts about God being clear to us. The good in this case seems to consist in the avoidance of an evil, namely, fanaticism.

Presumably, if God's hiddenness makes possible the achievement of some good, or the avoidance of some evil, it is fortunate that God is hidden. Or at any rate insofar as God's hiddenness makes possible the achievement of this good, or the avoidance of this evil, it is fortunate that God is hidden. According to theories that take this line, God would be harming someone by revealing God's self to them in a clear and unmistakable way.

But, as we have already seen, there are putative explanations of God's hiddenness that do not represent God's hiddenness as fortunate. Thus, attempted explanations that consist in saying that God's hiddenness is a function of our finitude or of some other lack or defect from which we suffer, or of God's infinity, may not appeal to any alleged good of mystery that is achieved by God's being hidden. Rather, they characterize the hiddenness of God as a by-product of certain states of affairs, whether it be something about God or something about us.

Still, perhaps it is better that these states of affairs obtain, even though they involve God's being hidden. Thus, for instance, if the explanation of God's being hidden from us is that we are very limited in our ability to understand God, perhaps it is better that human beings exist with the limited capacities we currently have than that we not exist at all, and better that we exist with these abilities than that we should exist with greatly enhanced abilities, in spite of the fact that God is hidden from us given our current level of abilities. Or, if this is too strong, there must at any rate be no awful consequences of our existing with the limited capacities we currently have.

Nevertheless, according to such an explanation, the hiddenness of God is a by-product of some state of affairs (which must be a good one, or at any rate not a disastrous one) rather than a means to the achievement of one or more goods of mystery. So it is useful, when considering explanations of God's hiddenness, to draw a distinction between explanations that appeal to goods of mystery and other attempted explanations of God's hiddenness. This is particularly so if we think of appeals to goods of mystery as involving both a specification of the benefits or advantages of God's being hidden and also an indication that the purpose of God's hiddenness is to achieve these advantages: in that case, God's hiddenness is thought of as something that has been brought about intentionally with a view to achieving such goods.

Putative explanations of God's hiddenness which do not present the fact that God is hidden as fortunate include some that present it as *unfortunate*, as a condition which should, if possible, be ameliorated. It could of course be fortunate in some respects and unfortunate in others. But whatever may be its ingredients, a convincing explanation must see God's hiddenness as something that God at any rate *permits*. For, as I have said, it seems obvious that God could do more to make God's presence known to us. Consequently, while considerations such as human defectiveness and divine transcendence may figure in the explanation of God's hiddenness, an appeal to goods of mystery must also be made. Only goods of mystery could account for why God is not even a little less hidden than is currently the case.

Here are three other ways to divide the field. First, as we will see, some theories of God's hiddenness have a capacity to explain why God's existence should be unclear to us, whereas some other theories have a capacity to explain merely why God's nature and purposes are unclear to us. Second, some attempted explanations imply that God's hiddenness is a result of God's hiding from us. They represent our situation as one that an agent, namely God, has chosen. Other attempted explanations do not present our situation in this way. Thus if the focus is on human blindness or on God's transcendence, there may be no such appeal to divine agency, although there may be room for an indirect appeal insofar as God is understood to have decided to bring into existence beings of our sort in circumstances such as ours. Third, some attempted explanations would also have a capacity to explain, or to contribute significantly to explaining why other facts in the area of religion should also be unclear, whereas others lack such a capacity. For instance, if the explanation of God's hiddenness were that it is important that people should be free to decide what to believe in the area of religion—an idea with many aspects, some of which I will explore in chapter 3—there probably would then be available to us an explanation of a phenomenon that is more general than the hiddenness of God, namely, that *none* of the facts that religions uniquely purport to describe are obvious to us, a phenomenon that I treat briefly in the rest of this chapter. For instance, in that case, the issues of whether we have souls and whether we will survive death would probably also be unclear to us. On the other hand, if the explanation of God's hiddenness were that God's nature is inaccessible to us, unclarity in this area might not infect other areas.

Here I introduce another piece of terminology. I have already distinguished between goods of mystery and other attempted explanations of God's hiddenness such as those involved in appeals to God's greatness or various human limitations. In considering whether we have an explanation of God's hiddenness, we also need, as mentioned earlier, to take account of various goods of clarity. Let us refer to *all* of the considerations that need to be addressed when considering whether there is an explanation of God's hiddenness (namely, goods of mystery, goods of clarity, and other attempted explanations of God's hiddenness) as *relevant considerations.*

7. Ambiguity

Discussion of the hiddenness of God is a contribution to discussion of all of those matters pertaining to religion about which there is ambiguity, or a lack of clarity. That the facts about God, if God exists, are unclear is just one aspect of the general unclarity that surrounds many central claims of the major religions. To say that God is hidden, therefore, is to say that religious ambiguity extends to the existence of God. In this final section of this chapter I turn to some discussion of this more general phenomenon.

Much of what I say in this book depends on my assumption that the world is religiously ambiguous. John Hick captures part of what I have in mind: "The universe is religiously ambiguous in that it is possible to interpret it, intellectually and experientially, both religiously and naturalistically. The theistic and anti-theistic arguments are all inconclusive, for the special evidences to which they appeal are also capable of being understood in terms of the contrary world view. Further, the opposing set of evidences cannot be given objectively quantifiable values."[20] Hick's view, if I understand him correctly, is not merely that it is *possible* to interpret the world in a variety of religious ways, and to interpret it naturalistically, but in addition that it is possible to do so without any loss of rationality.

A subject or phenomenon or area of inquiry might be said to be "perplexing" or "puzzling" or "mysterious" or "ambiguous." The second pair in this set of notions differs slightly from the first pair in the following respect. The claim that some subject or phenomenon or area of inquiry is mysterious and the claim that it is ambiguous are most naturally interpreted as descriptions of the subject, phenomenon, or area of inquiry under discussion, as distinct from descriptions of anyone's reaction to it or evaluation of it. And what I mean to make is a claim about a certain area of inquiry. On the other hand, the claim that something is perplexing and the claim that it is puzzling are most naturally interpreted as reports on the reaction of the speaker, or on the reaction of the speaker and of others known to the speaker, to an area of inquiry or a subject matter that elicits this reaction from them, perhaps because it is ambiguous or mysterious; such claims are most naturally interpreted as describing the *effect* that something has. As I say, my concern is with the phenomenon itself rather than with its effect. My concern is with what I take to be the ambiguous nature of much of the subject matter about which the religions purport to speak.

This religious ambiguity has a number of aspects. Consider God's existence. As already mentioned, not only does there seem to be neither a proof nor a disproof of God's existence; it also seems that neither the evidence for, nor the evidence against, God's existence is overwhelming. That there is relevant evidence is clear enough. The evidence, which I take to include every phenomenon and consideration that either supports or counts against belief, includes, for example, the religious experiences that people have and the presence of evil in the world. Perhaps there is *more* evidence on one side than on the other. But how are we to prove where exactly the balance resides, if indeed there is such a thing as the balance? As Hick rightly says, attempts to quantify the evidence seem very dubious. They have a remarkable tendency to yield results that confirm what was already believed.[21] One wonders, for example, how often the relevant calculation has resulted in a previously held religious position being rejected.

The world manifests ambiguity in that it is open both to secular and to religious readings, but also in that it is open to a number of religious readings. Thus, for example, our lives are ambiguous in that they may reasonably be interpreted in entirely secular terms or in religious terms, but also in that they may reasonably be interpreted using the concepts of various religious traditions. Thus a person might interpret her life as manifesting divine guidance, while another person might interpret her life as manifesting the operation of the law of Karma. People with intellectual integrity in different traditions look at the world around them, their own lives, their own experience, their inner states, their interaction with others, and all other phenomena in whose interpretation religious concepts are deployed, from the point of view of their tradition, without it seeming to them that what they experience is discordant with their interpretation of it. On the contrary, they look at all such phenomena from within the concepts and categories of their traditions, and they feel that their experience can be comprehended through those categories. So there are many competing alternative readings of those phenomena that religions purport to describe; and each reading meshes with the experience of a particular religious community, providing those who adopt it with a way to interpret what they experience, a way that feels right.

A striking feature of what it is to have deeply held religious beliefs often is that it feels to a person in this situation that there is no other reasonable way to perceive the world. Such beliefs seem obviously correct, and life without them seems to some degree unbearable. Yet we know that this feeling is not reliable, since people who share it actually subscribe to the tenets of traditions that make different, and largely incompatible, claims. Indeed, the presence of intelligent and reflective people in a number of traditions who have feelings of this sort and who are utterly convinced of the truth of their tradition both suggests that the world is religiously ambiguous and, in addition, is itself an aspect of the religious ambiguity of the world.

Presumably the religions have developed in such a way that they have a capacity to mesh with the experience of their adherents. Otherwise they would have been found by their adherents not to suffice to enable them to understand or cope with those phenomena with which religions uniquely enable people to deal. Presumably traditions that lack this ability either develop it or die off.

Religions that flourish over a long period, that are central to the lives of their adherents, and that influence many people—all of which is the case, by definition, for the major traditions—must also be well adapted to the culture and the biological circumstances of their adherents. For instance, the rituals associated with a tradition must be connected appropriately with events and phenomena that are important to its members. I assume that a religion that failed to provide an interpretation of, and hence a way to cope with, important events in people's lives such as birth, death, bereavement, coming of age, and so forth, would not survive. A religion, to put it in general terms, must be woven into the fabric of the culture with which it is associated, reflecting what the culture considers to be deeply important, and providing guidance in crucial areas.

Interestingly, to the extent that the shape that a religion takes involves its being molded in the shape of the culture with which it is associated, naturalistic interpretations of the origins and function of religion are plausible. For if a religion were a human construct—whether we take, for instance, a Feuerbachian or a Durkheimian reading of what this would involve, and whether we think of that religion as entirely or just as largely a human construct—it would reflect what matters to its adherents and what is most important to the society in which it develops: it will bear the trademarks of its source. The upshot is that there will always be something plausible about naturalistic interpretations of religion. Consequently, the interpretation of itself that a religious tradition offers will always be in competition with naturalistic alternatives with some plausibility. This, too, is an aspect of the religious ambiguity of the world.

Being well adapted to, or meshing with, the experience of the members of a tradition may usefully be thought of as having two aspects. On the one hand, the beliefs in question enable people to comprehend what they experience. People do not have a sense that their religious perspective is at odds with what they are encountering. On the other hand, the central claims of the traditions acquire this adaptability partly by avoiding specific predictions about the future experiences of their adherents. They thereby avoid the risk of making claims that will prove to be out of line with what occurs; the result is that the religious framework can accommodate whatever occurs.

Yet some of the claims of some of the traditions are just plain wrong, just as others are plainly correct. Thus the claim that an illness has been caused by witchcraft may be manifestly false, just as the claim that Jesus of Nazareth lived around two thousand years ago is manifestly true. It is useful to imagine the traditions being stripped of manifestly false ingredients. There may be some traditions of which there is little left after they have been so purged, but most traditions make claims about supernatural beings or entities or states or processes such as God or angels or Brahman or Karma or an afterlife we can enjoy, and their claims in such areas are not likely to be shown to be either manifestly true or manifestly false. When so purged, many religious traditions will still have most of their beliefs intact. The religious ambiguity of the world consists in part in the fact that the world may reasonably be interpreted in accordance with the beliefs of a number of traditions that pass this test.

Although I explore in parts of this book some aspects of this ambiguity, and in particular some of the attempted explanations of it from within the religious traditions, I do not make a systematic attempt to *show* that the world is religiously ambiguous. I am, however, contributing to such a case: for example, I do so by arguing in this chapter that God is hidden even from believers and by arguing, in chapter 10, that the religious experiences that people have fail to support uniquely the claims of any particular religious tradition.

What would an endeavor of a more systematic sort consist in? It would need to take into account all of the available evidence for and against the main claims of the various religions. This would of course be a truly daunting project. For instance, scrutiny of numerous arguments for and against the existence of God would be necessary. And since religions obviously make assertions in numerous other areas, with some not even positing a deity, there would of course be a lot more than that involved in showing that there is ambiguity. That there is a vast array of evidence and of relevant considerations to be taken into account is clear: a perusal of a dozen texts in philosophy of religion, including some whose purpose is to defend the claims of one or another tradition and some whose purpose is to call into question all religious traditions, suffices to show this to be so.

If the available evidence does not balance out, it must be hard for us to know whether or not it does so. For one thing, there has to be an explanation of how it is that large numbers of people with intellectual integrity who have reflected carefully have come to such different conclusions. It is obvious that for every Richard Swinburne who adds up what he thinks to be the relevant evidence and gets a result that supports theism, there is a J. L. Mackie who gets an entirely different result, and, in general, for every theist to whom the facts of her experience appear to confirm that God exists there are apparently equally well qualified nontheists, including members of nontheistic religions, agnostics, and atheists, to whom the facts of their experience have no such significance. Apparently painstaking attempts to assess the import of the evidence arrive at utterly different conclusions. While the notion that it is hard to know what the evidence adds up to is not the only conceivable explanation of why this is so, it is an excellent candidate for such an explanation. But if it is hard for us to tell what position the balance of the evidence supports, our situation is more or less the same as it would be if we knew the evidence to balance out.

I want to include among ambiguous situations not only those in which it seems to us that the available evidence balances out but also those in which it is hard to tell whether or not it does so. Actually I want to expand the notion of ambiguity still further to include certain cases in which the evidence seems somewhat more supportive of one side rather than the other, but these further conditions are also met: there is a lot of relevant evidence, some of it is complex, and it is difficult to add it all up and to discern what it amounts to, and in which—for all these reasons—there is a lot of room for error.

When there is ambiguity in an area that is of importance in the lives of many people, one's community is likely to be an important source of information about what to believe: in such circumstances beliefs are likely to need the support of a particular community for their transmission and preservation. And I take the fact that transmission by a particular community is essential if a certain body of beliefs is to endure to suggest that the area in question is an ambiguous one. Consequently, I take the fact that the role of tradition in the area of religion is very great, so that typically it is only if the traditions, practices, and institutions of a group are thriving that the beliefs associated with it are maintained and transmitted successfully, to suggest that the religions themselves manifest the fact that there is ambiguity.

To summarize, what I mean when I say that there is religious ambiguity is all of the following. On numerous matters about which the religions purport to speak, there is no proof that one side rather than the others is correct, and the available evidence appears not to be overwhelmingly on one side rather than the others. Our experience, both of the world around us and of our own lives, seems to be open to being interpreted in terms of the sets of concepts and categories that are available in different religious traditions. Further, even if some position seems to be supported by rather more evidence than the alternatives, this is so under circumstances in which there is disagreement among conscientious members of many other groups about how to interpret the evidence and under circumstances in which the available evidence is complex.

So these are our circumstances. To explore the hiddenness of God is to explore some aspects of this larger topic of religious ambiguity. The exercise of examining various theistic responses to God's hiddenness, which is what will occupy me in most of the remainder of part I of this book, is a contribution to the larger project of deciding whether members of the various religious traditions can account for the religious ambiguity of the world.

A final point about ambiguity and its implications. To say that the world is religiously ambiguous is to say that it is open to being read in various ways, both religious and secular, by intelligent, honest people. That this is so has two very different implications, one of which is supportive of participation in a religious tradition and one of which is not. The supportive part is that, in virtue of this ambiguity, it is reasonable for people in a number of traditions to live in accordance with the tenets of their tradition: for one thing, what they experience fits well with those tenets. But there is an implication that pulls in another direction: once one knows that members of traditions other than one's own also reasonably interpret the world around them, their experiences, and so forth, in accordance with their tradition, this should make a difference to the way in which one holds one's beliefs. I discuss the implications in part II of this book.

The latter recognition and the sensibility that it fosters are peculiarly modern phenomena. They arise in part from tolerance of a number of traditions and outlooks. But this hardly settles the question of whether they should be thought of as a case of seeing more deeply or as a case of blindness.

2

›—‹›—‹›—‹›—‹›—‹

GOD'S HIDDENNESS AND THE
POSSIBILITY OF MORAL ACTION

This and the next chapter focus mainly on the importance of human beings being able to exercise control of various sorts over their lives. In this chapter I consider a number of versions of the claim that God must be hidden if we are to be able to make morally significant choices. I focus in particular on the proposals of Kant and Swinburne, both of whom propose that there is an important good of mystery in the area of human moral autonomy. The next chapter concerns the importance of our being able to exercise control over what we believe.

1. The Importance of Being Responsible

There are a number of versions of the idea that if God were not hidden our moral agency would be undermined. I begin with these remarks from Eliezer Berkovits: "Since history is man's responsibility, one would . . . expect [God] . . . to hide, to be silent, while man is about his God-given task. Responsibility requires freedom, but God's convincing presence would undermine the freedom of human decision. God hides in human responsibility and human freedom."[1] Part of what Berkovits is suggesting here may be that God must be hidden if certain goods are to be achieved, namely, the good of our taking responsibility for the world around us, for people who are victims of cruel mistreatment, and so on. Berkovits may be thinking along these lines: if the facts about God—and in particular the facts about God's presence and about God's capacity to exercise control over everything, to intervene in every context, and to solve the problems that human beings try to solve—were very clear to us, our sense of re-

26

sponsibility would be diminished. In any case, let's consider this proposal, whether or not it is part of what Berkovits has in mind. I will call it the "loss of responsibility" problem.

The idea is that if God were not hidden, we would conclude that we do not need to concern ourselves with, say, people who are suffering the aftereffects of a natural disaster or who are being brutally treated, since, after all, God can easily take care of them. We would not believe that we are responsible, and we would lack a sense of responsibility. The outcome would be that we would not fulfill our responsibilities. We would fail to do what we ought to do, at least much of the time. Our situation would be somewhat akin to that of children who grow up always believing that their parents can take care of everything, and who consequently never develop a sense of responsibility.

But this suggestion is questionable. A conviction that God, being omniscient and omnipotent, is able to solve all or many of the problems of the world with less difficulty and effort than it would require for us to solve them is compatible with the idea that human beings have been delegated with certain tasks, such as the task of taking care of other people who are facing difficulties. It is not hard to think of reasons that it would be fitting for such tasks to be delegated to us. For example, such an assignment might be good for us. Again, even if it were thoroughly clear that there is a deity who is easily able to solve all or many of the problems of the world, it might nevertheless be apparent to us that the right way of life for us involves taking responsibility for others. We might believe that it is pleasing to God for us to adopt such a way of life. Or it might be that among the beliefs that would be clearly correct if, in general, the facts about God's existence and nature were clearer would be the fact that God wants us to take responsibility for others. Doubtless there are other possibilities. Moreover, if it were clear that God exists, people might be very confident on that account that they are on the winning side and that their contributions are part of a larger and more enduring project, one that will ultimately be successful. They may be more highly motivated on that account. They may feel that they have all the more reason to behave in a morally impressive way. So there is in fact a great deal that speaks in favor of the idea that we would actually have a stronger sense of responsibility, and take more responsibility for others, if it were clear to us that God exists.

How people will react actually seems to depend on what the deity is seen to be leaving undone: it might be clear that we ought to take on certain tasks in virtue of the fact that a clearly existing deity does not undertake them and is explicitly indicating that they are our responsibility. Consequently it is not a clearly existent deity that would have the untoward result under discussion: rather, it is a clearly existent deity who intervenes in all human crises, and who manifestly steps in to solve every problem that we would otherwise have to solve, thereby removing the burden of responsibility from us. But there is no justification for simply assuming that a clearly existing deity would so intervene. Consequently, a clearly existing deity would not, as such, be morally problematic, at least not in the respect under discussion.

But it is possible, I suppose, that people differ in the relevant respect and that some would be discouraged in the proposed manner. Even if God is not intervening, they may feel that God could do so. They may feel that even if they have had certain tasks delegated to them, there is no real need to carry them out since those tasks can so much more easily be accomplished by the deity.

Yet we also seem to have some weighty empirical evidence that counts against the loss-of-responsibility proposal. Theists, including some who appear to be ever so sure about the existence and nature of God, are not conspicuously absent in humanitarian and other morally motivated movements; if anything, they are often conspicuous by their presence. If the claim about the undesirable consequences of God's not being hidden were correct, we should expect less involvement in, for instance, attempts to ensure the betterment of the conditions of others to be a concomitant of a greater degree of certainty about the existence and nature of God. But that does not seem to be the case.[2]

There are of course many people who are entirely certain about the existence and nature of God but who do not distinguish themselves in the relevant respect; many even distinguish themselves by, for example, the hatred they have for those who disagree with them or for those whom they consider their enemies. But that is beside the point. The fact that there are such people does not bear on the challenge posed for the loss-of-responsibility proposal by the presence of many believers who are utterly convinced that God exists and convinced of some particular set of theistic beliefs (such as, say, those associated with Methodism or Hasidism or Shiism) and who are notable for their morally admirable conduct.

The force of this empirical evidence might be questioned. It might be suggested that the certainty that people have under present circumstances must be different in nature from the sort of certainty that people would have if the relevant facts were clear: in particular, certainty under present circumstances involves investing yourself in a certain system of religious beliefs when—at least for most people, most of the time—it is unclear that those beliefs are true. Certainty under present circumstances arises as much from a commitment of oneself to believe as it does from responding to what obviously is the case. Certainty under current conditions is certainty that is felt under circumstances in which the world is religiously ambiguous, whether or not believers recognize that this is so. Many people whose religious beliefs are certain under our current circumstances may therefore be aware at some level that what they believe to be true is not obviously true; perhaps this has a subconscious influence on them, so that their beliefs are somehow held in a different mode. If the certainty they feel is weaker, or the belief somehow takes a different form, this weakens accordingly an attempt to argue from the fact that theists are not currently discouraged from moral endeavors even if they are certain that God exists, to the conclusion that they would also not be discouraged if the existence and nature of God were very clear to them.

Yet the point remains that theists who, under current conditions, seem as certain as it is possible to be that their particular theistic system of beliefs is the correct one sometimes are people of the highest moral caliber, and are distinguished by the extent to which they take responsibility for others. If the loss-of-responsibility point were correct, you would expect a diminished sense of responsibility to accompany an increased sense of certainty. But there is no evidence at all that this is so. Hence it is hard to see why complete certainty should have the harmful consequences under discussion.

But perhaps the presence of theists who under current conditions distinguish themselves by the extent to which they take responsibility for others is actually in part to be explained by the hiddenness of God in that by their involvement in humanitarian and other morally admirable movements theists may hope to make known to others the existence, as well as the plans, purposes, and nature, of the being whom they worship. And for this sort of bearing witness to be something that is worthwhile, or even sensible, to do, God must be hidden. Consequently, it might be claimed that if God were not hidden our sense of responsibility for others would be diminished because of the certainty about God that would then be widespread, even though under our *present* circumstances (in which God is hidden) those who are certain of God's existence experience no such diminution of their sense of responsibility. What would otherwise be a morally harmful consequence of this certainty is mitigated by the need to respond in certain ways in the face of the hiddenness of God. This final point is not negligible in its force. It suffices, in particular, to reveal that the empirical evidence adduced above does not refute decisively the loss-of-responsibility proposal and thereby illustrates how difficult it would be to show that there is nothing to this proposal. Nevertheless, we have seen that the proposal extracted from Berkovits's remarks faces serious difficulties; while we have not refuted it, it seems to have little promise.[3]

2. Kant on the Need for God to Be Hidden If Morality Is to Be Possible

Next I turn to a related but distinct motif, one found in the work of Immanuel Kant and, more recently, in the work of Richard Swinburne. Kant thought that it would be morally disastrous if God's existence were known to us. It would undermine our capacity to act in a morally worthy way.

> [Our] faith is not scientific knowledge, and thank heaven it is not! For God's wisdom is apparent in the very fact that we do not *know* that God exists, but should *believe* that God exists. For suppose we could attain to scientific knowledge of God's existence, through our experience or in some other way (even if the possibility of this knowledge cannot be thought). And suppose further that we could really reach as much certainty through this knowledge as we do in intuition. Then in this case all our morality would break down. In his every action, man would represent God to himself as a rewarder or avenger. This image would force itself involuntarily on his soul, and *his hope for reward and fear of punishment would take the place of moral motives.* Man would be virtuous out of sensuous impulses.[4]

At the end of the *Critique of Practical Reason*, Kant comments again on what the consequences would be if our speculative reason were capable of solving "weighty problems" such as the existence of God, something which, he says, we wish were so. He says that it is fortunate this wish has not been granted, and he elaborates a little on why he thinks this to be so.

> Now assuming that [nature] . . . had here indulged our wish and had provided us with that power of insight or enlightenment which we would like to possess or which some erroneously believe they do possess, what would be the consequence so far as we can discern it? In so far as our whole nature was not changed at the same time, *the inclinations* (which under any condition have the first word) *would first strive for their satisfaction and . . . for the greatest possible and most lasting satisfaction under the name of happiness.* The moral law would afterward speak in order to hold them within their proper limits and even to subject them all to a higher end which has no regard to inclination. But *instead of the conflict which now the moral disposition has to wage with inclinations and in which, after some defeats, moral strength may be gradually*

won, God and eternity in their awful majesty would stand unceasingly before our eyes (for that which we can completely prove is as certain as that which we can ascertain by sight). Transgression of the law would indeed be shunned, and the commanded would be performed. But because the disposition from which actions should be done cannot be instilled by any command, and because *the spur to action would in this case be always present and external, reason would have no need to gather its strength to resist the inclinations by a vivid idea of the dignity of the law. Thus most actions conforming to the law would be done from fear, few would be done from hope, none from duty. The moral worth of actions, on which alone the worth of the person and even of the world depends in the eyes of supreme wisdom, would not exist at all.* The conduct of man, so long as his nature remained as it now is, would be changed into mere mechanism, where, as in a puppet show, everything would gesticulate well but no life would be found in the figures.[5]

Why exactly did Kant think that knowledge of God's existence would be so harmful? Why would our capacity for acting from duty be swamped, with the result that our actions would be emptied of moral worth? The answer is to be found, at least in part, in the italicized parts of the preceding quotations and includes the following three elements, the first of which seems most important.

First, Kant is making some psychological claims about how we would react to such knowledge: "hope for reward and fear of punishment would take the place of moral motives" (LPT, 123), and "the inclinations . . . would first strive for their satisfaction and . . . for the greatest possible and most lasting satisfaction under the name of happiness" (CPR, 152). The idea is that since we all have an intense desire for happiness, if we knew that God exists and if it were clear to us, as Kant claims it then would be, how to ensure our long-term happiness, we would be so consumed with pursuing that happiness that it would be impossible for us to do what is right *because* it is right. The benefits of doing what is right would be so great, and our desire to achieve those benefits so strong, that it would be impossible for us to do what is right because it is right. Since, according to Kant, an action is morally worthy only if we do it solely out of moral motives, morally worthy actions would become impossible: we would no longer act for the sake of duty. We would be incapable of doing what we ought to do solely because it is what we ought to do. The pursuit of happiness would contaminate our motivation, and our wish to achieve happiness would be at least part of what motivates us when we do what we ought to do.[6]

Kant may even hold the more extreme, and hence more difficult to defend, view that if we saw how to achieve our long-term happiness, the pursuit of that happiness would completely swamp all other motivations, thereby becoming the *sole* ground determining our wills. In that case other motives would cease to be efficacious and the takeover of our motivation by the desire for happiness would be complete.

It is also unclear whether Kant thinks that someone who has knowledge of God's existence would even be aware of his obligations qua obligations. Perhaps, in his view, such a person would just apprehend what it would take to achieve happiness, and then set out to achieve it. Or perhaps the idea is rather that such a person would be aware that what is necessary and sufficient for the achievement of happiness is doing those actions that we have an obligation to do, and would set out to do what he believes himself to have an obligation to do, conceiving of it as such.

Second, Kant says that among the unfortunate consequences of knowledge of the relevant sort would be that there would then no longer be "the conflict which now the moral disposition has to wage with inclinations and in which, after some defeats, moral strength may be gradually won" (CPR, 152; see also LPT, 116, 117, 118, 156). So in addition to the facts that under current circumstances our inclination to pursue our happiness is reined in, and room is left for moral motives to determine our behavior, it is also the case that we currently can develop a sort of moral strength as a result of coming through trial and error to act out of duty rather than out of inclinations. This process of development through trial and error would be out of the question if we had knowledge of God's existence. We would be too readily inclined to do what we ought to do.

Third, Kant also appears to think that it is important that we engage in a sort of fumbling around in the search for happiness, which is something that issues from our being uncertain about wherein our long-term happiness is to be found. His view seems to be that we are so constituted that if we could discern wherein our long-term happiness is to be found, we would pursue it at all costs and at the expense of all other goals we might have or other reasons that we might have for action.

The position of Kant and the position discussed in section 1 of this chapter—what I called the loss-of-responsibility point—differ in various respects. Both involve the claim that if God were not hidden, there would be untoward moral consequences; indeed, both involve the more specific claim that if God were not hidden, our freedom to make morally significant choices would be eliminated or at least drastically reduced. But the contention discussed in the last section is that if God were not hidden, our sense of responsibility would be undermined with the result, presumably, that we would do fewer morally right actions. Kant, on the other hand (and, as we shall see, Swinburne too), contends that if God were not hidden we would not have *enough* trouble doing morally right actions. And we would do them for the wrong reason. These views are undoubtedly in tension with each other, although there are ways to combine much of what matters to the advocates of each. For it could be that if we had knowledge of God's existence we would *both* do no right action for the right reason, which is Kant's concern, *and* do fewer right actions, which is part at least of what was at issue in the last section. Or it could be that one view is right with respect to some parts of morality while the other is right with respect to other parts. (The case discussed in section 1 had to do solely with our responsibility to others.) However, if I am right to think that the loss-of-responsibility point is very problematic, these last observations are moot.

What are we to make of the themes from Kant? It seems that what would actually be morally damaging, according to Kant, is certainty about what behavior would enable us to achieve our long-term happiness. Knowledge of God's existence—whether that is achieved through a proof or in some other way—would be dangerous just because, and only insofar as, it issued in certainty about whether or not actions that we are considering engaging in would help us to achieve our happiness. Such knowledge is not problematic per se; if it were not accompanied by certainty about which behavior will be rewarded and which will be punished, but were combined instead with uncertainty on this matter, there would not be the morally damaging results that Kant has in mind. So Kant's claims are plausible only if it is assumed that knowledge of God's existence would reveal, or would inevitably be accompanied by an awareness of, which behavior (among the possibilities we are contemplating in any situation) will be rewarded and which will be punished, and hence wherein our eternal happiness is to be found.

Moreover, if certainty about how to achieve our happiness were attained in some other way, a way that did not involve our having a proof of the existence of God, presumably it would be just as damaging as certainty that is achieved via a proof. That is, the problem that Kant identifies would arise in *any* circumstances in which eternal happiness is known to be a consequence of virtue.

My discussion proceeds as follows. I mention some difficulties that arise for Kant's views. Then I turn to Swinburne's proposal, which shares many features with Kant's position but is free of the difficulties.

First, the claim that knowledge that God exists, which would (allegedly) result in our being certain that virtue would be rewarded (etc.), would have the result that we would no longer act virtuously but would rather pursue our own happiness, is difficult to sustain given some other aspects of Kant's theory. According to Kant, an action that is done for some reason other than that it is in accordance with duty—such as, for example, in order to achieve a reward, to avoid punishment, to benefit a friend, or to please God—is not morally worthy. As mentioned earlier, Kant's view is that morally worthy actions are not merely morally right but in addition are actions that are done because they are morally right. Now if, once we knew that God exists, we would also know that we would be rewarded for morally worthy actions and not for actions that are morally right but not morally worthy, then we would know that if we are to achieve our long-term happiness, we had better not be motivated by the desire to achieve our long-term happiness.

Second, suppose that if we had knowledge of God's existence there would be less moral purity of the sort under discussion, and the pursuit of happiness would have a more dominant role in our behavior than it now has. The extent to which people *act* correctly might, however, be increased under these circumstances, for there would be a new and (supposedly) irresistible reason to act correctly. What would decrease is the extent to which what is right is done because it is right. But would it not be preferable for more right actions to be done even if this can be achieved only at the cost of less purity in moral motivation? Why should moral purity matter so much more than moral behavior and its desirable consequences? If, as Drabkin asks, mobsters, murderers, and extortionists are persuaded to abandon their ways and to act well, albeit for the wrong reasons, would this really be such a bad outcome?[7] These questions are sheer heresy for Kant, but the rest of us need to raise them: we have to be carrying a great deal of Kantian baggage in order for them not to arise.

Third, it is hard to reconcile what Kant says about the dreadful consequences of our having knowledge of God's existence with his claims about the positive role that theism plays in underpinning morality. The puzzles here include the following. Are Kant's remarks about the ill effects of such knowledge compatible with what he says elsewhere about the summum bonum, in which our level of happiness is brought ever more closely into conformity with our degree of virtue? Given his reasoning when he sets out to explain why knowledge of God's existence would be morally disastrous, how can he avoid the conclusion that a conviction that we will be happy to the extent that we are virtuous, which conviction he believes to be a necessary concomitant of moral effort, would also undermine, or at least diminish, our capacity to act morally? In general, how are Kant's claims about the disastrous consequences for morality of our having knowledge of God's existence to be reconciled with his claim that morality requires us to postulate God? This question in turn requires that we ask how Kant conceived of the epistemological status of our belief (if indeed he understood this to be a case of belief) in those things (God, freedom, and immortality) whose existence, he contended, must be postulated by each of us if we are to do what we are morally required to do.[8]

There would be less of a puzzle about how to reconcile Kant's remarks about the harmful effects of knowledge of God's existence with his contention that morality requires us to postulate God if his view were that morality requires that we *hope* that God exists or that we *believe it possible* that God exists, for example. But Kant repeatedly says that what morality warrants and requires is *certainty* (see, e.g., LPT, 42, 114, 122). Some of his remarks might be taken to suggest that the difference is that postulating God generates a level of certainty in us that is not of the highest caliber. Thus in a passage quoted earlier he asks us to consider how things would be if "we could . . . reach as much certainty through this knowledge as we do in intuition" (LPT, 123). Such a remark gives the impression that postulating God does not involve as much certainty about God's existence as might be achieved in some other ways. Yet he *also* says that a faith built on morality "is as certain as a mathematical demonstration" (LPT, 40). So if there is a difference here in the degree of certainty, it does not seem to be very great. In any case it is hard to imagine that it is a difference that matters so much that it is *essential* for morality that we achieve certainty of the lesser sort whereas it would be *disastrous* for morality if we were to achieve the greater degree of certainty.

Another puzzling feature of the situation is that while Kant says that a proof would contaminate our motivation, turning us into nothing but pursuers of our own happiness, the belief (if belief it is) that God exists that morality requires is valuable largely because it strengthens our moral motivation, enabling us to resist our tendency to act out of inclination. While morality stands on its own, requiring for its foundation no theological assumptions, in practice it requires the support of an "incentive" (LPT, 27, 31, 40, 111, 139, 141). We would be blinded by the dazzle of our sensuous impulses without the incentive provided by belief in God (LPT, 41). But if God must be postulated (whatever exactly this amounts to) in order to make it possible for morality to motivate us, how can it be that knowledge of God's existence would make it impossible for morality to motivate us? I am not sure that none of these (overlapping) questions about the relation between the moral case for postulating God and the case for the harmfulness of a proof can be answered adequately, but I do not myself see at present how to answer them.[9]

Fourth, two additional aspects of Kant's thinking deserve probing. As noted, he assumes that knowledge of God's existence would reveal, or would inevitably be accompanied by an awareness of, which behavior will be rewarded and which will be punished, and hence wherein our eternal happiness is to be found. Maybe we should concede this assumption. After all, if God's existence were clear to us, the moral properties of God might thereby be made clear to us, in which case much would probably also be made clear to us about how we ought to act. To believe that God exists is to believe that there exists a being who values and expects certain types of behavior rather than others. It seems inconceivable that there should be a form of theism that would have no moral implications or that would leave its adherents blind as to its moral implications; in fact such a view would not *count* as theism. So it seems reasonable to think that if God's existence were clear to us, God's will would be at least somewhat apparent to us and that this would have some moral implications. There probably would not be so many competing accounts of what God expects from us as there currently are.

Still, there is some room for debate here. Thus it might be that the general principles would be clear, but yet we might have room to discern how they should be applied in particular cases. For example, even if, in virtue of our enhanced knowledge of God, we would know that we ought to love our neighbors as ourselves, we might still have to make judgments about what this requires from us in many situations. Or it might be that some particular prescriptions and proscriptions would be clear but that much of the rest of morality would be less clear: the rules in certain areas of human life but not in others might be clear. So I think that the best thing to say is that a clear case for God's existence would have very considerable moral implications, although this might not result in our having a full account of how we ought to behave in all situations.

Finally, perhaps this reasoning is part of Kant's thinking: if, given knowledge of God's existence, the wish to promote our own happiness would become part of the basis on which we act, when we act in accordance with duty, then it would become apparent that duty alone was not enough to motivate us. However, even if knowledge of God's existence were to reveal that we are defective in this respect, this would not explain why it would be a bad thing for us to have this knowledge. Its availability would not bring it about that we need a motive other than duty. It would merely reveal that our motives were not pure. If we lack what is necessary to act for the sake of duty, then that is just a fact about us: the availability of knowledge of God's existence would not create this lack.

3. The Importance of Being Able to Be Immoral: Swinburne

Richard Swinburne's position is quite similar to Kant's but is free of the difficulties we have found in Kant. Thus Swinburne does not presuppose that we are preprogrammed to pursue our own happiness, once we see wherein it is to be found; nor does he presuppose that only action for the sake of duty has moral value. Many of Swinburne's relevant remarks occur in the course of his discussion of the problem of evil in his book *The Existence of God*.[10] His main purpose in this discussion is to explore the advantages of our learning what are likely to be the consequences of various courses of action through our observing the consequences that such courses of action typically have rather than as a result of God telling us what consequences they would have if they were to occur. The part of his case that is most important for my purposes here is his claim that if God were to give us this information directly, this would result in certain facts about God becoming clear, and his further claim that that would have certain unfortunate consequences.[11] The result would be that people would

> know for certain there was a God, with all that that involves . . . Whether morally good or bad, whether they would otherwise concern themselves with matters religious or not; the existence of God would be for them an item of evident common knowledge. Knowing that there was a God, men would know that their most secret thoughts and actions were known to God; and knowing that he was just, they would expect for their bad actions and thoughts whatever punishment was just. Even if a good God would not punish men further, still they would have the punishment of knowing that their bad actions were known

to God. They could no longer pose as respectable citizens; God would be too evident a member of the community. Further, in seeing God, as it were, face to face, men would see him to be good and worshipful, and hence would have every reason for conforming to his will. In such a world men would have little temptation to do wrong—it would be the mark of prudence and reason to do what was virtuous. Yet a man only has a genuine choice of destiny if he has reasons for pursuing either good or evil choices of actions; for . . . a man can only perform an action which he has some reason to do . . . God would be too close for . . . [men] to be able to work things out for themselves. (*The Existence of God*, 211–12)

So Swinburne's contention is that if we knew that God exists, wrong actions would not be chosen by us, or would seldom be chosen by us, because we would have no reason to choose them. Consequently we would have little temptation to do wrong and we would be deprived of a genuine choice of destiny.

But it is not quite right to say that under such circumstances we would have *no reason* to choose to do wrong actions.[12] If we were in circumstances in which the facts about God were plain for all to see, we might still have numerous reasons to do wrong. But we would also know that our bad actions and bad intentions would be evident to God. And to the extent that this is so, we would know that we could not get away with wrongful thoughts and behavior. This knowledge, Swinburne believes, would provide us with a powerful reason not to do what is wrong, a reason that is so powerful that it would render ineffective whatever reasons to do wrong we might continue to have under these circumstances. When he says that people in such circumstances would have no reason to do wrong, perhaps Swinburne just means that a reason that has been rendered ineffective is no longer capable of functioning for the agent in question as a reason that has a bearing on what she does. Swinburne also takes the Kantian line that if God were not hidden, good actions would also be robbed of much that is good about them. We would in fact have too many reasons to perform them, and their performance would come easily to us.

It is central to Swinburne's position that it is important that our reasons for acting wrongly should not lose their appeal.[13] He thinks it to be important that we should make a "genuine choice of destiny." And "to have genuine choice of one's own destiny one must be in a situation of temptation" (*The Existence of God*, 158). We will not be in such a situation unless wrong choices are appealing to us. (At least wrong choices must retain their appeal unless previous decisions have resulted in the gradual acquisition of a character that is resistant to their appeal.) And the problem with a world in which we know that God exists is that in it we would have little temptation to do wrong. In such a world it would be impossible, or virtually impossible, for us to be immoral; and in that case, we would be unable to choose not to be immoral. Rather, morally good actions and good intentions would come naturally. We would be unable to feel the pull both of good options and of evil options and then to choose the good options. We would consequently be unable to make a choice of destiny. Because we would live our lives knowing that God is always aware of what we are doing and thinking, choices of a profoundly important sort would be unavailable to us.[14]

It would be as if whenever you drove your car the chief of police were always present in the front passenger seat, observing all of your actions and ready to mete out punishments where appropriate. Or it would be as if we each had implanted in us a device that would announce regularly for all to hear what we had done that was wrong or unbecoming, as well as what we ought to have done but had failed to do, and even what wrong actions we had merely thought about doing or right actions we had merely thought about failing to do. Or it would be as if any respect in which we err would be broadcast immediately on the Internet. No doubt any of these circumstances would serve as a great barrier to wrongdoing and even to contemplating wrongdoing. A choice to behave wrongly, or a choice not to act correctly, or a mere thought about a wrong action or failure to act, and so forth—I will disregard most of these cases for the sake of simplicity—which is made in such circumstances would be a choice in which one is constrained in important respects, respects in which one would not be constrained if one thought that wrongdoing would go unnoticed. The appeal of right conduct would be so overwhelming and our pursuit of it so natural and spontaneous that wrongdoing would hardly tempt us at all.

The case where God, rather than other human beings, would know what we are choosing, and would be understood by us to know this, is of course somewhat different. It would be a matter of knowing oneself to be observed by someone with whom one is intimately connected, whose disposition toward one is of great importance, and whose respect and esteem are coveted. The relevant factors that would generate the inhibiting effect would include fear of punishment, awe, a wish not to displease God, and a wish not to be embarrassed or ashamed before God. The fear would not be of public exposure and embarrassment, as would be the case if we feared the consequences of being disapproved of by other humans, but how different would it be? This is not an easy question to answer: it is not easy to know how things would be if the existence and nature of God were clear to everyone and if we were in immediate and constant interaction of the requisite sort with a being such as God. It is hard to know exactly what this sort of intimate interaction would be like and hard to know exactly what effects such circumstances would have on those who experience them. But it seems reasonable to think that the effect of our being in such circumstances, and in particular the effect of our awareness that God would know what we are doing, considering doing, and so forth, would be at least as significant as the effect of knowing that our wrong actions would be revealed to other people, and that the consequences of our awareness of God's knowing of our wrongdoing would therefore be at least as serious as the consequences of others with whom we interact knowing of our wrongdoing. Certainly our circumstances would be different in a number of respects from our present circumstances, although, as I have said, we should not overestimate our ability to imagine what they would be like.

Presumably the reason that fear of public exposure restrains people from wrongdoing is that people wish to avoid being ashamed or embarrassed before others, being disapproved of by others, losing the respect of others, and in general suffering the various consequences of being found out, which might well include losses of a material sort. Many of these considerations would also seem to be relevant in the case of exposure before God.

I think that Swinburne's proposal has considerable plausibility. In particular it seems plausible that a permanent and intimate sense of the presence of God, with all that this would involve, would make a drastic difference to the options that confront people and hence to their behavior, limiting their options to a considerable degree in a way that would be morally damaging. Constant awareness that God is present, where this would be at least as clear and obvious as is our normal awareness that another human being is present would provide us with a powerful reason not to do wrong that we lack under present conditions. This might involve each of us carrying on constantly a private conversation with God, a conversation in which God's contributions have all or much of the clarity and immediacy that is typical of the contributions of our human interlocutors, with the result that we would know a lot about God's nature and about what God expects from us. This information could come from many sources, including what God is telling us directly. If we were constantly engaged in a conversation of this sort, we would have a constant companion who would be privy to our goings-on, private and public: perhaps the idea of having the person for whom you have the deepest respect always looking over your shoulder gives some remote sense of what would be involved.

There are indications in Swinburne's work that this is what he has in mind, and that he does not have in mind, for instance, the consequences of our having a sound deductive argument or a compelling inductive argument for God's existence. Thus he mentions on a number of occasions the ill consequences of God's speaking frequently and directly to us, and he thinks of this as a matter of our "seeing God . . . face to face" (The Existence of God, 212). This is entirely different from seeing that a certain conclusion follows from an argument whose premises seem to us to be true.

Another possibility is that God's existence might be apparent to us as a result of a massive and dramatic display of some sort. There is much to say about this possibility, but here I will just observe that it is most reasonable to think of grand displays as being morally damaging when they are understood to incorporate the sort of phenomena that, we have seen, are central to the most convincing reading of Swinburne. They would need to occur frequently. And they would need somehow to convey the sense that one was being observed by God—that certain behavior, for example, is expected of one, and will be rewarded, and so forth. It seems to be, for example, their constancy and the fact that they clearly convey the information that we are under surveillance, rather than their grandeur, that would render grand displays morally problematic, thereby drastically altering the character of our lives.

Another feature of the passage from Swinburne with which I began this section deserves mention. Swinburne says that in a world in which God's existence and nature are clear to us "men would have little temptation to do wrong—it would be the mark of prudence and reason to do what was virtuous." Presumably he means that in such a world people would not be tempted to do what they *believe* to be wrong but would instead have every reason to do what they *believe* to be right. The alternative is that he means that people would not be tempted to do what *is* wrong but would have every reason to do what *is* right. But in circumstances in which there is an ever-present awareness of God, these may coincide. After all, we presumably would then have an additional reliable source of information about what is right and wrong.

There is a related issue that also bears on Swinburne's points: to what extent do people who choose wrong actions understand themselves to be choosing wrong actions? In this context it is interesting to consider these insightful remarks from John Hick: "Our rejection of moral obligations which we are unwilling to accept does not typically take the form of a blank refusal to do what we see to be right, but rather of an evasion at the prior stage of cognition, the turning of a blind eye to the moral facts of the situation. We try to exclude from our minds an obligation which is beginning to dawn unwelcomely upon us."[15] The thought that I want to consider, and it is one that is at least consonant with Hick's remarks, is that someone who does a wrong action typically represents to himself the action in question as acceptable or good for some reason, and typically at most recognizes its wrongness as one of its many features, and probably not the dominant one. The idea is that people typically conceal from themselves the fact that their wrong actions are wrong, or at least the extent to which they are wrong, at least while they are doing them. (So what people do is typically "right in their own eyes.") So people who are doing wrong actions generally do not represent those actions to themselves as wrong; instead, they generally conceive of what they are doing in ways that exculpate them and that even represent their behavior as appropriate. This sort of creative redescription takes, for example, the form of representing victims of wrongful actions as hateful or as deserving of whatever is inflicted on them.

But if it is only, or mostly, actions that are viewed by those who engage in them as clearly evil (or wrong or unacceptable, etc.) that will be inhibited by an awareness of God's presence and by an awareness that God knows what one was thinking or doing, then an awareness of God's presence and the belief that God knows what one is thinking (etc.) may actually fail to deter most wrongdoing. Hence much wrong action might remain an option even if we were constantly aware of God's presence—due to the ease with which we can creatively redescribe what we are doing.

However it is not difficult to bolster Swinburne's proposal to deal with this possibility. First, it is likely that typically there is self-deception or dishonesty involved when wrong actions are creatively redescribed by their perpetrators. If God's existence and character were clear for all to see, such self-deception might be regularly unmasked just as, in general, wrong actions might be exposed. If we were familiar with the exposure of such self-deception, we probably would be less likely to engage in it. Second, if there are wrong actions about whose wrongness people are likely to deceive themselves, we might also be familiar with wrong actions of that particular sort being exposed as wrong, so that the relevant actions would come to be recognized as wrong, and self-deception with respect to them would therefore be more difficult. If God's existence and nature were clear, it might be more difficult to conceal the moral character of one's actions at the moment of action. Hence even if under current conditions most wrong actions are not conceived of as wrong when they are engaged in, this need not be taken to damage greatly Swinburne's proposal.

It might be said that Swinburne is assuming that what matters, or matters most, from the point of view of morality is making choices of the sort that he has in mind, namely, choices between good and evil alternatives, and that while everyone faces such decisions and it matters greatly that we should be able to make them, and that they should be made correctly, there are competing accounts of what it is to live a morally good life. For example, there are accounts that say that what matters is that we should cultivate certain virtues, such as honesty, kindness, and fortitude. Yet whatever such alternative account may be proposed, Swinburne's points can be reformulated accordingly. Thus the contention in this case would be that a clear and ever-present awareness of God would be oppressive and would alter for the worse the texture of attempts to cultivate such virtues. Moreover, the suggestion that morality might, as a whole, be construed in these ways that are, at first blush, less friendly to Swinburne's proposal, seems entirely implausible.[16]

The position under discussion faces a number of further difficulties, and these will be the focus of the remaining sections of this chapter. I will continue to refer to it as Swinburne's proposal because he has, I believe, given the fullest exposition of it. But others have endorsed similar themes. As we have seen, according to Joseph Butler, it is appropriate that we "should be placed in a state of discipline and improvement, where [our] patience and submission is to be tried by afflictions, where temptations are to be resisted, and difficulties gone through in the discharge of our duty."[17] Butler's view is that the process of disciplining and improving us, of fostering patience and submission in us, and of cultivating a capacity to resist temptations, is of profound importance: "Our province is virtue and religion, life and manners; the science of improving the temper, and making the heart better. This is the field assigned us to cultivate . . . [The] only knowledge . . . which is of any avail to us, is that which teaches us our duty, or assists us in the discharge of it" (241, 2). And this project of improvement works best, in Butler's view, when we have only a modest amount of evidence for our religious beliefs. Butler says that "the very notion . . . of a state of discipline and improvement . . . necessarily excludes such sensible evidence and conviction of religion, and of the consequences of virtue and vice" and that "the strict discharge of our duty, with less sensible evidence, does imply in it a better character, than the same diligence in the discharge of it upon more sensible evidence" (236).

4. Mesle's Objection

Swinburne's proposal as to why God should be hidden would be undermined if the claim that it is important for us to be able to do morally wrong acts were shown to be implausible. C. Robert Mesle argues that it would, in fact, be very fortunate if we were no longer free to choose to act in an evil way. Mesle's view is that "meaningful freedom can exist when there are meaningful choices between goods—as when someone decides between devoting their life to art or to science. Further I would argue that a good and omnipotent God should have created us with such a nature and in such an environment that we were free only to choose between goods."[18] It is the latter claim here that is important, for the view that meaningful freedom can exist when there are meaningful choices between goods is compatible with the view that much more meaningful freedom exists when a choice of evils is also available. Also, even if wrong choices lost their appeal, we might still be able to exercise some control over how heroic we will be; for instance, we might be able to make choices about how much of our time, energy, and resources to devote to the needs of others; and we might have a capacity to overcome any desires we may have to avoid actions that will demand a lot from us.[19]

Mesle challenges claims such as the following from John Hick:

[One] who has attained to goodness by meeting and eventually mastering temptations, and thus by rightly making responsible choices in concrete situations, is good in a richer and more valuable sense than would be one created *ab initio* in a state either of innocence or virtue . . . [It] is an ethically reasonable judgment, even though in the nature of the case not one that is capable of demonstrative proof, that human goodness slowly built up through histories of moral effort has a value in the eyes of the Creator which justifies even the long travail of the soul-making process.

> [Virtues] which have been formed within the agent as a hard won deposit of her own decisions in situations of challenge and temptation, are intrinsically more valuable than virtues created within her ready made and without any effort on her own part.[20]

Mesle's response is that freedom to be cruel, in particular freedom to be cruel to children, is just *obviously* without any value. The world would be a better place "if no one was emotionally free to violently assault children (or other people)."[21] Mesle says that he and his wife have tried to raise their own children so that they will be free of emotional urges to harm others. They wish it to be the case that "the very thought of cruel behavior never occurred to them, or else was so repugnant and incredible that they could never act upon it." (34). He points out too that in many contexts when people abuse their freedom, we think it correct to interfere and prevent them from harming others, even if doing so restricts their freedom. ("A child . . . begins to take toys away from a smaller child, or threatens to strike another child with a sharp stick. We surely expect that responsible adults would intervene, restricting the child's freedom"[41].) The world would simply be a better place if we lacked any inclination to harm others. Mesle's points consist in large part in an appeal to our intuitions: isn't it just obvious, he asks, that if we were constructed in such a way that we were free to make choices, but only with respect to options among which there are no harmful ones, then our situation would be better than the current one in which we are free to choose wrong, including harmful, actions? If Mesle were right, the correct response to Swinburne's contention that a clearly existing deity would make wrong actions much less available to us would be that we would not thereby lose anything of significance.

However, I do not think that Hick and Swinburne can be refuted so briskly. Their contention is that moral effort in circumstances in which we can choose to act morally correctly or morally incorrectly, and in which we are able to harm others, is very valuable, and that the development in us of a certain sort of character through that effort is also very valuable. A choice among supererogatory options, for example, is much less valuable.

At first glance it may seem counterintuitive or even paradoxical to suggest that it is good for us to be able to harm others. Yet there are reasons to think there to be great value in our being capable of harming or even destroying each other but generally forbearing to do so. One reason is that in that case we are responsible for each other to a greater degree than would otherwise be possible and it is therefore tremendously important what choices we make. If I can help you when you are in difficulty, or ruin you when it is to my advantage to do so, your future is in my hands in a way that it would never be if we were not vulnerable to each other. The notion that a world in which we have a great deal of responsibility for each other is better on that account is plausible.

This responsibility that we have for each other in circumstances such as ours, in which we are vulnerable to each other, has a number of aspects. There is the obvious fact that we can choose to benefit or to harm others around us, both in the subtle ways and in the not so subtle ways in which that can occur. (The subtle ways include, for example, whether we respond to the difficulties, needs, concerns, and so forth of others with encouragement and charity—or with cynicism, callousness, and a lack of charity.)

Others are also affected by the sorts of people that we are, by how we react to situations that we encounter and, in general, by the sort of society that we jointly create, which in turn holds out various possibilities for people and excludes others.

Also, by making certain choices, particularly over sustained periods, in such areas—how we treat others, how we look on others, what the subtleties of our interaction with others are, what ways of behaving we contribute to encouraging, and so on—we become certain types of people. In a world of the sort that Hick and Swinburne have in mind, our character is to a great extent the product of our own struggle and striving: our character is *ours* in a way that it can never be if it is produced in us in its final form. And it is not just the fact that our character is forged and refined through numerous experiences, errors, difficulties, encounters, and so forth, that is important, but that we forge our own character. Further, when our actions can hurt or benefit others greatly, there is much more at stake when the nature of our character is being settled. We can be people who are constantly and creatively seeking opportunities to address the difficulties of others, perhaps starting a movement that transforms the lives of millions. Or we can be indifferent and callous, allowing others to suffer without a care, or even treating them in a brutal fashion. In sum, a world in which we are vulnerable to each other is *our* world in important respects: the character of this world is to a large extent a product of our choices.

It is true that in a world in which evil options have no appeal (because the manifest and intimate presence of God renders such options unattractive or for any other reason), we might have a lot of control over, for example, the extent to which we would devote our time, energy, and resources to solving, say, the most pressing social and environmental problems, over the extent to which we would cultivate, say, the virtue of courage and, in general, over what sort of people we will be. So there would be room for certain forms of heroism. But in our current conditions there is room for additional forms of heroism and for additional important types of choice. Moreover, in a world in which the manifest and intimate presence of God has rendered wrong options unavailable, the value of the forms of heroism that remain available may also be reduced: they may, for example, take on the character of something that is to be expected.

However, my aim is not to argue that this is how things *are*. It is the more modest one of pointing out that Hick and Swinburne have resources at their disposal that provide a way for them to deal with Mesle's objection.

5. Schellenberg's Objections

Some additional objections to Swinburne have been advanced by J. L. Schellenberg. It is important to see the context in which Schellenberg presents these objections. His contention is that a loving God would render nonbelief unreasonable. And, as I discuss in chapter 5, he contends that the fact that nonbelief is reasonable provides the basis for a weighty case against the existence of a loving God. A loving God would render nonbelief unreasonable by providing evidence, perhaps in the form of religious experiences, that adequately supports belief by rendering it probable. (Actually Schellenberg's view is that this is so only in the case of those who are capable of relating personally to God; I will ignore this qualification here.) Since belief is involuntary, a person con-

fronted with evidence that renders belief probable will believe, unless she culpably re-
sists belief.

Schellenberg considers various putative reasons why a loving God would *not* render
nonbelief unreasonable, and it is in the course of considering such reasons, all of which
he finds unconvincing, that he introduces and considers Swinburne's proposals. Now it
is important to notice that Schellenberg is here considering whether Swinburne's arguments serve a purpose for which Swinburne did not design them. And it may be that
Swinburne's arguments fail to serve the purpose that Schellenberg has in mind while
they serve the purpose for which Swinburne intended them. Indeed, I think that this is
in fact the situation: Swinburne's arguments are quite successful at explaining why we
do not each constantly have a sense of the intimate presence of God but are less successful when it comes to explaining why the facts about God are not (merely) sufficiently
clear that nonbelief is irrational. This is so just because it is not clear that the various ill
consequences that Swinburne reasonably believes would arise if God's existence were
very apparent to us after the fashion discussed earlier would also arise if it were merely
the case that nonbelief were irrational. Consequently, it probably is true that Swinburne's case is not very effective at showing that it would be very unfortunate if nonbelief were irrational. But we need to consider whether Schellenberg's objections suffice
to show that Swinburne's arguments fail to serve the purpose for which Swinburne intended them.

Schellenberg considers first the possibility that we read Swinburne as saying that it is
fear of punishment that would restrain people from wrongful behavior if God's existence
were clear for all to see. The following difficulties arise, he suggests.[22] Even if there is fear
of punishment, the punishment might be believed to be in the distant future. Or it might
be believed to be imposed in virtue of one's conduct throughout one's entire life. Or it
might be that in the heat of the moment, when one is about to engage in a wrongful act,
one would deceive oneself into thinking that God would be lenient in this particular case.
Even if the punishment were thought to be immediate, one might be so consumed with
a desire to do a wrong act that in the heat of the moment an awareness of punishment to
come would be temporarily blotted out. Again, one might deceive oneself about the
wrongness of the act in question or about the likelihood of punishment, or about some
other feature of the situation. Schellenberg's view is that "it is only if an individual believes that God's policy on punishment implies that a failure to do good actions will in the
here and now result in bodily harm or loss of life . . . [that is] correlated with each bad
action . . . that the motivating effect of his belief can be plausibly viewed as great"
(124). Schellenberg might also have mentioned that there often is genuine uncertainty
about which actions are wrong. This is a further reason that knowledge that wrong actions will have unfortunate consequences would sometimes fail to deter people from actions that are genuinely wrong. It has the result that even if they know that wrong actions
will be punished, and even if the knowledge that they would be punished for a particular
wrong action would deter them from that wrong action, they may nevertheless not be
deterred from some wrong actions.

The claim that if it is fear of punishment that would have morally harmful consequences, then it matters greatly how we conceive of the punishment in question, is a
plausible one. However, Schellenberg's next move is more questionable. He writes as
follows:

Why should God's goodness be taken to imply that he will harm us severely each time we do wrong? It seems much more reasonable to suppose that persons met in experience by a loving God would come to believe (correctly) that God desired their deepest well-being, and that they would, in consequence, be left without a clear belief about the ultimate implications of resisting the good or with the belief that God would never refuse anyone a second chance (or, at the very most, with the belief that only after persistently, over a long period of time, rejecting the good, the likelihood of well-being in the hereafter would be greatly diminished). (125)

Schellenberg argues that this is how people would think of God, and of the punishment that they might expect. In particular, a person who is so situated would either (a) lack a clear belief about the consequences of wrongdoing, or (b) believe that God would always provide a second chance, or (c) believe that only persistent wrongdoing would lead to punishment. And their expectations would be confirmed by what they observe in human life: they would see that whatever punishment is inflicted is not immediate, for example. Hence they would not be deterred from wrongdoing after all. Schellenberg concludes that "[the] Swinburnian case fails . . . when stated in terms of punishment" (125).

The question is this: would the sort of intimate relation to God that we are assuming while discussing Swinburne's claims be likely to have the effects suggested by Schellenberg? It probably is the case that a person who is so situated would come to believe that God desired his deepest well-being. Every episode in his constant interaction with God would help to deepen his sense that this is so.

Of course, what beliefs people form about the effects of wrongdoing under the specified conditions would depend on the sort of punishment that God would actually be seen to impose. (Schellenberg in effect acknowledges this when he says that expectations of the sort he mentions would be confirmed by what is observed in human life.) So the form that punishment would take would no longer be a matter for speculation if we enjoyed constant intimate interaction with God. The question is: what reason do we now have to think that it would take one form rather than another?

Actually, there are what we might think of as conflicting pressures here in that it is likely that fear of punishment will deter wrongdoing most effectively (by reducing most considerably the attractiveness of engaging in wrongdoing) if the punishment in question is understood to be inflicted both immediately and on account of particular infractions, whereas a loving God is most naturally thought of as not inflicting punishment of this sort but instead as providing second chances and multiple opportunities for reform. Nevertheless, a loving God may reasonably be expected to inflict punishment that would drastically reduce our capacity to behave morally incorrectly. Even if the punishment is not connected to particular cases of wrongdoing, and is not immediate, a loving God might inflict punishment that is sufficiently immediate and sufficiently linked to particular cases of wrongdoing that it would be a significant deterrent to wrongdoing. Being thoroughly immediate and being linked clearly to particular actions, and being thought of as such, are not necessary for being a significant disincentive to wrongdoing and for having a powerful inhibitory influence on agents, even if diminished immediacy (etc.) would diminish the deterrent effects. Moreover, punishment that is immediate and linked to particular cases of wrongdoing may itself be a catalyst for reform and therefore may actually be what makes it worthwhile to provide a

second chance. So it is a mistake to assume that if God wishes to provide us with opportunities for reform then God will not impose punishment that is both immediate
and manifestly imposed in virtue of particular actions.

Schellenberg also considers an alternative reading of Swinburne, namely, that it is an
awareness that God will think badly of us if we act wrongly, rather than fear of punishment, that would make impossible a choice of destiny. "Desiring to be well thought of
by God, whom we knew to be aware of all our actions and thoughts, we would have little temptation to do evil. It would be *easy* to do the good in every situation, and so we
would be left without a genuine choice of destiny" (126).[23] Schellenberg's response to
this theme is that there is a conflict between the belief that God would think badly of
us under certain circumstances and "the notions of equal regard and unconditional
acceptance"—notions which we "naturally associate with perfect love" (126). He thinks
that someone who has an experience of God of the sort that he has in mind (and presumably the same holds a fortiori of someone who has an ongoing intimate relationship of the sort that we need to assume if Swinburne's position is to be presented in its
strongest form) will believe that God "accords to each of us a basic dignity and value
which is not altered by our actions, good or bad" and views each of us as "irreducibly
valuable" (127). Schellenberg contends that this notion of God seems to conflict with
conceiving of God as thinking well of us insofar as we are good and thinking badly of
us insofar as we are bad.

But there is no such conflict. Consider a simple analogy. A mother can value her children equally, accepting each child unconditionally, and for that matter viewing the welfare of each as equally important, while thinking less well of some than of others. Her
thinking less well of some than of others might, for example, take the form of thinking
that some have a stronger character than others, or are more admirable or more clever, for
example. The fact that she values them equally, on the other hand, may be evinced by the
fact that her feelings of concern for the welfare of each of them are equally strong. Equally
valuing them is compatible with a host of comparative judgments. All that is necessary for
Swinburne's purposes is an account of some respect in which we might be badly thought
of by God—such that our awareness that we would be thought badly of in that respect if
we were to behave badly would have an effect on our behavior—but which is consistent
with the idea that we are equally valued by God. And that seems easy to supply. An evaluation of us as moral agents, with some scoring better than others in this respect, is a different matter from according us a basic level of respect that is due to everyone.

Schellenberg makes the further point that even if we believed that we would be
thought less well of by God, there are various reasons why our bad desires might not be
overwhelmed. Here his criticisms parallel those offered in his discussion of punishment. Similar forms of self-deception might be operative: for example, one might deceive oneself about the moral status of an action. Or one might focus attention on the
approval of flawed human beings rather than on the disapproval of a thoroughly good
God. Or one might convince oneself that particular episodes of bad behavior would not
be repeated in the future and hence would not have serious consequences. And so forth.
My response here is as it was in the case of punishment. Factors such as these may indeed reduce the extent to which an awareness of how God would think of us would
inhibit wrongful action, but there is no reason to believe that they would reduce it
drastically or even greatly.

An additional line of criticism, also mentioned by Schellenberg, brings us back to a theme that was discussed in the first section of this chapter. For here, too, there is relevant empirical evidence; and it may seem to count against Swinburne's proposal. Those who under present circumstances are sure of God's existence and nature seem very capable of wrong actions. This seems true both for those who believe they have a proof of God's existence and for those who are convinced that God is aware of their every move. The situation of those who believe that they have a proof, even if they are wrong, seems relevantly similar to what would be the situation of those who both believe they have a proof and actually have a proof. The same goes for those who under current circumstances, in which it is not clear that God is aware of their every move, are convinced that this is so. And if certainty about God's existence (etc.) when the facts are not obvious is not destructive of one's capacity to act morally, why would it be destructive for there to be such certainty when God is not hidden and the facts are obvious?

But there are responses that are open to Swinburne. The points that were made in response to the empirical evidence that was adduced against the loss-of-responsibility proposal merit repetition here. First, under current circumstances there is a consideration that may serve as an incentive to moral action and that might well be absent if God's existence were apparent to us, namely, that by engaging in morally admirable behavior, believers may hope to make known a hidden God. Second, someone whose theistic beliefs are certain under current circumstances may be aware at some level that what she believes to be true is not obviously true; perhaps this has a subconscious influence on her. The idea is that however firmly she may believe at present, and however certain she may be, she is certain under conditions in which there is room for uncertainty and doubt. And that difference may make a difference to the extent to which people feel that they can get away with wrong actions. For example, it may make possible a sort of mental distancing from the entire idea of God's existence.

Moreover, Swinburne can simply allow that people who under present circumstances are certain of God's existence may actually be somewhat inhibited from wrong actions. The fact that people who are certain of God's existence do wrong actions tells you little about the extent to which this certainty has actually operated as a restraining influence, diminishing the appeal of wrong options. And if people are inhibited to some degree from wrong actions under our present circumstances—in which the existence of God is not clear, in which even those who claim they have a proof or who claim that for one or another reason they are certain of God's existence, are to some degree aware that the existence of God is not clear, and in which belief that God exists can consequently be repressed or ignored—then they would be yet more inhibited if God's existence, and whatever facts about God's nature might be accessible to us, were plain for all to see.

Lastly, the relevant empirical evidence is less clear in this case than it was in the case of the loss-of-responsibility problem. That people with great certainty about God's existence suffer no apparent loss of a sense of responsibility for others seems clear: we can tell that this is so from their behavior. But whether wrong options have a diminished appeal for people who are certain about God's existence is harder to assess. In summary, Schellenberg's points may weaken Swinburne's case somewhat, but there is no reason to think that they undermine it entirely.

6. Conclusion

This by no means exhausts the objections to a case such as Swinburne's. Thus it might be objected that if too much evidence for God's existence would be harmful, perhaps the best situation would be one in which there is no evidence at all for God's existence or even weighty evidence against it. In that case, it might be said, there would be room for *real* moral heroism, for we would have no religiously based reason at all to think that we would benefit by behaving morally. If a lot of evidence would be really harmful, then would a little bit of evidence not be a little bit harmful, so that least harmful of all would be the case in which we have no evidence at all?

However, the obvious response is just that someone who thinks that it is fortunate that we do not have a proof or a clear case for God's existence need not be committed to the view that it would be fortunate if we had no evidence at all for God's existence. There may be a relevant threshold below which the amount of evidence must fall if the bad consequences that Swinburne discusses are to be avoided; yet there may be no further advantage (with respect to morality) in falling yet further below it, and there may even be significant disadvantages to doing so.

Again, it might be asked how theists are to square a belief in heaven, which is understood to be both an ideal state of affairs and a state of affairs in which people would automatically do what is right, with the claim that it is of great importance that we make choices such as the choice not to harm others in circumstances in which we could do so. One response is simply to point out that from the fact that it matters greatly that wrong options should be open to us now it does not follow that they should always be open to us.

But here are four additional objections that deserve to be taken more seriously. First, the force of Swinburne's points is diminished somewhat if we assume that what God would be believed by us to want from us, if God's existence and intimate presence were constantly manifest to us, would be actions which are done because they are right, and that actions that are done because we, for instance, wish to avoid punishment or wish to avoid being badly thought of by God would not be enough. For a recognition that what matters is that we engage in right conduct because it is right might have the result that we would take steps to ensure that our right actions would be done because they are right, and not for some other reason. And all of this might mitigate the harmful effects that Swinburne says would arise from the facts about God being clear to us.

Swinburne might reply that it is all very well to say that we would take such steps, but that if God's existence were clear, we simply would be unable to do what is right because it is right, even if we *were* to recognize that what God wants from us is that we do what is right because it is right. But he would need to explain why this is so.

Second, according to the school-for-character-development line of thought under discussion, we are in the midst of a great ongoing developmental adventure in which our character is tested and tried. But is our situation fair? In virtue of their genetic endowment, family background, cultural context, educational opportunities, and so forth, some people are much better equipped than others to face the challenges, difficulties, temptations, and so forth, that come their way. For example, for some people it comes naturally to be generous to others, whereas for others even a small step in this direction would be a major achievement.

This is, however, hardly a knockdown objection. One response is to think of what is necessary for success in the school-for-character-development as relative to each individual so that one's native endowment—where one is starting from—is taken into account. Another response, or rather a variation of the same theme, is to point out that those who are especially well endowed in the relevant respects may have their own attendant hurdles to overcome. Here are some likely candidates: thinking that one is special or important or superior to others, or thinking that one somehow deserves to occupy the privileged position of being better equipped in the relevant respects, or lacking empathy for others who are not as fortunately situated in those respects, or thinking that one's interests or welfare matters especially—so that the very characteristics that equip one to succeed along certain dimensions have a dark underside and carry their own set of challenges and lessons to be learned. What puts one in a better position has its own possibilities for egotism and for exercising the will to power.

Third, as I have intimated above in section 2 of this chapter, there may also be goods of clarity in this area. It is after all something of a commonplace in the theistic traditions that more knowledge of God would be morally beneficial. For example, the importance of doing what is morally right might be more apparent to us and less easily forgotten if the facts about God were clear to us. Or we might be more morally resolute. As a result, there would be fewer wrong actions and, presumably, fewer bad consequences. And there would be more morally correct actions and morally good consequences. So perhaps the situation is that—for the reasons proposed by Swinburne—some ill moral effects would result if the facts about God were clear, but there would also be some beneficial moral effects. However, someone who thinks with Swinburne that there are moral goods of mystery can accept that there are also moral goods of clarity.

Of course the moral implications of God's hiddenness are just one of many relevant areas. There may be other goods of mystery and other goods of clarity. Because this is so it could be that the moral goods of clarity might actually outweigh the moral goods of mystery even while all the goods of mystery, taken together, suffice to account for God's hiddenness. In that case the moral implications of God's hiddenness would not be beneficial. I discuss the general topic of the overall balance of good and bad consequences of God's being hidden in chapter 6, and I postpone further discussion of it until then.

Fourth, it may be that theism requires that God would produce the best world that God could produce. If that is so then, if God exists, this world in which we are free with respect to evil options and have a concomitant vulnerability to each other and responsibility for each other is a better world than any in which there are no beings that are free with respect to evil options, where that includes both worlds in which there are no free beings and worlds in which there are free beings who are so constructed that evil options are not open to them. In considering whether this is so, you have to weigh into the relevant calculation the sorry history of human cruelty and viciousness and all of its consequences for innocent people and animals. At the end of the twentieth century the calculation must include the annihilation of other species, the destruction of their habitat, and all the harm we are doing to the ecosystems we inhabit. You also have to take into account whatever is good about good choices that are made by beings who are free with respect both to good and to evil options; this would include the good consequences of such good choices, but there may be more involved than that. And it is far from obvious what would be the outcome of a complex calculation that would take all of this into account. However, since this is not obvious, it is also not obvious that Swinburne's proposal is to be rejected on this count. Moreover, it is not clear that we should assume that God would produce the best world that God could produce. I also return to this last theme in chapter 6.

To draw this survey of objections to a close, my view is that, taken together, while they do not suffice to *refute* Swinburne, their cumulative effect is to weaken his proposal considerably. Nevertheless, it remains a possibility that Swinburne's proposal about certain morally valuable states of affairs may contribute something to an explanation of God's hiddenness. As we have seen, the putative goods of mystery that seem worthy of discussion in this context include the good that consists in our not being fawning sycophants who do what is right to please God and the related good of our facing certain choices between good and evil under conditions in which both options are open to us. My view is that a case of this sort is likely to be a part of any plausible theistic response to God's hiddenness.

Swinburne's case is most compelling as a way to show that it would be harmful for us to have continuous intimate interaction with God. It does not provide reason to think that, for example, more evidence than is currently available would be harmful. We have seen little reason to believe that it would be unfortunate for God's existence to be somewhat more apparent than is now the case. For all that has been shown to the contrary, this could occur without any bad moral consequences. Moreover, perhaps God's existence could be considerably more apparent without any extremely bad moral consequences. It is difficult to make the case that the ill effects that, Swinburne suggests, would accompany a great degree of intimacy between us and God would also occur in various weaker scenarios. If there would be morally harmful consequences in these weaker cases, they probably would be less harmful. Thus our capacity for the sorts of choices that matter to Swinburne might be reduced somewhat without being eliminated. God's presence, God's awareness of one's actions, God's relevant intentions, and so forth, might be more easily ignored. The factors that would reduce the fear of punishment, for example, would be more likely to come into play; and the factors that would reduce the significance of the wish for God not to think badly of us would also be more likely to come into play. Consequently the appeal of evil options would be reduced to a lesser extent, if at all. Lastly, Swinburne's arguments are less compelling as a case against, say, our having a proof or a strong inductive argument for God's existence. We might have either without having the sort of constant sense of God's presence that we have seen to be central to his proposal.

3

GOD'S HIDDENNESS, FREEDOM TO BELIEVE, AND ATTITUDE PROBLEMS

1. God's Hiddenness and Freedom to Believe

In this chapter I consider the merits of the claim that it is good and appropriate that the facts about God's existence and about God's nature should not be clear to us on the grounds that this enables us to exercise control over what, if any, religious beliefs to hold and in particular whether to believe that God exists. I probe various versions of this claim and various objections to these versions. The important questions for my purposes are these: Is there an important good of mystery to be found in this area? Is there something here that could contribute to an explanation of God's hiddenness?

The account of God's hiddenness that I will consider here has a number of parts, including the following claim:

> (A) If there were available to us a clear case for God's existence, it would be impossible for us to exercise control over whether we believe that God exists.

According to this account, it is also a good and valuable thing that we exercise control over what we believe in this area, and it would be bad and unfortunate if the belief that God exists were forced on us. This account assumes, too, that we are capable of exercising control over what we believe about such matters. Presumably if we have this capacity with respect to religious belief, we have it in other areas too. I refer to the view that we are able to exercise considerable control over what we believe as "volitionalism."[1] And for ease of discussion I refer to the larger theory about God's hiddenness that is under discussion, and that consists of a number of parts including volitionalism and (A), as "cryptovolitionalism"; and I call someone who advocates it a "cryptovolitionalist." This chapter is devoted to an exploration of this possibility.

Here are two statements that involve cryptovolitionalism. The first is from John Hick and the second from Alasdair MacIntyre.

> Why should God want to present himself to his human creatures in such an indirect and uncertain way instead of revealing himself in some quite unambiguous fashion that would permit no possible room for doubt as to his reality? Perhaps the answer is that God is leaving men free in relation to himself. Perhaps he has deliberately created an ambiguous world for us just in order that we shall *not* be compelled to be conscious of him.

> [If] religious belief was the kind of thing that could be presented as the conclusion of an argument, we should either have too much certitude or too little for the belief in question to be a religious belief. For if we could produce logically cogent arguments we should produce the kind of certitude that leaves no room for decision; where proof is in place, decision is not. . . . If the existence of God were demonstrable we should be as bereft of the possibility of making a free decision to love God as we should be if every utterance of doubt or unbelief was answered by thunder-bolts from heaven. But this kind of free decision is the essence of the Christian religion.[2]

I say that these remarks *involve* cryptovolitionalism, since Hick and MacIntyre both have more than cryptovolitionalism in mind. MacIntyre thinks that the price we would pay for certitude would not only be that we would be unable to make a decision to believe that God exists; in addition, certainty would deprive us of an opportunity to make a decision to love God. This, too, MacIntyre says, would be forced on us if God were not hidden. Other remarks from Hick suggest that he, too, has something more comprehensive in mind.[3] And what Hick says here is not precisely that it may be important that the world should be ambiguous so that we will be in a position to exercise control over what we believe, but rather that in virtue of this ambiguity we are not compelled to be *conscious* of God. Hick thinks that God could have created us as beings who are conscious of God, but that it is better that we should develop this consciousness, as well as various admirable qualities of character, by choosing to do so. To use terms that Hick himself has made familiar, our cognitive freedom requires that the world be ambiguous. But I presume that (a) being conscious of God involves holding certain beliefs about God and that (b) Hick's view is that part of what would be wrong with our having consciousness of God imposed on us would be that the beliefs in question would then be forced on us. It seems, therefore, that part of what is being said by both authors is that if God were not hidden, we would not be in a position to make up our minds about the facts about God. So there is a cryptovolitionalist component in the thinking of both authors. And this is the aspect of these remarks from Hick and MacIntyre on which I propose to focus. In any case my concern is with the position itself rather than with whether Hick or MacIntyre advocates it.

I will not say much about volitionalism. The remarks that I make about it in this section serve at best as an indication of some of the questions that arise once one begins to consider its truth. All that actually matters for my purposes is that we should be able to exercise control, of some sort or other, over our beliefs. If there is no way in which we are able to do so, the claim that it is an advantage of God's hiddenness that it enables us to exercise such control is nugatory. There are, I will suggest, two ways in which we appear to be able to exercise such control.

We are not able to bring it about that we hold a belief simply by willing that we shall do so. That is, we are unable to move from entertaining a belief to holding it merely by trying to do so. So *direct* volitionalism, at least, is mistaken.[4]

By introspection we can see that we do not enjoy much success when we try to will directly that we should believe a proposition. Efforts of this sort appear not to work.[5] But we can do more than appeal to introspection. There are also reasons that this is out of the question as a matter of principle. Here are two relevant considerations.[6] First, to believe a proposition is, in effect, to register something about how things seem to be: it is to register what seems to be a fact about the world. And typically you cannot make things seem—that is, really seem—to you to be a certain way merely by willing that this should be so. So what is wrong with direct volitionalism can be seen just by reflecting on what it is to believe something to be the case. Second, if we were to bring it about that we held a belief just by willing that we should do so, we would typically know we had done so, and it is impossible to believe p while knowing that it has come about that you believe p *via* your own efforts. You would know too much about how the mental state in question had come about for it to be a case of belief. So direct volitionalism is out of the question, at least in cases in which one would be aware of having directly caused oneself to have the belief.

William P. Alston says that not only are we unable to bring it about that we hold a belief by willing it as a basic act, that is an act that can be done without doing anything else; in addition, we are unable to bring it about that we hold a belief as a nonbasic act—that is, by doing something else. I can wave my hand as a basic act. I can also greet my neighbor by waving my arm, thereby greeting my neighbor as a nonbasic act. But I cannot bring it about that I hold a belief in either way.[7]

This much seems correct. Just as we are unable to bring it about that we hold a belief in a direct and immediate way, by willing that we shall do so, we are also unable to acquire a belief as a single nonbasic act. Nevertheless, it seems that we are able to exercise a good deal of *indirect control* over our beliefs, including control over whether we will acquire a belief. It seems that to a considerable extent we can bring about, or fail to bring about, changes in our beliefs by making, or failing to make, changes in something else. The view that we can exercise this sort of indirect control is usually known as *indirect volitionalism*.

For instance, to borrow from what Pascal says in his discussion of the Wager, if I were a Roman Catholic Christian who is experiencing doubts, I might know that if I were to join a religious order in which I would be surrounded by serious, reflective, and supportive Catholics, I would probably shed my doubts, just as I might know that my doubts are likely to increase if I spend my spare time associating with freethinkers or reading works that poke fun at Catholicism, or at Christianity, or at religion in general. Again, I might know that many reasonable people have been persuaded that a certain view is correct by reading certain books, and I might set out to read those books with a view to acquiring the belief in question.

That people bring it about through indirect means that they hold various beliefs is in fact a fairly obvious feature of religious life. For example, many people choose to join a religious tradition. Part of what they are doing, when they choose to do so, is choosing to go along with the relevant beliefs. They take on board the whole package, including the lifestyle and the rituals, but also the beliefs. This happens frequently. In some such cases acquisition of the relevant beliefs probably is best understood as an unintended by-product of something else that one has chosen, such as active participation in a certain religious community. But there also appear to be cases in which, knowing that participation will eventually involve belief, in choosing to participate one thereby indirectly chooses to believe.

Again, we may be able to focus our attention on some aspects of a situation or issue rather than others, perhaps by focusing on some particular body of evidence and ignoring or downplaying the significance of other evidence; and in this way we may be able to control, or at least to exercise some control over, how we interpret it, and consequently over some of our relevant beliefs. This particular idea is nicely expressed by Pascal:

> The will is one of the chief organs of belief, not because it creates belief, but because things are true or false according to the aspect by which we judge them. When the will likes one aspect rather than another, it deflects the mind from considering the qualities of the one it does not care to see. Thus the mind, keeping in step with the will, remains looking at the aspect preferred by the will and so judges by what it sees there. (*Pensées*, 218)

Volitionalism presupposes that we can exercise a good deal of control over our beliefs, whether this control be exercised directly or indirectly. And to say that we can, at least sometimes, do so indirectly is fairly uncontroversial. While it seems that belief is willed neither as a basic act nor as a nonbasic act that is achieved by a single basic act, we seem to be able to bring it about that we acquire a belief by pursuing a certain strategy—in the course of which we will do various basic acts.[8]

In my own case, for what it is worth, it seems to me that I can to some extent exercise the following sort of indirect control. I can draw myself toward my own religious tradition, both with respect to my general attitude toward it and, in the process, with respect to holding the beliefs that are associated with it, thereby coming to believe more strongly. I can do so by reading the writings, and imbibing the ideas, of authors who (a) argue for that tradition, or for other traditions that resemble it, in ways that are insightful and do not rely on fanciful speculation, and who (b) do not claim to know more than, it seems to me, people are typically in a position to know, who (c) are knowledgeable in relevant areas and fair-minded in their approach to the relevant issues. I can also bring about these effects by focusing on the aspects of my tradition that seem to me to be especially precious and therefore worthy of preservation. Yet again I can do so by reading works that attack religion in an unfair, dismissive or extreme way, since that puts me on the side of the position that is being unfairly attacked.

On the other hand, I can distance myself from my tradition, in the various respects just mentioned, by reading authors who oppose religious positions in a fair and balanced way, or who give plausible accounts, in terms lacking all religious presuppositions, of phenomena that religions have thought themselves uniquely able to explain. I can also do so by reading authors whose defense of religious claims manifests an obliviousness to any difficulties that such claims need to confront, or who are dogmatic or pompous or unreflective in their conviction that they are right. (It would not be surprising if these and other types of literature were to affect different people in different ways. And of course to talk in general terms about these "types of literature" is to fail to distinguish a multitude of subtly different genres and works.) Yet again, I can distance myself by failing to bother to focus on relevant matters.

Indirect volitionalism raises further questions. One intriguing question concerns how we are to conceive of the status that a proposition p has for a person S when S indirectly wills that S will believe p. For one thing, if when S does so, S already thinks that p is true, then S *already* believes p: so what is there here to will? For example, if S already believes that modern factory farming is morally unacceptable, it is senseless to think that S would set out to acquire that belief. And if S does not believe it, why would S set out to try to acquire the belief?

However, S may have reasons for wishing to believe p that do not have to do with the truth of p: for example, an acceptance of p might seem to S to be essential for the kind of life that S wishes to live, or for membership in a social group or religious tradition to which S wishes to belong. S may have numerous reasons of this sort—reasons that are not directly connected with a recognition that p is true—for desiring or even longing to believe that p.

Yet an awareness of the truth of a proposition may also play a role here. For instance, S might form the view that it is because of the improper influence of one or more inclinations that S has heretofore resisted the belief that p—while all the while more or less believing p to be true. In this sort of case S seems already to half-believe that p. The inclination in question might be an inclination not to accept the belief per se. Or it might be an inclination to do something that S feels (rightly or wrongly) he will be prevented from doing, or unable to do, or that will become more difficult, if he accepts the belief in question. Thus, by way of an example, S might be aware that the easy and inexpensive availability of meat, which S greatly enjoys eating, has prevented him from fully facing up to a recognition that most of the meat he eats has been produced using morally unacceptable methods and that he ought to desist henceforth from consumption of all such meat.

Under what circumstances can we exercise indirect control over our beliefs? To see what is meant by this question we need to take a short detour. Situations in which S might believe a proposition p can be categorized as follows. There are situations in which p seems to S to be more probable than not; these include cases in which p seems certain. And there are situations in which p seems to S to be less probable than not, including cases in which p seems to S to be clearly mistaken. There are also situations that seem ambiguous to S. Thus the available evidence may seem to S to balance out and not to support one reading or interpretation rather than another; or it may seem to S that it is hard to tell which position the balance of the evidence supports; or a certain proposition may seem to S not to be implausible, and yet S may find that he does not have much relevant evidence, one way or the other. Perhaps someone tells S that p is true, but the person in question has a mixed record, either in general or in cases of this sort, sometimes telling the truth and sometimes not, and this is S's only source of information about p; so all in all the relevant evidence is mixed.

I will ignore cases in which p seems to S to be more probable than not. In many such cases, and especially if p seems to S to be much more probable than not, S will believe p, and no act of will on S's part is necessary to do so. (There probably are exceptional cases, such as cases in which S sees that p is much more probable than not but is strongly inclined to disbelieve p, and will believe p only if this inclination is resisted.)

Let us say that *weak* volitionalism is the view that S can exercise control over what S believes in situations that seem ambiguous to S. *Strong* volitionalism, on the other hand, is the view that S can in addition bring it about that he believes p in circumstances in

which p seems less probable than not or even seems false. Versions of strong volitionalism differ over the extent of this control.

Weak volitionalism is obviously a lot easier to defend than strong volitionalism. (So
among the positions discussed so far, the easiest to defend is weak indirect volitionalism.) A version of cryptovolitionalism that requires for its truth only weak volitionalism
is therefore easier to defend than one that requires strong volitionalism, all other things
being equal. Since being weak and strong in the relevant sense are matters of degree
and are not properties that are had either completely or not at all, it is more accurate to
say that *weaker* versions of volitionalism are easier to defend, as are the versions of cryptovolitionalism that incorporate them. Least plausible and hardest to defend are the
strongest of the strong versions, those that say that we can bring it about that we believe
p in circumstances in which p seems clearly false.

So, to conclude this short detour, part at any rate of the answer to the question of
under what circumstances we can indirectly exercise control over our beliefs is that the
claim that we are able to do so in ambiguous circumstances is easier to defend than the
claim that we can do so with regard to a belief that seems false. I will say more about
this idea later in this chapter.

Next I want to distinguish two ways in which we might exercise control over what
we believe. It might be a matter of making an effort either to acquire or to avoid acquiring a particular belief that one entertains. Control is exercised, in other words, with
respect to whether one holds a certain belief that one has already identified. Some cases
of control of this sort also occur in conjunction with a selection from among an array
of possibilities of one belief as the belief that is to be acquired. When that feature is
present, there is more involved than bringing it about that one says "yes" or "no" to a
particular proposition; there is also a process of selecting the proposition in question
from among a number of alternatives.

Then there are cases of a different sort: cases in which S's belief that p comes about,
either wholly or to a considerable extent, as a result of the fact that belief that p fits with
and is an expression of one or more of the following: S's purposes or dispositions or inclinations or attitudes or character, or what S considers to be important, or what interpretations of situations S is inclined toward. (Let us assume that there is a considerable
degree of unity among S's relevant attitudes and inclinations [etc.].) I will refer to all
cases of this sort—cases in which S's belief that p has come about at least to a considerable extent as a result of the fact that belief that p fits with and is an expression of S's
purposes or dispositions or inclinations (etc.)—as cases of *autonomous* belief. Cases of autonomous belief differ from each other in an important respect. S may have exercised a
considerable degree of control over the purposes, dispositions, attitudes (etc.), that are
reflected in the belief that p. In other cases S may just find herself having the purposes,
dispositions (etc.) in question.

One feature of autonomous belief is its relative effortlessness. One confronts alternative beliefs as a person with certain attitudes or interests or with a certain character, and
the adoption of one among the alternatives comes naturally. And cases of this sort need
not involve any prior identification of the relevant proposition as the one that is to be
believed or any attempt to bring it about that one will hold any belief.

If it were clear that we are not able to exercise any control of the relevant sort, or if it
were incoherent to suggest that circumstances in which we would want to do so might

arise, cryptovolitionalism would be implausible and we should not bother to discuss it further. But that is not the case, so at least on this score it should not be eliminated from consideration. We seem in fact to be capable of exercising two sorts of control: one involves indirect willing, and the other is control of the sort that is involved in autonomous belief.

Earlier I noted two difficulties for direct volitionalism. We need to ask whether these difficulties confront the two possibilities mentioned in the last paragraph. Those difficulties were that (a) to believe a proposition is to register something about how the world seems to you to be, and typically you cannot make the world seem a certain way just by trying to do so, and that (b) if we were to bring it about that we held a belief just by willing that we should do so, we would typically know we had done so, and it is impossible to believe p while knowing that you believe p just because you have chosen to do so: you would know too much about how the mental state in question had come about for it to be a genuine case of belief.

Neither difficulty confronts autonomous belief. Such belief arises in response to how the world seems to be. Yet how the world seems to be is, in such cases, to some considerable extent, a function of the character, dispositions, and so forth, of the person who acquires the beliefs. This takes care of the first difficulty. As for the second, the fact that one's character has entered into one's acceptance of autonomous beliefs is just the sort of thing that is likely not to be apparent.

Both difficulties also have diminished force in the case of indirect volitionalism. Thus, in the case of the first difficulty, one can imagine a belief being established gradually and incrementally as a result of steps taken with a view to bringing this about, so that the belief in due course confronts one as something that has to be accepted. Also, the force of the second difficulty is diminished in the case of indirect willing: it would be easier to conceal from oneself the fact that a belief has been acquired as a result of one's own efforts if the route to belief is a circuitous one—one that involves taking a series of steps, each of which can be regarded perhaps as having another rationale. Also, if the process is a gradual one, the new belief may gradually squeeze out the awareness that it has been adopted as a result of an effort to acquire it.

Moreover, in all those cases that I have characterized as cases in which one already "half believes" that p, neither the first nor the second difficulty arises.

In any case, the main conclusion so far is that the proposal that it is important for us to be able to exercise control over what we believe is not undermined by the fact that we are incapable of bringing it about directly by an act of will that we hold a belief. Other sorts of control on our part are possible. However, cryptovolitionalism faces other challenges. Next I consider another challenge to its central component:

(A) If there were available to us a clear case for God's existence, it would be impossible for us to exercise control over whether we believe that God exists.

2. Penelhum's Objection

Terence Penelhum has, in effect, argued against (A). His arguments are presented in *Problems of Religious Knowledge* and in *God and Skepticism*.[9] The target of Penelhum's objection is the cryptovolitionalist who argues that there could not be a proof of God's existence because "[a] successful proof coerces acceptance of its conclusion . . . [but] God . . . does not coerce his creatures into believing in him but respects their freedom," (PRK, 45). Penelhum points out that there can be a sound argument for a proposition p, and one can recognize that argument as such, and yet reject p: "[Facts] which proved [the] . . . existence [of God] . . . where this is understood to mean merely that they entailed it or made it overwhelmingly probable, so that disbelief was thereby shown to be irrational, . . . do not compel assent . . . because men are irrational and do deceive themselves" (PRK, 47; see also GS, 110ff.). So it could be proven that God exists, S could recognize that this has been proven, and yet S could exercise control over whether to believe that God exists. Hence it is wrong to think that a proof would force its conclusions on anyone, even on those who recognize it as a proof.[10] Penelhum's view of the status of a proposition p which has been proven to S, but which S does not accept, appears to be this: S recognizes that p follows from premises which S accepts, but S refuses to accept p. S, we might say, sees that p follows from premises that S accepts, but S does not draw the conclusion that p. Penelhum's point is just that this is a possible state of affairs.[11] (He says that "[proof] merely places hearers in a position where the only barriers to it are the self-imposed barriers of irrationality and self-deceit" [GS, 99].) (A), according to which a proof or clear case for God's existence would make it impossible for us to exercise control over what we believe, is therefore wrong. It is wrong because we deceive ourselves and we can be irrational. Even if we had a proof of God's existence, therefore, we could still bring it about that we would not believe that God exists.

3. Responses to Penelhum's Objection

Two ways in which it is open to the cryptovolitionalist to respond to this criticism, the second of which is the more impressive of the two, are as follows. First, the cryptovolitionalist might question the extent to which we would be in a position to exercise control over what we believe if we had a proof of, or a compelling case for, God's existence. For one thing, if the proof or case in question were obvious, so that to reflect on it at all would result in one being overwhelmed with a sense of the truth of its conclusion, it may be virtually impossible to resist belief. The contrast is with cases in which there is a proof whose comprehension requires grasping a long series of complex premises and their relation both to each other and to the conclusion: here there seems to be more room for us to exercise some control over whether we accept the conclusion. Perhaps in some cases in which there is a proof of some complexity, and one recognizes it as a proof, one could manage not to believe that God exists, although doing so would require gross self-deception and elaborate strategies for avoiding what would clearly be the case.

But could one bring it about that one believes under such circumstances? Everything would speak for the existence of God. Generally speaking, you simply *would* hold this belief. It would be one of a very large set of beliefs that we have that it is hard for us to resist and which most of the time we just find ourselves accepting. Beliefs about what I now see before me, for example, are in this category, as are many obvious and commonsensical beliefs about others and about the world around us. In such cases belief is so spontaneous, natural, and unavoidable that talk of having control over the process that results in your acquisition of a belief, seems idle.[12]

Still, there might be *some* room here for control to be exercised: thus if one had an almost overwhelming urge *not* to believe a conclusion that one could see was entailed by an argument that one had decided was sound, or that rendered its conclusion very probable, one might set out to resist that urge and to acquire (or keep) the belief. In fine, the cryptovolitionalist's first response to Penelhum is that if we had a proof, or a compelling case, our capacity to exercise control over whether to believe would be at least diminished to a very significant extent, for those with access to the proof or compelling case. And if the case were particularly compelling, that capacity might be eliminated entirely.

The second and more decisive response is as follows. The cryptovolitionalist may reasonably make the following proposal about the *sort* of control over belief that it is important for us to have. He can say that what matters is not exactly that it should be possible for us to exercise control over whether we believe, but rather that what matters is that it should be possible for us to do so in circumstances in which either option is rational. That is, the cryptovolitionalist can say that

(B) if there were available to us a clear case for God's existence, it would be impossible for us to exercise control over whether we believe that God exists in circumstances in which either option is rational.

To say that either option is rational is to say that there is some evidence for each position and that the available evidence does not provide the basis for a convincing case for or against either position.[13] (If there is ambiguity, then both the belief that p and the belief that p is false are rational in this sense.) There is therefore an important sense in which it is reasonable to adopt either position.

The cryptovolitionalist can reasonably claim that it is not ad hoc to replace (A) with (B) by way of responding to Penelhum's objection. For (B) reflects the importance of the fact that we are rational beings. If we are able to avoid believing some proposition p only if we are irrational, then while there is on that account a respect in which we are able to avoid believing p, obviously we are able to do so only insofar as we are prepared to compromise our rationality. (B) would explain why a proof, or a case that would render nonbelief much less rational than it now is, is not available to us. So even if Penelhum is correct and it is mistaken to infer that there cannot be a proof of p from the importance of our having control over whether we believe p, control of the sort mentioned in (B) would not be possible if there were a proof or a compelling case. And this, the cryptovolitionalist may reasonably contend, is the sort of control that counts.

So, to summarize, the cryptovolitionalist can respond to Penelhum's objection in either of two ways. The first is to insist that (A) has not really been shown to be wrong, since a proof of p, or a compelling case for p, would at least greatly reduce our capacity to influence whether we believe that p. This amounts to a significant qualification of Penelhum's claim that a proof would not undermine our capacity to exercise control over what we believe. The second is to substitute (B) for (A); this approach amounts to a rejection of Penelhum's claim that a proof would not undermine our ability to exercise control over what we believe on the grounds that a proof would undermine our ability to exercise control of the, or at least an, important sort.

I will refer to what you get when you substitute (B) for (A) as *revised* cryptovolitionalism, and to what you have prior to this substitution as *unrevised* cryptovolitionalism. An attractive feature of revised cryptovolitionalism is that (B), its central ingredient, requires for its plausibility only weak volitionalism, the view that it is possible to exercise control over whether you believe p when the relevant evidence is ambiguous.[14]

My strategy in the rest of this chapter is as follows. In the next section I argue that both forms of cryptovolitionalism face a difficulty. It is not clear whether unrevised cryptovolitionalism can cope with this difficulty, but it seems that revised cryptovolitionalism can do so. I go on to examine further difficulties for revised cryptovolitionalism, and in the final section of this chapter I suggest a promising way of combining this view, or at least some if its central ingredients, with some rather different themes.

4. The Varieties of Religious Belief

The difficulty for both of the forms of cryptovolitionalism that I have just mentioned arises in virtue of the differences between various sorts of belief. This difficulty reflects the fact that you can believe something to be the case and yet have room for maneuver with respect to how you react to what you believe.

Here we need to introduce two fairly obvious distinctions. The first distinction is between what I will call full theism and what I will call minimal theism. The second, which is as familiar as it is obvious, is between *belief that* God exists and *belief in* God.

A full theist takes seriously the belief that God exists and focuses on and pays attention to the nature of God. This belief is central to, rather than peripheral to, his system of beliefs. It dominates, or at least heavily influences, that system and is the focus of much of his attention. Minimal theism, on the other hand, has minimal significance for one's other beliefs. That is, its role in the system of beliefs of the person who holds it is minimal: it makes little difference to the rest of her beliefs and is in this regard rather isolated. It may be a belief whose content has numerous connections with the content of other parts of one's system of beliefs, and it may even be believed by the person who holds it to have those connections. But the role it actually plays is minimal. It has little influence on other beliefs and little influence on behavior. A minimal theist unreflectively accedes to the proposition that God exists, but does so in a detached and uninvolved way, paying little attention to the significance of the belief.

It is likely that minimal theism will also be minimal in its *content*. Given the limited role that minimal theism has in the life of a person who subscribes to it, it would be surprising if it were to be very rich and elaborate in its content. But that is not altogether out of the question. Someone might have learned an elaborate and rich religious story and be able to answer ("by heart" and yet without heart) questions about the details of this story without any of this meaning much to him.

But there must of course be enough content for the belief to count as *theistic* belief. To be a minimal theist is to accept that God exists. A being would not be God unless it were thoroughly good, powerful, wise, and kind (etc.). To believe that God exists obviously does not require believing there to be a being who is understood to have *all* of the attributes that are traditionally ascribed to God, not to mention all of the attributes that are actually possessed by God if God exists. But to believe that God exists requires believing some subset of the total set of propositions that are typically believed about God, and in particular it requires that one hold certain important and key beliefs within the total set. The beliefs that God is good and powerful, for example, are good candidates for inclusion within that essential subset, as are the beliefs that God is the creator of all things, cares about you, and knows and wishes what is best for you. At any rate there has to be some such set of properties which a person believes God to possess in order for her to believe that God, as distinct from some other being, exists; and moral properties have to be included here as well as other properties. There is, in short, a minimal content that must be present in order for belief to count as theistic belief.

There must, in addition, be enough substance for what is going on to count as theistic belief. To see what is meant by this, it is useful to distinguish between minimal and what we might call nominal belief. Nominal belief is belief only in name, involving mere verbal assent. Minimal belief, on the other hand, is a type of belief, but belief that does not matter much to the person who has it.[15]

There seem to be both full theists and minimal theists. Actually it is more accurate to think of there being a spectrum of possibilities between full and minimal belief, but I will just consider the two extreme cases. As will be clear from the ensuing discussion, it suffices for my purposes that there should be a distinction of this general sort to be drawn. It does not matter that we get it absolutely right, if indeed there is such a thing as getting it right. (So it actually does not matter, for instance, whether we define minimal theism as theism with minimal content.)

The distinction between minimal and full belief obviously has application to beliefs in areas other than the area of religion. The same belief can generally be held in either a minimal or a full way, although, as I will mention shortly, there are some beliefs that seem inherently suited to being held in a full way.

The second distinction is the familiar but important one between, on the one hand, belief that God exists and, on the other hand, belief in (faith in, trust in, reliance on, commitment to, etc.) God. (In this chapter I will sometimes refer to belief in as trust, although in doing so I am aware that I may be obscuring some subtle differences between the two notions. I consider the notion of trust in more detail in the next chapter.) Belief in or trust of the sort that I have in mind is an interpersonal phenomenon: it is directed toward a person or persons and presupposes that the person or persons in question exist.

Trust need not be thought of in this interpersonal way. "I trust that you will get well soon" (and other such statements) are sometimes made without anything more being expressed than confidence or hope that the person to whom this is said will get well. (However, the use of this particular locution to express confidence or hope probably derives from its use to refer to interpersonal trust.) But this is not how the term will be used here. Again, trust may be invested in a cause or movement (Marxism, Irish nationalism, the spread of New Age thinking) rather than in a person or being. But I will restrict my attention to trust in a person or being. There are also other uses of "belief in." Thus it is common for people to say that they believe in the existence of God or in the existence of some other being. To say that one believes in the existence of God, I take it, is just to say that one believes that God exists, and to signify that the relevant belief is held in circumstances in which one might reasonably doubt that God exists, or in which there is dispute about God's existence, or something of this sort.

Now that we have these distinctions before us, the objection to be addressed can be introduced, and it is just this. Even if your ability to exercise control over whether or not to be a theist were diminished by a proof or a clear case, you would still have abundant room to exercise control over what you believe in the area of theistic belief: in particular, you could do so with respect to whether or not to have full theistic belief and whether or not to believe in God. (You might also, for instance, be in a position to decide whether to love God or to worship God.) There might also be numerous beliefs, including, for instance, both beliefs about the nature and activities of God and beliefs about numerous other religious matters, with respect to which we might still have a lot of room for maneuver even if, say, we had a proof. And the more minimal we think minimal belief to be, the more room for maneuver in all of these areas there would be.

This objection is closely related to the objection from Penelhum discussed in the previous section. For Penelhum's objection is that you can have a proof of p and yet deny p. The objection under discussion is that you can have a proof of p, and as a result of the availability of this proof come to believe p in the minimal way, and yet have room for maneuver of other sorts with respect to your belief that p. The objection is, further, that the remaining room for maneuver is good enough. So the claim that the facts about God must be unclear in order for us to decide what beliefs to hold appears to face a serious difficulty. Let's call this objection, which arises in virtue of the varieties of belief, the "varieties objection."[16]

5. Responses to the "Varieties Objection"

How is an advocate of cryptovolitionalism to respond to this objection? One response might be that an ability to exercise control even in the case of minimal theistic belief is *itself* important and valuable, and that an ability to exercise control with respect to full theistic belief and belief in God, however valuable these may be, is not enough. But it is not so easy to see what could be so important and valuable about minimal belief that God exists, and hence what could be so important about our having an ability to control whether we adopt such minimal belief. It is easier to see why it would be important that we should respond appropriately once we have the belief that God exists, and why it would be important that we should be able to choose, or exercise control over, whether to so respond. Moreover, even if minimal theism were very important, full theism and trust in God presumably are at least as important. So the question would remain: Why would control over whether we have belief of these varieties not be enough?

A response to the varieties objection that takes a bit of sorting out but that in the final analysis is, I think, unconvincing is as follows: while there is a distinction, at least in theory, between minimal and full theism, if one accepts the former there is no room (or little room, or significantly less room) for choice (or for choice of the right sort, or for exercising the right sort of control) about whether to accept the latter. And the same holds for the relationship between belief that God exists and belief in God. According to this response, the different types of belief cannot be detached from each other in the way required by the varieties objection.

Consider the following case. Imagine a parent who wishes to ensure that his child will have a minimal belief in the truth of Marxism, and who therefore takes steps to ensure that the child will accept that Marxism is true. (The child is sent to summer camp for Marxist youth, where the old songs are sung with gusto around the campfire, and where all the children come under the influence of good Das Kapital–believing Marxists.) The parent also wishes his child to be deeply committed to Marxism and to believe fully in its central claims, but wishes to leave to the child the matter of how deeply to take belief in the truth of Marxism, and the further matter of whether to believe in Marxism. Yet the steps that would ensure that the belief that Marxism is true is inculcated in the child seem to be such that they would reduce greatly the amount of control that the child would have over how deeply to take belief in the truth of, and over whether to believe in, Marxism.

Let us probe a bit further. There are at least two reasons to think that the different types of belief cannot be detached from each other in the way presupposed by the varieties objection, and these reasons are closely related. One thought is that certain causal relations obtain: minimal theism might lead (or lead in the case of many people, or often lead, etc.) to full theism and to belief in God. If so, to adopt minimal belief would be, or often would be, in effect to adopt the other sorts of belief. This would mean that minimal theistic belief is only possible, or usually is only possible, in theory.

Second, it might be thought that people, or most people, would find any belief that God exists to be of such great import for them, and would find it to make such a difference to how they see things, that once they have that sort of belief it would not be possible for them to retain control over whether to be full theists or whether to believe in God. To be a theist at all, even a theist of a very minimal variety, is to accept that there is a creator of all things who cares about you, knows what is in your interests, wishes what is best for you, and so on. It is also to have some awareness that you are a member of God's creation, however exactly you may cash in this notion. And this will normally involve submission or a willingness to submit to the will of such a being. So the suggestion is that belief that God exists is inherently unsuited to being held in the minimal way. Minimal theism, in short, exists only in theory, and is to all intents and purposes out of the question; a belief would not count as belief that God exists unless it involved full belief and trust. The suggestion is also that belief that God exists and trust in God are more of a piece than the advocate of the varieties objection recognizes.

There are various other beliefs that seem to be inherently more than minimal. Imagine that you were somehow to be persuaded that your real parents are not the people whom you have known from childhood but rather are Queen Elizabeth II and the Duke of Edinburgh. Or imagine that you came to the conclusion that most people are worthy of trust, having previously thought otherwise. It is unlikely that you could believe such propositions in the minimal way. Such a belief will matter a lot to the person who holds it. Again, a belief that someone is your friend is likely to be interwoven with a commitment to, and awareness of the appropriateness of, certain ways of interacting with this person as well as with a recognition of the importance of advancing their interests and of supporting them in various ways. That someone is your friend is a proposition that cannot be believed in a detached way and with minimal import for your beliefs and behavior. In short, for this belief to be held, there must in fact be something more than the belief involved: there must be, for instance, a commitment to a certain behavioral response.

So there seems to be something to the suggestion that there are beliefs such that minimal acceptance of them is out of the question. But the problem that confronts the proposal that theism is of this nature is just that there appear to be minimal theists. There appear to be people who believe that God exists, but for whom that belief has little weight. So the causal claim, at least in its strongest form, is wrong. It is not true that theistic belief is inherently more than minimal. (We could of course decide to restrict the term "theistic belief" [or "belief that God exists," etc.] to belief that is full as distinct from minimal, or to belief that involves trust, but this would just be to stipulate that these terms are to be used in a new way.) Moreover, the suggestion that theism is inherently more than minimal because, for example, to be a theist of any sort is to accept that there is a creator of all things who cares about you, knows what is in your interests, and wishes what is best for you, or because theism of any sort involves some awareness that you are a member of God's creation and a willingness to submit to the will of such a being, is dubious. For the minimal theist may not go into such matters: he may be inattentive and fail to focus on the character of the being he believes to exist, and on the implications of its existence. This may be irrational, or unsatisfactory in some other way; yet it seems to occur all the time.

Furthermore, the varieties objection seems to raise a particular problem for *revised* cryptovolitionalism. A proof of, or convincing case for, God's existence would make it irrational not to be a theist. If it is irrational not to accept the belief that God exists, not to accept minimal theism, presumably it is also irrational not to accept full theism. One might be able to see that there is a proof without letting that have much weight with one; that is, one might be *capable* of believing that God exists (in a merely minimal way) and manage to avoid being a full theist. But there is at least something to be said for the idea that one could not do so without being irrational. If it is irrational not to accept that God exists, then it is irrational not to accept that there is a creator of all things who cares about you, knows what is in your interests, wishes what is best for you, and so on; it seems that the rationality of not being a full theist (that is, in effect, of not taking this belief seriously) would be greatly diminished if not eliminated entirely.[17]

It is hard to judge the precise force of these responses to the varieties objection. One complication is that the fact that there are minimal theists might be thought merely to *weaken* the varieties objection. For example, there may be causal factors of the relevant sort that are often or generally at work, and theism may be inherently suited to being held in more than a minimal way, and yet some people may manage to hold it in a minimal way. Perhaps there is something to the idea that once you believe at all that a being with many of God's properties exists, then you will in effect be launched in the direction of full belief and trust. Another thought is that some of what may seem to be minimal theism may merely be nominal theism, or theism only in name. Still, I am inclined to think that the varieties objection suffices to show that cryptovolitionalism, in all of the forms of it discussed so far, is flawed. But whether or not this is so, there is an independent and insurmountable difficulty, one that requires that this proposal be either abandoned or modified drastically.

6. The Trouble with Cryptovolitionalism

Cryptovolitionalism appears to imply that belief that God exists is especially virtuous, or especially valuable in some way, when the facts about God are unclear. It says that it is better to become a theist when it is unclear whether theism is true than to do so when it is clear that theism is true. Revised cryptovolitionalism, in particular, seems to involve the assumption that there is something good about people becoming theists when a number of the relevant available options are rational. The notion that, in general, to believe p when it is unclear whether p is true is somehow preferable to believing p when it is clear that p is true and only one position—namely, the belief that p—is rational, is ridiculous.

A simple example, although one is hardly needed. It is not clear, particularly to a layperson, which among the various competing theories of the destruction of the dinosaurs around sixty-five million years ago is correct. Suppose that you believe what seems now to be the majority view, namely, that the cause was a climatic change resulting from a comet striking the earth. Compare this belief, held under circumstances in which it is not clear which of the available competing theories is correct, with the belief that dinosaurs existed, a belief for which there is an abundance of evidence and about which there is no serious disagreement. On the face of it, the notion that the former belief is in any respect preferable to or better than the latter, in virtue of the presence of ambiguity or uncertainty in the former case and of clarity and the absence of ambiguity in the latter, is absurd. Further, if it were good to believe that God exists when it is not clear that this is so, wouldn't it also be good to believe all manner of other propositions for which the evidence is unclear? We have here a recipe for epistemic promiscuity. And would it be best if we also had to decide who our parents are, or what sort of government is in power in our society, or what are the laws of our society, in circumstances in which the relevant facts of the matter in these areas are also unclear? There is little to recommend such proposals. Mesle makes the main point here nicely: "[This position] forces us into the religiously, ethically and philosophically offensive position of saying that God considers it a virtue for us to believe without sufficient evidence and has intentionally created the world so that such blind belief is the only way we can come to believe in God . . . [It involves] a shallow and arbitrary conception of freedom."[18]

Moreover, according to revised cryptovolitionalism, we should be able to exercise control over whether we believe in circumstances in which both choices are rational. But if both options are rational, how much room is there for regarding a failure to believe as unacceptable or even as unfortunate or regrettable? If both belief and nonbelief are rational, it seems that even if one option is correct and the others incorrect, there is—since both are rational—something acceptable about both, including the wrong option. The revised cryptovolitionalist, therefore, has an important reason to reject the traditionally central theistic claim that to be a nontheist is to be in a less than respectable position.

The advocate of (B)—the view that if there were available to us a clear case for God's existence, it would be impossible for us to exercise control over whether we believe that God exists in circumstances in which either option is rational—may be happy to jettison this traditional claim, in the process greatly reducing the stigma that is attached to nonbelief. But that is not the end of the problem. If rival positions on an issue are rational, why should we even make up our minds about it? If the facts are unclear, it seems that what we ought to believe is just that the facts are unclear: agnosticism seems to be the right response, and we have good reason not to take a particular position. Why not sit on the fence if you are comfortable there and have no pressing reason to set off in any particular direction?[19] These questions are particularly apt in the case of issues that are disputed among groups that include reflective and serious individuals. In such cases it seems likely that there is something to be said for each side. If so, why not just observe what is to be said on each side and reserve judgment? These questions are also particularly apt in cases in which the disputed issue is an important one about which it matters what people think. For in such cases there is additional reason not to jump to conclusions which may not reflect everything that needs to be taken into account.

Perhaps the idea that bringing it about that you believe that God exists is especially virtuous, or especially valuable in some way, when the facts about God are unclear, derives from a failure to keep distinct the notions of belief that God exists (whether it be minimal or full) and *belief in*, or trust in, God. It may be a good thing for us to exercise control over wherein to place our trust: trust that is freely given is more valuable on that account. But from the fact that there is value in our exercising control over wherein to place our trust, or who to believe in, it hardly follows that there is value in our exercising control over what to believe about the relevant facts. Moreover, we can responsibly exercise control over wherein to invest our trust only if the relevant facts about the being in whom we might trust are clear.

It is possible that the idea that belief that God exists is especially virtuous or valuable when the facts about God are unclear also derives some of its appeal for theists from another erroneous line of thought. Most people, whether or not they are theists and indeed whether or not they are religious in any sense of the term, would agree with the following simple intuition. Acting correctly when there is no concern about being observed or with gain of any sort, and the main concern is with doing what is right, is more valuable than acting correctly when the motive includes a concern to be viewed with respect by, or to impress, someone by whom one would like to be respected, or whom one would like to impress. Now theists hold that to believe that God exists is to act correctly. There may therefore be a tendency to think that this too is more worthwhile and has more value when it is uncertain whether there is a deity (who is morally superior to us, would know all about us, including our behaviour, and so forth) than it would be if it is clear that there is such a being. But this line of thought has little to recommend it—so little, in fact, that one wonders if the error under discussion is ever actually made. Even if it is clear in general that it is best that one does what is right without an awareness that anyone or any being is taking note, and even if it is right to believe that God exists, it cannot be that the value of believing that God exists increases as there is less evidence that God exists. *This* particular case of right conduct is an exception to the general rule.

7. Attitude Problems

The best strategy for the cryptovolitionalist to adopt in response to the flaws that have been pointed out is to propose that (a) while there may be various alternative positions that are rational, the evidence overall is somewhat more supportive of God's existence than it is of the alternatives and (b) it requires a considerable exercise of judgment, as well as certain attitudes and ways of thinking, to recognize this to be so.

There are a number of themes here that fit well together. There is the emphasis on the importance of our having control over what we believe. This emphasis can profitably be combined with the idea that while the world is religiously ambiguous, with real discernment one can see what the facts with respect to it are. Revised cryptovolitionalism is compatible with the claim that with the right attitudes it is possible to discern which view is correct; for to say that a number of rival positions are rational is to say that it is not possible to provide a convincing case for any of them; and this is compatible with its being possible under certain circumstances to discover that one position is correct. But if it does become clear to those who have the right attitudes what position ought to be taken on various religious matters, this appears to involve something like seeing what is faintly there to be seen, or reading certain hints in a particular way, rather than seeing that one position is obviously correct. At least this is so if theism is the right position to take for, as I argue in chapter 1, if God exists, God always remains hidden even from the believer, or at least from most believers most of the time.

Cryptovolitionalism is most plausible when it is understood to involve the view that a certain set of attitudes or a certain character is necessary to discern that one side has more going for it than the others. For this would provide an explanation, or at least contribute to an explanation, of why the process in question is important: its importance would be at least in part a function of the fact that adopting the right belief requires you to be a certain sort of person.

Let us refer to this combination of ideas—revised cryptovolitionalism combined with the claim that with the right attitudes it is possible to discern which view is correct—as "extended cryptovolitionalism." The version discussed in the last few pages—what I have called revised cryptovolitionalism—can not cope with objections such as those introduced in the last section. Extended cryptovolitionalism, on the other hand, avoids the criticism that it assumes that arbitrary or random belief is virtuous. It enables us to make sense of what would otherwise be unintelligible, namely, that it might be better to believe some proposition when it is unclear to many people whether we ought to believe it, than it would be to believe that proposition when it is clear to all that it ought to be believed. The key is that it is not thoroughly unclear, what ought to be believed and, further, that it will become discernible what ought to be believed once we approach the relevant subject matter with the right attitudes (etc.). If it were clear what ought to be believed, what attitude one approached it with would be less important.

To appeal to the ill effects of various human attitudes is to resort to what I referred to in chapter 1 as a human defectiveness theory. Human defectiveness theories say that our arrogance, or self-centeredness, or disobedience, or—in general—certain flaws that we have, are the reason that we do not know more about God. Human defectiveness theories generally locate the explanation of God's hiddenness in quite a different area from where cryptovolitionalism locates it, since the latter represents the hiddenness of God as a fortunate state of affairs that makes possible a certain important good, namely, our being able to make a certain type of choice. But there is no reason that such considerations may not be combined; what is under consideration here, therefore, is a mixed theory with elements from these two distinct lines of thought.

8. The Problematic Attitudes

These passages from Pascal and Alston are interesting in this context, although Pascal exaggerates greatly the extent to which the facts about God are clear to those "who sincerely [seek] him . . . and . . . who desire . . . to see":

> If he had wished to overcome the obstinacy of the most hardened, he could have done so by revealing himself to them so plainly that they could not doubt the truth of his essence, as he will appear on the last day with such thunder and lightning and such convulsions of nature that the dead will rise up and the blindest will see him. This is not the way he wished to appear when he came in mildness, because so many men had shown themselves unworthy of his clemency, that he wished to deprive them of the good they did not desire. It was therefore not right that he should appear in a manner manifestly divine and absolutely capable of convincing all men, but neither was it right that his coming should be so hidden that he could not be recognized by those who sincerely sought him. He wished to make himself perfectly recognizable to them. Thus wishing to appear openly to those who seek him with all their heart, and hidden from those who shun him with all their heart, he has qualified our knowledge of him by giving signs which can be seen by those who seek him and not by those who do not. . . . There is enough light for those who desire only to see, and enough darkness for those of a contrary disposition. (*Pensées*, 79–80; see also 101)

> Let them at least learn what this religion is which they are attacking before attacking it. If this religion boasted that it had a clear sight of God and plain and manifest evidence of his existence, it would be an effective objection to say that there is nothing to be seen in the world which proves him so obviously. But since on the contrary it says that men are in darkness and removed from God, that he has hidden himself from their understanding, that this is the very name which he gives himself in Scripture: *Deus absconditus* . . . ; and, in a word, if it strives equally to establish these two facts: that God has appointed visible signs in the Church so that he shall be recognized by those who genuinely seek him, and that he has none the less hidden them in such a way that he will only be perceived by those who seek him with all their heart. (*Pensées*, 155)

> God is not available for voyeurs. Awareness of God, and understanding of His nature and His will for us, is not a purely cognitive achievement; it takes a practical commitment and a practice of the life of the spirit, as well as the exercise of cognitive faculties.[20]

> [The] details of this vary, but it is generally acknowledged in the tradition that an excessive preoccupation and concern with worldly goods, certain kinds of immorality—particularly self-centeredness and unconcern with one's fellows—and a mind that is closed to the possibility of communion with God, are all antithetical to an awareness of God's presence.[21]

The idea that is common to these passages and that is especially relevant here is that certain attitudes, motives, dispositions, or beliefs might keep God hidden from people, or from certain people. I refer to attitudes (etc.) that have this effect as "inhibitors." One way to set out to determine which attitudes, motives, or beliefs are inhibitors would be to see what attitudes (etc.) might be involved in acknowledging that God exists (or, if we push this thinking further, are involved in trusting God)—let us refer to these as "facilitators"—and then to see what other attitudes or states of mind would inhibit the occurrence of these attitudes. And the analysis can be extended to other more specific beliefs about God's nature and activities, including activities in relation to oneself. For example, an awareness of being guided by God might require a sense of needing guidance or a willingness to be guided.

There may be *beliefs* that are inhibitors. For example, if you are inflexibly entrenched in the view that God does not exist, or that theism is sheer nonsense, or that believers are in it for the comfort it brings, or on account of some other dubious purpose, or if you are not even slightly open to the possibility that a being of this sort might exist, then you may be unable to be aware of such a being, or your capacity for such an awareness may be reduced. The same might hold if your motives, when you reflect on or discuss matters pertaining to theism, are, for instance, solely to discredit and disparage: it may be inevitable that God will be hidden if that is the case. There are plenty of other cases in which beliefs or motives preclude a type of awareness.

Awareness of God may require a certain type and degree of attentiveness. Failing to take the time and trouble to attend, to focus in the right way, may mean that God will be hidden, or hidden to a greater extent than would otherwise be the case. It seems that you can live your life, or most of it, without focusing on religious questions at all, just as you can live without ever cultivating an aesthetic sensibility, although the deficiency in the case of religion will seem of greater moment to anyone with a serious interest in religion.

Next I want to consider the proposal that there is an array of *attitudes* that function as inhibitors and, correspondingly, other attitudes that function as facilitators. Such attitudes as a willingness to worship and obey God, if God exists, a willingness to acknowledge one's status as a creature who is subservient to God, and a measure of humility and openness to possibilities that one does not understand, or even a willingness to be assessed or judged by God, if God exists, may be essential for acquiring even a rudimentary awareness of God. You might say to yourself: even if God were to exist, be the creator of everything, care about my interests, and wish me and others to flourish, I would not be interested. And even if you never articulate such thoughts to yourself, and hence perhaps cannot properly be said in a full-blown sense to have such attitudes, your dispositions may be such that this would be the way in which you would respond. If you would be entirely unwilling to conform to a divine plan, if there were such a thing, how could you acknowledge that there is a divine plan? A willingness to say "not my will but thine," a willingness to shift away from focusing on your own wishes, may also be essential to acknowledging that God exists. To accept that God exists is to accept that there is a being who has produced everything else. You might even be in love with yourself to such an extent that you could not acknowledge there to be such a being: if you were very self-absorbed there might be no room in your vision for a being in comparison with whom you are as dust. If, so to speak, your *real* God is yourself, or your loves, or your future as you conceive of it, there may not be room for any other. If you are comfortable and self-satisfied, there may be no room to acknowledge a being whose presence would require you to change your priorities in a way that you find disagreeable.

If we need to have certain attitudes or a certain character in order to recognize certain facts that are easily missed, our relevant beliefs are in part a product of something about us. In particular, in the case of theism, this would make belief in God, and failure to believe in God, an expression of our judgment and character (etc.). This would be consistent with, and may illuminate, the claim, sometimes made by theists, that faith is a response of the whole person; and the same would hold for not having faith.

There are various ways to conceive of how various attitudes might inhibit awareness of the facts about God. They might result in a sort of blindness so that what would otherwise be apparent is concealed. On this analysis the wrong attitudes would prevent you from perceiving what you otherwise would perceive. Berkeley's remarks, quoted in chapter 1, that "to an unbiased and attentive mind, nothing can be more plainly legible, than the intimate presence of an all-wise spirit" are suggestive of this analysis. (They also suggest that given the right attitudes what was previously concealed will become altogether clear and obvious whereas, for reasons I have given, I think we should eschew this particular claim and assume that, at most, one would be able to discern with difficulty the facts about God.)

Another way to conceive of the harmful effects of the wrong attitudes goes with thinking of the development of the right attitudes as involving something like the acquisition of a skill, a skill that is necessary to achieve an awareness of the relevant facts. On this analysis to have the wrong attitudes is akin to failing to acquire the relevant skill. The preceding remarks from Alston suggest this analysis. Again it might be that the inhibitory attitudes result neither in a perceptual defect nor in a lack of a certain skill but rather in a refusal to accept a certain belief. These analyses are not mutually exclusive, however. Different inhibitors, and even the same inhibitor, may function in more than one way.

It may not be apparent to someone what her relevant attitudes are, or that certain of her attitudes are inhibitors. It may require careful or even painful introspection, and it may not be feasible at all for some people. A closed mind or a refusal to believe or a cynical dismissal may be difficult to discern. Self-love, in particular, may be very hard to see for what it is. Questions such as this need to be asked by someone who wishes to probe whether such attitudes may play a role in her thinking: With what attitude do I approach the relevant issues? Am I open to perceiving the force of arguments for positions that differ from my own?

There may in fact not be any immediately obvious difference between the experience and feelings of someone who genuinely has no reason to accept a belief such as the belief that God exists and, on the other hand, the experience and feelings of someone who has such reasons and yet does not hold this belief in virtue of the presence of inhibitors. In both cases there would be an outlook that would feel both correct and natural. The phenomenal states may be much the same. Casual self-scrutiny might not tell you which description you satisfy. It seems that if, say, certain attitudes were holding you back from having a belief which you would otherwise have, this is something of which you would be unlikely to be aware, and with respect to which you would be likely to deceive yourself. Indeed, it might be important that your relevant attitudes should be difficult to discern, even for yourself; for if this were not so it might be apparent to you which of your attitudes were barriers to accepting which beliefs, and hence which beliefs were true. But if all of that were apparent, having the right attitudes would not after all be necessary for seeing which beliefs are true; and the wrong attitudes would not result in the facts being hidden. So an inner refusal, an inner saying no, would have to disguise itself.

Still, there is no reason that your relevant attitudes should be utterly impossible to discern. They might be manifested in, for instance, which types of evidence you greet with enthusiasm and which you greet with a lack of enthusiasm. So it might be useful to ask yourself whether you are pleased, and whether it sits better with you, when you hear of evidence for the claims of some religious tradition, such as your own tradition, or when you hear of evidence against those claims. You might ask yourself: For which positions do you seek support, and which positions do you probe for weaknesses when you are engaging in reflection about religious matters? There seem to be various steps and various lines of inquiry that someone can take that would at least help one to discern what his relevant attitudes are.

To the extent that the relevant character, attitudes (etc.) are under our control, additional content is provided for the idea, central to cryptovolitionalism, that some of our beliefs are under our control to some extent. And if the reason you do not believe some proposition is that you lack the attitudes or perspective that would facilitate recognition of its truth, and that lack is culpable, then the notion that nonbelief is something for which you may reasonably be held responsible has some plausibility after all, at least in this sort of case.

However, whether the lack in question is culpable is a separate matter from whether it has inhibitory effects. In order for it to be culpable there must, I think, be reasons to have the facilitating attitudes that are quite independent of their facilitating role and these must be recognizable as reasons to have those attitudes even by someone who has no awareness of their function as facilitators. And in the case of certain attitudes it is not hard to come up with such reasons: thus the attitudes in question may benefit us; or they may grease the wheels of social intercourse. Consequently, one might have a moral obligation to acquire those attitudes. Hence someone who is completely unaware that the attitudes (etc.) in question are facilitators, or that his current attitudes are inhibitors, could be blameworthy for not having the facilitating attitudes.

Correspondingly, insofar as the inhibitory attitudes (etc.) are a product of states over which one has no control, perhaps because they are caused by cultural factors or one's genetic endowment or original sin, then one cannot properly be blamed for such attitudes. In that case people with the wrong attitudes obviously cannot be held responsible for not holding the beliefs in question. Given their attitudes, they just could not make out the relevant facts; and they do not have control over their attitudes.

Finally, there are many other beliefs that you could not adopt unless you had particular attitudes or a particular character. These are beliefs that go with a response of the whole person. Consider, for example, the belief that the interests of other people matter greatly, and about as much as your own interests. You could not go from believing that you ought to look out primarily for your own interests to embracing this belief without becoming a different sort of person and opting for a certain way of life, thereby undergoing a certain reorientation of character.

9. Problems

The proposal, to summarize, is that the facts are clear enough that with the right attitudes and approach you will be able, with difficulty and effort and without achieving clarity, to make them out. Part of what the lack of clarity involved may amount to is this: it may be somewhat unclear to the person involved that they are actually observing something that is there as distinct from imposing a reading on what they observe. In any case, the ambiguity will be extensive enough that there is room for us to exercise considerable control over which way to go in circumstances in which a number of options are rational. The emphasis on the need for certain attitudes if the facts about God are to be apparent fits well with the idea, alluded to in chapter 1, that belief in the area of religion requires cultural support. The requisite character, attitudes, proclivities (etc.) that are necessary for the relevant sorts of awareness may be encouraged in some contexts, discouraged in others.

At first glance an appeal to human defectiveness in an attempt to account for God's hiddenness is unappealing. Apart from seeming insulting to nontheists, in some of its formulations it has an unfalsifiable and hence unimpressive air about it. This is so insofar as it consists in the claim that if you lack an awareness of God, that *shows* that you are in a defective state. But on closer inspection, and especially when attention is paid both to the ways in which various attitudes might have an inhibiting effect and to how an account of those attitudes may be combined with the more plausible version of cryptovolitionalism, it is more plausible.

So perhaps extended cryptovolitionalism provides part of the explanation of the hiddenness of God. This theory is not incoherent or implausible, is not clearly at odds with generally recognized facts, is not at odds with any standard theistic assumptions, and, hence, is not disqualified for that reason from being part of a plausible theistic response to the hiddenness of God.

A full theory in this area would need to deal with the question of why, from a theistic point of view, it is appropriate that the world should be set up in such a way that extended cryptovolitionalism is true. An account of the advantages of this sort of process would need to be provided. The fact that we go through it must not result in our losing anything of great importance for our well-being and flourishing. The most promising area for further reflection is, I think, as follows. It might be better that we discern certain things for ourselves—in the special sense that we have to make ourselves to be a certain way in order to discern them. In this way we have more of a hand in charting our own course than would otherwise be possible. It may also be, for example, that facilitators are good in themselves.

But I am a lot more confident that what we have here is a coherent proposal than I am that this proposal, in all its parts, is correct. There are many considerations to keep in mind at this point, including some that actually call into question this entire line of thought.

First, we have hardly settled the question whether certain attitudes (etc.) will, as a matter of fact, permit us to discern, say, that there is more to be said for theism than against it. This remains merely a possibility. The opposition will claim that the opposite is in fact true and that the right attitudes will enable us to see that there actually is more to be said against theism than for it. Indeed, this sort of attempt to, as it were, pull out the rug of epistemic respectability from under one's opponents, and to say that they are not in a position to form a reliable judgment about a disputed matter, is one that can easily backfire: on the face of it, and in the absence of further argument, it is no more plausible for theists to make this move than it is for opponents of theism to say that theists are under the mistaken impression that there exists a hidden God as a result of, say, wishful thinking and self-deception. Neither move settles the issue. All we have here is a possibility.

A full assessment of this proposal would require an attempt to determine to what extent the existence and nature of God are clear to those who lack what it is reasonable to consider to be the inhibitory attitudes. As far as I know, such an investigation has never been conducted. It is hard to know what results it would yield. It would have to take account of the fact that there have been, and are, cultures in which nontheistic religions have flourished or in which theists have been few or have been absent entirely, but in which the beliefs, attitudes, dispositions (etc.) that may facilitate belief are not entirely lacking. In the absence of the sort of evidence that such an inquiry would yield, this entire proposal is a matter of speculation. My own suspicion, and it is only that, is that the relevant evidence is mixed. People who believe themselves to be aware of God's existence seem to include both arrogant and self-satisfied types as well as saintly types (with humility, a willingness to obey God if God exists, etc.). It seems entirely unrealistic to suggest that theism always or even usually involves the allegedly right attitudes. And those who claim to lack any sense of God's existence seem to include saintly types with all the right attitudes. (Interestingly, I have found that the step that people usually take when reflecting on a matter such as this is to consider the people with whom they are personally acquainted. Maybe there is no alternative, but the widespread tendency to rely on such a dubious procedure calls into question the reliability of judgments in this area.)

One might resort to saying that someone who appears humble and appears to seek the truth may be very clever at concealing his arrogance, even from himself, and that someone who appears arrogant and self-satisfied may merely be keeping up a brave front. But if we are so inept at making the relevant judgments about the character of others, it is hard to see how we are to evaluate the proposal under discussion. And is it not reasonable to think that we can make some progress with judging the relevant aspects of people's characters? It might be said that the correlation between character and God's existence being clear should not be too obvious since an obvious correlation would give the game away, actually making the existence of God clear. But even a very close correlation of the relevant sort might not make it obvious that God exists. For example, it may be that insight which is akin to the insight necessary for seeing the facts about God is necessary to recognize the presence of the right sort of character and hence of the relevant correlation.

Second, a deep difficulty for the proposal under discussion is that there obviously are competing religiously based accounts of what you will be aware of if you have the right attitudes (etc.). Many traditions contend that their account of reality will be apparent to anyone who has the requisite attitudes. Each of them will wish to stake its claim to having the insights that will become apparent to a seeker with these right attitudes. While the presence of a number of such traditions—each of which claims that its insights will be available to one who approaches with the right attitudes (etc.)—by no means suffices to show that there is no single tradition that is unique in that only in its case is this really true, it does call into question the claim of each tradition to be that one.

Third, theism simply is not a live option for many people. And this is not merely because their attitudes may inhibit them in such a way that they do not acquire it. Rather their culture and circumstances are such that they are not confronted with theism as a live option. It seems obvious that a lot of people do not even get to the point where inhibiting attitudes *could* prevent them from being theists. Correspondingly, it is equally obvious that the reason most theists are theists is that this is what they have been taught; they have been brought up to hold theistic beliefs just as they have been brought up to behave in certain ways. It simply is not a matter of anything about them as individuals. People are generally presented with a certain view of the world; it is presented to them and received by them as the obviously correct view of the world and entirely sincere people accept it as such; just as obviously, what the correct outlook is thought to be varies across societies. It flies in the face of human experience to suggest that *in all cases* it is the presence of certain attitudes or character or inclinations that has brought it about that certain individuals adopt theistic belief and that it is the absence of those attitudes (etc.) that has brought it about that others fail to do so.

Fourth, here is a troubling thought. The "right attitudes" are such that it is hard for us to have them, and we will at best be able to achieve them to a limited extent. Hence a theist who endorses the line of thought under consideration in the last two sections of this chapter will always have some basis upon which to argue that the extent to which any particular nontheist has achieved the right attitudes is not good enough. Hence theism can always insulate itself: it can say that there are reasons of the sort under discussion that someone is unaware of certain facts, and an account of these reasons will always resonate to some extent with human experience.

What we have here, nevertheless, remains a possibility that has to be taken seriously. As I have said, it is not obvious that the proposal under discussion is correct, just as it is not obvious that it is incorrect. But then if it *were* correct this is something that probably would not be obvious. So the fact that it is not obviously correct has no clear implications, one way or the other, for whether it is correct. In spite of the various concerns I have considered, it appears to remain a possibility that extended cryptovolitionalism explains, or contributes to explaining, why God is hidden from some people.

4

TRUST AND OTHER GOODS
OF MYSTERY

1. Divine Hiddenness and Human Trust: Adams and Adams

In this chapter I consider first the claim that trust in God requires God to be hidden. Then I consider some other proposed goods of mystery.

All of the theistic traditions emphasize the importance of trust in God. This is sometimes said to be what faith in God consists in.[1] More often trust in God is considered to be a central ingredient in faith in God, in which case another central ingredient in faith is usually understood to be belief that certain propositions about God are true. Since chapter 3 was devoted to an analysis of the claim that God must be hidden if we are to come to believe, or at least come through the right steps to believe, that certain propositions about God are true, by the end of this discussion of trust, therefore, we will have in effect discussed the idea that if it were plain that God exists, there would be no room for faith, or at least we will have discussed much of what such a claim generally consists in.

I use some remarks that Marilyn McCord Adams has made while discussing the problem of evil as a starting point for this exploration of trust. Adams presents what she considers to be a distinctively Christian response to evil. She says that the phenomenon of martyrdom, and in particular Jesus' crucifixion, contributes to our understanding of various evils. But she also says that God's goodness is a mystery: "the divine nature is eternally beyond the creature's conceptual grasp." She wants to emphasize how limited is our human comprehension of God. Our lack of comprehension is partly a result of our status as created beings, but it is also "part of God's deliberate design, since it is necessary to make possible the relationships He wants with us and for which we were created." Adams says that "what God wants most from us is wholehearted trust and

73

obedience. Yet it is conceptually impossible to trust someone if you know in advance every move that he will make."[2] I wish to examine these claims about trust.

Adams's immediate concern in her essay is with the degree of mystery surrounding the *goodness* of God, but if her remarks are convincing they amount to an explanation or at least a partial explanation, of why it is appropriate that other aspects of God's nature that have a bearing on what God does in relation to us are mysterious. The line of thought which I will explore in Adams seems to give no reason to think that the *existence* of God should not be altogether clear to us. What we have here, therefore, is a potential explanation, or potential partial explanation, of the lack of clarity that surrounds God's *nature*.

Adams's view is that believers derive *some* sense of God's nature from Scriptures and from other sources: "while we cannot get a simple, clear analysis of divine goodness that will enable us to trace the hand of God in every situation . . . we can get a general idea of God's character, purposes and policies from the collective experience of God's people over the centuries" (252). So her view is certainly not that everyone needs to be, or is, altogether in the dark about God's nature. Adams probably would agree that, in general, trust permits some knowledge of the being who is trusted. Indeed, she may even agree that trust *requires* some knowledge of the being who is trusted. There are at least two considerations that support the view that this is so. The first is just that as a matter of psychological fact, trust in a being about whom nothing is known will be more or less impossible. Trust is a demanding attitude, and people probably will not be able to display it with respect to a being about whom so little is known that it is entirely unclear that trust is deserved. The second consideration is that *trust in God* requires some understanding of God's nature. That is, someone trusts in God only if he understands himself to trust in God. And in order to understand oneself to trust in God, one needs to have some grasp of what would be involved in being God, and one must conceive of God as a suitable recipient of trust.

Adams says, however, that there must be some uncertainty about what someone is going to do if we are to trust him. "If you know in advance every move that [someone] . . . will make [then] . . . it is conceptually impossible to trust that person." From this it follows that there must be some uncertainty about the nature of the trusted being. So the relationship that God wants to have with us requires mystery. Is this a plausible claim? Can this point contribute anything to an explanation of God's hiddenness? An attempt to answer these questions requires that we clarify the notion of trust and that, in doing so, we distinguish some types of trust.[3]

Trust is an attitude that involves, or issues in, a measure of assurance or confidence that something has been, is being, or will be taken care of. When there is trust, there is a person who is trusting and a person who is trusted.[4] (Since you can trust, or fail to trust, yourself, these can be the same person.) Trust also involves something with respect to which one is trusting. This can range from something specific, such as escaping from a deranged attacker, to something general, such as living one's life in a useful and significant way. The most specific sort of trust occurs when someone or some being is trusted to do something in particular in a particular situation. It is somewhat more general when someone is trusted to respond to some situation, but is not trusted to do anything in particular in response to that situation. And it is entirely general—let's call it global trust—when the other person is just being trusted or relied upon in general.

Let us take a first stab at considering Adams's claim that trust requires some uncertainty. Consider some simple cases. Suppose I leave town for a few months, and a thoroughly reliable friend promises to feed my chickens. Does my confidence that my friend will do exactly as she has promised in any way inhibit, or make more difficult, my trust in her? Not at all. Compare this with a case in which I leave home and entrust my chickens to a well-intentioned but rather absentminded (featherbrained), and hence somewhat unreliable, colleague. The suggestion that trust is more difficult if I am certain that the chickens will be fed seems plainly wrong.

Or suppose that you trust the best surgeon in the world to perform some difficult and important surgery that involves great risk to you. Suppose you are sure, and reasonably so, that the surgery will go well. There is nothing at all conceptually problematic about the idea that you can trust the surgeon, in spite of the fact that you have no uncertainty about the surgery. This is so, too, in the case of a surgeon who has never made a single mistake, and about whom it is justifiably believed that he is very unlikely to make a mistake, and if in addition the surgery is easy to perform, unimportant—minor cosmetic surgery, maybe—and involves little risk. Further, there is nothing conceptually problematic about the idea that you might trust a surgeon whose decisions about what procedures to undertake will all be made while you are unconscious and the surgery is under way, with the result that you are trusting the surgeon concerning some situation but not relying on him to perform a particular, prearranged procedure.

The last two paragraphs indicate that the claim that there can be trust only when you do not know what moves someone will make can be seen to be false in a variety of types of cases. In some of these cases the assignment that has been entrusted to someone is difficult, whereas in others it is easy. In some of these cases someone is being trusted with respect to some specific course of action, whereas in one case at any rate this is not so. Again, in some cases the consequences of the person who is trusted failing to do what they have been trusted to do would be serious, whereas in others they would be fairly insignificant. (An example in this last category is the case of unimportant surgery that is not risky. It is not hard to come up with other cases in this category: thus assume that in either of the chicken cases I have backup plans so that if the trusted party were not to come through, others would step in at once and save the day.)

2. Varieties of Trust

Nevertheless, if I am certain what will be the actions of a being whom I trust, this obviously precludes a certain sort of trust, namely, trust that involves (a) uncertainty about how things are going to go, (b) reliance on the being in whom I trust to select the outcome, and (c) reliance on the trusted being to bring about the selected outcome. Let us refer to trust that satisfies these conditions as "complete trust." So complete trust involves something being out of one's control in three distinct respects: first, in the sense that you do not know in advance how it is going to go, second, in the sense that another's decisions will settle how it is going to go and, third, in the sense that another's actions will bring about whatever occurs.

Just in virtue of the uncertainty about what will be done that it involves, complete trust is somewhat general. It is not a matter of trusting S to do some particular action a, although it may be a matter of trusting S to do something to solve a particular problem or to take care of a particular situation. And if it extends to every area of life, it will be global as well as complete.

Incomplete trust, on the other hand, only has one of these elements, namely, reliance on the trusted being to deliver a prearranged outcome. Incomplete trust, in other words, involves certainty, or something close to certainty, about what the trusted being is going to do. The explanation of how it is that there is room for trust even when there is certainty, or something close to certainty, about what will occur is just that it is the being or beings who are trusted that will bring about what they are being trusted to bring about. The desired outcome requires that person's cooperation. Thus if I share a confidence with someone, trusting her to keep it, I hand over control of the keeping of this confidence to her. She, not I, will decide whether or not the confidence is kept. Even if I am as sure as it is possible to be that she is going to keep it, it is under her control and not under mine. Again, suppose that you are a very inexperienced climber who is in a very hazardous location, and that you have no choice but to rely on a very experienced guide to get you out alive. Only if you follow his moves and take exactly the steps that he indicates are you going to survive. If his track record in such situations is excellent, you may be very confident that he will get you out alive. Yet there is ample room for trust here because you have to rely on the guide every step of the way.

So the question is: Why is complete trust more valuable than its incomplete counterpart? For it is only the former that has any capacity to contribute to an explanation of God's hiddenness.[5]

The value of uncertainty, which is central to complete trust, is emphasized by Adams. She says that there is a danger that people would try to manipulate God if they knew what God is going to do: "[Knowledge of God's nature] . . . would be a source of great temptation. For example, if God were known to have a fixed policy of rendering temporal goods for well-doing and temporal evils for wickedness, then the observant might even try to manipulate the equation to use God as a means to their ends" (251). The idea here is that if we knew what reactions there would be to our actions, we might be tempted to try to act in whatever way was necessary to produce those reactions. So it is a good thing that we do not know enough about God that we can predict what God is going to do. If it were otherwise, we might try to manipulate God. Our uncertainty excludes the possibility of the sort of manipulation that you can engage in if you can predict how someone will react in various situations.

However, this point about manipulation, and hence this particular case for the importance of uncertainty, and in turn for the value of the sort of trust that incorporates it, seems questionable. For example, in the case of the surgeon whose record is so impressive that he can hardly be imagined making a mistake, the surgery may be complex and difficult: in such a case to say on account of the fact that it is reasonable to predict success that you are therefore manipulating the surgeon, or would be tempted to try to do so, rings hollow. Moreover, there is an important reason that the need to avoid a situation in which we can manipulate God may not require that we be unable to tell what God is going to do: it could be that if we learned a great deal more about what God would do if we acted in certain ways, part of what we would learn is that manipulative behavior will not work with God, that attempts to manipulate God will backfire. This suggestion that attempts to manipulate God would backfire is not ad hoc but rather fits well with other theistic beliefs, including beliefs about God's knowledge of human intentions, purposes, and expectations.[6] It seems that a case for the value of complete trust in God, is not to be found here.

Robert Merrihew Adams also probes these themes and does so in a way that holds some promise for revealing what might be valuable about the sort of trust that involves uncertainty. He expatiates upon the relationship between trust and control in his essay "The Virtue of Faith."[7] He discusses our wish to have control over our lives and circumstances, and some ways in which this wish influences us. In particular our wish to have control leads us to want to know what to expect and leads us to avoid the unexpected. It creates a barrier to our having trust in "[God's] power and goodness in general, without having a blueprint of what he is going to do in detail" (20). The wish to know what is coming next, in other words, keeps us back from a certain type of trust. Robert Adams suggests that one aspect of the sort of dependence that trust of the complete sort makes possible is that it involves the trusted being to some extent defining what the good is for the person who is trusting, or on whose behalf someone is trusting. Trust of the more thoroughgoing sort also has the advantage that the uncertainty that it involves helps us to avoid the dangers that arise from our wish to make ourselves secure and to avoid the unexpected.

The point about our wish to have control over our own lives and circumstances, a wish that leads us to want to know what to expect and to avoid the unexpected, certainly squares with a strand that is found in Christianity as well as in the other theistic traditions. According to these traditions the believer should not concern himself with the future and should graciously accept whatever befalls him.

However, more needs to be said about the idea that in cases in which there is complete trust, the trusted being defines the relevant good, and about how this point would bear on the value of the trust that is thereby facilitated. Consider first some cases in which the character of the relevant good is specified in advance. Compare the following two cases, in both of which you are trusting a surgeon to do something to rectify a condition from which you suffer. In one case you do not know what steps the surgeon will take, and you have complete trust in the surgeon. In the other case you trust the surgeon to carry out a procedure whose precise nature and expected outcome have been explained. Assume that in both cases you are certain that the surgeon's successful execution of whatever he undertakes to do can be counted upon. Why would the former sort of trust be more valuable than the latter? Both of these instances of trust involve a sense of dependency and of a lack of self-sufficiency, of vulnerability, and of being at the mercy of another. In addition, both provide possibilities for confirming over time that it is appropriate to rely on the being in question. Are these shared features not more important, from a theistic point of view, than the uncertainty about what is going to come next that is characteristic of the former, more complete, sort of trust? What does complete trust, with the uncertainty that it involves, add that is so valuable?

What it is important to see here is that there can be differences between complete and incomplete trust that are not revealed by such cases. The reason is that in cases such as these it is clear wherein your good is to be found: you suffer from a particular condition, and what is good for you is that it should be alleviated. So you are trusting with respect to the alleviation of a particular problem and it is quite clear that the relevant good consists in its alleviation. Consequently the difference between complete and incomplete trust in such a case as this is just the difference between trusting that a certain good that is specified in advance will be achieved somehow or other and trusting that it will be achieved in a particular way.

The differences between complete and incomplete trust are more significant in cases in which the good in question is not specified in advance, and especially in cases in which the being who is trusted to some extent defines the good in question. This is, in effect, to say that the less specific and the more global a particular case of trusting is, the greater will be the difference between complete and incomplete trust. Cases in which this additional dimension is present include, for instance, cases in which you trust someone to aid and guide you in *whatever* situations may arise in the future. For this will involve trusting both with respect to the discernment of what the good is in many situations, as well as with respect to its achievement.

In the surgeon case you are certain that the surgeon will achieve the good in question, which is the alleviation of the condition from which you suffer. But if the trusted being is "defining the good," part of what he is doing is deciding how to respond to some problem or situation. So trust that has this extra dimension is trust that something will be done by way of solving a problem or assisting in a certain situation, even if the person who is trusting has no idea what will be done. In cases of this sort, in which there is more room for complete trust because of uncertainty about what will be done, and hence room for the trusted being to pick out the solution to a problem—in virtue of the fact that it is not specified in advance—we can see the point of suggesting that it is important that we should have complete trust. For in such cases it is possible to put yourself in the hands of another to a much greater extent.

Suppose, again, that aging parents are deeply distressed about the future of their retarded child. They do not know how the child will fare when they are no longer able to take care of him. They wonder if the child will be treated with kindness, with indifference, or with cruelty. Suppose that they trust God to watch over the child—not to do anything in particular, but rather to look after the child in whatever circumstances may arise. Trust has a different texture in such a case.

Yet it is worth noting the limited extent to which the being in whom complete trust is invested defines the relevant goods, even in cases in which this occurs. The reason is just that there is something with respect to which someone might be trusted only if there is something that needs to be taken care of, only if there is some area of difficulty or perplexity or danger, or some problem to be solved, for example. Hence implicit in the very possibility of trust of any sort, even of the global sort, there must be some awareness of what needs to be taken care of, and of what it would be for it to be taken care of. And to that extent the relevant good is already specified and understood. That the relevant goods are specified in advance is clearly the case for the more specific sorts of trust, which include, for instance, trust that a particular problem will be alleviated. So at least in the case of the more specific sorts of trust, complete and incomplete trust are not likely to differ greatly in this particular respect. Still, the more general the trust, the greater the room for difference between the two sorts of trust and the easier it is to make a case for the importance of complete trust.

However, while it is clear that there are cases in which the differences between complete and incomplete trust are considerable, what is less clear is that it is reasonable to believe complete trust to be a good of mystery, and to believe that its importance serves to explain, or to contribute to explaining, God's hiddenness. For while the trust of the aging parents who trust God to watch over their retarded child has a distinctive character in virtue of being complete, what is not so clear is what is so valuable about it. Why is it so important to put yourself in the hands of another in the particular respects involved here?

There are additional problems with this proposal. First, complete trust with respect to some area of life or with respect to some difficulty requires only that we not be able to foresee exactly what will be done to solve that difficulty: that is, mystery must surround the nature of the trusted being only to the extent that this is necessary for us to be unsure what this being will do. And this condition may be met even when we know a great deal about the nature of the being in question, particularly if it is a complex being. Indeed, it might be that we would not be able to discern what God is going to do in many situations even if we knew *everything* that can be known by beings like us about God. The fact that we can be intimately familiar with other human beings and still not know how they will react in many circumstances provides strong reason to think this to be so: since this is so in the case of other human beings, who are quite like us, there is all the more reason to think that it would hold in God's case. (There are various possibilities here. For example, we might fail to grasp the implications of what we already know about God. Or we might fail to know whatever we would need to know to draw the relevant inferences.) This is a compelling reason to doubt that the appeal to the importance of complete trust can contribute much to explaining the hiddenness of God.

Second, I assume that it is only when the person whom we are being urged to trust is one whom it is reasonable to trust, one who merits trust and is seen to merit trust, that complete trust is important and should be urged on us.[8] This may not be necessary for complete trust to be possible, but it is necessary for it to be reasonable. There must be reason to believe that the being in whom one is trusting is reliable, in spite of the fact that one does not know precisely how things are going to go. Complete trust involves abandoning yourself to the mercy of another being: if you are to cast yourself on the mercy of someone, you ought to know, or have very good reason to believe, that he is merciful. So in the case of complete trust in God, God's nature ought to be apparent to us to a considerable extent, it seems. It is interesting to note, for instance, that in the book of Psalms in the Bible exhortations to trust God are accompanied by statements about what it is about God that makes this trust appropriate, such as the fact that God is just and is a "refuge" and a "fortress." In general, theists believe that it is a good and fitting thing to put your trust in God because God is merciful, just, reliable, and so forth. That is, it is in virtue of what is understood to be known about God that trust is urged on us, not in virtue of what is understood not to be known. Indeed, it is not unreasonable to suggest that complete trust in God would actually be promoted to a greater extent than it now is if there were less mystery than there now is about God and about God's nature and actions. If so, an appeal to the value of complete trust seems suited to being included in a case for the value of God's being *less* hidden than is currently the case. However, it is not out of the question that while more knowledge of S's character would promote trust of S, there is also a valuable sort of trust that is possible only when you cannot predict how S will act.

Third, there does not seem to be anything inherently bad or problematic about a wish to be safe and secure and to avoid unpleasant eventualities, or about an attempt to

ensure the safety and security of others about whom one cares. The situation is otherwise with, say, excessive concern with making oneself safe and secure, excessive concern about the safety and security of those to whom one is closely related, excessive
concern of either sort combined with indifference to others, and attempts to manipulate or control others: these seem inherently bad.

Moreover, trust in God, whether of the complete or of the incomplete sort, will
probably issue in a sense of security and in a sense that while one may encounter the
unexpected, one will not encounter the completely disastrous or utterly ruinous. So it is
not plausible for theists to say that a measure of security in such areas is inherently bad
or problematic.

To return to a theme mentioned at the outset of this chapter, while complete trust
requires uncertainty about what the trusted being will do, it seems to require—at least
if it is to be something that it is reasonable to expect—complete certainty about the *existence* of the trusted being. In fact it seems that the appeal to complete trust will serve as
a plausible justification for the nature or character of the trusted person being unclear
only if the existence of that being is taken to be certain. Hence a case for the value of
complete trust in God is weakened to the extent that it is not clear that God exists; as we
have seen, that it is not clear that God exists is evinced by, for example, the fact that the
theistic traditions have endeavored to explain *why* this is not clear.

It is, perhaps, not utterly out of the question that the appeal to trust—and in particular the case for the importance of complete, and relatively global, trust—contributes
something to an explanation of the hiddenness of God. But the pickings seem slim.

3. Some Other Alleged Goods of Mystery

Next I survey some further considerations that may have a capacity to contribute to an
explanation of God's hiddenness, although I will suggest that none of them contributes
very much. Some of these additional proposals have been advanced by important and
influential authors, although their value is in some cases inversely related to the importance of the authors who have espoused them. I will consider a few other goods of
mystery, starting with three themes mentioned by J. L. Schellenberg.

First, let us consider the Diversity Argument, according to which religious diversity
would be greatly reduced if the facts about God were clear to us. (In his discussion of
this topic, as throughout the rest of his book, Schellenberg restricts his attention to the
possibility that there might be available a case for God's existence that would make it irrational not to believe that God exists, and to the apparent consequences of that being
so, so I am modifying his point somewhat.) In the view of someone who proposes the
fact of diversity as a good of mystery, it would be unfortunate if religious diversity were
reduced: the idea is that the world would be a poorer place if this were to occur.

Schellenberg considers two versions of the Diversity Argument. According to one
version, the good in question consists in the presence of the various religious traditions
that actually exist. According to the other, it consists in the fact that our current circumstances permit "the free expression of religious imagination, creativity and devotion."[9]
Schellenberg correctly objects that even if the facts about God were clear to us, there
might still be a great deal of religious diversity. The religious traditions that would

emerge under those circumstances might vary as much as, say, the various forms of Judaism that currently exist. They might differ, for instance, with respect to their understanding of Scriptures or in their moral or political teachings. In fact they might differ to a greater extent than the varieties of any historical religion have differed, or currently differ from each other, since the emergent strands would presumably thrive in a great multiplicity of historical periods, economic circumstances, geographical locations, climates, and so forth, so that there would presumably be especially fertile conditions for the development of new and different varieties. Schellenberg observes, and here again he is convincing, that if the reason it is important that there should be diversity is that it is important that religious imagination, creativity (etc.) should have free expression, this could be accomplished within the more limited set of alternatives that would emerge if it were clear that God exists. In order for religious imagination, creativity (etc.) to have free expression, it is not necessary that there be traditions as various as Judaism, Christianity, Hinduism, Buddhism, the various forms of polytheism and animism, and the whole panoply of radically different alternatives that we know as the religions of the world.

But there may still be something to be said for the idea that the diverse set of traditions with which we are familiar is worthwhile for its own sake. Undoubtedly this diversity makes for a richer and more colorful world. In this respect it resembles, for instance, the diversity of languages and of species of plants and animals. To be sure, there would still be variety if all languages were, say, dialects of Irish and if every animal were a type of mouse. But things would not be quite the same and in either case our world would be greatly impoverished. It seems, therefore, that there is something to be said for what we might call the *aesthetic* version of the Diversity Argument. And this is so even if we concede that there is nothing special, or especially worthy of being preserved, about the particular array of traditions that currently exist: we can still think it important that there be some such array and that the relatively narrow set of alternatives we would be faced with if some version of theism were obviously correct would be a poor substitute. This consideration may have a capacity to contribute something modest to an explanation of God's hiddenness, although it would be odd for orthodox theists to make much of it. The sensibility that it manifests is really an aesthetic one *rather than* a theistic one. Many theists would find it a little awkward to celebrate the fact that their tradition has so many vibrant competitors. Presumably most theists would contend that the aesthetic good in question is far outweighed by the costs associated with widespread participation in traditions which, they believe, make false claims and are incapable of delivering or facilitating salvation, or at any rate are less effective in this regard than is their own tradition.

So much for the Diversity Argument. Second, I turn to what we might call the argument from the *Importance of Searching*.[10] This is the idea, which is related to the central themes in the last chapter, that there is great value in people searching for God and engaging in their own process of investigation. A somewhat similar theme is mentioned by John Wesley: "I have sometimes been almost inclined to believe that the wisdom of God has, in most later ages, permitted the external evidence for Christianity to be more or less clogged and incumbered for this very end, that men (of reflection especially) might not altogether rest there but be constrained to look into themselves also, and attend to the light shining in their hearts."[11]

Of course our present circumstances require just such a process of searching, so we have good reason to engage in it. However, there are points that can be made in an attempt to make a case for the importance of our doing so. One suggestion is that it might help to ensure that people will not be lackadaisical or careless in their believing and that it helps to make us aware of our status relative to God.

Yet the appeal to the importance of searching faces some difficulties. One obvious difficulty is that the very conditions that allegedly are justified by the appeal to the importance of searching may in some cases actually give rise to a lackadaisical or careless attitude. And if the goal of the searching process is that people should become theists by their own route, the process is not very successful. For it is clear that what happens is that people who engage in a search come to all manner of different conclusions. So part of the cost of our being in circumstances in which a search is necessary is that many people fail to discover important truths.

How would you decide whether the advantages of our engaging in such a search outweigh the disadvantages? I see no reason to be confident one way or the other. It depends, for example, on what are the consequences of our failing to discover important truths. There is no way to rule out the possibility that the advantages of our engaging in a search may outweigh the disadvantages, and hence no way to rule out the possibility that the appeal to the importance of our engaging in such a search might, on balance, contribute something to an explanation of God's hiddenness. A further difficulty, as Schellenberg notes, is that if the facts were more obvious there might still be a lot of room for searching, including perhaps searching out the will of God in a particular situation. But obviously there would not be, say, room for the particular sort of search that is possible only if our circumstances are such that both theistic and nontheistic options are rational, and if the choice of one position rather than the other is to reflect our attitudes and character, as discussed toward the end of chapter 3.

Third, there is the "reasonable nonbelief and actual existents" argument, which Schellenberg disposes of with commendable dispatch.[12] This argument is based on the plausible claim that if nonbelief were unreasonable (or, we might add, if it were clear to us that God exists), the world would be sufficiently different that we, the human beings who actually currently exist, would not exist. The assumption is that if very different circumstances had obtained in the world—as would have obtained if God's existence had been clear to us—the history of the world would have been different: different couples would have mated, different children would have been born, and the people who now exist would not have existed. So it is just as well for us, at any rate, that God's existence is not clear to human beings. *We* have nothing to complain about.

The main difficulty for this line of thought is that the hiddenness of God need not be thought of just as a problem for the people who now exist. That is, the question is not: Why, if God exists, is God hidden from *us*? Rather the question is: Why, if God exists, is God hidden from whatever beings of our sort there are? So the fact, if it is a fact, that if God were not hidden then we—the people who now exist—would not exist, is beside the point.

Fourth, next I come to some proposals that have to do with the importance of worship and with the worship-worthiness of God. Consider, first, the claim that if God were not hidden, worship of the sort with which we are familiar, and whose practices reflect the fact that God is hidden, would be impossible. And worship of this sort—so it is said—is appropriate and valuable.

Now it may be true that if God were not hidden, worship of the sort with which we are familiar would be impossible. But we need a reason for thinking that that would be unfortunate. To argue that the relation between human beings and God must be a certain way just in order that worship of the sort that currently is engaged in will be possible is to "put the cart before the horse." The institutions of worship that are to be found in the theistic traditions have developed in circumstances in which, if God exists, a great deal of mystery surrounds God's existence and nature, and the forms that those institutions take reflect this fact. But must worship take these forms? And even if they must, might there not be, for instance, forms of respect, or reverence, or certain other modes of interaction between human beings and the deity, that would be just as valuable and which could take the place of worship if there were less mystery? Indeed, isn't theism of all varieties committed to there being forms of worship that are available only in heaven and that are superior to anything currently available to us—in part at least because what we now see "through a glass darkly" will then be seen "face to face"?

Distinct from this unimpressive appeal to the value of worship as currently practiced, there is a more promising point concerning the qualities that a being must have in order for it to deserve to be worshiped. Worship, according to this latter proposal, involves awe, reverence, and adoration, for example. We cannot worship a being—so this point continues—unless it is different from us, entirely other, at a distance, inscrutable and sacred. Worship involves an emotional and attitudinal prostration of ourselves; and it involves keeping our distance. These remarks from Rudolf Otto and Paul Ricoeur are interesting in this context:

> The truly "mysterious" object is beyond our apprehension and comprehension, not only because our knowledge has certain irremovable limits, but because in it we come upon something inherently 'wholly other', whose kind and character are incommensurable with our own, and before which we therefore recoil in a wonder that strikes us chill and numb.

> [The] transcendent is that before which man cannot stand; no one can see God—at least the God of taboos and interdicts—without dying. It is from this, from this wrath and this terror, this deadly power of retribution, that the sacred gets its character of separateness. It cannot be touched; for if it is touched—that is to say, violated—its death-dealing power is unleashed.[13]

However, if a being would be worthy of worship only if it is surrounded by a degree of mystery, it is not clear that this mystery needs to pertain to the *existence* of the being in question. On the contrary, it seems that the more mystery there is about its existence, the more doubtful it is that we should worship (revere, adore, prostrate ourselves before, etc.) it. As with the point about trust discussed earlier, we have here a consideration that at most could contribute to an explanation of the degree of mystery surrounding the *nature* of God.

Nevertheless, there may be a point of some substance in this neighborhood: it probably is true that a being would not be worthy of worship unless it had plans and purposes and so forth that we are at most capable of dimly understanding. If we could see precisely what such a being was about, we would be able to understand as much as it understands. And why should we worship a being whom we can understand? Being worthy of worship, it seems, requires a considerable degree of mystery.

But, contrary to the point with which I began this fourth line of thought, it is not as if God is hidden *because* this is necessary for worship. The connection, rather, is as follows. Some of God's qualities, in virtue of which God is worthy of worship, such as God's wisdom, goodness, and justice, and especially the combination of these with God's omnipotence and omniscience, are bound to generate a great deal of mystery for beings with our cognitive abilities. *Both* the mystery that surrounds God's nature, or at least some of it, and the fact that God is worthy of worship are a function of these facts about the divine nature.

The suggestion that worship-worthiness requires incomprehensibility is complicated, but not called into question, by the fact that our sense of the worship-worthiness of God would presumably also be *enhanced* by a greater appreciation of the wisdom, justice, power, and so forth, of God. A further difficulty is that it is a matter for speculation whether the level of comprehension of which we are capable would bring us into the danger zone in which our sense of the worship-worthiness of God would be compromised. Still, perhaps there is to be found in this area something that, again, can contribute modestly to an explanation of God's hiddenness.

Fifth, Hilary Putnam draws attention to another line of thought in Kant that has some bearing on God's hiddenness, this time from Kant's *Religion within the Bounds of Reason Alone*. Putnam writes as follows: "Kant makes the remarkable statement (many would say that it is an absurd statement) that it would be a bad thing if the truths of religion could be deduced by reason, because that would produce fanaticism."[14] Putnam actually says that the passage in Kant in which he makes this statement is "the most revealing passage in perhaps all of Kant's moral writing" (49). He continues as follows:

> [In *Religion within the Bounds of Reason Alone*,] Kant is saying—and with deep psychological insight—that what makes the fanatic a fanatic isn't that his beliefs are necessarily wrong or his arguments incorrect. It is possible to have true beliefs supported by correct arguments, and still be what Kant calls a 'fanatic'; it is possible to have the kind of undesirable intolerance, intensity, in short, hostility to others thinking for themselves, that represented 'fanaticism' to the Enlightenment, and still be perfectly logical. (49–50)

I doubt that there is much to be said for this idea. Of *course* what makes the fanatic a fanatic is not the fact that his beliefs are wrong (or necessarily wrong) or his arguments incorrect. More important, the claim that it is *possible* to be perfectly logical and to have true beliefs that are supported by correct arguments, and yet to be a fanatic, is obviously a weaker, and more easily supported (and much less controversial and less interesting) claim than the bold but less plausible claim that "it would be a bad thing if the truths of religion could be deduced by reason, because that would produce fanaticism."

On the face of it, and in the absence of further argument, the claim that a proof of God's existence would induce fanaticism is no more convincing than the following three contrary claims. First, if the truths of religion could be demonstrated, this would *reduce* fanaticism because once the facts were obvious, there would not be as much room for dispute, and there would be no need for each of the competing sides to excite themselves so about the defense of their preferred alternative. Second, the availability of a proof would reduce fanaticism because it is holding on to, and committing yourself to, beliefs that go beyond what may clearly be seen to be the case that generates fanaticism. Third, since we presently lack a proof of the existence of God, and there is no shortage of fanaticism, if anything we have some reason to believe that it is the *absence* of such a proof that is conducive to fanaticism. I do not wish to defend any of these three claims, but I suggest that each of them is about as plausible as Kant's view.

The sixth and seventh points on which I will comment are gleaned from the work of the great Reformer Martin Luther. The hiddenness of God was an important theme for Luther, although his orientation is different from that of most of the authors whose ideas I have considered. Luther would think that to regard the hiddenness of God as a problem for theism is to go seriously astray. He writes from what I have called a biblical perspective, from which God's existence is taken for granted, and God's hiddenness does not need to be justified or explained. His appeal is in part to God's infinite nature, and in part to the fallenness of human nature. I will briefly discuss just two of the themes that were important to Luther and that have not come up so far in my discussion, but I will make no attempt to give a comprehensive account of his views.[15] Neither theme, I suggest, holds any promise for contributing to an explanation of the hiddenness of God.

The first theme occurs in his essay "The Bondage of the Will," which Luther wrote in opposition to Erasmus. Here Luther distinguishes between, on the one hand, "God preached, revealed, offered to us, and worshipped by us" and, on the other hand, God "not preached, nor revealed, nor offered to us, nor worshipped by us."[16] The latter involves "the dreadful hidden will of God . . . [which] is not to be inquired into, but to be reverently adored, as by far the most awesome secret of the Divine Majesty. He has kept it to Himself and forbidden us to know it" (190). Luther continues as follows:

> Wherever God hides Himself, and wills to be unknown to us, there we have no concern. Here that sentiment 'what is above us does not concern us', really holds good. . . . God in His own nature and majesty is to be left alone; in this regard, we have nothing to do with Him, nor does He wish us to deal with Him. We have to do with Him as clothed and displayed in His Word, by which he presents Himself to us. (190–91)

Luther says that it is important to distinguish "the Word of God" or "God preached" and "God Himself" or "God hidden." His purpose in introducing this distinction is to explain how it can be that God can will some people to be damned. The explanation is that "God preached . . . desires that all men should be saved, in that He comes to all by the word of salvation, and the fault is in the will which does not receive Him." God hidden in Majesty, on the other hand, "neither deplores nor takes away death, but works life, and death, and all in all; nor has he set bounds to Himself by His Word, but has kept Himself free over all things." God "does not will the death of a sinner . . . in His Word; but He wills it by His inscrutable will" (191). Luther thinks that we should not expect to understand the purposes and actions of God, at least insofar as God's inscrutable will is concerned, and indeed that it is presumptuous for us to think that we might do so: "as Paul says in Rom. 11: 'Who art thou that repliest against God?'" (192).

We should be clear about what Luther is not saying. He is not just saying that without revelation we would be completely in the dark about God. This idea could be expressed colorfully by saying that there is a God of revelation who is not hidden and a God without revelation who is hidden. Nor is he merely saying that God as he is known through revelation appears very different from God as he is known through what Luther regarded as futile attempts to know God by the use of our own reason and other abilities. Nor again is he just saying that there are various features of human experience, perhaps specifically of religious experience, that provide support for the idea that God is hidden.[17] Nor, finally, is he just saying that it is theologically useful or therapeutic or advantageous in some other way to look on God in both of these ways, with each way of looking at God having its own special role, and perhaps being appropriate at some times and not at others.

Luther's view goes beyond all of these relatively plausible proposals. He says that God actually is both hidden and revealed. A hidden God exists, side by side as it were, with a revealed and not hidden God. But how could this be? As B. A. Gerrish points out,

> Luther's argument ends up by jeopardizing his own theological starting point. He insisted at the outset that he proclaimed nothing but Christ crucified. . . . But one of the doctrines that Christ crucified brings with him [namely, the doctrine that God saves some and damns others] finally forces us to acknowledge an inscrutable will of God behind and beyond the figure of Christ . . . [The] problem is not merely that there is a hidden will *alongside* of the revealed will of God, but that the two are found to be in apparent *contradiction*. . . . [The] Incarnate God must weep as the Hidden God consigns a portion of mankind to perdition. . . . It is not easy to respond, except with agreement, to those who proclaim the collapse of Luther's doctrine of God at this point.[18]

Luther needs to answer a simple question: What is God's nature really like? If God is utterly hidden and inscrutable, then the Scriptures misinform us when they say that God desires that we should be saved. And if the Scriptures do not misinform us, but instead accurately reveal that God desires that we should be saved, then God is not altogether hidden and inscrutable.

The second theme in Luther's thinking on which I will comment briefly is connected with the biblical theme that "man shall not see me and live" (*Exod.* 33:20). As long as we are unregenerate, so this idea goes, we cannot see God and live. God is utterly different from us, and contact with God would overpower us. The attitudes that it is appropriate for us to have toward God include awe and perhaps even terror. God's unknowability is part of the awe-inspiringness of God. God is powerful, full of majesty, splendid, and even destructive. Who are we to question God, to ask whether or not things are set up in the best way? We should plead for mercy and not try to insist on what we think is rightfully ours. ("[He] who has not denied himself and learned to subject his questions to the will of God and hold them down will always keep asking why God wills this and does that, and he will never find the reason. And very properly. Because this foolish wisdom places itself above God and judges His will as something inferior, when actually it should be judged by Him."[19] In a letter to Melanchthon Luther puts the point that "man shall not see me and live" as follows: "[We] are not able to endure Him when He speaks. . . . As if the [Divine] Majesty could speak familiarly with 'the Old Adam,' and not first slay him and dry him out, so that the evil odor of him would not be a stench in his nostrils; for He is a consuming fire."[20] However, some people can endure God's speaking, namely, those in whom the Old Adam has died. These are people whom Luther refers to as "prophets." How can you tell who is a genuine prophet? "Would you know the place, the time, the manner of God's talks with men? Then listen:—'As a lion He hath broken all my bones'; . . . 'I am cut off from before thine eyes'; 'My soul is full of troubles and my life hath drawn near unto hell'" (85).

So we have a number of interconnected themes here. Luther says that a broken and tried spirit is necessary: you have to be broken, to be humiliated, to abandon yourself, in order to get a glimmer of what God is like. We have to abandon the authority of reason and abandon the hope of mastering such issues by our own ability. For we lack the requisite ability. Further, we are incapable of knowing much about God, at least while we are unregenerate.

Among the problems that arise for this proposal are the following. Suppose it is true that direct contact between God and the unregenerate would have the awful consequences described by Luther. What about indirect contact? It is hard to believe that there are not ways in which the facts about God's existence and nature could be made clearer to us without the destructive effects described by Luther. Furthermore, this reaction which consists in part in saying "give up on reason" is medicine that is prescribed by many physicians, each of whom has his own diagnosis of what ails us: there are at least as many prescriptions as there are religious traditions. As it stands, therefore, this reaction is not very impressive, and there is no particular reason to think that any one tradition should see it as lending support to its unique position. Finally, perhaps the best response to the emphasis on self-abasement that is to be found here is not argument but protest.

Eighth, and last, I will just mention the following unimpressive move. It might be suggested that because God is so different from us, we can proceed only by way of negation when characterizing God, saying that God is not this and not that. However, the suggestion that in characterizing God we must proceed by way of negation can contribute to an explanation of God's hiddenness only if it consists in the view that everything we know about God is of a negative character. For if negative theology were just one of a number of routes to information about God, so that there were in addition positive theology, of whatever sort, we would not have here a contribution to explaining God's hiddenness. But the obvious problem is that God is worthy of worship only if God is, for example, good, just, all-knowing, and so forth. If all we knew about God were that God is not this and not that, and such negative claims are never to be cashed in in terms of any positive ones, why should we concern ourselves about God? Indeed, there is not to be found here anything that can contribute to an explanation of God's hiddenness because the problem of the hiddenness of God is the problem of how it is that God, who is understood to be a certain type of being (namely, one who cares about us, wishes us to have faith, and so on) is hidden from us. But if we do not know anything about the nature of God other than what God is not, and if this negative information cannot be reformulated in terms of positive attributions, this puzzle does not arise. This is a puzzle about God, not a puzzle about a being about whom we can only say what it is not.

4. Unknown Goods of Mystery

Next I want to consider an important category of goods of which as yet no mention has been made, namely, goods of mystery of which we are not aware, or what I will call "unknown goods of mystery." Is it reasonable to believe that there are such goods?

Unknown goods might take either of the following forms. They might be goods of which we are incapable of being aware. Or they might be goods of which we are capable of being aware but of which, for whatever reason, we are nevertheless unaware. The notion that we are *capable* of being aware of a good, or of anything, is a murky one. Suppose, for example, that it is necessary to devote most of your adult life to the study of some arcane topic in order to be aware of something, or suppose that it would require brain surgery. Are you in either case capable of being aware of the object in question? There is no clear answer to such questions. However, we can obviate the need to settle such questions provided we count as unknown goods both (a) unknown goods that we are capable of being aware of and (b) unknown goods that we are incapable of being aware of. I also assume that to be aware of a good is to be aware of it *as* a good. Hence something of whose existence we are aware, but of whose status as a good we are unaware, is to be classified as an unknown good.[21]

It is important to consider unknown goods, since, if God exists, it is likely that there are manifold goods that are unknown to us but known to God. They might include goods that are enjoyed by creatures of whose very existence we are unaware. They might also include goods that God enjoys. Might there be goods of mystery among the unknown goods?

If there were unknown goods of mystery, then it would not be surprising that we do not understand why God is hidden. If we even have grounds to *suspect* that there may be such goods, we ought not to conclude from the fact that we do not understand why God is hidden—if it is indeed the case that we do not understand why God is hidden— that there are no good reasons for God to be hidden.

In a discussion of this topic J. L. Schellenberg usefully draws on, and extends, a relevant debate between William Rowe and Stephen Wykstra.[22] Actually Schellenberg's discussion focuses on a narrower set of goods, namely, those that are inscrutable, which is to say that we are incapable of being aware of them or that they are beyond our grasp. Since, as mentioned, there could be goods of which we are ignorant but for reasons other than that they are inscrutable, I will continue to consider the more inclusive set of *unknown* goods.

Schellenberg correctly points out both that there can be goods that are unknown to us but that do not serve to justify *any* evils, and that if we think of God's hiddenness as part of the problem of evil, then even if there are unknown goods that serve to justify some evils, they may not justify the particular form or instance of evil that consists in God's being hidden. Evils come in many shapes and sizes, and we have no particular reason to think that unknown goods will explain the *particular* sort of evil that consists in God's being hidden even if (a) there are unknown goods, (b) unknown goods explain the occurrence of some evils, and (c) God's hiddenness is an evil. Of course this consideration hardly settles the question of whether unknown goods of mystery might contribute to the explanation of God's hiddenness.

Schellenberg, adopting a point from Rowe, proposes the following reason for doubting that there are unknown goods of mystery. He says—and here I paraphrase—that if such goods are to contribute to an explanation of why God is hidden from *us*, they must be human goods. They must bear on our salvation or at least on our welfare. The idea is that if they were, say, goods that consisted in benefits to other beings, it would be unfair to impose on *us* the burdens of God's being hidden from us in order to achieve the benefits in question. So any goods whose occurrence justifies God's being hidden from us must benefit us. And, so this thought concludes, if a good is a human good, we ought to be acquainted with it or at least we are more likely to be acquainted with it than we would be in the case of other goods.

The claim that a good that would justify, or contribute to justifying, the hiddenness of God would be one that would benefit us does not have anything special to do with *unknown* goods of mystery. Rather, it bears on all attempts to explain God's hiddenness that appeal to some good that is achieved by God's being hidden. That there is something right about this claim is confirmed by the fact that the goods that have so far seemed to be the most promising candidates for inclusion in the explanation of God's hiddenness are indeed goods that involve some benefit to us, whether this be a matter of facilitating our moral autonomy, a matter of our being able to exercise a certain sort of control over our beliefs, or something else. In fact, even the unpromising candidates surveyed display this feature.

The claim that goods of mystery would be good for human beings, and that consequently we ought to know about them, has some force, but I do not think that it suffices to show that unknown goods cannot contribute to an explanation of the hiddenness of God. First, even if it is true both that unknown goods of mystery would be goods that benefit us, and that the fact that goods involve benefits to us increases the probability that we will know of them, it hardly follows that there are no unknown goods of mystery. For one thing, we may not know enough about our welfare or destiny to recognize them. For another, we may enjoy them in the future. Second, it is not clear that goods whose occurrence justifies God's being hidden from us *must* benefit us. Perhaps it is enough that we would be satisfied with them as an explanation of God's hiddenness if we understood them, even if we ourselves do not benefit from them. Or perhaps it is enough that we *ought* to be satisfied with them. So this proposed reason to believe that goods of mystery of which we are unaware are incapable of contributing anything to an explanation of God's hiddenness is unconvincing.

In reflecting further about this possibility we should bear in mind that just as there may be unknown goods among the goods of mystery, there may also be unknown goods among the goods of clarity: these would be advantages that would attach to the facts about God being clear but that we are currently unaware of, either because they are beyond our grasp or for some other reason. Since we do not know what unknown goods there are, we do not know in which of these two categories, if either, they are to be found.

At first glance it may seem that we have as much reason to include the one as the other in our calculations. It may seem, therefore, that we have no reason to think that *all* of the unknown goods, if they are all taken into account and considered together, will explain or help to explain God's hiddenness as distinct from providing, or helping to provide, an explanation of why God ought *not* to be hidden. Nevertheless, there is some reason to think that unknown goods are somewhat more likely to be among the goods of mystery than they are to be among the goods of clarity. For it might be essential to the hiddenness of God that we not see precisely which goods are served by God's being hidden. The idea is that if we could see precisely which goods were achieved by God's being hidden, then, in effect, God would not be hidden at all. And there seems to be no corresponding reason to think that we would need to be ignorant of goods of clarity. This point hardly provides conclusive reason to think that there are unknown goods of mystery but no unknown goods of clarity. Still, it lends an element of support to the thought that unknown goods of mystery may contribute to an explanation of God's hiddenness and that we should not just ignore them on the grounds that it is also possible that there are unknown goods of clarity. Moreover, this reason to believe that unknown goods are more likely to be among the goods of mystery than they are to be among the goods of clarity is also a reason to believe that unknown goods are more likely to be among the goods of mystery than they are to be among the goods that account for the occurrence of evil—or evil of other sorts, in the event that God's hiddenness is counted as an evil. Consequently, if we count God's hiddenness as an evil and if we think that some evils may be accounted for by appeal to unknown goods, we actually have some reason to expect that this particular evil, the hiddenness of God, will be among those evils that are accounted for by appeal to an unknown good.

5. Implications of the Possibility of Unknown Goods of Mystery

It may seem that if God exists, we ought to be able to explain why the facts about God are not clear to us. The fact that theists have proposed various putative explanations of God's hiddenness suggests that this thought is a widely shared one. Presumably the fact that so many explanations have been offered signifies that it has been thought necessary or important or useful (or something of that sort) to provide an explanation; implicit in that thought is the further thought that it ought to be possible to provide an explanation. But this may not be possible. Unknown goods of mystery may contribute significantly to the explanation of God's hiddenness. If we are incapable of being aware of the goods in question, then clearly we are incapable of explaining why God is hidden. If the goods in question are merely goods of which we are *currently* ignorant, and we are not permanently incapable of knowing them, then we are (only) currently incapable of explaining why God is hidden.

Another reason to doubt that theists ought to expect to be able to understand why God is hidden was mentioned at the end of the last section. If there are good reasons that the facts about God are not clear to us, there probably are in addition (and consequently) good reasons for it not to be clear to us what those good reasons are. In that case, it would be important that the relevant goods of mystery or other relevant considerations that explain God's hiddenness should be unknown to us. Our lack of an adequate explanation would be a natural concomitant to the combined facts that God's existence is not clear to us and that there are good reasons for this to be so.

More exactly, if we were to see what exactly is the explanation of why God's *existence* is not clear, then the existence of God would in effect be rendered clear to us. Thus if we knew that it is just because it is necessary for our moral autonomy that it is not clear to us that God exists, then we would in effect know that God exists. Indeed, we would know that God exists if it merely is clear that *there is* an explanation that actually accounts for the fact that the existence of God is not clear to us.

On the other hand, we could see what would suffice for an explanation of why it is unclear to us that God exists, and we could have access to what we have reason to believe may be the explanation, or to what we understand to be possible ingredients in such an explanation, without it becoming clear that God exists. The availability of a *plau-*

sible story would not provide reason to believe that God exists: it is the availability of the actual explanation, where this is recognized to be the actual explanation, that would have this effect.

As things are, no one is in a position to be sure that they know what the actual explanation is. In fact, it seems that we would be able to go beyond making our best guess about what seem to be the most promising candidates, and beyond a speculative and exploratory stage in our reflections, only if the actual explanation were known by us to be revealed to us by God. Yet if we knew that God had revealed it to us, then we would know that God exists. If, say, it were merely planted in our minds without our knowing its origin, then how would we know that it was not just an idea that had occurred to us? We would have no special reason to take it seriously.

In the case of other facts about God, we might be able to grasp the explanation of those other facts not being clear without those facts actually becoming clear in the process: thus it might be unclear (a) what the will of God is in some situation and (b) why this is unclear, without our thereby coming to know the will of God in that situation. So there certainly are some facts about God that might be unclear, and we might see clearly why they are unclear, without the unclarity surrounding those facts thereby being dissipated. But as far as the *existence* of God is concerned, if there is good reason for God's existence not to be clear to us, there is therefore good reason for it also to be unclear to us what those good reasons are.[23]

So we have two lines of thought that ought to diminish our confidence that we ought to be able to understand why God is hidden, if God exists. One appeals to the possibility of unknown goods of mystery. Another appeals to the connected idea that if it were clear what factors account for God's hiddenness, then God would no longer be hidden. These considerations provide reason to doubt that, if God exists, we should be able to understand why God is hidden.

If it is unlikely that we would be able to understand why God is hidden if God exists, then the fact that we are unable to do so, if this is indeed a fact, has a quite different significance from what it would have if we had every reason to be confident that if God were to exist and there were an explanation of why the facts about God are not more clear, then we would know what that explanation consists in. It also has the result that it is unreasonable to say that theists must provide an explanation of why God is hidden if they are to avoid the charge of irrationality or of going wrong in some other way.

Finally, I am sure that by the end of this chapter I have not surveyed all the explanations of God's hiddenness that are worthy of serious consideration.[24] But what I have considered in this and the last two chapters are, I believe, the most promising candidates, the most important proposals that one will encounter in a search of the relevant literature and in conversation with believers from the theistic traditions.

5

THE HIDDENNESS OF GOD AND ARGUMENTS FOR ATHEISM

In general I am approaching the issue of the hiddenness of God as an internal problem for theism. I am probing the various putative explanations of God's hiddenness that theists offer and attempting to assess their credibility. But doesn't the ambiguity that surrounds the existence of God provide evidence against God's existence? Some argue that we ought to deny the existence of God for reasons that are at least related to the fact that the world is religiously ambiguous. They contend, in effect, that the fact that people do not know more about God provides the basis for a case for atheism. I will consider, and reject, two arguments of this sort, one that Thomas V. Morris has discussed in his essay "The Hidden God"[1] and one that has been advanced by J. L. Schellenberg in his book *Divine Hiddenness and Human Reason*. My general position here is that although the mystery that surrounds the nature and existence of God is a serious problem for theism, it does not provide the basis for a convincing case for atheism.

1. The Case for Epistemic Atheism

The argument that Morris discusses is based on what he calls the Hanson-Scriven thesis (HST):

> For any rational subject S and any positive existence claim p, if S is in possession of no good evidence or any other positive epistemic ground for thinking that p is true, then S ought to adopt the cognitive relation to p of denial. (12)

This thesis is the foundation on which an attempt has been made to establish what Morris calls "epistemic atheism." Epistemic atheism is the view that given HST and the fact (and epistemic atheists claim that it is a fact) that we lack good evidence or any other positive epistemic ground for thinking that God exists—a fact which (epistemic atheists say) theists misrepresent when they say that God is hidden—we should all be atheists. Theism, agnosticism, suspension of judgment, for example, are all unacceptable.

HST squares with our intuitions in cases of certain sorts. Presumably the reason we ought to deny that, say, there are any large dinosaurs still living on our planet has everything to do with the fact that we are in possession of no good evidence for thinking that such creatures still exist. Again, the reason I ought to deny that, say, there is an elephant in my garden has a great deal to do with the fact that I am in possession of no good evidence or any other positive epistemic ground for thinking that there is an elephant in my garden.

2. Being Well Situated Epistemically

Morris rejects HST and the case for epistemic atheism that depends on it. His main point, and it is a convincing one, is that one ought to infer that p, a positive existence claim, is false from the fact that one has no good evidence or any other positive epistemic ground for thinking that p is true only if one also reasonably believes that one is in a good position to know of whatever grounds there are for p. That is, one ought to deny p on finding that one has no reason to believe p only if one reasonably believes that if there were good reasons to believe p, one would know of them. Morris refers to the position that you get when you qualify HST to take account of this fact as HST′, and he states HST′ as follows:

> For any rational subject S and any positive existence claim p, if S rationally believes himself to be in good epistemic position relative to p, and S is in possession of no good evidence or any other positive epistemic ground for thinking that p is true, then S ought to adopt the cognitive relation to p of denial. (15)

Morris does not endorse HST′. His point is rather that it is the closest principle to HST that is plausible. In light of HST′, Morris says, people who find that they lack good evidence or any other positive epistemic grounds for a metaphysical existence claim, such as the claim that God exists, generally ought to conclude only that either the existence claim in question is false or it is true but they are not in a good epistemic position to recognize its truth. The contrast is with all cases in which we have every reason to believe that we are well situated epistemically, as in the elephant in the garden case, in which cases HST′ would warrant a negative existential claim. Once one's epistemic situation is in doubt, the case for the negative existential claim is weakened accordingly.

Morris also says that theists can provide an explanation of why the person to whom God is hidden is not in a good epistemic position relative to the existence of God. In particular, Morris suggests, the theist can develop the following themes from Pascal. People need to be at a certain stage in their spiritual development in order to know about God's existence and nature. They need to be humble, to realize they lack self-sufficiency, and to seek the truth with all their energies. Morris's position is that it is reasonable for the theist to say that God is hidden from all, and only, those who are spiritually undeveloped in such respects. The idea is, further, that it would be dangerous for God not to be hidden from people who are spiritually undeveloped: it would lead to pride and to an inflated sense of self-worth.

I think that Morris is right about the unsatisfactory nature of HST and about the need to replace it with HST′. In cases in which our intuitions seem to square with HST, such as the case of the elephant in my garden, part of what gives it appeal is the combined facts (a) that we know what would count as evidence for the presence of an elephant, (b) that no such evidence is available to us, and (c) that we know that we are sufficiently well situated epistemically that we would know of such evidence if it were available.

Once we are unsure about such matters, including (c), HST loses its appeal. Thus we have much less reason to be sure that we are well situated epistemically with respect to detecting the existence of extraterrestrial life, and it is accordingly much less reasonable to conclude from our lack of evidence for such life that there is no such life. In general, in circumstances in which we have reason to doubt that we are in a good position to know of whatever reasons there are for thinking that some existence claim is true, there is little to be said for HST.

Morris is also right when he says that an effective case for epistemic atheism is unlikely to be based on HST′. For whatever we may think of the Pascalian suggestion that God is hidden from all, and only, those who are spiritually undeveloped in virtue of their lack of humility or their excessive sense of self-sufficiency or their failure to seek the truth with all their energies, we have at any rate reason to be uncertain whether we are well situated to be aware of whatever evidence there is for God's existence. And that alone calls into question the viability of any attempt to base a case for atheism on HST′.

In chapter 3, I indicated what we should say about the Pascalian suggestion. Briefly, it seems that we could make some progress in discerning who is humble, who is aware that he lacks self-sufficiency, and who energetically seeks the truth. And we can tell whether people who score well in such respects report that God is not hidden to them. An investigation of this sort would require looking at different cultures and at different periods in history. There have been, and are, cultures in which nontheistic religions have flourished or in which theists have been few or absent entirely, but in which these virtues (humility, searching for the truth, etc.) are not entirely lacking. In the absence of the sort of evidence that such an investigation would yield, the Pascalian proposal remains speculative. As it is, the relevant evidence that we have seems rather mixed. However, my most serious reservation about this proposal is that it presupposes that God is not hidden from those who are at the right stage in their spiritual development, who are humble, realize that they lack self-sufficiency, and seek the truth with all (would much be enough?) of their energies. It seems a bit too easy and even a trifle self-congratulatory for the theist to say that the reason that God is hidden from nontheists is that they are so undeveloped spiritually. Moreover, the presupposition that God is not hidden (at all) from those who are at the right stage in their spiritual development is not plausible for reasons discussed in chapter 1. So, at least in the form in which it is discussed here, the Pascalian theme is not very appealing, although, as indicated in the last two sections of chapter 3, a theory that is roughly of this sort may be correct.

3. Having "No Good Evidence" for p

Actually there are other reasons why HST′ is very unlikely to serve as an adequate basis for epistemic atheism, and it is instructive to probe these. According to HST′, if S rationally believes himself to be in a good epistemic position relative to p, then S ought to deny p if S has no good evidence or any other positive epistemic ground for thinking p to be true. But what is it to have "no good evidence or any other positive epistemic ground" for thinking p to be true? Morris regards this as equivalent to having "no clear evidence or any other sufficient positive epistemic ground" for p (13). But these notions of good evidence, clear evidence, and positive epistemic grounds are all ambiguous in the same respect. When, for instance, is there clear evidence for p? Is there clear evidence for p if there is some evidence that clearly provides some support for p, or must there be evidence which, all things considered, suffices to convince us of the truth of p? Or would something in between be clear evidence for p? Is the clarity of the evidence a matter of its actually providing some epistemic support for p? Or is it a matter of the abundance of the evidence?

If the notion of having clear evidence for p—and the same goes for the other notions—is interpreted as involving anything more than having any evidence at all that provides some epistemic support for p, HST′ is very implausible. HST′, so interpreted, would imply that one ought to deny p when one has some, but insufficient, grounds or evidence for p. But there is no reason to accept this claim. Why ought you to deny a claim for which you have some evidence, but lack good evidence, so construed? If S has some positive epistemic grounds for p, but not enough for it to be clear to S that p is true, perhaps S should, for example, suspend judgment about p, or examine her belief that p, or doubt p, or believe p with less enthusiasm.

HST′ is plausible if S is understood to be "in possession of no good evidence or any other positive epistemic ground for thinking that p is true" only if S has no reason whatsoever to accept p. That is, there must be nothing whatsoever to recommend p to S. In order to make this point explicit, we might restate HST′ as follows, and call this HST″:

> For any rational subject S and any positive existence claim p, if S rationally believes himself to be in good epistemic position relative to p, and there is nothing whatsoever to recommend p to S, then S ought to adopt the cognitive relation to p of denial.

Under what circumstances is there nothing whatsoever to recommend a positive existential proposition p to S? This would certainly be so if S had a disproof of p or if it were clear to S that a necessary condition for the truth of p is not met. The idea of there being nothing whatsoever to recommend p can be further clarified by examining some respects in which there might be something to recommend p to S. Thus p might have something to be said for it in virtue of (a) the epistemic support that is provided for p by other beliefs that S holds, or (b) the credibility of the source from which S has acquired p, or (c) p's relation to relevant experiences that S has had. (The latter might, for example, be a matter of S having experiences in which S believes himself to perceive that p is true; or p may be a part of a theory that S reasonably believes to provide the best or most natural account of experiences that S enjoys.) (a), (b), and (c) are hardly an exhaustive list of the possibilities, but they are at any rate considerations that should figure in such a list. So HST″ is the claim that if p has nothing to be said for it in any such areas as these—other beliefs that S holds, the source from which S received p, and experiences which S has—then S ought to deny p.

It does seem that if p fares badly in all such respects, then—assuming that the other conditions stated in HST″ are met, so that, for example, S rationally believes himself to be in good epistemic position relative to p—it is reasonable to conclude that S ought to deny p. But I take it as obvious that most theists do not find themselves so poorly situated with respect to their theistic beliefs. Few theists will find that there is nothing whatsoever to recommend theism to them. There is no disproof of theism, nor is theism likely to appear false to them given the other beliefs that they hold on adequate grounds. Most theists find, in fact, that their theism fits with their experience at least to the extent that their theistic beliefs provide a framework within which they are able to make sense of much of their experience. That alone means that it is not true that there is nothing whatsoever to recommend theism to them. There is also, for instance, the fact that others who appear to be honest claim to experience God. And almost everyone who encounters the belief that God exists does so by hearing it from a source that they have found to be at least fairly reliable. One's family or community or friends, or some such source whom one respects and knows to be reliable on many issues, and whom one generally has no compelling reason to believe to be unreliable in this particular area, is the source of the belief that God exists. It seems, therefore, that HST″ is unlikely to provide the basis for a case for atheism.

It might be objected that while there may be some apparent evidence for theism, such as evidence provided by religious experience or by testimony, there are available to us defeaters which undermine the probative value of each such piece of apparent evidence. Hence there is after all nothing whatsoever to recommend theism to us: it only *looked* as if there were. Hence the conditions specified in HST″ are satisfied—S rationally believes himself to be in good epistemic position relative to p, and there is nothing whatsoever to recommend p to S—and HST″ is relevant after all. Hence S ought to adopt the cognitive relation to p of denial.

However, it is not enough to mention possible defeaters: it has to be shown that there is a defeater for each piece of evidence that appears to provide reason to believe that God exists. Until this task has been discharged, the burden of proof is on those who think that HST″ can provide the basis for a case for atheism to show exactly how each apparent ground is to be defeated; and this is no easy task.

Another possibility is that there is *something* to be said for p and yet on balance this epistemic support for p is utterly outweighed by other considerations, so that S ought to deny p. Here the idea is that a belief need not fare badly in *all* respects mentioned for it to be plausible to claim that one ought to deny it. (For example, it need not be altogether lacking in epistemic support from other beliefs that S holds on adequate grounds, or from credible sources, for example.) S may have undefeated grounds for accepting p—that is, particular grounds that are undefeated—and yet the case against p may be overwhelming. But, once again, why think that theists find themselves in that situation? The relevant sources of support for their beliefs are various, and there is little reason to think that they are utterly outweighed in this fashion.

Yet another possibility is that in virtue of the absence of a particular piece of evidence for p, S ought to deny p. Thus even if the sacred texts with which I am familiar, or the revered elders whom I recognize, tell me that there is an elephant in my garden, if I fail to see an elephant there—search as I may behind the gooseberry bushes and in the corner behind the overgrown buddleia—I ought to deny that there is an elephant in my garden, assuming of course that I rationally believe myself to be well equipped to spot an elephant in the garden, which as a matter of fact I do believe myself to be. What is distinctive of such a case is that the absence of a particular crucial piece of evidence for p provides decisive evidence against p. But there does not appear to be any such crucial piece of, or body of, evidence in the case of theism.

There is another reason that neither HST′ nor HST″ is likely to provide a basis for epistemic atheism. Both say that S ought to deny p if, among other things, S rationally believes himself to be in a good epistemic position relative to p, so that if there were grounds for p, S would know of them. This requirement is not satisfied, therefore, whenever we have reason to doubt that we are in a good epistemic situation with respect to some claim. And we do have reasons to doubt this in the case of God's existence. The theistic traditions provide such reasons when they offer putative explanations of God's hiddenness. Some of these explanations appear to have some promise; their very availability provides reason to doubt that we are in a good epistemic situation with respect to God's existence.

Epistemic atheism is difficult to defend because it is so demanding. It says that under the conditions specified earlier, one has a duty to be an atheist. However, the view that under such conditions atheism is, for example, rational or acceptable, or is one of a number of options that are rational or acceptable, is more plausible and easier to defend.

4. Schellenberg's Case for Atheism: The Central Argument

In his book *Divine Hiddenness and Human Reason*, J. L. Schellenberg argues that theists are unable to explain God's hiddenness. More exactly, what Schellenberg says is that theists are unable to explain why nonbelief that God exists is rational or reasonable. For it is, he says, the fact that nonbelief is rational that makes it impossible for many people to enter into a personal relationship with God. In this section I outline his main argument. In the remainder of the chapter I discuss that argument.

Schellenberg contends that a loving God would want all human beings to have a personal relationship with God at all times at which they are capable of it. Such a relationship is not to be identified with the beatific vision: it admits of change and growth, and it may be shallow or deep, depending on the human response. What Schellenberg has in mind is something along the lines of close friendship. He says that "[if] I love you and so seek your well-being, I wish to make available to you all the resources at my disposal for the overcoming of difficulties in your life. But then I must also make it possible for you to draw on me *personally*—to let you benefit from my listening to your problems, from my encouragement, from my spending time together with you, and so on. In other words, I wish to make available to you the resources of an intimate personal relationship with me" (18). One of Schellenberg's arguments for the view that God would seek a personal relationship with us is that the best sort of love between human beings involves reciprocity and mutuality. God would seek such a relationship with us because it would "immeasurably enhance our well-being" (18), bringing with it ethical, experiential, and other benefits, and also because such a relationship is worthwhile in itself. Almost everyone, in most stages of their lives, is capable of some degree of such a relationship (24).

However, it is impossible for us to have a personal relationship with God unless we believe that God exists. So God would provide everyone who is capable of a personal relationship with God with evidence that adequately supports belief that God exists. This evidence would render at least probable the belief that God exists (33–35). If we had such evidence, nonbelief would be unreasonable. Moreover, anyone who had such evidence would believe, unless his culpable acts or omissions caused him not to believe, for belief is involuntary and arises in response to the perceived evidence unless one chooses to resist it.[2]

God, being onmipotent, could cause people to believe that God exists even if they lack evidence that is adequate to support belief: Thus God could conceal from people the fact that the evidence thay have is not adequate, it that were indeed the case. But this would be deceitful and therefore is out of the question for God. And if a lack of adequate support for belief were discoverable by us, we might actually discover it, in which case nonbelief would then be inculpable for us.

So God would provide evidence that adequately supports belief, evidence that renders the belief probably true, thereby rendering nonbelief unreasonable. God would thereby elicit belief in everyone who is capable of a personal relationship with God and who does not culpably choose to resist it. One way to provide the evidence in question would be to bring it about that all people who are capable of a personal relationship with God "have an experience as of God presenting himself to them, which they take to be caused by God and which is caused by God presenting himself to their experience" (48–49). Schellenberg characterizes the experience in question as "an intense [nonsensory] apparent awareness of a reality at once ultimate and loving which (1) produces the belief that God is lovingly present (and ipso facto, that God exists), (2) continues indefinitely in stronger or weaker forms and minimally as a 'background awareness' in those who do not resist it, and (3) takes more particular forms in the lives of those who respond to the beliefs to which it gives rise in religiously appropriate ways (for example, the believer who pursues a personal relationship with God may describe his experience as that of the forgiving, comforting, or guiding presence of God)" (49). The experience might vary in its force as is necessary, say, to compensate for challenges to belief, such as are provided, for example, by the problem of evil, thus preserving at all times sufficiency for belief. The experience could also be universal and uniform. If we knew that many others had the same experience, this would help to confirm the conclusions each person would come to on the basis of such experience. However, since we can be unreasonable, and can resist God's overtures, we might fail to believe even if God were to provide us with this sort of experience. But nonbelief would then be irrational and culpable.

In summary of the aspects of his argument that I have mentioned so far, Schellenberg writes that

> If God exists and is perfectly loving, then for any human subject S and time t, if S is at t capable of relating personally to God, S at t believes [that God exists] on the basis of evidence that renders [God's existence] probable, except insofar as S is culpably in a contrary position at t. (38)

However, evidence that is sufficient to produce belief in everyone who is capable of belief and whose nonbelief is not culpable has not been provided. Instead, nonbelief is reasonable. So we have reason to believe that God does not exist. There is reason to believe that "[the] weakness of our evidence for God is not a sign that God is hidden; it is a revelation that God does not exist" (1; see also 212).

Schellenberg considers the possibility that culpable acts or omissions of each person who does not believe that God exists have caused her nonbelief. In his response he does not focus on the easiest cases, such as people in nontheistic cultures who have never been exposed to theism, or for whom theism is at any rate not a live option, and whose nonbelief obviously is not a product of their own acts or omissions. Instead he goes to some trouble to argue that for people in a culture such as ours, *doubt* (by which he means in this context uncertainty generated by the belief that neither the proposition that God exists nor the proposition that God does not exist is epistemically preferable to its denial) is sometimes inculpable.

To summarize, part 1 of Schellenberg's book, whose contents I have sketched thus far, presents "an argument of considerable force from the reasonableness of nonbelief to the nonexistence of God" (83). It does so by making a prima facie case for the soundness of this argument for atheism (A):

1. If there is a God, he is perfectly loving.
2. If a perfectly loving God exists, reasonable nonbelief does not occur.
3. Reasonable nonbelief occurs.
4. No perfectly loving God exists.
Therefore, there is no God.

But A is open to defeat: it would be defeated if we came up with an important good, or set of goods, whose achievement would require nonbelief to be reasonable. If there were such goods, premise 2 of A would be false. Schellenberg's view, however, is that we are unable to come up with any such goods. He thinks that an analysis of goods such as those I have examined in chapters 2 to 4 shows that they are unable to contribute to an explanation of the occurrence of reasonable nonbelief under conditions in which a perfectly loving God exists. Hence by the end of his book, by which point he has canvassed the relevant goods, Schellenberg understands himself to have presented an undefeated argument for atheism from the reasonableness of nonbelief. He says that "unless it can be shown plausible to suppose that there are countervailing considerations . . . [the] conclusion, that God does not exist, goes through" (91).

In assessing the force of his case it is especially important to consider the status of premise 2 in Schellenberg's argument. His view is that if premise 2 is true, then A is sound (84). Premises 1 and 3, he says, are clearly true; premise 4 follows from premises 2 and 3; and the argument is valid. So it all rests on premise 2, for which he understands himself to have given a prima facie case in part 1 of his book. He says at the end of part 1 that "the reasons . . . [I have given] for supposing that God, if perfectly loving, will prevent the occurrence of reasonable non-belief are clearly sufficient to warrant the conclusion that he *will* do so unless an adequate defense of that claim's denial can be mounted. It follows that A must be viewed as sound unless such a defense can be given. There is, in other words, a presumption in favor of its conclusion which is defeated only if our support for [premise 2] is defeated" (84).

So Schellenberg does not understand himself to have shown conclusively that A is sound and that God does not exist. Rather his position is the somewhat weaker one that what we have after the various attempts to defeat premise 2 of A have been found want-ing is an undefeated presumption in favor of believing that premise 2 is true and that A is sound. Hence, for now, it is reasonable to think that A is sound although it remains possible that a way to show premise 2 to be false will be found in the future.

Schellenberg says that what one should conclude depends on whether one thinks oneself to have independent evidence for theism and on how much of it one has. (By "independent evidence" he means evidence that is distinct from the evidence consid-ered in his book: thus someone would have such evidence if, say, he had encountered a convincing version of the argument from the "fine-tuning" of the universe to God's ex-istence or if he enjoyed striking theistic religious experiences.) If a theist had strong in-dependent evidence for God's existence, then the argument of his book should merely "exert a certain evidential pressure" (210), and it certainly ought not to be ignored and is a serious challenge. It may be that it ought to lead to perplexity or doubt. As for someone who lacks overwhelming independent evidence for theism, which is the situation in which, he believes, most people find themselves, "[the] final claim of the book is . . . [that] the argument from the reasonableness of nonbelief goes through, providing good grounds for atheism" (3). It is unreasonable for such a person not to be an atheist. For such a person his arguments provide "good reason to suppose that a lov-ing God does not exist" (9). And A, the main argument of the book, will retain this force until someone comes up with a defeater of premise 2, and hence a refutation of A, which is something that Schellenberg thinks is not about to happen, since he has ex-plored the likely candidates and has found them all to be wanting.

5. Objections to Schellenberg's Argument

It seems obvious that if God exists, God could do a lot more to make God's existence more apparent to us. To this extent Schellenberg is right. He is also clearly right to think that the fact that nonbelief that God exists is reasonable is a difficulty for orthodox the-ism. But, as I have suggested in earlier chapters, his estimation of some of the relevant considerations is open to question. And while he is right to think that there are reasons to believe that a loving God would arrange things so that nonbelief is irrational, there are also reasons to deny this. Next I present some objections to his views.

A. Even if a personal relationship with God would immeasurably enhance our well-being, perhaps it would be best that we achieve it in the future, such as when we are in a more advanced state of development. It is an intuitively plausible idea that different goods would be suitable for us at different stages in our development, with the greatest goods available to us when we are most developed.

Schellenberg considers, and rejects, this possibility, and in the course of doing so quotes these remarks from Marilyn Adams:

> For each created person, the primary source of meaning and satisfaction will be found in his/her intimate personal relationship with God. This relationship will also be the context in which a created person can be best convinced of his/her worth, because it is the place where God's love for the individual is most vividly and intimately experienced. Christians naturally see it as to everyone's advantage to enter into this relationship as deeply as one can in this world, as soon as possible. [3]

By way of supporting the claim that God would want to be personally related to us here and now, which is indeed a fairly standard theistic claim, Schellenberg also says that "if there is a God, my deeper well-being lies in a deeper relationship with him" (26). He says that God is "self-giving, unconditionally accepting, [and] relationship-seeking" (11) and that "the proper explication of 'God loves human beings' must include the proposition 'God seeks to be personally related to us'" (23). And he says that "[a] loving God . . . would bring us into existence so that he might enter into fellowship with us—for our sakes, but for its own sake too" (26). He concludes: "[We] have, then, reason to suppose that there is no time at which some human being is to some extent capable of personal relationship with God but at which God does not wish the potential represented by that capacity to be realized" (26). He thinks that God would seek a personal relationship here and now rather than in the future because such a relationship would be good for us and because such a relationship is worthwhile for its own sake.[4]

But it does not follow from the combined facts that our having a personal relationship with God is a great good, and a good that brings with it numerous benefits for the human participants in the relationship, and a good whose achievement is central to the purpose of our existence, and that we are capable of such a relationship, that it is right that we should achieve it now. For a start, we may be capable of it only in the sense that we could acquire the ability to achieve it, but not currently be able to do so. In that case we would be capable of it in the sense in which I am currently capable of speaking at least a few phrases of, say, Tagolog, a language with which I am presently entirely unacquainted; learning to do so require some study and training or the opportunity to listen to native speakers.

Even if we are now capable of a personal relationship with God in the fuller sense that we are currently in a position to enjoy it, we may not be ready for it now. It may not be suitable for us at the present. Or most, or many, people may not be ready for it now.[5]

The fact, if it were a fact, that we are not ready for such a relationship even if we are fully capable of it would provide excellent reason for a loving God not to do what is necessary to achieve such a relationship with us now, whatever its importance. It would not follow that it is right that we should achieve this good now even if our having a personal relationship with God were the sole purpose of our life.

B. Schellenberg's basis for believing that the vast majority of people are at some point in their lives capable of a personal relationship with God is that what this requires is that we have "the cognitive and affective equipment required to hold religious beliefs and exhibit such attitudes as trust, gratefulness, obedience, and worship" (24). And most people, he says, have that equipment. But this is at least debatable. For instance, if the line of argument developed at the end of chapter 3 is correct, theistic belief requires a set of attitudes that many people lack.

C. Schellenberg says that even weak belief that God exists would suffice for a personal relationship with God (32f.). A weak belief differs from a strong belief in that, among other things, it involves more openness to the possibility that one may be wrong and the disposition to feel that the belief is true is weaker. To believe p, however weakly, is to be disposed to feel it true that p, and to think in terms of p rather than merely to think about p. Weak belief would be made possible for us if the available evidence were to render the existence of God even marginally more probable than not. Schellenberg says that "[even] a weak belief that God exists is compatible with gratefulness, love toward God, trust, contemplation and the like, for even a weak belief involves a disposition to feel it true that [God exists] . . . If I feel, however weakly, that it is true that there is a God, I may be moved to praise him and to struggle with him in prayer in ways that would be ruled out were I to, for example, be uncertain whether [God exists]" (32). So Schellenberg accepts that the difference between strong and weak belief would be reflected in different prospects for personal relations, and he concedes that an intimate personal relationship would require something more than weak belief. While it is true that we can feel some measure of gratitude, love, trust, and so on toward a being whom we only weakly believe to exist, and while we may praise this being and struggle with him in prayer, all of this will have a different tenor if the belief supporting it is weak rather than strong. Weak belief that God exists may suffice for exploration, for testing of the waters, even for worship of a sort. But because of the extent to which it involves openness to the possibility that one may be wrong—even about the existence of God—a personal relationship would be facilitated to a lesser extent.

What would it take for it to be possible for us to have personal relations with, say, extraterrestrial beings with intelligence that is merely somewhat greater than ours and capacities that are merely somewhat greater than ours? Certainly it would not be enough for it to seem more probable than not that they exist. Nor would it be enough for it to seem more probable than not that they want to communicate with us. We would need, in addition, to have a sense of their presence and some awareness that we are interacting with them and that they are involved in our lives. Extensive interaction with them would in fact be necessary.

For us to have a personal relationship with God, we would need to be aware in a constant and forceful way of God's relating personally to us; we would need to have a constant and palpable sense of God's presence. We would need to be intimately aware of God in a permanent and ongoing way. This would be very invasive. And the more invasive it would be, the easier it is to make a case against its being desirable that we should currently be in such a state. Such a case may appeal to moral autonomy, to the goods spelled out in the cryptovolitionalist argument advanced at the end of chapter 3, or to unknown goods, for instance. For such reasons a personal relationship with God may not be such a great good for us as we are presently constituted—even if it would be beneficial to us in various respects, even if it is good in itself in various respects, and even if, in the end, it is part of the purpose of human existence.

D. Is it really true that the best sort of love between human beings involves reciprocity and mutuality? Surely I can seek your well-being in the best possible way without in the process making available to you an intimate personal relationship with me. I may think that it will do you more good to have such a relationship with someone else. Or I may think that an intimate relationship, or another intimate relationship, is not what you currently need. A loving parent might judge that what a child needs at a certain stage in his development is intimacy with children his own age rather than with himself. Each of us can have intimate personal relationships only with a few people. Must our love for all others be of a second-class sort; or is it just of a different sort? Further, even if the best love between humans involves reciprocity and mutuality, this may be a poor model for love between God and us. Love between humans is love between equals, or at least beings in the same general category, whereas love between God and us is love between the worship-worthy creator of everything and a small part of his creation.

E. We need to consider the possibility that unknown goods may explain, or help to explain, why nonbelief is rational. It is of course difficult to know how much weight to give this possibility. And we should bear in mind that there might also be unknown goods among the consequences of nonbelief being irrational. Nevertheless it remains the case that the possibility that there are unknown goods among the benefits of nonbelief being rational calls into question Schellenberg's main argument. (Schellenberg considers this possibility and rejects it. I have discussed his reasoning in section 4 of chapter 4.)

6. The Possibility of a Cumulative Case

I am especially unpersuaded by Schellenberg's rejection of the possibility of an explanation of the rationality of nonbelief that would involve a number of considerations. There is reason to doubt that any single attempt to account for how it is that nonbelief is rational is alone capable of providing an adequate explanation. But this leaves unresolved the issue of their cumulative import. Schellenberg's strategy, when he considers the possibility of a cumulative case, is as follows. He provides this list of potential explanations of why nonbelief is rational, on each of which he has already commented by the time he considers the possibility of a cumulative case, and all of which I have at least mentioned at one point or another in previous chapters:

> (i) the possibility (for many) of a Kierkegaardian subjectivity of uncertainty; of venturing, risking all, in the search for God; (ii) the possibility (in many cases) of choosing to investigate God's existence (or failing to do so) in the absence of any clear reason to believe that there is a religious reality at all; (iii) the existence of the actual religious traditions, that is, Hinduism, Buddhism, and so forth; (iv) the existence of those human beings who actually exist; and (v) the responsibility (for some) of transmitting evidence sufficient for belief to individuals who would otherwise lack it and so lack the benefits made possible thereby. (205)

Schellenberg contends that goods that are *roughly* of these sorts would actually be available if and only if nonbelief were irrational. So even if the goods mentioned in this list are available only if nonbelief is rational, there are other goods that would be available only if nonbelief were irrational and that are just as valuable. (These are roughly what I have called goods of clarity.) In order to keep in mind Schellenberg's point in introducing them here, let us call them *counterpart* goods. A good cannot contribute anything to the explanation of why nonbelief is rational if there is a counterpart good that is roughly of equal value. Schellenberg argues that in addition to there being a counterpart good corresponding to each good of types (i) to (v)—a counterpart that would actually be available if and only if nonbelief were irrational—the following additional good of considerable import is also available only if nonbelief is irrational: "the possibility for all at all times of personal relationship with God" (205). Hence, he contends, it is not reasonable to argue for the importance of nonbelief being rational by appealing to the cumulative value of goods such as (i) to (v) above.

Here is an example of Schellenberg's reasoning. Even though goods of type (i)—that is, the possibility (for many) of a Kierkegaardian subjectivity of uncertainty; of venturing, risking all, in the search for God—would be unavailable if nonbelief were irrational, there would in that case be "the possibility for all . . . of cultivating the inwardness of belief; of striving to know God more fully" (206). Maybe this is right. Maybe the good of striving to know God more fully under conditions in which it would be irrational not to believe that God exists is about as worthwhile as the good of risking all in a search for God under conditions in which it is rational not to believe that God exists. Such a judgment is, as Schellenberg rightly says (206), difficult to make. Still, the suggestion that these goods are roughly equivalent seems fairly plausible.

However, I have two reservations about Schellenberg's reasoning. First, unknown goods may contribute to a cumulative case. As mentioned, there may be counterpart goods that are benefits of nonbelief being irrational. And this in turn raises the possibility that the unknown goods in these two categories might be roughly equivalent. However, not only is there no particular reason to think there to be such an equilibrium, in addition we have seen that there is some reason to believe that unknown goods are more likely to be found on the side of goods of mystery, or among the benefits of nonbelief being rational, than they are to be found on the side of goods of clarity, or among the benefits of nonbelief being irrational. The burden of proof, in any case, is on someone who holds that unknown goods do not contribute to a cumulative case. Moreover, any theist who has reason to be a theist, whether this be provided by religious experiences or by something else, has, as a result, reason to believe that there is an explanation of the rationality of nonbelief. Consequently if such a person does not know what this explanation is, she has reason to believe that there are relevant unknown goods or, at any rate, goods that are unknown to her.

Second, to return to another earlier theme, if there is something to be said for the idea that in our current circumstances we are not ready for an intimate personal relationship with God, then it is wrong to include among the advantages of nonbelief being irrational "the possibility for all at all times of personal relationship with God."

So what general conclusions should we come to? We have no precise way to measure the force of the relevant goods and considerations. Hence we have no basis on which to be confident that premise 2 in Schellenberg's argument A is true, and hence that A is sound. Not only have we no precise way to measure the force of the relevant goods and considerations; we also have no precise way to decide what to include on each side. As far as goods (as distinct from other relevant considerations) are concerned, we have no way to add up the value of the goods on each side, one with another, just as we lack a precise way to compare the goods on one side with those on the other. In the next chapter I explore the implications of this fact.

So while Schellenberg is right when he says that if God exists, God could do much more than God has done to make God's existence apparent to us, the case for atheism that he presents for our consideration is not compelling.

6

THE HIDDENNESS OF GOD: IMPLICATIONS

1. The Hidden Emperor

Once upon a time, in a faraway and geographically isolated land, there was a small community that had lived without contact with other communities for so long that the very memory that there were other peoples had been lost almost entirely. Only a few of the elders could recall from their childhood the stories that used to be told of visitors from afar, of distant peoples and communities, of powerful princes and lords, and of their vast empires. Some of the very oldest people with the best memories could recall that back in the old days there were some who said (or was it that they remembered hearing reports about its having been said?—it was so long ago and so hard to tell) that their territory was actually itself part of one of those great empires, and one that was ruled over by a great and good emperor. But these stories had not been told for so long that even the old people had difficulty remembering them, and the young were down-right skeptical.

And then one day there arrived an outsider who claimed to be an emissary and who bore astonishing news. He declared that some of the old stories were true. He said that the small, isolated community was indeed part of a great empire, an empire that stretched farther than anyone could have imagined. And—more astonishing still—the ruler of all this, the emissary said, pointing to the familiar hillsides and fields, to the rude dwellings and away to the horizon in all directions, is a great and wise emperor who deserves loyalty and obedience from all his subjects. And that includes you, said the visitor. And—could it be yet more astonishing?—the emperor is generally known to his subjects throughout the rest of the empire as the "Hidden Emperor," for he never lets himself be seen clearly by any of his subjects. Not even his closest, most loyal, and most devoted servants are sure exactly what he looks like. But it is widely believed that he travels incognito throughout the empire, for he has various remarkable powers that make this possible, including the power to make himself invisible, the power to travel from place to place with great speed, and even the power to understand what people are thinking. Indeed, *so* great are his powers in these respects, said the visitor, that it is hardly an exaggeration to say that he is always present throughout the entire empire.

Never had anything quite like this been heard. Mouths were agape, eyes were wide in astonishment. What are we to do, what does the emperor want from us and what are we to expect from him? people asked. "He wants your loyalty, trust, and obedience, and he offers protection and help in time of trouble," replied the emissary.

At this point a man in the crowd, a tallish bearded man with a puzzled expression, and of the sort that is inclined to twiddle with his beard in an irritating way, replied as follows. "But why," he asked—and the emissary knew what was coming, for he had been through this many times and knew that in every community there is a trouble-maker or two and that beard twiddling and a puzzled expression are among the best in-dicators that trouble is brewing—"why does the emperor have to be hidden? Why can't we see the emperor for ourselves? I know that it is not my place to ask"—a familiar line to the seasoned emissary, who has heard it all before and can recognize false modesty at a glance—"but why couldn't the emperor's existence and presence be as clear as *your* presence and existence? And"—now for the coup de grâce, thought the emissary, the sign that we are contending here with a *serious* thinker—"if it is important for the em-peror to be hidden, why are you here informing us about him?"

After the tall bearded man had spoken, there was silence for a few minutes. The fact was that no one quite knew what would happen next, or what it was proper to say to the emissary. Had the bearded man gone too far? Had he spoken improperly? Would he be reprimanded or punished? Would they all be reprimanded or punished? Should he be silenced?

Then an old woman, known for her wisdom and insight, and of that generation among whom belief in the great emperor had not entirely been lost, spoke up. "I, for one, think that things are much better this way. As long as the emperor, and may he and his blessed relatives live for ever," she added, with a glace at the emissary, "as long as the emperor is hidden, we have a type of freedom that would otherwise be unavailable to us. We are free to decide whether or not to believe that there is an emperor. If the facts of the matter were clear to us, and it were just plain obvious that the emperor exists, belief would be forced on us. As long as the facts are unclear, we are in a position to ex-ercise control over what we think. And even though our esteemed visitor has come to explain the situation to us, we are still in a position to decide whether or not to believe what he says."

At this the bearded man became downright exasperated, saying, "Listen here. What is so great about being able to make up your mind in conditions in which the facts are unclear? Surely if the facts are unclear, we ought simply to believe that the facts are un-clear. It's absurd to suggest that there is something especially admirable or good about deciding that the emperor exists under circumstances in which it is unclear whether the emperor exists. Do you think that it would also be good for us to be able to choose whether or not to believe, say, that two plus two equals four in circumstances in which *that* is not clear, or for us to be able to choose what to believe about who our parents are in circumstances in which *that* is not clear?"

"This may seem absurd to you," interjected the woman, "since you are the sort of man who likes to strut around as if you had all the answers to life's questions even though nobody else has quite noticed, but what you have to understand is that this arrangement has the great advantage of permitting our willingness to acknowledge our status as subservient underlings in the emperor's realm to play a role in determining whether or not we believe that the emperor exists."

"And I will tell you," said the woman, warming to her theme and enjoying the attention of the crowd, and what she took to be the approving look of the visiting emissary, "I will tell you about another benefit of our current situation. The fact that we do not know what the emperor looks like permits him to come among us, looking like one of us. Long ago, when I was a little girl, it used to be said that when you entertain a stranger, you should remember that you might be entertaining the emperor. In fact people used to say, 'Every poor stranger is the emperor.' I don't suppose that they really meant it, but you can see what they had in mind. And there was another saying, too, now that I remember it. We used to say, when we wished to show respect for someone, that 'You are He.' Of course, if you knew that a visitor in your house really was the emperor, you would be quite dazed and overwhelmed, and even ashamed by how little you had to offer such a guest."

"Damn it all," said the man with the puzzled look, "this is all nonsense. If the emperor wanted us to believe in him, he would make his existence apparent to us. Don't listen to that old bag. It's as simple as this. If the emperor existed, he would want us to know him and to know about him. If so, he would make his presence apparent to us. He does not do so even though he could do so. The only sensible conclusion is that *there is no emperor. There is no emperor! There is no emperor!*"

After this intemperate outburst yet another voice was heard from the crowd, the voice of one who prides himself on taking a sober, comprehensive, and balanced view of things, and in the process takes himself much too seriously. "Maybe we *are* part of the empire," said this new interlocutor. "Certainly we have some evidence that this is so, not least of which is the fact that our honored visitor, who appears to me to have an open and trustworthy countenance, has come to tell us that this is so. The recollections of some of our senior members are also relevant here. Surely they give us some reason to believe there to be an emperor. But if there is an emperor—and I certainly do not rule out this possibility—it is hard to believe that it matters to him whether we believe that he exists. If it mattered very much to the emperor that we believe that he exists, then surely it would be clearer than it now is that there is an emperor. After all, where has the emperor been all this time? Furthermore, the beliefs that we hold about the emperor under current conditions, if we hold any, ought to reflect the fact that they are held under conditions of uncertainty. Any beliefs we hold in this area ought in fact to be held with tentativeness, and with an awareness that we may be wrong."

In the fullness of time, and after the emissary had gone his way, it came to pass that three schools of thought developed, each of which embraced one of the views that were expressed on that day. There were those who agreed with the old woman, and who were known by their opponents as the "Imperialists." Then there were the Skeptics. All of their bearded members had a strong inclination toward beard-twiddling. And there were the Tentative Believers. They were known to their detractors as "the half-baked believers." So who was right?

2. Implications of God's Hiddenness

In this chapter I argue that it is unclear whether theists can account for God's hiddenness, and I argue that this fact has certain implications for theistic belief. I suggest that theists should recognize that there is considerable reason to doubt that it is important that people should hold theistic beliefs and, a fortiori, that there is considerable reason to doubt that it is important that they should hold any particular set of theistic beliefs, such as those associated with Judaism or Islam. Moreover, whatever beliefs are held in this area probably ought to be held tentatively.

Along the way I ask what sort of explanation of God's hiddenness theists should expect to be able to provide; I ask whether theists should take the view that the world is set up in the best possible way as far as the hiddenness of God is concerned; and I consider some more general claims that bear on this one, including the claim that theism requires that the world is, in general, set up in the best possible way, as well as the claim that theism requires that the world should be set up so that we are not deprived of any good that is essential for our flourishing.

3. Explaining God's Hiddenness

An attempt to explain God's hiddenness might make reference to just one consideration or to a number of considerations. Also, if God exists, there may be considerations that have some potential for contributing to an explanation of God's hiddenness but that nevertheless are not part of the actual explanation. So the question whether some argument or line of thought is capable of contributing to an explanation of God's hiddenness and the question whether it is part of, or even the whole of, the actual explanation of God's hiddenness are two different, if related, questions. By the "actual explanation" I mean the factor or factors that as a matter of fact explain God's hiddenness. There is of course an actual explanation only if God exists.

An adequate explanation of God's hiddenness is one that alone is capable of providing the explanation of God's hiddenness. There could be a number of adequate explanations available, only one of which is the actual explanation. Another possibility is that there are a number of adequate explanations that together constitute the actual explanation. In that case the situation would be similar to one in which someone does a certain action and has a number of reasons to do that action, any one of which reasons would alone suffice to account for his doing it, but of all of which mention must be made if a full answer to the question why he did the action in question is to be given. However, both of the possibilities mentioned in this paragraph are rather far removed from what we know to be the case.

In virtue of what it would take to be God, there are definite limits on what can serve as an explanation of why God is hidden. Thus presumably God would not make various facts about God, such as the fact that God exists, unclear to us for no good reason, just on whim, for example. Acting on whim, I take it, is inconsistent with being God, at least in the case of any matters that bear on the welfare of created beings. Whatever reasons God has for actions, and especially for actions that bear on the welfare of created beings, must be good reasons.

There are, however, different conceptions of what it would be to explain why God is hidden. We might take this to be a matter of (a) specifying God's reasons for being hidden—that is, saying what God is aiming to achieve (and hence, presumably, is actually achieving) by being hidden—or (b) saying what are the goods involved that outweigh the various costs so that it is overall a good thing that God is hidden, or (c) explaining what are the factors or conditions—such as God's transcendence or human finitude—that have caused God's hiddenness.

If God exists there has to be an explanation in the sense of a *cause* of God's being hidden, and of God's being hidden to the extent that God is hidden. That is, there must be factors or conditions of some sort (such as God's transcendence, or our limitations, or the fact that God has chosen not to make the facts about God clearer to us) that have resulted in things being the way they are in this respect—just as there must be factors or conditions that have resulted in things being the way they are in any other respect. Or, if this is too sweeping, there must at least be factors or conditions that have resulted in things being the way they are with respect to the intentional conduct of any agent, including God. And we have reason to believe that the explanation of God's hiddenness will make reference to God's intentional actions or omissions, given that however difficult may be the subject matter, and however limited may be our capacities to comprehend it, it seems that the facts about God's existence and nature could be more apparent to us, if God exists.

If there is an explanation in the sense of a cause, there is at least something to understand, although it certainly does not follow that we can understand it. And since in God's case there has to be an explanation that is consistent with God's nature, there must be reasons—probably reasons that have to do with goods of mystery—that explain why God is hidden.

It is not likely that the explanation of God's hiddenness will consist in an appeal to such considerations as the inherent unclarity of the subject matter or our limited abilities. For surely God could do something to make the facts clearer to us than they currently are even if, for example, in virtue of our very limited capacities we are not well equipped to comprehend God or God's plans and purposes. Presumably God could choose to make the facts about God much more clear to us if God elected to do so.

The relationship between explanations of types (a) and (b) requires comment. Consider first the following fact. There seem to be important differences between God's actions and ours in the following area. The actions of human beings can result in good consequences that are both unforeseen and unintended by the agent who engages in them. On the other hand, presumably there are no benefits of God's actions that are unforeseen by God. This sort of good fortune is out of the question for God. Yet there might be benefits of God's actions that are not part of God's reasons for action. If so, there might be benefits of God's being hidden that are not part of God's reasons for being hidden. So God's reasons for being hidden might not be exhaustive of the reasons that it is best for God to be hidden. Thus God could choose to be hidden because this affords us a certain sort of moral autonomy or because it achieves some unknown good, and yet God's hiddenness might have one or more additional benefits that are not part of God's reasons for being hidden. However, God presumably foresees these additional benefits. But God may foresee such benefits without intending them. Or, if the benefits in question are intended, they may nevertheless be distinct from God's reasons for action. Yet if we are weighing the costs and benefits of God's being hidden, with a view to deciding whether the benefits outweigh the costs, such a good has to be included on the benefits side of the calculation—even if it is not a part of God's reason for being hidden.

While there is room for a theoretical distinction here between two sorts of explanation, (a) and (b), God's reasons to do any action *a* may in fact include everything that is relevant to whether it is good that *a* should be done. If that were so, God would take everything relevant into account—in which case (a) and (b) would amount to the same thing. At any rate, there is much to be said for the idea that if God had reasons to do *a* that were greatly outweighed by the benefits of not doing *a*, so that the costs of doing *a* would be very high, then presumably God would not do *a*. Let us assume for now that (a) and (b) amount to the same thing.

Some of the considerations adduced in the foregoing chapters are at least candidates for inclusion in the actual explanation. We have before us, therefore, what are at least possible ingredients in such an explanation. It is time for some assessment of their import. By way of a reminder, among the considerations that appear to have at least some capacity to contribute to an explanation of God's hiddenness are the following. The appeal to moral freedom appears to have some promise, in particular when construed as the claim that God must be hidden if we are to avoid being fawning sycophants whose main preoccupation is with pleasing God but rather are to be confronted with choices among options that include some that are both wrong and appealing to us. Another consideration that has some promise is what I called extended cryptovolitionalism, which is a combination of the claim that it is important that we should be in a position to exercise control over what religious beliefs to hold in circumstances in which various options are rational, with the further claim that the discerning observer, with the right character and attitudes, will be able to recognize—with difficulty and without achieving certainty—that God exists, and be able to tell a certain amount about God's nature. I have also suggested that the appeals to religious diversity, to the importance of searching, and to worship-worthiness may also contribute something, however modest, to an explanation. The appeal to unknown goods or, more broadly, unknown relevant considerations, may also so contribute, and may do so very significantly. Obviously it may be that a number of promising considerations, which taken individually do not have the capacity to account for God's hiddenness, would have the capacity to do so when taken together.

The considerations mentioned are promising partly because they are free of fanciful and speculative components. They impute to God purposes, intentions, and other mental states that fit with standard theistic beliefs about God. In general, it is reasonable for us to consider an explanation to be adequate only if its ingredients square with what theists typically believe about God. Thus merely to think up some good that we can imagine might be very important (for reasons of which we lack any idea) or whose promotion (for reasons we do not claim to begin to understand) requires God to be hidden, would not be to make much of a contribution to a theory that it is reasonable to count as adequate. Nor would the imputation to God of purposes that we could think up but that are alien to traditional theism. An adequate explanation must in addition specify considerations that seem sufficiently important that they might reasonably be thought to make a significant contribution to an explanation of how it is that God is hidden. Actually all of the conditions for being considered part of an adequate explanation that are mentioned in this paragraph are fairly minimal necessary conditions; but it is worth noting that the goods that have emerged as promising from the discussion of the foregoing chapters satisfy these minimal requirements.

As noted in chapter 5, the availability of the various promising considerations that have emerged from the discussion in chapters 2 to 4 renders unsatisfactory the suggestion that the only reasonable response to God's hiddenness is atheism. If there were no such promising considerations, the situation for theism would be much as it would be if there seemed to be no way to begin to reconcile with theism the fact that in the world there is evil—or, if God's hiddenness is a sort of evil, evil of other sorts. (However, as noted in chapter 4, there would be this difference: if there is reason to believe that it is good that God is hidden, there is in that case reason to believe that it is good that we do not understand why God is hidden; and there seems no reason to think that analogous reasoning applies in the case of evil.) Correspondingly, theism is that much stronger if it looks as though we may have some ingredients of an adequate explanation of God's hiddenness and that much stronger again if we seem to have an adequate explanation in its entirety.

So far, so good. But what do the promising considerations that emerged in chapters 2 to 4 add up to? My view is that it is not clear what they add up to. There are a number of unresolved puzzles. First, there is the question whether the richest and most comprehensive set of promising considerations that we can come up with amounts, when its ingredients are added up and taken account of, to an adequate explanation of God's hiddenness. The considerations that have emerged from the foregoing discussion as apparently having some capacity to contribute to an explanation of God's hiddenness may not constitute this richest and most comprehensive set. But they are at least an approximation to it. And it is unclear whether this set of considerations is adequate, or even close to adequate, to account for God's hiddenness. There is no way to measure the precise force of such considerations, not least because it obviously is impossible in principle to know what, if any, weight to give to unknown goods. In general, there is no way to measure the relevant costs and benefits with any precision.

Second, there is the question whether a particular promising consideration (that is, a consideration that appears upon scrutiny to be able to contribute to an explanation of the relevant sort) actually contributes anything to the explanation of God's hiddenness. To show that a consideration has a capacity to so contribute is one thing; to show that it actually does so—that is, to show that it actually is part of the reason that things are as they are—is quite another. As it is, we do not know if any of the promising considerations that have emerged from the foregoing discussion is part of the actual explanation. It is hard to tell whether considerations such as those adduced in previous chapters, and even the promising ones among them, might not be best understood merely as after-the-fact rationalizations, as advantageous by-products of the fact that the claims that the religions make are not more clearly true. The religious ambiguity of the world has various consequences, and some of these consequences seem good from a theistic point of view. The result is that if we are in the business of seeking good reasons for God to be hidden, we at least have something to point to.

Third, even if it were certain (which it isn't) that we have an adequate explanation, we might not know whether it is the actual explanation of God's hiddenness. If God exists, then there is such a thing as the actual explanation of God's hiddenness. And if we know that God exists, then we know there to be an actual explanation of God's hiddenness. But even if we know that God exists, and even if we have an explanation that appears to be adequate, we might not know whether it is the actual explanation.

Fourth, it is also unclear whether the promising considerations that have emerged from the foregoing discussion suffice to explain why God is hidden *to the degree that God is hidden*. In fact, some of these promising considerations have no capacity whatsoever to contribute to an explanation of the particular degree to which God is hidden. Thus the case for the importance of a robust moral freedom that emerged in chapter 2 seems most effective as a way to show that it would be morally damaging to us to have ongoing intimate communication with God of a sort that would involve our knowing that we are constantly being observed. There is less reason to think that a proof or, say, a onetime grand and magnificent revelation would be as damaging in this particular respect. And there is no reason to think that if the facts were even slightly clearer than they now are, there would be any such unfortunate consequences. It is very doubtful that we have as much as a good candidate for an adequate explanation of why God's existence is not even a little more apparent than it currently is.

Some theists will be inclined to say in response to the availability of anything that looks like, or approximates to, or has the merest whiff of, an adequate explanation, that there is no need to ask for anything more. But the maneuver that consists in rushing to the conclusion that the problem is solved and the maneuver that consists in rushing in the opposite direction and concluding that it cannot be solved are equally unimpressive. The situation is less clear than either side would have it. Although this is not decisive, the very fact that reasonable people embrace each of these positions itself suggests that this is so.

Finally, I have generally operated on the assumption that if there is an explanation of God's hiddenness, it is the same for all people at all times. But this might not be so: for example, it might be that in the case of some people the arguments of chapter 3 play a role while for others this is not so. The possibility that different factors might bear on different people complicates the situation, although I do not see that we can go much beyond mentioning this possibility. However, the thought that it all balances out, so that while some factors work in the case of one person or group and other factors work in the case of another, everyone is, in the final analysis, equally well situated with respect to their prospects for theistic belief, seems altogether fanciful.

4. The Balance of Goods and the Importance of Belief

If it were clear that God exists, various goods of clarity that are currently unavailable would then be available to us. The goods of clarity in question may include our holding the true belief that God exists, and our having a personal relationship with God, as well as certain moral benefits: thus it may be that more people would be more willing to do what they ought to do if it were clear that God exists. It probably would also be clearer to us wherein our long-term happiness is to be found; and that would probably be to our advantage. Some people would also include on this side of the ledger—that is, among the goods of clarity—the fact that it would be easier for us to achieve heaven and to avoid hell; for it would be clear, or clearer, to everyone what would be necessary to do so. Further, the goods of clarity might include other cognitive goods in addition to our knowing that God exists, such as our knowing important facts about the origin and purpose of the world and of human life, of which we would otherwise be unaware or at least less sure. And I have mentioned other goods of clarity in chapter 1: for instance, if God exists and if the facts about God were clear for all to see, there would be less opportunity for hucksters to set themselves up as religious experts and to enrich themselves by duping gullible people with their supposed insight, and for ecclesiastical authorities to acquire and exercise power over others. These last considerations are of no minor significance in the lives of many people throughout human history. The possibility of unknown goods of clarity also requires mention.

There is some reason to think that, if God exists, the goods of mystery and other relevant considerations that have a capacity to contribute to an account of God's hiddenness, when taken together, outweigh the goods of clarity. At any rate let us assume for now that this is so. (Let us call this the "balance of goods assumption." In the next section I ask whether this is a plausible assumption.)

If the goods of mystery are more valuable than the goods of clarity, then a fortiori they outweigh any particular good of clarity, such as the good of believing that God exists or the good of a personal relationship with God. In other words, if God exists, not only does no particular good of clarity outweigh all of the goods of mystery: in addition, the goods of clarity, taken together, do not do so.

Hence there is considerable reason to doubt that any particular good of clarity, such as our believing that God exists, or our having a personal relationship with God, has the great importance that the theistic traditions think it to have. (Even if it is wrong to classify either belief that God exists or a personal relationship with God as a good of clarity, the same reasoning applies.) When it comes to goods of mystery, we have plenty of promising hints and interesting lines of inquiry, but we have nothing that is terribly impressive. This provides us with reason to doubt the importance of any goods that we are unable to achieve, or are less able to achieve, because of God's hiddenness. Also, because we have little reason to think that we have an explanation of why God is not somewhat less hidden, we also have little reason to think that any good that would be more accessible to us if God were somewhat less hidden is terribly important.

There is, then, some reason to think that, if God exists, it must not matter greatly to God whether we believe. This applies to belief that God exists, to various standard theistic beliefs about God, such as beliefs about the activities and character of God, and to belief in God. At least that we should hold such beliefs, or enjoy this or any other good of clarity, here and now and under our current circumstances probably does not matter greatly. There is also considerable reason to believe that it is not important that everyone should accept any particular form of theism, such as Judaism or Islam. If it were very important that we should accept theism or any particular form of theism, our circumstances probably would be more conducive to it.

So there is this important lesson here for theists: there is considerable reason to believe that it does not matter very much whether people agree with them about the existence of God, and about other religious matters. If God exists, no particular good of clarity, such as our believing that God exists or our having a personal relationship with God, is of momentous importance. If it were, it would outweigh the relevant goods of mystery, and in that case the facts about God would be more apparent to us. As it is, it appears that no such good is either the sole purpose of human life or even an extremely important purpose of human life. The situation, in effect, probably is that either God does not exist or God exists, but it is not terribly important that we believe here and now that God exists or that we enjoy any other good that is made possible (either now or later) by our presently holding such belief.

As I have said, we have no way to measure precisely the force of the promising considerations that have emerged from the discussion of the previous chapters. It is not clear that they add up to an adequate explanation of God's hiddenness, even when they are viewed collectively and even when the possibility of unknown goods is included in the calculation, and it is not clear that any of the promising considerations that have emerged here is an ingredient in the actual explanation. If it were clear that there were an adequate set of goods of mystery, and if, in addition, we knew such an adequate set to constitute the actual explanation, then we would have an explanation of why we are deprived of various important goods of clarity. Goods of mystery that clearly are very important would suffice to outweigh a very important good of clarity. As it is, it is not clear that there are very important goods of mystery; consequently, we have reason to doubt that there are goods of mystery that are capable of outweighing a very important good of clarity. Hence we have reason to doubt that any such good is outweighed. Even when taken together the goods of mystery surveyed may not amount to much; if they do not amount to much, and if God exists, it must not actually take much to outweigh the costs associated with God's hiddenness; hence these costs must not be so great; so there is reason to think that human nonbelief, for example, must not matter that much, even if God exists.

Moreover, God's being even somewhat less hidden than is currently the case would promote belief. The fact that it is not clear whether we have an explanation of why God is hidden to the extent that God is hidden also calls into question the claim that it is important that belief should be promoted. For the good of moral autonomy might account or help to account for, say, our not having an intimate relationship in which we are constantly aware of being observed by God. The importance of our being able to exercise control over what we believe in conditions in which various options are rational might account or help to account for our not having a great deal more evidence than we currently have. But neither would help to account for our not having a little more evidence than we currently have.

However, we need to tread with caution here for at least three reasons. First, while (a) it is not clear that the various goods of mystery that we have identified either add up to an adequate explanation of God's hiddenness or are part of the actual explanation and (b) this gives us reason to doubt that the goods of mystery suffice to outweigh any important goods of clarity, this thought has to be qualified in virtue of the further thought, discussed at the end of chapter 4, that there are reasons to think that we ought not to expect to be able to understand why God is hidden. We noted two relevant considerations at the end of chapter 4. First, unknown goods of mystery may contribute to explaining why God is hidden; if the unknown goods in question are very important, conceivably they might constitute the entire explanation. And to vary this theme a little, if some or all of the goods of mystery that have been identified were much more important than they seem to us to be, they might have a capacity to outweigh an important good of clarity. Second, there may be an in-principle sort of obscurity here: if there are reasons that it is good for God to be hidden, there may also be reasons that it is good that we do not know what those reasons are.

Hence it may be that the explanation of why we do not recognize that there are deeply important goods of mystery that suffice to outweigh an important good of clarity is not that there are no such goods of mystery. For there are good reasons not to be confident that if there is an explanation of God's hiddenness, we will know of it. Hence our lack of an explanation is far from giving us overwhelming reason to conclude that there is no explanation.

Of course we do not know that either of the two lines of thought mentioned actually helps to account for our lack of an explanation. For example, that there are any unknown goods of mystery at all is a matter of speculation; and that there are very important goods of this sort is all the more so.

Second, we should not lose sight of the fact that extended cryptovolitionalism, as discussed in chapter 3, may be part of the explanation of God's hiddenness, so that it is only if, for example, one has certain attitudes that one will be in a position to recognize that certain subtle and easily missed states of affairs obtain. Hence belief might be important after all. This would explain, in addition, why theistic belief under conditions in which God is hidden is an especially good thing. (Conceivably there might even be other goods of the same general sort: that is, goods that would explain why belief under conditions in which God is hidden is an especially good thing, although I have no particular good in mind here.)

Yet extended cryptovolitionalism is just a possibility, and we do not know that it is part of the actual explanation of God's hiddenness. There are, in addition, various competing theories about what you will discern if you approach the situation with the right attitudes, including both nontheistic religious theories and nonreligious theories. Also, as noted in chapter 3, there is something dubious about the way in which extended cryptovolitionalism blames human beings for God's hiddenness.

Moreover, even if it were known to be part of the explanation of God's hiddenness that this would afford us various opportunities to respond, and even if it were true that belief would be feasible only if one had certain attitudes, it would not follow that belief is important. It might be that what would matter would be (a) that we exercise control over whether we believe in circumstances in which both alternatives are rational; or (b) that we search for God under such circumstances; or, more broadly, (c) that under those circumstances we make an honest and careful attempt to work out what, if any, religious beliefs to hold.

Third, if, say, the good involved in extended cryptovolitionalism is even fairly important, and the good involved in moral autonomy has some importance, and some other goods—including perhaps some unknown goods—also have some importance, together these may amount to something that could outweigh even a fairly weighty and considerable good. This is especially likely to be so if the goods of mystery are more numerous than the goods of clarity. It is possible that many fairly important goods of mystery *barely* outweigh very few goods of clarity of considerable importance, although we lack much of a reason for thinking this to be so.

So the situation is that the puzzles that surround God's hiddenness provide us with some reason to doubt that it is important, even from God's point of view, that we should hold theistic beliefs. Since it is not clear that any of the goods of mystery is very important, this calls into question the importance of any of the goods of clarity—or, more generally, any state of affairs that is possible only if there is clarity. However, I doubt that we can *show* that theistic belief is unimportant, given our circumstances. I doubt that we can reasonably deal in the currency of proof and disproof in this area.

5. Disaster Avoidance

In the preceding section I took it for granted that if God exists, the goods of mystery outweigh the goods of clarity. (In doing so I downplayed, for reasons I have given, the possibility that considerations other than goods of mystery might contribute to the explanation of God's hiddenness.) The idea is that if it were not so, God would not be hidden.

But should theists believe that things are set up in the best way as far as God's hiddenness is concerned, so that if the goods on the side of mystery outweigh those on the side of clarity, there is mystery and, correspondingly, if the goods of clarity were to outweigh those of mystery, the facts about God would have been clear, or clearer than they now are? Or can a theist reasonably believe that, although God is hidden, it would be better if God were not hidden? And can a theist reasonably believe that it would be better if God were hidden to a lesser (or greater) extent than is now the case? More generally, should theists say that this is the best world that God can create?[1] So here I am questioning what I referred to in the last section as the "balance of goods assumption."

My contention will be that even if the balance of goods assumption is not plausible, a weaker principle, which I will call the "disaster avoidance principle," is plausible. And the disaster avoidance principle has much the same implications for the importance of belief.

It is possible that there should be two or more worlds that are best among the worlds that God can create, perhaps because they have different arrays of goods that are equally valuable, or because they differ with respect to features that do not bear on their goodness. In either case there would be no single best world that God can create. In that case the question would be: Must God create *one* of the best worlds that God can create? But let us ignore this possibility and assume that there is a single best world that God can create.

The best world that God can create may not be as good as various other possible worlds. For one thing, for reasons that are familiar from the work of Alvin Plantinga and others, it may be that the best of all possible worlds is not a world that God could create. If the best of all possible worlds would exist only if created beings who are free with respect to morally significant choices make certain choices rather than others, then created beings determine whether or not the best of all possible worlds exists. If created free beings were to go wrong in every world in which they exist even though, if they had chosen otherwise, they would never go wrong at all, the best world that God can create would not be as good as, and might even be considerably worse than, the best of all possible worlds. If created beings would go wrong in every other world in which they exist to a greater extent than they do so in our world, our world would be the best world that God could create. (Or at least this would be so provided that the worlds in question differ in terms of goodness only insofar as created beings behave well or behave badly.)

If our world is the best world that God can create, the best array of goods that is achievable by God is achieved in it. If so, there presumably are goods of mystery or other relevant considerations that account for the fact that, and the extent to which, God is hidden. And insofar as the considerations that bear on God's hiddenness are all either goods of mystery or goods of clarity, the former must outweigh the latter. If there are good reasons for God to be hidden to the extent that God is hidden, then the search for such reasons is more likely to be successful, although this is hardly to say that under these conditions success is guaranteed. As we have seen, unknown goods of mystery may provide part of the story.

So *should* theists accept the following claim, (H1)?

(H1) God would create the best world that God could create.

According to (H1), if more beauty would, all things considered, make the world a better place, and if God could bring it about that there would be more beauty, then God would bring it about that there is more beauty. The only reason for not adding more of some good-making quality, such as beauty or love or enjoyment, would be that to do so would do more harm than good, perhaps by inhibiting the occurrence of some other, more important, good.

At first glance it seems natural that theists should be well disposed to (H1). There is something intuitively plausible about the idea that if there were a world that God could have created that would have been better than this world, perhaps because it would have had more of some good such as beauty or less of some evil such as suffering in it than there is in our world, then God would have created that world.

Further, in defense of (H1)—or at least in anticipation of a misdirected objection to it—it is worth noting that it need not depend upon the assumption that God has an obligation or duty to create the best world that God can create. The claim that God has this or that obligation is open to challenge on a number of grounds. For instance, it might be claimed that any obligation that God might have concerning the world would be an obligation to us or to members of other created species, and it might be claimed further that the creator does not have obligations to creatures or that, in our case in particular, whatever obligations there were, or might have been, have been undermined by human sin. But it may be true that God would create the best world that God can create even if God has no obligations to us, or even if God has no obligations at all. God might do so, for instance, just because doing so comes naturally to God, given God's nature.

The considerations just discussed are not negligible in their force. But they hardly provide decisive support for (H1). And in any case we have independent evidence against (H1). At least we have independent evidence against (H1) on the assumption that God exists. In particular it seems obvious that there are evils in the world whose removal would make the world a better place, all things considered, just as it seems obvious that there are goods that are absent even though their addition would make the world a better place, all things considered, and just as it seems—in turn—obvious that God would be able to remove the evils and supply the goods in question. Consequently, it seems that if God exists, God has not created the best world that God could create. It appears that if God exists, (H1) is not true.

We have no way to prove this claim: it is always possible that the suffering of every brutally treated innocent child or brutally treated animal is actually for the best, and that the same goes for the absence of every good that we can imagine being supplied. This is a complicated matter because a person of faith often perceives something that may appear to a nonbeliever as an unmitigated evil as, instead, a valuable and purposeful event, perhaps as an opportunity for reform, or correction, or reflection, or solidarity with other sufferers. The person of faith may also feel that the true character of the event is apparent only in retrospect or only from a perspective that is difficult or even impossible to achieve. But surely the burden of proof is solidly on those who say that all evils in the world may be transmuted thus. (In fact, given that many of the evils that are present and goods that are absent seem to be the sort of thing that it would be well within the abilities of an omnipotent being to control, if it were clear that God would create the best world that God could create, then we would have considerable reason to believe that God does not exist, since there is considerable reason to believe that God has not created the best world that God could create.)

There are weaker alternatives to (H1). Consider the claim that

> (H2) with respect to features of the world that bear on our welfare, God would create the best world that God can create.

One reason for accepting (H2) has to do with how a creator may reasonably be expected to treat created beings. An emphasis on God's concern for human beings and for other created beings is generally central to theism. And any version of theism that lacks this ingredient, or an ingredient of this sort, seems unsatisfactory just because God seems worthy of worship only if God is concerned with human welfare and with the welfare of other created species; and it is central to theism that God should be worthy of worship.

But (H2) faces more or less the same difficulty as (H1). It seems that it is not the case that God has created the best world that God could create as far as many aspects of the world that bear on our welfare are concerned. To believe otherwise is to believe, for example, that all human suffering—or at any rate all suffering that is not a consequence of wrong human choices—is necessary for the avoidance of some greater evil or for the achievement of a good that outweighs the suffering in question. And that, too, seems very hard to believe. (However, if God does not exist, (H1) or (H2) may be true: if God does not exist, it may be true that, if God were to exist, God would act in the fashion specified by either proposition.)

There is, however, a related position here that does not face this difficulty, namely, that

> (H3) as far as our prospects for achieving the deepest and most important aspects of our welfare are concerned, God would create the best world that God can create.

(H3) says that God would not permit any feature or aspect of the world (that could be removed or altered) that would prevent our flourishing in the ways that are most important for beings of our sort. Rather, God will do whatever God can do to ensure that we will flourish in such ways, achieving the deepest and most important goods that we can achieve. These are the goods that really matter for beings of our sort and without which we will not achieve our full potential. (H3) says that if God exists, we are not deprived of such goods, assuming that this is avoidable.

(H3) is not subject to the difficulty we have seen to confront (H1) and (H2). While the conditions that we observe all around us in the world give us reason to doubt and even to deny that God has created the best world that God can create, just as they give us reason to doubt and even to deny the more limited claim that God has created the best world that God can create as far as every aspect of human welfare is concerned, they provide little, if any, reason to believe that we live in conditions that frustrate the achievement of the deepest and most important aspects of our well-being. For while there are evils that we experience that we would be better without, and there are evils that the world as a whole would be better without, there is little reason to believe that we live in conditions that frustrate the achievement of the deepest and most important aspects of our well-being. Whether or not this is so depends on factors that are not clear to us here and now, including, for example, whether there is an afterlife and, if there is, what bears on our prospects in it.

That there are no insurmountable barriers to our flourishing in the ways that matter most for beings of our sort is also, I take it, a working assumption among the major religions of the world, differ as they may in their conceptions of what it is for us to flourish, of what conditions prevent us from flourishing, of how those conditions may be ameliorated, and so forth. It is much less clear that the major theistic traditions are committed to (H1) or (H2). The traditions have, after all, generally considered it to be part of their mission to help their adherents to cope with the vicissitudes of life: perhaps they thereby acknowledge that the world has much that is deeply and genuinely wrong with it, including much that has a bearing on our welfare.

Further, what I offered as reasoning in support of (H2) actually better supports (H3). For a creator who brought it about that creatures of a certain sort exist but failed, when it was possible to have done otherwise, to bring it about that they are in conditions in which they might flourish, in the ways that matter most for beings of their sort, would be irresponsible. I infer that a deity would not permit any arrangement under which people would systematically be deprived of the most important goods, provided that this could be prevented from occurring. The case for (H3) seems strong. According to (H3), everything possible will be done to ensure that we will flourish in such respects.

However, this idea, too, needs to be qualified. If the deepest and most important goods of which we are capable were neither very deep nor very important, it would not matter much whether we achieved them. (Most important could be fairly unimportant.) So let us assume that we are able to enjoy deep and important goods: let us assume, in other words, that we are capable of a sort of flourishing that is rich, extensive, and inherently worthwhile. That this is so is also accepted by all the religious traditions, theistic and nontheistic alike, so once again we are not here taking for granted anything that is alien to the traditions.

Also it is at least conceivable that there are great goods that can be achieved, or great evils that can be avoided, only if God does *not* create the world that is best (among the worlds that God can create) as far as our prospects for achieving the deepest and most important aspects of our welfare are concerned. It is hard to be sure how seriously to take this concern. When I mention it, I do not have in mind any particular good (or evil) that might play the relevant role. On the other hand, we lack any compelling reason to believe that there is no good (or evil) that would play this role. However, we can circumvent this difficulty by switching attention to a claim that is related to (H3), but for which this difficulty does not arise:

> (H4) God will arrange it so that we are not deprived by our circumstances of any good that is necessary for our long-term flourishing.

(H4), which I will call the "disaster avoidance principle," specifies a condition that must be satisfied in order for it to be reasonable to proceed with the creation of a species. If there is a good, g1, that is so important that the life of a created being would be thoroughly blighted without it, there is no need to consider the possibility that there might be some other good, g2, that is so important that the achievement of g2 would justify our not achieving g1. For even if there are goods that are more important than our achieving the good in question, the point is that without g1 our lives will be disastrous and, after all, we need not have existed.

Actually, (H4) is to be thought of as the combination of two further principles, each of which makes reference to a possible type of disaster. First, there is the idea that it would be unacceptable that our lives should be thoroughly blighted, as would be the case if, say, we were all constantly in excruciating and entirely demoralizing pain. Second, there is the distinct idea that it would be unacceptable for us to be deprived of any good that is crucial to our thriving as beings of our sort. The goods in question are those that are essential for us to flourish in the deepest and most important ways in which beings of our sort are capable of flourishing. This distinction is important because it might be that our lives would still be good and worth living, on balance, even though we are excluded from the richest sorts of flourishing of which we are capable. So a situation is understood to be disastrous if either our conditions are terrible or our lives are still worth living but we are deprived of the richest and most important forms of flourishing of which we are capable. So disaster, in this context, can take either of two forms. The proposal is that a worship-worthy creator would ensure that we will avoid disaster.

6. Disaster Avoidance, the Hiddenness of God, and the Importance of Belief

(H4) specifies a standard below which it is unacceptable that a creator should fall with respect to how parts of the creation are treated. Whereas (H1) says that God will produce the best world that God can produce, (H4) says that God will avoid creating certain bad worlds. If (H4) is the relevant principle, it could be that the goods of clarity outweigh the goods of mystery but the best arrangement has not been achieved. However, if God exists, disasters (of the sort explained) will not occur. So the effects of not achieving the greater good would not be disastrous.

But there is a problem here. The notion of a good that is essential to our flourishing is puzzling in the context of a discussion of creation. Consider first a case such as the following. If I breed dogs, it is normally the case that I am not doing anything wrong if I do not attempt to breed dogs that can run longer and faster than other dogs of their sort, or if I do not aim to breed dogs that will be prizewinners at the county show, or even purebreds. (The exceptions obviously include cases in which I have promised to do something of this nature.) But under normal circumstances if I knowingly breed lame dogs or dogs that will never be able to run properly, I am doing something very wrong. This is obvious to us because we have acquired from observation a good idea of what it is for a dog to flourish and of what it is for a dog to fail to flourish.

In the case of human beings, we think it is all right for God to create human beings who are very poor athletes or who can barely hold a tune even though presumably God could have created beings that are generally like us but for whom singing as well as Maria Callas or running as fast as Sonia O'Sullivan is normal. Theists do not think that God has failed us by not giving everyone such abilities. We do not take our idea of what it is to flourish from exceptional performances. Nor do we take our idea of what it is to flourish from imaginary feats that no one can achieve. If all beings of a certain sort are unable to do something or to achieve a certain state, as in the case of the human inability to run a two-minute mile, we do not consider the fact that we are all created with this inability to deprive us of something that is necessary for our long-term flourishing. On the other hand, creating people who are all constantly in excruciating and demoralizing pain seems wrong. Our intuitions here are, once again, a function of the fact that we have a fairly clear idea of what it is for beings of our sort to flourish, what it is for one of us to do exceptionally well, and so forth. Our thinking here seems to have an awful lot to do with what we are used to.

In the case of creation, however, the creator decides what sort of nature a type of being will have and hence what it will be for a being of that type to flourish, what an exceptional creature of its sort will look like, what it will be for it to do very badly, and so forth. (In the breeding case, on the other hand, one works within the confines of a notion of what it is to flourish that is already settled, or much of which is already settled.) Hence it is difficult to see what would distinguish (a) a case in which a being that is capable of a certain sort of flourishing is deprived of it from (b) a case in which an otherwise similar being is not capable of that sort of flourishing. Because the creator decides what sort of being to create, the goalposts seem to change with each creative decision. Ideas of what is normal, and of what it is to flourish, seem not to have any particular content once we detach them from the types of creatures with which we are familiar.

The way to circumvent this particular problem is just to focus on a standard theistic line about what constitutes flourishing for us. The theistic traditions generally say that our deepest good consists in, or at least includes, our believing that God exists and our having fellowship with God here and now. So let us consider this possibility.

(H4) says that we will not be deprived of anything that we need to flourish in the ways that matter most for beings of our sort, when it could have been arranged otherwise. Hence God's hiddenness does not so deprive us even though all signs are that it has the result that many people do not believe that God exists. If our flourishing re-quired knowledge of God here and now, then many people would be deprived here and now of the ability to flourish in virtue of God's being hidden. God would not create a being who is capable of, but avoidably deprived of, a good that is so crucial for our well-being. In fact, a being who would permit such a state of affairs would not be God: it is not the sort of thing that a being who is worthy of worship would permit. The fact that some cultures provide little encouragement for theistic belief would be especially unfair. If theistic belief or a personal relationship with God were very important, each person, surely, would have an equal shot at it. That this is not the case is part of the ar-gument for the goods in question not being of the greatest importance. Schellenberg's arguments, as discussed in the previous chapter, are therefore right to this extent: if it were of the greatest importance that, for example, we have a personal relationship with God here and now, or that we believe that God exists, then God's hiddenness would be unfair.

Hence we arrive via another route at the conclusion that if God exists, it must not matter that much whether we believe, at least here and now, whatever facts there are about God to which we would have access if God were not hidden, including the fact that God exists, as well as various facts about God's nature. Nor does it matter greatly whether we have a personal relationship with God. For if God were not hidden, the facts about God would be more widely believed than they are now and the relationship in question would be more common.

Some theists may opt at this point for saying that it may not be important to the deity that everyone believe, and believe correctly, but that it does matter that *some* people believe. This is a reasonable suggestion only if belief is not a prerequisite for salvation or some other such profoundly important good. If belief is a precondition for salvation, to say of some people that it does not matter whether they believe is to say that it does not matter whether they achieve salvation. But a being who would discriminate in favor of some and against others, so that there would be some whose salvation matters and oth-ers whose salvation does not matter, would not be admirable and would not be worthy of worship and therefore, once again, would not be God.

God's being hidden must not deprive us of any really important good. But it may de-prive us of less important goods, goods whose loss does not matter that much. So human belief that God exists or human fellowship with God here and now, or our knowing now whatever facts about God we are capable of knowing, may be among such less important goods. (H4) does not provide reason to believe that we are not de-prived of any such less important good.[2]

We have three routes to the conclusion that it is likely that it is not important that we hold theistic belief.

1. There is the fact of religious ambiguity. This alone, and taken at face value, suggests that theis-tic belief is not important. That is, the very fact that there is so much unclarity surrounding God's existence and nature itself gives some reason to believe that it is not very important that people should hold theistic beliefs.
2. If God would create the best world that God could create, then, if God exists, this world in which there is ambiguity, with the result that some believe and some do not believe, is better

than a world in which it is clear that God exists. If so, it is not likely that belief as such is very important: if it were, it probably would be clearer than it now is that God exists.

3. If God would not create the best world that God could create, then at least the disaster avoidance principle is true. If so, and if God exists, we are presently avoiding disaster. If so, God's hiddenness does not deprive us of any good that is essential if we are to avoid disaster, in spite of the fact that it has the result that many people do not hold theistic beliefs.

It seems not to be part of the purpose of human life that we here and now hold theistic beliefs, and a fortiori that we hold any particular set of theistic beliefs. This is, incidentally, compatible with its being good to believe that God exists. It is also compatible with its being beneficial to us in various ways to believe that God exists: thus it may make for a happier life. It is even compatible with its being true that the ultimate purpose of human life is that we live a life of worship and adoration of God. Yet it remains the case that it probably is not important that we believe here and now.

Someone who comes to the conclusion about the importance of belief for which I have argued may regard the emphasis that the theistic traditions place on the importance of belief as a relic of a period in which God's existence, and numerous claims about God, were regarded as obvious. If the existence and nature of a worship-worthy God were thought to be obvious, then to fail to believe that God exists would reasonably be thought to be as foolish as any other failure to accept the obvious. And to fail to believe in God and to worship God, under those circumstances, would be to fail to fulfill an obvious duty. But those are not our circumstances.

7. God's Hiddenness and Tentative Theistic Belief

Next I want to say something about the *type* of theistic beliefs that people should have, given God's hiddenness. Given the religiously ambiguous nature of the world, certain sorts of belief rather than others probably are appropriate. It is unlikely that *certainty* about the details of the doctrine of any particular religion about God is either obligatory or appropriate, and it is likely that tentative belief, at most, is appropriate.

Sometimes people point to the mystery that surrounds many central religious claims as making possible nontentative faith, as facilitating a sort of hurling of oneself into faith in the face of uncertainty. But the mystery that surrounds God's existence and nature as well as numerous other religiously significant topics and areas has in fact a quite different significance. More specifically, the fact that God is hidden (if God exists) suggests that one ought to be wary of the claims that the theistic traditions make about God: they probably are claims that exceed what may reasonably be said with confidence. The additional unclarity that surrounds the issue of whether we have an adequate explanation of God's hiddenness, while it is far from warranting atheism, further supports this wariness.

The situation might be otherwise if it were clear that a particular set of goods of mystery is adequate to account for divine hiddenness, and especially if we had before us what seemed to be the actual explanation of God's hiddenness and if it appeared to be adequate. However, a case for belief remaining tentative, at least with respect to *certain* religious matters, might still be available even if we were very confident we had discovered the explanation of God's hiddenness. This would be so if certain particular ingredients figured prominently in the actual explanation. For example, if a certain sort of human defectiveness is emphasized as a factor that contributes significantly to God's hiddenness, this would contribute to the case for tentative belief. If our ability to see the truth is very defective, it seems plain that we may easily go wrong.

The sort of belief that is appropriate, given our circumstances, will not be dogmatic. It will view different accounts of the nature or purposes of God, especially the details of those accounts, as equally likely to be true, as stabs in the direction of something about which it is difficult to be certain. The implication is that theists ought to be skeptical of many of the claims about God that are made by the dominant theistic traditions, including their own tradition. The problem is not just that the traditions cannot all be correct in their claims about God (although that is certainly the case, and it will be the focus of much of my discussion in chapters 7, 8, and 9) but rather that since God is hidden, we should look with some skepticism on the claims of those who believe that they have a clear account of God's nature—who carry on, in short, as if God were not hidden. A suspicion that the theistic traditions go too far in their pronouncements about God is therefore in order, and it is natural to consider in this context the possibility that beliefs that are shared by many religious traditions, such as the belief that there is some sort of superior being or reality or state, are correct, whereas the claims that are specific to a tradition, such as the uniquely Christian claims about God the father of Jesus Christ, or the uniquely Islamic claims about Allah, go beyond what may reasonably be asserted. One might look on the claims that are unique to the various traditions as claims that all have an equally good chance of being correct. In any case any particular form of theism ought to take a relaxed attitude to the presence of nonbelievers, to nonbelief as a phenomenon, and to the presence of other traditions and positions.

In general, the dominant characteristic in faith ought, therefore, to be hope or exploration rather than certitude. One sort of belief is appropriate when one sees the whole picture, when one "sees face to face." Mystery, on the other hand, requires a more tentative, more modest, more agnostic faith. Indeed, given the extent of the mystery that surrounds the existence and nature of God, it is striking that religions do not emphasize what they do not know as readily, as eagerly, and as vigorously, as they insist on what they claim to know. The mystery that surrounds these matters is in striking contrast to the great confidence with which religions purport to speak.

In chapters 7, 8, and 9, I will have a lot more to say both about what this sort of belief amounts to, and in defense of it. A main project in this book is to present a case for tentativeness in beliefs about religious matters. It is, however, to a considerable degree a religiously based case, operating with many of the assumptions of the dominant religious traditions (especially the theistic varieties), taking seriously many of the things that these traditions take seriously, and in addition holding out the possibility of a form of theism while rejecting the conventional varieties.

II

RELIGIOUS DIVERSITY

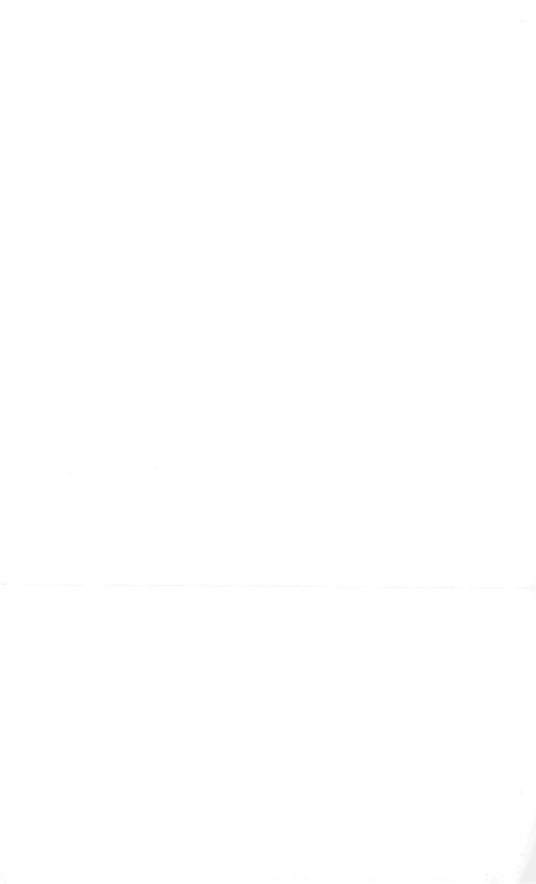

7

RELIGIOUS DIVERSITY

Introduction

1. "The Other Side"

Once upon a time, in an isolated region that was surrounded by steep and almost impassible mountain ranges, there lived a small community of a few thousand people. Since this region had an abundance of food and other resources, and since transportation methods were primitive, and the people were generally contented with their lot, there had not been much pressure to face the dangers of crossing the great and forbidding mountains—"the great divide," as they were known.

As is to be expected among the sons and daughters of men, there was disagreement within the community about what lay beyond the mountains. A number of traditions had developed over the years, each of which had its own interpretation of what was on "the other side," as the region beyond the mountains was called. Some spoke of lush and verdant lands rich in game, others of kind and friendly natives who would welcome an explorer for a meal, others of cannibalistic savages who would also—but alas in another sense—welcome an explorer for a meal, and yet others of great oceans. There were even some who insisted that beyond the mountains there was nothing at all, and that their cozy little homeland was the sum total of all that there was.

Each group was sure that it had the right account. Some claimed to have had visions and dreams that, they believed, confirmed their account of what was on the other side. It was also common for each group to say things like "I just know that I am right," or "the people that I have most respect for tell me that things are as I believe them to be," or "there will come a day when we will finally reach the other side, and you will see that I am right." (Truth be told, from time to time there was even an element of swagger in these pronouncements.)

Imagine that you were to belong to one of these groups. Having an inquiring mind, you wonder aloud to another member of your group: "How can we be sure that *our* account of what is on the other side is correct? See how many theories there are, and see how many intelligent people accept each theory . . ." You are not at all impressed by the two-part rejoinder that you do not need evidence for your position, since (a) *some* beliefs must be held without evidence and (b) your beliefs about what is on the other side have not been shown by anyone to be unsuitable for being held without evidence. You want to know why the beliefs of your group deserve your allegiance. You want to know what is special about them. Is it not clear that the presence of the other traditions ought to have some significance for the way in which you hold your beliefs? Is it not clear that you ought to probe various dimensions of the disagreement between your group and other groups? Perhaps the only responsible course of action would be to examine your beliefs about what is on the other side of the mountains, to see what is to be said for and against them, to see how they compare with the competing beliefs, and to see what sort of procedures can be developed for deciding which beliefs are correct.

2. Disagreement about Religion

Consider a simple example that is closer to home. I believe that Yeats was a great poet, and almost everyone who knows his work would agree. (We might even go further and say that someone who did not agree was not really familiar with his work.) But consider an issue about which there undoubtedly is disagreement, such as whether Yeats was a greater poet than Eliot. There is, I am sure, disagreement about this even among experts, some of the obvious experts in this case being students of twentieth-century poetry. What are the implications of this disagreement for the beliefs of either side? Or suppose that someone whose judgment you generally take seriously disagrees completely with you in your evaluation of the character of a mutual acquaintance. What are the implications for your evaluation?

And consider beliefs about religion. There have been times when it has been easier than it now is for a group within which there is agreement on a particular religious issue to ignore the opinions of other such groups. But now we know more about each other. Or, if we don't, at least we know that we could learn more about each other. And we have to confront the significance of what we learn, or know we could learn. In addition, the simple fact that people in many groups in some parts of the world are now more tolerant of other groups, and of their views, has the important consequence that they are more inclined to take seriously the beliefs of those groups.

In the discussion that follows I use the expression "beliefs about religion" (or "beliefs about religious matters") to refer to a large category of beliefs, including the beliefs that are held in virtue of membership in any religious tradition, as well as agnostic and atheistic beliefs. This is a little cumbersome and even open to misinterpretation: "beliefs about religion" might be misinterpreted to refer, for instance, to the beliefs that an external observer such as a social scientist might have about the religions of other people or about the phenomenon of religion in general. But, on the other hand, "religious beliefs" would leave out too much, including atheistic and agnostic beliefs. Hence my use of the more comprehensive, if more cumbersome, term.

It is obvious that intelligent, reflective, and sincere people hold conflicting beliefs about religious matters. There are large groups with long histories and unique traditions and practices on each side in such disputes. Whatever beliefs about religious matters they may hold, people typically hold them with great conviction, and they typically build their lives around them. It is an interesting fact that the great diversity of such beliefs generally appears not to raise questions in the minds of those who accept any particular set of them. How is it that, say, Northern Irish Presbyterians are so sure that they are right in their religious beliefs and so sure that, for instance, the intelligent Roman Catholics all around them are deeply mistaken, and vice versa? How can the unreflective Muslim be so sure that her views about religion are right when all around her there are, for instance, convinced Jews, Christians, Hindus, Buddhists, atheists, and so forth? How is it that the beliefs of other groups, the conviction and assurance that they have of being right, is not seen to raise fundamental questions about the beliefs of one's own group about religious matters? Is there a sort of blindness, a failure of imagination, involved in being unable to appreciate the appeal of the worldviews of others?

It is not just the fact that there are diverse beliefs that is striking: it is the fact that wise people who think carefully and judiciously, who are intelligent, clever, honest, reflective, and serious, who avoid distortion, exaggeration, and confabulation, who admit ignorance when appropriate, and who have relied on what have seemed to them to be the relevant considerations in the course of acquiring their beliefs, hold these diverse beliefs. Let us say that such a person has *integrity*. I want to focus on the implications of disagreement among people with integrity, and particularly on the implications of disagreement among groups that include such people.

Disagreement on the part of people who lack integrity does not have the same significance: beliefs that have not been reflected on do not have the same claim on our attention. The assumption is that the process of being reflected on, particularly the process of being reflected on by people with integrity, is a winnowing process, one that increases the likelihood that beliefs that have been subjected to it are true. The further assumption is that people with integrity have not been careless in their believing.

As I have said, if religious views that are inconsistent with ours are held by people who lack integrity, the pedigree of the beliefs in question is such that the extent to which we should take those beliefs seriously is reduced. This fact is complicated a little, although in no way called into question, by the further fact that one way in which we decide whether a person has integrity of the relevant sort is by looking at her beliefs. Some beliefs are so outlandish, so wildly at odds with what we know, that the mere fact that someone holds them disqualifies that person, giving us reason to believe that they do not have integrity, or at least giving us reason to believe that whatever integrity they have does not extend to the particular area to which the beliefs pertain. This is a complicating factor in an area such as the area of religion since people's beliefs in this area, as well as the behavior in which their beliefs are played out or with which they are associated, often strike others as absurd.

Given the extent of the disagreement on religious matters, the confidence with which people make pronouncements on matters of religious importance, and the conviction with which their relevant beliefs are held are remarkable. Many people seem *positive* that their beliefs about religion are right. Often the views of others are thought not only to be wrong but even to be unintelligible or deserving of scorn and ridicule.

From the point of view of many members of many traditions, it is unthinkable that they should become a member of another tradition or be anything other than just what they are. Within each major tradition there are smaller groups with a distinct message whose members are sure that *they* are the ones who are right. It is striking how many people live—and die—in full confidence that they are right.

There are various respects in which members of the various traditions believe themselves to be right. They typically believe the way of life associated with their tradition to be the right way of life. And they typically believe the ceremonies and rituals they participate in to be the right ceremonies and rituals. But my concern is primarily with the belief that one's tradition provides a true account, an account that fits with the facts, of those things that it purports to describe, such as what, if any, supernatural beings there are, how it came about that there is a universe, how it came about that there is intelligent life, what sort of beings we are, and what, if anything, we will experience after we die. I take it for granted in what follows that religions, or at least many religions much of the time, understand themselves to be stating what is true on matters such as these. In addition to this deep sense of being right that is shared by most members of most religious traditions, there is also an equally widespread sense that one's beliefs fit with, account for, and are supported by many of the events and experiences in one's life.[1]

A major part of the explanation of the fact that the world religions differ to such an extent, in my view, is simply that the matters about which religions speak are open to so many different interpretations. It is obvious that a complete explanation of the variety of beliefs about religious matters would also make reference to, for instance, cultural, economic, social, historical, political, and geographical factors. All of these have an influence on the development of views. But these factors might not have much of an impact were it not the case that the matters that religions purport to describe are ambiguous. One can imagine there being but one plausible interpretation of those things that religions attempt to give an account of, such as human nature, death, suffering, and the origins of the universe. It might have been that there was not a lot of room for different interpretations, that someone who doubted the tenets of, say, the one obviously correct religion would be as foolish as someone who doubted the existence of other people or of the external world. But things are not like that.

So the fact of religious diversity and the fact of religious ambiguity are intimately linked. That there is ambiguity is a very promising explanation of the phenomenon of diversity, although there are other possible explanations. Thus it could be, for example, that the facts in the area of religion are plain for all to see but many people persist in misinterpreting them. (There could also be ambiguity even if there were no disagreement. This would be the case if, under our currently ambiguous circumstances, the adherents of all but one religious outlook were to die off or to convert to that one outlook.) Yet it seems clear that religious diversity is, at least in large part, a product of ambiguity.

In this and the next two chapters I explore some of the implications of religious diversity. In the course of this discussion I take it for granted that many of the claims of the different traditions contradict each other. For instance, Christians and Muslims typically hold opposing views about the significance of Jesus and about the significance of Muhammad. If Jews are right about God's nature and activities, or the nature of the afterlife, then atheists, Muslims, Hindus, and others too, are wrong, or at least are wrong in many of their beliefs. I recognize that there are disagreements that are *merely* apparent. That is, there are some religious claims that look as though they are inconsistent with each other, but that turn out on closer inspection to be consistent. For instance, it may be that some apparently conflicting descriptions of God are all actually true of God in virtue of God's being a complex being.[2] But there are numerous other cases in which the disagreement is genuine and does not admit of an analysis of this sort.

A full account of the nature and extent of the disagreement that there is among the religious traditions would be long and complex. Disagreements differ, for instance, with respect to the extent to which the beliefs involved are central to the traditions whose members endorse them: some disagreements are about peripheral matters, whereas other disagreements are about central and crucial matters of doctrine. Disagreements between some traditions extend across numerous matters of doctrine, whereas between others there is much agreement and only pockets of disagreement. But I do not need to provide a full account of these matters here. Suffice it to say that there is not a single claim that is distinctive of any religious group that is not rejected by other such groups, with the possible exception of vague claims to the effect that there is something important and worthwhile about religion, or to the effect that there is a religious dimension to reality and that however the sciences proceed certain matters will be beyond their scope. Obviously even claims as vague as these are rejected by nonreligious groups.

I recognize that some religious statements should not be taken at their face value. Their "surface grammar" may mislead us. One has to understand their role in the lives of those who assert them. Some contend that what religions are really all about is a matter of recommending or making possible certain ways of life, and that the function of much of what appear to be statements of belief actually is something else, such as declaring an intention to live in a certain way or providing ways of thinking that will support a certain way of life. Thus, it might be said, someone who says that "God is love" may mean to express a willingness to live in a loving way. If a contention such as this amounts merely to the claim that what is especially interesting or worthy of discussion (or something of that sort) in religious assertions is the fact that they express certain intentions, or the role they play in supporting certain practices or ways of life, this contention stands a chance of being right and certainly is worth considering. But if it is offered as an account of what people who make such assertions actually are doing, or—worse—of what people who make such assertions actually think themselves to be doing, it is utterly implausible. Typically people who make an assertion such as this are attempting to describe reality, and typically they think themselves to be describing reality. They may think themselves to be doing more than that. And they may be doing more than that. But they are attempting to do that much at least.[3]

It is clear, therefore, that large numbers of people have held, and now hold, false beliefs in the area of religion: for, to state a truism as true as they come, if two views are incompatible, at most one of them can be true. So on many of the issues on which there is disagreement, many of the disagreeing groups hold utterly mistaken views. And since so many people hold false beliefs in the area of religion, it would seem, therefore, that all groups need to consider the possibility that their beliefs in this area may be mistaken.

It is somewhat unfortunate that so many people hold false beliefs in the area of religion because the beliefs in question generally are precious to the people who hold them, are central to their lives and are a source of comfort, and often provide the basis for their deepest hopes. In itself the fact that people derive comfort and hope from false beliefs may not be unfortunate. The comfort they draw and any other psychological benefits they derive are in themselves a good thing. But what is unfortunate is the fact that the hope they invest and the comfort they draw are typically predicated on the assumption that the beliefs in question are true: this is unfortunate, since for the most part they are not true.[4]

We might approach the issues to be discussed in this and the next two chapters as follows. In general we try to avoid internal inconsistencies among our beliefs. Presumably one reason we try to do so is that we know that if two of our beliefs are inconsistent, then one of them is false, and we care about having beliefs that are true. But what is the significance of what we might call *external* inconsistency—that is, inconsistency between our beliefs and the beliefs of others? We cannot be expected to take the beliefs of others as seriously as we take our own beliefs. To expect us to do so would be to expect us to detach ourselves from our own beliefs and to look on beliefs that are at odds with beliefs of whose truth we are convinced as equally worthy of acceptance. But are we justified in not taking them seriously at all? If we ought to take them seriously to some extent, we might think of this as being a matter of the wish for consistency being extended to the set that consists of our beliefs and other people's beliefs.

Next I want to dispose of an objection that I have encountered. This is the objection that my approach, even in the little that I have said so far in this chapter, implicitly favors, or at least is written from the point of view of, a tradition that puts a lot of emphasis on *beliefs*. But—so this objection goes—some traditions put more emphasis on a way of life or on participating in certain ceremonies, or on membership in a certain community, or at any rate on something else other than holding certain beliefs. Beliefs as such may have a fairly minor role. My focus on beliefs shows—so this objection concludes—that I am working within a fairly narrow framework, a framework that has more to do with traditions such as Christianity and Islam, for example, than it has to do with traditions such as Judaism or Hinduism. And—so the charge is further elaborated—if we try to tease out beliefs in the case of those traditions that do not emphasize them, and then line up traditions side by side as though there were beliefs in each of them that play the same role and function in the same ways, we will in the case of some traditions be concocting something of our own creation, something that is different from what the tradition actually amounts to. We ought to pay attention to what is important to the members of the tradition, not to what is important to us.

I see this objection as sounding a cautionary note. Certainly it would be unwise to assume that beliefs have the same importance and the same function in different traditions. One response would just be to limit the entire discussion to those traditions that emphasize beliefs, and to think of the discussion as not bearing on other cases. But even this step is unnecessary as there is not a serious difficulty in this area. For one thing beliefs may be implicit, and it may just be that not a lot of attention has been paid to them. If there are practices that seem to have a life of their own, and not to involve any particular beliefs, it may emerge, perhaps in response to questioning, that various beliefs underpin those practices. Why, we may ask those who are engaging in the practices, are they doing what they are doing? It is possible that they will not be able to tell us, but that presumably will be the exceptional case. If those who engage in the practices had nothing at all to say, this would obviously be puzzling, although even in such a case, we might think of the very existence of the tradition, with its silence on matters about which we may have a lot to say, as something of a challenge to our own tradition. Moreover, even if people are unable to tell us why they are following certain practices, it may be that certain beliefs figure in the explanation of why they are doing what they are doing. (Perhaps the memory of the rationale for much of what they do has been lost; perhaps we have come across a remnant of a previously flourishing group or some of the less articulate and less reflective members of the group.) There may of course be people in any of the traditions who accept their tradition in such a superficial way that they lack much of a sense that their position is correct. Perhaps they say to themselves: "Well, this is just our way of getting on, or a way we have of dealing with momentous events in our lives, a way that our ancestors developed and we continue," and perhaps they do not focus much attention on the relevant issues, giving mere perfunctory verbal assent to the tenets of their tradition. But I take it that most people, or at any rate most people in the major religious traditions, are not like that.

If we *were* to change things, perhaps by questioning the practitioners, so that beliefs that previously existed only in an inchoate and undeveloped form are made explicit and concrete, it is important not to exaggerate the *extent* to which in doing so we would change the tradition in question. It is not as though beliefs that previously had *no* grip on members of the tradition would come to be embraced by them in response to our questioning. It is more likely to be a matter of what was implicit becoming explicit. Further, nothing I say implies that being religious *primarily* involves holding certain beliefs, or that what religions are *mainly* concerned with is that people hold certain beliefs. I do not need to commit myself to any particular view of how central the belief part of religion is. My view is just that beliefs are very central to many traditions. Which beliefs are important, and what are the ways in which they are important, may vary both in obvious and in subtle ways.

3. Deep and Widespread Disagreement

The fact that there is deep and widespread disagreement about religious matters has considerable significance for our beliefs about those matters. By saying that a disagreement is deep, I mean that there are large-scale systems of belief that differ considerably from each other. There is not just an appearance of disagreement, and there are not merely some isolated issues about which groups differ. For the most part, if the beliefs of one tradition are true, those of the other traditions are false. By saying that a disagreement is widespread, I mean that there are sizable groups on each side, each of which has its own traditions and practices. Disagreements among individuals are not my concern, although one would expect that sometimes their significance is somewhat akin to that of disagreement among groups. My main interest, of course, is in beliefs about religion that matter to large groups of people, and in particular beliefs that are associated with the major religious traditions or with secular responses to, and interpretations of, religion.

I understand cases in which one group believes p, a proposition about an issue of religious import, and others have no belief in this area, neither asserting nor denying p and perhaps not even having an opinion about p, as well as cases in which a group does not care much about p, to have much the same import as cases in which one group accepts while one or more other groups reject, p. Or at least there are *some* cases in which this is so. I have in mind in particular cases in which a group regards some religious belief as profoundly important, and as being such that they cannot imagine a life, or at least a meaningful life, to which its acceptance is not central. But then they find that what is precious to them is thought by others to have little value, is not taken seriously by them, and plays no role in their lives; rather, others have beliefs of their own that play as central a role in their scheme of things and in their lives. Something like this seems to be the situation with respect to many of the world's religions. For throughout the history of the respective traditions Christians typically would not have denied, say, Buddhist doctrines about Nirvana; nor would Buddhists typically have denied, say, Islamic beliefs about the prophet Muhammad. They would have had no views on such matters at all, not knowing enough about the particular doctrines of others to reject them.

So I mean to introduce a broad notion of disagreement, taking in much more than the case in which one group believes, and one or more other groups deny, various propositions. My reason for introducing this broad notion of disagreement is just that, for example, it is not merely the fact that other groups reject central Muslim beliefs that should give Muslims pause, but also the fact that there are plenty of people who get on perfectly well without having any position about, and without ever having considered, and indeed without ever having thought there to be any need to consider, the beliefs that are central to Islam. This is part of the challenge that each tradition provides for the others. But to avoid the need to allude constantly to different types of cases, I focus much of my discussion on cases in which one group believes p and one or more other groups deny p.

As indicated earlier, it is disagreements in which there are people with integrity on each side that are my main concern. But if some of the disagreeing parties clearly are qualified to talk about a disputed issue and others clearly are not, disagreement in that case does not have the same import: it may merely reflect confusion or ignorance on the part of one or more parties to the dispute. I want to focus on disagreements in which the disagreeing parties do not include one or more that clearly has the relevant expertise while the others clearly lack it. Of course when there is deep and widespread disagreement, one of the disputed questions is likely to be precisely the question of who has the relevant expertise. Thus in the case of religious questions there is no agreement about who are the experts. Methodist ministers? Roman Catholic priests? Muslim imams? Buddhist monks? Mormon elders? Hindu priests? Billy Graham? Marx? Pope John Paul II? Freud? Bertrand Russell? Clifford Geertz? Peter Berger? You or I?

In spite of the difficulties surrounding this question, we can agree on some of the characteristics of an expert. An expert will display integrity in the particular area in which she is an expert: we might think of this as *local* integrity. Global or general integrity obviously is not enough: since there is so much to know, anyone with general integrity lacks expertise on numerous issues. Being an expert in an area involves something like this: having reflected on the relevant issues, having made an attempt to understand them, and having worked out views on them with some care. We should probably also include the requirement, in cases in which there is, and is known to be, disagreement, that some attempt has been made to understand the point of view of those who disagree.

Should we include the requirement that there has been some progress in understanding the disputed issue? That is, does being an expert require something like this: knowing the facts about an issue, or at least knowing more of the facts than many others know, as distinct from *seeming* to oneself, or to others, to know? And is recognition by a community necessary for expertise: Is an expert someone who is recognized by a group as an expert? There seem to be various different, equally sensible, ways to answer these questions. Since my main concern is with the kind of disagreement that exists among the various religious communities that we are all familiar with, I will simply restrict the discussion to expertise that *has* been recognized by a community. However, I assume that the process of becoming recognized as an expert by a community is one that will at least increase to some extent the likelihood that there will be genuine understanding: that is, this process will select to some extent for genuine understanding. If so, the experts that are relevant to my discussion may well have made some progress in understanding the issues on which they are experts. So while being an expert may not require genuine progress in understanding, it increases the chances of it.

In many contexts in which we form beliefs we can help ourselves to discern whose views are to be taken seriously in the following way. In addition to seeing whose belief acquisition and maintenance practices are generally good, we can see whose judgments in areas which have a bearing on, or connection with, the disputed area are generally reliable. For example, suppose that you are wondering whether you should take seriously the views of some other group concerning some particular moral or social issue. If you know them to be of sound judgment in their thinking about other social and moral issues, this provides reason for you to take seriously their views on this particular issue. (We might think of this process of checking for expertise in contiguous areas as a step that we can take that will permit us to avoid the whole question of who is an expert in the disputed area, or—and I think this is more natural—we might think of it as being a matter of checking for expertise.) The idea is that competence extends to contiguous areas more readily than to remote areas. The more connections there are between areas of known competence and a new area, the more "carryover" there is likely to be.

But in the area of religion this maneuver faces an insurmountable obstacle. For it is not clear what are the contiguous areas. To put it mildly, there is a great distance between, on the one hand (for example), a good understanding of other people or of various areas in science, or being in general a person of judgment and sensitivity and, on the other hand (for example), a good understanding of whether there is a creator and what its nature is like. In fact it seems doubtful that competence in *any* other area is an indicator of competence in the area of religion. (If it were otherwise, we might be faced with a different difficulty: it might be unclear whether any particular tradition has the greatest concentration of individuals who are competent in the contiguous areas.) Hence this sort of help seems unavailable in the area of religion.

There is another way to approach what is essentially the same question of who is qualified to talk about a disputed issue. If a disagreement is deep, each side probably has at its disposal what I shall call *discrediting mechanisms*, which are techniques that are used to discredit or explain away the views of others, typically by imputing a defect of some sort to those who hold them. The defects that are imputed to others are of different sorts. The familiar ones include, for instance, an inability to see beyond class interests, lack of imagination, carelessness, intellectual cowardice, intellectual conformity, wishful thinking, stubbornness, and sin.

Discrediting mechanisms are used to render other views unconvincing, and hence unthreatening. The existence of such mechanisms is one case of a general tendency to insulate systems of belief from attack, to resist challenge or even inspection, a tendency that is hardly unique to beliefs in the area of religion. Discrediting mechanisms seem pervasive in the case of large-scale systems of beliefs that purport to explain a lot, be they religious, political, scientific, or of some other sort, and that matter to the people who hold them.

Attempts to insulate a religious system typically involve an attempt to account for the failure of nonbelievers to accept it. Those who do not accept it are characterized as, for example, misguided or religiously blind. Discrediting mechanisms also typically characterize the defect that is thought to be responsible for the failure of the opposition to accept the favored beliefs as a defect whose significance is likely not to be apparent to those who suffer from it.[5]

It is obvious that not all discrediting mechanisms are such that it is reasonable to rely on them. Some are mere manifestations of prejudice. Some can be summarily dismissed on the grounds that they involve an imputation of a defect to others solely on the grounds that their views are at odds with the views of one's own group. ("Since you hold religious beliefs that I do not take seriously, you *must* be self-deceived or under the influence of wishful thinking," or "since you don't believe what we believe, you *must* be blinded by sin.") We can easily distinguish between the notion of plausible and the notion of implausible discrediting mechanisms, although it is quite another matter to specify relevant criteria and on that basis to say which are which. For the plausibility of discrediting mechanisms is usually part of what is at issue in large-scale disagreement; that is, disagreements about discrediting mechanisms are likely to be as widespread and as intractable as disagreements in other areas. Still, it is worth saying that the sort of disagreement whose significance I will endeavor to probe is disagreement that does not involve one party whose discrediting mechanisms successfully discredit the views of the others, thereby showing them not to be competent. (Actually this is implicit in what has been said, for if the relevant defect were to contaminate the acquisition of beliefs in general, then the group in question would lack integrity. And if the defect were one whose effects bore specifically on the acquisition and possession of some particular belief, or on a cluster of related beliefs, the person would lack *local* integrity.) Let us say that a group with integrity whose views on some topic have not been effectively shown to be unreliable by appeal to some discrediting mechanism is *apparently competent* with respect to that topic, or has *apparent relevant competence*.

A final point about discrediting mechanisms. Some people will say that they do not need to consider other points of view, since they have not been acquired in a satisfactory way: they will say that since the procedures that typically have been relied upon in acquiring those other points of view have not been the right ones, there is no reason (or a lot less reason than there otherwise would be) to take those points of view seriously; their ancestry disqualifies them from serious consideration. Naturally people who deploy this sweeping and—in the absence of argument—altogether unimpressive discrediting mechanism exempt their own case: their beliefs, they claim, are not subject to this criticism. They have based their beliefs on the evidence, whereas the beliefs of others are a product of wishful thinking or of strategies that will enable them to cope in times of difficulty, or have been influenced by economic conditions or psychological needs, or whatever. Thus a friend, who is known locally for his vehemently antireligious views, wrote in the margin at the relevant place in a draft of this chapter that "people seldom acquire religious beliefs for reasons." Remarkable! How does he know this? I claim no such universal familiarity with how people have acquired their beliefs in this or in any other area. Indeed, I assume that there are many mechanisms at work and that beliefs about religious matters are acquired in different ways by different people, just as is the case for beliefs in other areas.[6]

4. Importance

Disagreement of the sort I have in mind is also about important matters. There are various respects in which a belief may be important. Thus a belief may be important in virtue of the fact that it has numerous ramifications for our other beliefs: in virtue, that is, of the role that it plays in our system of beliefs.[7] A belief has this sort of importance when a change with respect to it will issue in many further changes in beliefs. I refer to this as *cognitive* importance.

A belief may also be important in virtue of its implications for how we live, with an important belief in this area being one that makes a big difference to our own lives. I refer to this as *personal* importance. A belief with cognitive importance probably will also have personal importance. But there may be exceptional cases in which this is not so: an example of an exceptional case in which there is cognitive importance, but not personal importance, might be a belief about strategy in chess that has implications for many other beliefs, but only for beliefs about chess, and hence does not make much of a difference to a person's life in general.

A belief that has personal importance might not have cognitive importance; or at any rate it might have less cognitive importance than it has personal importance so that it is very significant to the person who holds it (for example, eliciting strong feelings from him or often being reflected upon by him) and yet being fairly isolated and having few connections with other beliefs. It could be dropped or modified without extensive repercussions for the rest of his beliefs.

A belief may also have great significance for how we deal with others: I refer to this as *interpersonal* importance. Crucial respects in which beliefs are often interpersonally important include the fact that they bear on how we treat others, and on what we say to others. Beliefs that are likely to make a difference to what people tell others, perhaps in virtue of the influential social roles of those who hold them, are likely to score highly in terms of interpersonal importance.

These types of importance overlap considerably. As I have said, to make a lot of difference to other things that we believe, or to make a lot of difference to how we deal with others, typically is, in effect, to make a lot of difference to our own lives.

Unimportant beliefs are unimportant in *all* these respects, although there probably is

no such thing as an entirely unimportant belief. Every belief will have some implications for other beliefs, some bearing on what will be said to others, and so forth. And
talk of importance in general is shorthand for a combination of these sorts of importance, and for others if there are others. Also, importance is a matter of degree, although
for convenience I present it as an all-or-nothing affair.

Importance of each of these three types that I have distinguished is person-relative.
That is, the personal, impersonal, and cognitive importance of a belief may vary from
one person to another. But there are beliefs which, just in virtue of their content, are
likely to be important in some of these ways to anyone who holds them. For example,
some beliefs are such that in virtue of their content it would be very surprising if they
did not have cognitive importance. This may be so in virtue of the extent of the connections that obtain between their content and the content of many other beliefs that
are held by the same person. Again, beliefs that have far-reaching implications for, say,
how we see others, such as a Calvinistic belief in the depravity of human nature or a
Nietzschean belief in the inferior nature of the "herd" or a Marxist belief about the role
of economic considerations in determining human behavior, are likely to score highly
in terms of interpersonal importance. Since importance is sometimes either wholly
or partly a function of the content of a belief, we might say that—to that extent—
importance is belief-relative. That is, there are beliefs whose content is such that, whoever may have them, they are likely to be important in one or other of the three respects
I have distinguished, to whoever holds them.

How important a belief is to someone cannot just be read off from the significance it
has for, say, his behavior in some particular area of life. It may have lost its capacity to
make a difference to behavior in some particular area of life and yet remain very important to a person who holds it, making a great deal of difference in certain other areas.
There may be change in these respects over time. Thus a person's religious beliefs may
remain profoundly important in his private experience even though they have come to
have less significance in his public life. Such changes may lead to misunderstanding by
others. Or religion might lose its significance in the workplace and yet remain deeply
important in private areas of life. The lesson is that we must beware of facile judgments
in this area and pay close attention to the actual beliefs and practices of different
groups.

When I talk about *disagreement* in what follows, what I have in mind is widespread and
deep disagreement about an issue of importance among those with integrity and with
some apparent relevant competence. It seems obvious that the beliefs that people hold
about religious matters frequently are important in each of the three respects that
have been distinguished.[8] More generally, whatever beliefs we may hold about religious
matters, they obviously are beliefs that are held in circumstances in which there is
disagreement.

5. The Critical Stance: The E-Principle and the T-Principle

Suppose you are, for instance, a serious Anglican or Catholic or Jew or Muslim or
Hindu, or a convinced atheist. You are sure that your beliefs about religious matters, of
whatever sort they may be, are correct. Yet however you may have acquired those be-

liefs, you have never subjected them to critical scrutiny, either at the time of their acqui-sition or subsequently. You have never asked what is to be said for them, never consid-ered the appeal of alternative beliefs, never considered seriously the possibility that you might be mistaken, never asked how it has come to be that others accept different and incompatible beliefs.

Is someone who is in this exceedingly common situation failing to do something that he ought to do? Does each of us have obligations in this area? If so, of what sort are they? What must one do to discharge them? And if we have such obligations, why do we have them? What is their basis? I will attempt to cast some light on these issues and to make a case for the importance of examining, questioning, and comparing our be-liefs about religion.

We can imagine having a fully articulated and comprehensive theory of what we might call the "ethics of inquiry." Such a theory would include, among other things, a full account of when we ought to examine our beliefs, of the extent to which we ought to do so, of when we ought to examine the beliefs of others, and of which types of be-liefs are especially deserving of scrutiny. I propose to offer a fragment of such a com-prehensive theory. A full theory of the ethics of inquiry would in turn be part of an even more comprehensive theory, namely, a full-scale ethics of belief, or what we might think of as a full-scale account of belief management. The proposals that I advance in the remainder of this and in the next two chapters are also fragments of that larger theory. A full-scale theory of the ethics of belief would presumably include a part that deals with the acquisition of beliefs and a part that deals with management of beliefs that we already hold: we might say that these would deal with our belief-acquisition and our belief-maintenance practices, respectively. The claims that I make in this and in the next two chapters about an obligation to inspect our beliefs bear on both of these areas.

In making a case for the importance of examining beliefs about religion, I have a number of targets against which I wish to direct my arguments. One is the claim which is sometimes made in religious circles that we ought to accept without challenge or scrutiny the teachings of some favored book or tradition or religious authority, whether it be, for instance, the Bible, the Church, the Qu'ran, a group of religious leaders, or a single religious leader who is believed to be inspired.

Another target is the more sophisticated approach of some contemporary philoso-phers of religion, the approach known as reformed epistemology. This approach in-volves a set of claims, including the claim that religious belief can be rational even if it is a basic belief, that is, a belief that is not based on any other belief; the claim that be-liefs which entail that God exists may properly be held as basic beliefs; and the claim that it is proper for these beliefs to be basic in virtue of the conditions in which they are held. Some advocates of reformed epistemology may not be unsympathetic to the claim that beliefs about religion ought to be examined. But it is also clear that an em-phasis on the need to subject your beliefs to scrutiny and examination is at least some-what antithetical to the spirit of reformed epistemology.

In any case it is clear that many people, including some theologians, philosophers, and religious leaders, would oppose the idea that there is an obligation to subject be-liefs about religion to critical scrutiny, although this claim may be thought more palat-able when made of the beliefs of others! It also seems clear that if there is an obligation of this sort in this area, numerous people, both within and without the various religious traditions, fail to fulfill it. Indeed, they never consider that they might have such an obligation. For these reasons, among others, the possibility that there might be such an obligation is worth discussing. In any case, my concern is with making a case for the importance of examining beliefs about religion, and not with who may agree or disagree. But the current rise in religious fundamentalisms around the world suggests that there is a need to reinvigorate what is essentially an Enlightenment sensibility, but one which is informed by, and partly motivated by, a new appreciation of other traditions.

I will defend the following principle, which I call the "E-principle":

> Disagreement about an issue or area of inquiry provides reason to think that each side has an obligation to examine beliefs about that issue.

What is the relevance of the E-principle for beliefs about religious matters? Clearly there are in the area of religious belief disagreements of the relevant sort—that is, deep and widespread disagreement about matters of importance between groups of people with integrity and with apparent relevant competence, or at least between groups that include people of this sort. Beliefs about religion—be they theistic, nontheistic, or atheistic—generally are important in all of the ways I have identified. They greatly influence how we live: they typically make a lot of difference to what we consider a good life, to what sort of society we want to live in, to what we tell our children about various issues that are central to our lives and will probably be central to their lives too, and that may make a difference to how they fare in the world. They influence to a great extent how we see, and interact with, others. And they have numerous implications for our entire system of beliefs. There can be no question about their importance, at least for many people.

The issue of competence is more difficult. It will always be possible to question the competence of other groups, and to say that they suffer from some defect. It will always be open to one side or the other to say of their competitors: "But they actually do not know what they are talking about" or "We are right, and everyone else is misguided by sin" or "We are right, and everyone else is engaging in wishful thinking." I have no argument to refute the position of those who dig in their heels and dismiss the views of other groups and traditions: indeed, there is no such argument to be had. But if we cannot prove mistaken the position of someone who automatically attempts to discredit the views of all other groups, perhaps by appealing to their alleged wishful thinking or their alleged sinfulness, we can show how far one has to go in order to hold it. And there are suggestions that may at least have therapeutic value. While these suggestions would not refute such a position, they may help to rid someone of it. Being persuaded by the main lines of thought in this and the next two chapters, might serve this purpose. Here are other suggestions. The exact procedure that is being followed while the views of others are being discredited should be laid out for examination. On closer examination, perhaps it will be seen to be unsatisfactory and thereby lose some of its appeal. Moreover, there are claims that sometimes it will be reasonable to expect those who dismiss the views of others to concede, including, for instance, the claim that other groups have integrity, are concerned with finding the truth, have been serious and careful and honest about what they believe, and are not morally inferior. Conceding these claims may at least make the discrediting mechanisms work less smoothly: it may make it more difficult to dismiss others and their views.

Nevertheless, the "we alone know" and "their judgments don't count" attitude in the intellectual sphere has much the same unassailability as has ethical egoism, the view that the interests of others do not matter, in the moral sphere. There seems to be no way, in either case, to *show* to be mistaken someone who refuses to accept that, in the one case, the judgments or, in the other case, the interests of others should be taken seriously. (But, honestly, isn't either position *embarrassing*?) I understand my project in this and the following two chapters, therefore, to be one of chipping away at the "we alone know" attitude, of confronting it with a series of difficulties, rather than one of refuting it. For no refutation of it is possible.

In this and the next two chapters I shall also discuss and defend the following claim, which I call the "T-principle":

> Disagreement (of the sort under discussion) about an issue or area of inquiry provides reason for whatever beliefs we hold about that issue or area of inquiry to be tentative.

The T-principle says that if certain conditions hold, including the condition that the conflicting views are held by people with integrity of the relevant sort, there is reason to think tentative belief to be appropriate.[9] Belief is tentative when it involves a recognition that one may be wrong about it, when it involves openness to revision and openness to inquiry. In the next chapter I go into more detail about the character of belief of this sort.

The T-principle pertains to belief in general, and hence to beliefs about religion. So disagreements about religious issues, including disagreements about the activities and purposes of God, about whether there is an afterlife, and what its nature is, and so forth, provide reason to think that on such matters, tentative belief, at most, is appropriate.

The T-principle is a normative claim, but there is a related descriptive claim that may also be defensible. The descriptive claim is that encounters with other groups lead, or tend to lead, to tentativeness: it says that this is how people, or many people, react or tend to react, and it says that views, including religious views, are toned down in a situation in which a variety of alternatives confront people, perhaps because they find that even without being fully aware of it, they are entering into an inner dialogue with those alternatives. The descriptive claim probably is correct, at least some of the time, although sometimes a conservative "head-in-the-sand" response is elicited in response to the availability of alternatives. There are, however, versions of the descriptive claim such that if we knew them to be true, there would be little, or less, point in making the normative claim. For example, if it were certain that the inevitable reaction to encountering groups with other views—especially groups that include people with integrity— would be tentativeness, there would not be much point in making a case for tentativeness. ("Ought" implies "can avoid.") Since it is not clear that any such sweeping claim is correct, the normative claim is worth making.

The two principles are different in that the E-principle requires us to *do* something, namely, to engage in a certain process of examination, whereas the T-principle requires us to *be* in a certain state with respect to how we hold our beliefs. The two principles seem especially different if we consider that any number of outcomes may occur as a result of subjecting your beliefs to examination. For example, you may conclude that you have more reason than ever to think that those who disagree with you are mistaken. The conclusion that you ought to be tentative in your beliefs is just one of a number of possible conclusions that may develop as an outcome of the process of examination; where you will end up depends on what you find when you carry out the process of examination. But to a certain extent the difference between the two principles is one of emphasis. For the E-principle requires not just that we should go through a certain process but also that we be in a particular state with respect to how we hold our beliefs: in particular, it requires that one be open to the possibility that one is wrong on matters about which there is disagreement. It also requires attention to and openness to alternatives and openness to revision. Further, the presence of ambiguity gives reason to think that the outcome of following the E-principle will be tentativeness. What motivates the E-principle is an awareness that is in accordance with the T-principle. And the achievement of the state required by the T-principle will probably require that one take certain steps, do certain things, to achieve it. Given these various connections, it is not surprising, as will be clear in the next two chapters, that considerations which provide the basis for a case for subjecting to examination beliefs about which there is disagreement should also provide the basis for a case for holding those beliefs tentatively.

Together the E-principle and the T-principle constitute what I shall call the *Critical Stance*. Religion in accordance with the Critical Stance is religion that is conducted more in the mode of longing and aspiration than in the mode of confident declaration. It has progressed from "knowing" that it is right to acknowledging how limited is our ability to know about religious matters, and to recognizing both the ambiguity of our circumstances and the variety of responsible responses to those circumstances. Yet it seeks to carve out a territory that permits faithfulness to a tradition.

The next two chapters are devoted to elucidating, advocating, and defending the Critical Stance with respect to beliefs about religion. In the next section I explore some approximations to, or anticipations of, the Critical Stance in the work of Reinhold Niebuhr, Peter Berger, and others. In the remaining two sections of this chapter I comment on the sort of examination that we should understand the E-principle to require, and I raise the question of who should be expected to adopt the Critical Stance.

6. Allies and Anticipations

In *The Children of Light and the Children of Darkness*, Reinhold Niebuhr advocates a certain approach to the presence of religious diversity, an approach which, to my knowledge, he never develops elsewhere. The central component of this approach is humility.

> It demands that each religion, or each version of a single faith, seek to proclaim its highest insights while yet preserving an humble and contrite recognition of the fact that all actual expressions of religious faith are subject to historical contingency and relativity. . . . According to the Christian faith the pride, which seeks to hide the conditioned and finite character of all human endeavour, is the very quintessence of sin. Religious faith ought therefore to be a constant fount of humility; for it ought to encourage men to moderate

their natural pride and to achieve some decent consciousness of the relativity of their own statement of even the most ultimate truth. It ought to teach them that their religion is most certainly true if it recognizes the element of error and sin, of finiteness and contingency which creeps into the statement of even the sublimest truth. . . . Religious toleration through religiously inspired humility and charity is always a difficult achievement. It requires that religious convictions be sincerely and devoutly held while yet the sinful and finite corruptions of these convictions be humbly acknowledged; and the actual fruits of other faiths be generously estimated.[10]

Niebuhr's position has much to recommend it. My main complaint is that he does not go far enough. The humility involved is directed, it seems, at the authoritativeness of the current formulations of the tenets of one's faith: this sort of humility requires us to concede that as of yet we may not have managed to articulate or express our faith in the best possible way.[11] I want to endorse the idea of a humility that recognizes that even the most central tenets of one's tradition, as distinct from the details of their current formulation, may be mistaken.

The sociologist Peter Berger, whose work examines in an insightful and imaginative way the changing role of religion in modern society, has also proposed a position that in some respects resembles the Critical Stance. In order to see what he has in mind, we first need a little background. Combining what Berger says in two of his works (*The Heretical Imperative: Contemporary Possibilities of Religious Affirmation* and *A Far Glory: The Quest for Faith in an Age of Credulity*), we get the following picture.[12] When different religious groups coexist peacefully and interact socially to a considerable extent, it is inevitable that there will be "cognitive contamination":

The thought obtrudes that one's traditional ways of looking at the world may not be the only plausible ones—that maybe these other people have a point or two. The worldview that until now was taken for granted is opened up, very slightly at first, to a glimmer of doubt. This opening has a way of expanding rapidly. The end point may even be a pervasive relativism. There are few certainties, convictions become mere opinions, and one becomes accustomed to considering just about any different view of things. . . . Pluralism creates a condition of permanent uncertainty as to what one should believe and how one should live. (FG, 39, 45)

Berger's claim about the inevitability of "cognitive contamination" seems mistaken. Whether cognitive contamination arises from interaction depends on numerous factors, including these: the extent to which mechanisms that are used to discredit the beliefs of others are at work; the antecedent degree of conviction; the extent to which people belong to a religiously vibrant community whose ways of thinking are resistant to change and are constantly reinforced by a community of like-minded people; and whether there is, for example, rapid social change and economic uncertainty, in the face of which many people may be inclined to turn to and embrace wholeheartedly their traditional beliefs. No doubt there are many other factors that may mitigate, or for that matter enhance, the corrosive effects of pluralism. What is plausible, however, is a weaker claim such as this: extensive interaction is conducive to cognitive contamination and sometimes creates uncertainty.

In any case—and here we come to the point that is important for my purposes—it is Berger's view that extensive social interaction confronts cultural groups with certain options, including one that Berger prefers. Combining, once again, what he says in the two works under discussion, the options he identifies are these. The deductive option, which he also calls "cognitive retrenchment" (FG, 41, 43f.) and which occurs in more than one form, "reasserts the authority of a religious tradition in the face of modern secularity" (HI, 56). This option is deductive because it proposes to read off from some canonical version of the tradition its implications for contemporary life. The reductive option, or "cognitive surrender" (FG, 42f.), reinterprets the tradition in modern secular terms and substitutes the authority of modern secular thought for the authority of a religious tradition. "[Modern] consciousness and its alleged categories become the only criteria of validity for religious reflection" (HI, 57). Then there is "cognitive bargaining" (FG, 41f.), which involves ditching some beliefs and maintaining others.

Berger convincingly rejects the deductive and the reductive options: the former being, for example, the stance of Barth and Kierkegaard and of many conservative Christians and Muslims, and the latter being the stance of "demythologizers" such as Bultmann, of radical critics of religion such as Nietzsche, of "death of God" theology, of those who reduce religion to its ethical content, and of those who offer social scientific reductions of religion, be they psychological, economic, or whatever. He also diagnoses accurately the perils of the "cognitive bargaining" option.

Finally, there is Berger's favored alternative, which he calls the "inductive option" and which is "the only one that promises both to face and to overcome the challenges of the modern situation." It involves "[turning] to experience as the ground of all religious affirmations—one's own experience, to whatever extent this is possible, and the experience embodied in a range of traditions" (HI, 58; also FG, 138ff.). Some of Berger's remarks in this context are suggestive of the Critical Stance:

> [Induction] means here that religious traditions are understood as bodies of evidence concerning religious experience and the insights deriving from experience. Implied in this option is a deliberately empirical attitude, a weighing and assessing frame of mind—not necessarily cool and dispassionate, but unwilling to impose closure on the quest for religious truth by invoking any authority whatever—not the authority of this or that traditional Deus dixit, but also not the authority of modern thought or consciousness. The advantage of this option is its open-mindedness and the freshness that usually comes from a nonauthoritarian approach to questions of truth. The disadvantage, needless to say, is that open-mindedness tends to be linked to open-endedness, and this frustrates the deep religious hunger for certainty. The substitution of hypothesis for proclamation is profoundly uncongenial to the religious temperament. (HI, 58)

Berger also says that "[the] core of the inductive model is . . . the assertion that a specific type of human experience defines the phenomenon called religion" (HI, 124). He says that the inductive option reasserts "the human as the only possible starting point for theological reflection and a rejection of any external authority (be it scriptural, ecclesiastical, or traditional) that would impose itself on such reflection" (HI, 141). The inductive option takes "human experience as the starting point of religious reflection, and [uses] the methods of the historian to uncover those human experiences that have become embodied in the various religious traditions" (HI, 115). It "entails . . . taking . . . a deliberately naive attitude before the accounts of human experience in this area, trying as far as possible, and without dogmatic prejudices, to grasp the core contents of these experiences. . . . [It entails a] turn from authority to experience as the focus of religious thought" (HI, 59). The sort of "return" to experience

Berger advocates is something that, he thinks, members of all of the religious traditions can and should engage in (HI, 140).

On Berger's preferred approach it is clear that all eggs are to be put into the basket of religious experience: all that there is to build up from inductively is just "momentary experiences that can only be maintained precariously in recollection" (HI, 138). He says that "there are . . . experiences of contact with the supernatural that carry within them absolute certainty, but this certainty is located only within the enclave of religious experience itself. As soon as the individual returns from this enclave into the world of ordinary everyday reality, this certainty is retained only as a memory and as such is intrinsically fragile. This is true even of those individuals who claim to have had the most intense encounters with the divine—mystics, say, or prophets" (HI, 138–39).

There actually seem to be three classes of experience to which appeal is to be made in the course of engaging in Berger's inductive method. First, there are the experiences of the original founders of a tradition: with the aid of historical research, an attempt is to be made to unearth these experiences and to understand their character. Second, there are the religious experiences of current members of the tradition: these are the "intrinsically fragile" experiences that yield certainty only at the moment they occur. A third type of experience that is relevant to the inductive process seems to be introduced when Berger says that the process he recommends involves "sifting and testing." In sifting and testing, the focus will not be primarily on the practical implications of what is believed on the basis of experience; the emphasis is more likely to be on confronting what is experienced religiously "with the total context of experience"—by which I take him to mean in part that what is understood to be encountered in religious experience must be assessed on the basis of other experiences.[13] The "sifting and testing" process will involve "[weighing] the insights purporting to come from the experience on the scale of reason" (HI, 134–35). Berger says that while the inductive approach acknowledges that the experience itself is "beyond all rationality," if we are looking for "criteria for distinguishing 'true' religious experience from its flawed imitation . . . nothing better can be suggested than sober rational assessment" (HI, 135).[14]

So the process of returning to the original experience, combined with sifting and testing of what it yields, should occur within each of the major traditions. Yet Berger eschews the idea that these procedures for sifting and testing will yield findings that will show that a particular religious tradition is the one whose claims are correct. This is so, I think, for reasons that also account for his endorsement of a view that is close to the Critical Stance. He emphasizes an "open-endedness" that "frustrates the deep religious hunger for certainty," one that substitutes "hypothesis for proclamation." Berger seems to believe that the attempt to unearth the original formative experiences of a tradition by historical investigation is doomed to uncertainty. This appears to be the import of the dark statement, which Berger quotes from Troeltsch, that "the historical and the relative are identical" (HI, 136). In addition, the experiences that are currently enjoyed by the members of a tradition are at best episodic and easily forgotten.

Another contemporary scholar who espouses some themes that anticipate the Critical Stance is Ian Barbour. In his *Religion and Science: Historical and Contemporary Issues*, Barbour considers a variety of responses that religious traditions can make to the presence of a diversity of traditions. Among these, he opts for what he calls "Pluralist Dialogue." He explains what it means for him, as a Christian, to take this approach.

> Pluralistic Dialogue allows us to give preeminence to revelation and salvation in Christ with-
> out denying the possibility of revelation or salvation in other traditions. It . . . [involves
> great] openness to the possibility of distinctive divine initiative in other traditions. It also
> goes further [than other responses to diversity] in accepting the historical conditioning of
> our interpretive categories. . . . It brings liberation from the quest for *certainty*. . . .
> [Certainty] is not possible, . . . and all understanding is historically conditioned.[15]

Barbour favors an approach that encourages "humility and openness, avoiding the dogmatism that has often been present in historical religious traditions" (97).

Finally, while identifying allies and anticipations, I would just draw attention to
these remarks from Alvin Plantinga: "Philosophy itself is a good candidate for a certain
measured skepticism: in view of the enormous diversity of competing philosophical
views, one can hardly claim with a straight face that what we have in philosophy is
knowledge; the diversity of views makes it unlikely that the relevant sections of the design
plan are sufficiently reliable."[16] My concern is, of course, with religion rather than with
philosophy; and what I will defend is a type of belief rather than a type of skepticism.

7. Examining Beliefs

According to the E-principle,

> Disagreement about an issue or area of inquiry provides reason to think that
> each side has an obligation to examine beliefs about that issue.

What will be involved in the process of examination that the E-principle says we ought
to go through when there is disagreement of the sort under discussion? It will involve
an attempt to assess the evidence for and against both your beliefs and competing beliefs. It will involve exposing yourself to other perspectives, trying to get a sense of their
appeal and of the concerns of those who advocate them. This process of examination
should involve an exploration of strategies that might be adopted in the attempt to resolve the conflict. This, in turn, may involve both an attempt to lay bare the procedures
that you have used in acquiring your beliefs and an attempt to understand what procedures those who disagree with you have followed in acquiring their beliefs.

This is an extremely difficult task. When you have embraced a certain system of belief, such as atheism, for example, and particularly when you have embraced it in a
wholehearted way, it is difficult to open yourself to the appeal of the alternatives, especially if the alternatives are alien to you or hard for you to comprehend, or if their acceptance would require you to change yourself in significant ways.

There are various purposes you might have in examining your beliefs. The differences between these are important, partly because the different purposes are associated
with different conceptions of the project of examining your beliefs. What purposes are
being pursued will probably make a difference to how the process of examination will
proceed and to what findings it will yield.

For instance, you might have it as your purpose to deepen your understanding of
your beliefs or to learn better how to interpret them. Or your purpose might be to promote your own appropriation of them: that is, to ensure that they will be more impor-

tant to you, matter more to you, and be more central to your life. Or you might have as your purpose the acquisition of useful material for defending your beliefs from attack, or for explaining them to others, or for showing them to be correct or superior to the beliefs of others. Let us think of these possibilities as exemplifying the *conservative* approach to examination.

The conservative approach would probably go hand in hand with an attempt to refute the views of others insofar as they disagree with one's own view: it would not be surprising if it were accompanied by a process of probing the beliefs of others with a view to finding where they have gone wrong, where their weaknesses are, and hence where they can be most readily attacked, and by an attempt to persuade others of the correctness of one's views. The conservative approach is likely also to involve the assumption that the rules for inquiry (or the rules for this particular sort of inquiry) such as rules concerning what you should take for granted, how far you should go in your investigation, what sort of findings you should be satisfied with, and what you conceive of as the purpose of engaging in the process, are dictated by the tradition to which you belong.

There may be good reasons to engage in the conservative sort of examination: for example, doing so will contribute to making people understand better their own beliefs and the implications of those beliefs. But the sort of examination which I conceive of as being part of the Critical Stance and for which I wish to make a case in this and the next two chapters requires more than this. It requires, in particular, a considerable degree of openness to the possibility that your antecedently held beliefs, along with their attendant rules for inquiry and so forth, may be mistaken in important respects as well as to the possibility that alleged sources of authority may need to be called into question. It requires an awareness of these possibilities: that one may not have the complete account of the relevant issues, that one may have much to learn from other groups, that even beliefs that seem obviously right actually may be wrong. Further, these possibilities are not to be thought of as remote or merely logically possible, but rather as possibilities that stand some significant chance of turning out to be the case.

I also want to eschew an approach that is at the other extreme from the conservative approach and which I will call the *radical* approach. According to the radical approach, the attitude with which one should approach such an inquiry is that of regarding everything as "up for grabs"; one's prior commitments are to be seen as just one of numerous possibilities, and as being on a par with the other possibilities. Someone who takes the radical approach assumes that what he has believed in the past is no more likely to be true than what others who have disagreed with him have believed. Whether your approach is conservative or radical probably will make a considerable difference to, for example, what you tend to notice, as well as to what conclusions you will come to in the course of examination.

The process of examination for which I wish to make a case is between these extremes: it does not require that we assume that our antecedently held beliefs are no more likely to be true than the beliefs of those who disagree with us. One need not detach oneself from one's position in the fashion required by the radical approach in order to carry out the process of examination for which I am making a case. On the other hand, because of what motivates it, the process of examination under discussion needs to go beyond what is countenanced by the conservative approach: because there is disagreement, which is in part to say that there are various traditions with wise and intelligent members, and so forth, each of which has its own position, there needs to be a critical attitude even to one's own beliefs.

However, the approach to examining beliefs that I am proposing is to be understood to leave room for a variety of attitudes toward your beliefs while you examine them. You might be disposed to hold on to as many of them as possible: indeed, you might be willing and eager to keep them intact to the extent that you can do so. Or you might engage in examination and scrutiny without any such dispositions or even without any preconceptions about how many of them you can hold on to, how many will survive the process of being subjected to critical scrutiny: you might be somewhat indifferent on these counts, letting the chips fall where they may. Or you might have a hierarchy among your antecedently held beliefs such that there are some that you will abandon easily, some you will abandon only if pressed, and some you will not abandon at all. And there are various other possibilities. The process of examination for which I am making a case may be carried out with a variety of such attitudes, or sets of attitudes, to your antecedently held beliefs. It is also worth mentioning that we should not assume that it is obvious even to oneself what one's relevant attitudes are. For example, you might think that you are approaching the process of examination with an open mind when that is far from being the case.

We can say something about what will be found by people who engage in scrutiny of their beliefs about religion. Atheists, theists, and members of nontheistic religions alike, if they do a decent job, will encounter objections to, and difficulties for, their beliefs. Responses, at least partial responses, to these objections will have to be found. Adjustments in the beliefs held will probably have to be made. There will be a thinking through of the issues, inspection of the point of view of others, and discussion with others, and perhaps a deepening of one's understanding of what one believes. I have argued that there is a considerable degree of ambiguity surrounding both the existence and the nature of God, and surrounding all of those phenomena which religions uniquely posit; this is a conclusion that, it seems to me, people should come to if they examine the plausibility of theism. That is, inquiry will uncover reasons to be a theist and reasons not to be a theist. I do not think of every step alluded to here—thinking through the issues, inspection of other points of view, discussion with others—as part of what is required by the E-principle; but its various ingredients are at least likely to be a product of doing what is required by the E-principle.

The process of examination requires certain attitudes, including humility, avoidance of dogmatism, and recognition that one does not have the whole story and that one may be off the mark in certain respects. Inquiry of this sort is a risky business, whatever convictions you bring to it. Who is to say in advance what will happen? You may change your beliefs as a result of it; you probably will change the way in which you hold your beliefs. On the other hand, the outcome of subjecting your beliefs to examination may be a deepened conviction that your beliefs were more or less right. You may actually move farther away, in terms of the content of your beliefs, from those with whom you are in disagreement. This might occur as a result of developing a more fully worked out and more ramified version of the position with which you began. Another outcome of going through the sort of process for which I am making a case probably will also be that one will be less at the mercy of whatever objections one may subsequently encounter: one probably will emerge with a more stable position. And whatever changes occur, they may occur whether or not you wish them to occur.[17]

8. Observations on the E-Principle and on Its Implications for Beliefs about Religion

To whom do the E-principle and the T-principle apply? In addressing this question in this section, I will focus primarily on the E-principle; corresponding points can be made in the case of the T-principle. The E-principle applies most clearly to intelligent, educated, reflective, well-informed adults who have the leisure, ability, and opportunity to subject their beliefs to scrutiny. I will refer to such a person as a *privileged* person. Such a person ought to be aware that there is disagreement about religious matters. The claim that it is appropriate to adopt the Critical Stance is most plausible in the case of privileged people.

Being privileged is a matter of degree. Being adult, well educated, well-informed, having opportunities to reflect, and so forth, make for being privileged in the relevant sense. The greater the extent to which one satisfies these conditions, the more privileged one is. And the stronger is the case for the Critical Stance.

I generally restrict my attention to the case of privileged people, although there is another category of people in whose case the claim is about as plausible. These are people who are not educated, or not reflective, or not well informed, or not aware there is disagreement in some area, but whose failings in any such respect are something for which they can reasonably be held responsible. For instance, someone does not avoid having the obligation specified in the E-principle in virtue of being carelessly and culpably ill-informed on the relevant issues. Such a person is to be blamed *both* for not being privileged *and* for failing to do what she ought to do if she were privileged. But for ease of discussion I restrict my attention almost entirely to the case of the privileged.

We can expect more of the privileged with respect to their beliefs, and perhaps in other areas too. The more privileged one is, the more stringent is one's obligation to examine those beliefs which one has an obligation to examine and the more, in general, may integrity, as defined, be expected of one. The less privileged one is, the more likely, and the more apt, it is that one should rely on experts—provided the experts seem to have integrity, some relevant expertise, and no apparent relevant defects—at least in areas of belief in which it is easy to go wrong. But even quite unprivileged individuals and groups are likely to be in a position to assess to some extent the relevant data and to assess to some extent expert opinion so that they can at least choose among experts.[18] And they certainly can be expected to be reflective and serious about their beliefs.

Emphasis on the privileged as the main bearers of the obligation to examine their beliefs about religion, or as those to whom the case for the Critical Stance is mainly directed, and even the very identification of a certain group as being privileged, might be thought to be elitist. But the point is simply that it is wrong to expect people who, say, are for good reason wholly preoccupied with practical matters, or who know little of any system of beliefs other than their own, to subject their beliefs to examination. They may not be in a position to do so. Many people probably are too preoccupied with matters of survival, business, family, and so forth, or are too limited in their knowledge or experience or reasoning abilities, or have too many practical difficulties to overcome to engage in much reflection about how things appear from the point of view of others, especially others whose worldview is very different. The idea just amounts to "ought implies can": one ought to do so only to the extent that one is in a position to do so. In short, the obligation is on those who are (or—in the case of those whose failure to be in a position to fulfill the obligation is culpable—ought to be) in a position to fulfill it. But since almost everyone is in a position to fulfill it to some extent, this means that the obligation is on almost everyone to some extent. I should also add that I have little invested in the notion of an *obligation*: the E-principle can be restated by saying that there are powerful reasons that beliefs about religion ought to be examined, or simply that there are powerful reasons to examine those beliefs.

There is one other factor that bears on the issue of who has the obligation in question, and that is worthy of emphasis. As discussed, this obligation pertains to *important* beliefs, and beliefs are important in a number of respects: I have mentioned cognitive, personal, and interpersonal importance. Beliefs vary in their importance in each of these respects. Now some beliefs have great interpersonal importance in virtue of the extent to which certain people who hold them influence others. It is particularly important that people who preach, lecture, speak on television, or write about religious matters should have made an effort to fulfill this obligation since what they say is especially likely to make a difference to others. So the group about whom it can be said that it is *most* important that they should fulfill this obligation is the group of privileged people who influence others. In this category are, for instance, many intellectuals, many scholars and teachers of religion, as well as many priests, rabbis, ministers, imams, evangelists, and other religious officials. So those who influence others have the obligation in a particularly robust form; but others are also subject to it. The obligation may also be thought to fall on religious groups, especially on groups that include many people upon whom the obligation individually falls.

The picture that emerges is this. How much the E-principle requires of a person with respect to a particular belief is a function both of facts about the person in question, such as the extent to which he is privileged or the extent to which the belief is important to him, and of facts about the situation in which the belief is held, such as the extent to which there is disagreement about the belief. To say all this, however, is to leave a lot unspecified: for instance, it may be clear that you and I ought to subject our belief that p to some examination, but it may not be clear what is the *right* amount of examination for either of us. And there are other unanswered questions. For instance, what is the currently available relevant information that one needs to have before one? If I am, say, a devout Catholic, do I need to have information about Protestant beliefs, Jewish beliefs, Islamic beliefs, Marxist beliefs . . . ? It would be foolish to suggest that everyone who has a position on religious matters ought to become a scholar of comparative religion, however much gainful employment for one's colleagues and friends this would create. And the relevant information includes not just knowledge of other religions but also, for instance, knowledge of many areas in science and history. However, the fact that it is difficult to give an account of important aspects of the obligation in question, and in particular of how much it demands of people, obviously is not a reason for denying, or even doubting, that there is such an obligation.

The obligation is also one about which it may be very hard to know whether you have fulfilled it adequately. One reason for this is that the extent of your obligation is dependent on facts about you and your situation, and these facts themselves may require some interpretation. Another reason arises from the presence of discrediting mechanisms as part of any large-scale system of beliefs. A convinced Buddhist, for instance, would probably have to work very hard to get to the point where she can examine carefully, say, the Muslim system of beliefs. (And of course there is no *one* such set of beliefs that needs to be taken into account.)

The process will involve considering the beliefs of others. But what is it to consider, to really consider, the beliefs of others? A mere cursory glance in their direction, backed up by all of one's prejudices and defenses will not suffice. It is all too easy to say—and which of us has not often heard it said?—that you have looked at the alternatives and have found them wanting, so that you are now more convinced than ever that your beliefs are superior. But with what attitude have you approached them? Have you really listened, have you really tried to enter into that alien point of view? This is a subtle matter, even in your own case. Perhaps the feature of it that is clearest is that it allows great room for self-deception.

To fail to examine your beliefs when you ought to examine them is to fail to be rational in an important respect. This claim does not require for its defense the articulation of a full theory of rationality. It merely requires that we assume that any adequate account of rationality will include this claim.[19]

There are features of beliefs in the area of religion that tend to conceal the fact that we have this obligation. For one thing, such beliefs tend to be insulated from attack, to be protected in such a way that they resist challenge and inspection. An aspect of this that I have mentioned is the fact that they are generally accompanied by discrediting mechanisms, or procedures for rendering unconvincing, and therefore unthreatening, the views of other groups. These procedures are used to explain away dissent and to discredit the views of those who disagree, thereby keeping them at arm's length. Another aspect is the tendency of those with strongly held beliefs about religion to take various steps to strengthen and confirm those beliefs: Muslims tend to read Muslim books and to associate with Muslims, Christians tend to read Christian books and to associate with Christians, and when it comes to finding something to read about religion, atheists seem to have a marked preference for, say, Bertrand Russell over Pascal or C. S. Lewis. The same goes for other groups. It is no exaggeration to say that an effort is generally made to turn one's system of belief into an impregnable fortress. Yet another consideration that is important to keep in mind is that we seem not to examine beliefs around which we build our lives, which it seems against our interests to call into question, and from which we derive security. I suggest that the more evidence there is that such tendencies are present in the case of a particular belief, or set of beliefs, the more aware we should try to be of whatever relevant obligations we may have in this area, and the more diligent we should be in our efforts to fulfill them.

A few final points. First, there are bound to be cases in which conditions that generate an obligation for someone to examine her beliefs obtain, but in which she is unaware that this is so. (This might be so for various reasons. For example, someone might not recognize that conditions such as those in which she is aware that she holds her beliefs are conditions that generate such an obligation, or she might recognize that conditions of the sort in which she holds her beliefs generate such an obligation, but fail to recognize that those conditions actually obtain.) There may also be cases in which conditions in which beliefs are held do not generate an obligation to inspect them, but in which it is falsely believed by the person who holds the beliefs that there is an obligation to inspect them. (This, too, might be so for various reasons. For example, someone might believe that her beliefs are inconsistent with those of others and believe that this fact contributes crucially to the presence of an obligation to examine her beliefs, although it is actually the case either that the relevant beliefs are not inconsistent or that they are inconsistent but that this fact does not have the significance which it is believed to have.) I will not pursue such cases further.

Second, by and large, it seems, religious disagreement is not perceived by the members of any of the religious traditions as a problem for acceptance of the beliefs associated with their tradition. No doubt the availability of discrediting mechanisms plays a large role in ensuring that this is so. Advocates of large-scale systems of belief that include discrediting mechanisms are not in a position to appreciate the appeal of systems of belief they think to be discredited. They are not likely to be able to give them a fair and sympathetic hearing. I suggest that when there is disagreement (of the sort under discussion), it is parochial and unsatisfactory to fail to take other perspectives seriously. Yet to take them seriously is to open the door to great change. I realize of course that many will claim that they alone are the experts, or the people with most expertise. I do not aim to prove that they are wrong, since I do not think that that can be done, but I wish to put pressure on their position. Someone who contends that it is obvious or very clear to her that the facts in the area of religion are as she believes them to be ought to recognize that other people consider to be obvious beliefs that are inconsistent with her beliefs. Being sure that you are right, even being sure that you are obviously right, simply is a poor guarantee that you are right, at least in any area in which there is disagreement, including the area of religious belief.

Third, there are many remaining questions. For example, what would it be to be Christian or Jewish or Buddhist, for example, and to adopt the Critical Stance? What would be left of the traditional notion of membership in the tradition? I address these questions in the next two chapters. Thus in chapter 8 I explore sorts of religious commitment that are compatible with the Critical Stance. The project of developing the Critical Stance is an exploration within religion; it is not supposed to be destructive of all religious commitment; rather, it is an attempt to indicate the form that involvement in a tradition should take in our era. So there is a negative part and a positive part. The negative part includes a rejection of the sort of certainty that the theistic religions, in particular, expect of their adherents and often urge on others, too. I argue that this expectation of certainty is a mistake. The positive part includes the attempt to spell out types of commitment that are compatible with the Critical Stance.

Fourth, I assume that many people have reasons to be in the religious tradition in which they find themselves. Their tradition probably fits with their experience in a general sort of way, which is one of the sorts of religious experience that I discuss in chapter 10, and it may in addition be buttressed by, for example, perceptual experience of the sort that I discuss in chapter 11. People also often feel a sense of obligation to be faithful to their community, to their tradition, to the ways of their ancestors, and so forth, and they have every reason to take these feelings seriously. They may have a strong sense that doing so is extremely important. They are also aware of themselves as members of a particular historical community of like-minded individuals, whose way of life is valuable and worthy of preservation. This may in fact be the community in which they have acquired their evaluative criteria and their outlook in life; so membership in it may be partially constitutive of who they are. So these are some examples of factors that speak in favor of continued participation in a tradition, with all that that involves. But people have these reasons to believe in circumstances of ambiguity and in circumstances in which there is disagreement, and that makes a difference to how their beliefs should be held.

8

THE CRITICAL STANCE I

Tentative Religious Belief

In this chapter I discuss at some length what is involved in tentative belief, explaining how it differs from other sorts of belief. I ask whether *religious* belief can be tentative. I ask whether belief of this sort is compatible with religious commitment, and I probe various respects in which this is so. I conclude with some discussion of the relationship between belief of this sort and tolerance.

1. Tentative Religious Belief

According to the T-principle,

> Disagreement about an issue or area of inquiry provides reason for whatever beliefs we hold about that issue or area of inquiry to be tentative.

By "disagreement," as explained in the previous chapter, what is meant is widespread and deep disagreement about an issue of importance among those with integrity and with some apparent relevant competence. But what does tentative belief amount to, and what would tentative *religious* belief be like?

Tentative belief has a number of components. It involves a recognition that the belief may need revision and may be mistaken. It also involves a concomitant openness to alternative beliefs and an awareness that some of these alternatives may be plausible, and that one or more of them may even be correct. If I recognize that a belief of mine may be wrong, then I recognize that its negation may be right. And in a situation in which there is a well-defined set of viable alternatives, to recognize that the position one had thought to be correct may be wrong is in effect to recognize that one of the other positions may be right. (If it seems that either the butler or the gardener or the maid did it, and if I have hitherto believed that the butler did it but now become tentative in this belief, this is in effect to become more open to the possibility that the gardener or the maid did it.)

The tentative attitude involves openness to further discussion and openness to exploration. (We might refer to it as "open belief" rather than as "tentative belief.") Belief of this sort permits you to entertain as live hypotheses various alternatives to your own position. It involves an attitude such as this: here is how I see things, but views that are quite different from mine may instead be right, and my view and my tradition may be wrong. When we believe in this way, we are less surprised if it turns out that we are wrong than we would be if we believed nontentatively, for the belief already is accompanied by an awareness that it may be mistaken.

Tentative belief that p assigns to p a lower probability than strong belief that p assigns. Correspondingly, it assigns a higher probability to the claim that one may be wrong about p. It also involves a psychological component, namely, that one is less convinced of p. One will give up p more readily. So there is a part that has to do with your judgment about the proposition and the extent to which it is justified, and there is a particular psychological state involved; in both cases what is involved may be reflected only dispositionally.

A recognition that there is some *remote* chance that one may be wrong might not result in diminished conviction. As long as the belief remains above a certain level epistemically, even if it does not have really top-class status, it may be reasonable to be firm and confident about it. But tentative belief, as it is understood here, involves an awareness that one may very well be wrong and that alternative views may very well be right. This awareness will, I think, inevitably involve a less confident and less firm attitude to the belief. In any case, the tentative belief for which I will make a case involves both a reduced estimate of the probability of the proposition in question and diminished psychological certainty.

With a qualification that I shall add later (four paragraphs hence), I understand tentative belief to share the features that Gary Gutting says are distinctive of "interim assent," which he distinguishes from decisive assent as follows.

> Interim assent . . . accepts p but without terminating inquiry into the truth of p. Its effect is to put me on the side of p in disputes about its truth. However, my endorsement of p is combined with a commitment to the epistemic need for continuing discussion of p's truth. . . . Decisive assent to p is defined by the fact that it terminates the process of inquiry into the truth of p. This does not mean that I no longer think about p, but my thoughts are concerned with developing its significance (analyzing its meaning, determining its implications) rather than establishing its truth. Nor does it mean that I am unconditionally committed to p, i.e., that I intend to maintain p no matter what evidence subsequently presents itself. Rather it means that I view the present case for p as allowing me to end the *search* for reasons for and against believing p.[1]

Gutting's term "interim assent" may suggest that to assent in this fashion is in effect to be *on the way to* decisive assent and that this sort of assent is a halfway stopping point on the route to something more, or at least to something else. I mean this connotation to be absent from the notion of tentative belief.

Clearly the extent to which we are open to the possibility that we might be wrong about a belief admits of degrees. There is a spectrum of possibilities that extends from, at one extreme, a recognition that a belief could conceivably need revision to, at the other extreme, thinking it sufficiently likely that we are wrong about it that we barely hold on to it. Tentative belief covers part of this range, occupying an area between these extremes, especially toward the latter end of the spectrum. And it, too, is a matter of degree. It involves more than a mere occasional recognition that you could conceivably be wrong: rather, the "I could be wrong" that is part and parcel of it is a permanent and prominent feature of it and not just a thought that may once in a while accompany it. So a mere acknowledgment that a belief could conceivably be wrong does not suffice for it to be tentative. On the other hand, since it is a form of belief, it can only go so far in the direction of admitting that it may be wrong. Thus, for instance, tentative belief that p involves something more than a mere suspicion that p is true or mere entertainment of p.

In addition to varying with respect to the extent to which it is accompanied by a recognition that it may be wrong, tentative belief can also vary in its nature along a number of other dimensions. For example, it can vary with respect to the extent to which it is accompanied either by an awareness of a need for further inquiry or by an actual process of inquiry. To cast further light on what I have in mind here, it is useful to recall a remark by Gutting and also to look at some rather similar remarks from Gilbert Harman. Gutting, as we have seen, characterizes "interim assent" as involving endorsement of p "combined with a commitment to the epistemic need for continuing discussion of its truth." Harman thinks of tentative acceptance as a matter of accepting something as a working hypothesis; it involves an experimental attitude to the belief in question.

> To accept something as a working hypothesis is to "try it out," to see where one gets by accepting it, to see what further things such acceptance leads to. Accepting a particular working hypothesis is fruitful if it allows one to make sense of various phenomena; if it leads to solutions to problems, particularly when there are independent checks on these solutions; and if it leads naturally to other similarly fruitful hypotheses."[2]

There may even be a suggestion in what Harman says that one might merely dabble with the belief, "trying it out" without taking it very seriously. Harman also emphasizes the concern with the fruitfulness of the belief: it is with a view to its fruitfulness that one is experimenting with it.

So both Harman and Gutting have in mind a rather active and engaged state, one that involves continuous, "never-ending" inquiry.[3] However, tentative belief, as I understand it, may be a more stable and settled condition. (It is on this point that I wish to qualify significantly my acceptance of what Gutting says about interim assent.) Tentative belief is accompanied by an awareness of the sort "this is how it seems to me, but I could be wrong," by a willingness to engage in inquiry and examination, and by an openness to change. It need not be approached with an experimental attitude. Nor need it be accompanied by constant inquiry or even by an awareness of the need for constant inquiry. Harman's idea is that one should focus a lot of attention on the process of testing and checking to see if the belief is fruitful, and so forth; I mean these implications to be less central. While I argue for the importance of examining beliefs about religion, I do not see that it is necessary to be permanently in an examining mode. So what Gutting and Harman think of as a defining feature of tentative belief, I think of as just one point on a dimension along which tentative belief can vary. It may be accompanied by a strong sense of a need for continued inquiry, but it may instead be held in such a way that it is open to that sort of inquiry. And there are various options between these alternatives.

To say that certain of our beliefs are open to revision is to say we may be wrong about their content. If we recognize that we may be wrong about their content, the details of their content are likely to be less important to us. In saying this, I assume a distinction between "the big picture," or core beliefs, that is accepted by the members of a tradition and various details that are typically accepted by those members. This is imprecise but not without content. Thus the beliefs that God exists, that Jesus rose from the dead, and that the Papacy has some religious authority, are beliefs that are part of the "big picture" that is accepted by Roman Catholic Christians; the details in this case would include, for example, the belief that priests ought not to marry or that the mother of Jesus was immaculately conceived. Part at least of what is definitive of the latter category is that one can imagine someone abandoning entirely beliefs of the latter sort and yet remaining in the tradition. Indeed this happens all the time. But to abandon core beliefs seems to be to step outside of the tradition.[4]

I understand tentative belief to involve or at least permit agnosticism about the details, and a feeling that it does not matter much what position one takes on such matters, that the various options on matters of detail are perhaps worth pondering but not of great moment. Thus a tentative Muslim will not just recognize that she may be wrong about core beliefs such as the belief that Muhammad is the seal of the prophets or that the Qur'an was revealed to the prophet Muhammad; she may also think that it does not matter what position she takes on matters of detail such as what is experienced by a believing Muslim directly after death. So tentative belief, as I understand it here, involves a lack of concern, and even perhaps agnosticism, about many of the details in addition to the various components I have mentioned, such as a willingness to revise and openness to alternatives.[5]

Since being a religious believer is as much a matter of experiencing the world, one's own life (etc.) within the categories of one's religious tradition as it is a matter of believing certain propositions to be true, it is important to say something about the significance of tentativeness for this aspect of what it is to belong to a religious tradition. There are bound to be implications in this area, not least because to experience, say, an illness that one has had as, say, the result of the operation of the law of Karma or as reflecting divine judgment is in effect to accept certain beliefs, including of course the belief that the illness in question was caused in the way specified in the interpretation.

I will give just two simple examples of the impact of tentativeness for this experiential aspect of belief. Suppose that while walking in the country someone notices some beautiful wildflowers. A nontentative theist might be inclined to see at once the hand of God in creating such beauty and to thank God for having done so. A tentative theist, on the other hand, would be more inclined to respond by combining an awareness that God may have created the flowers with an awareness that the beauty of the flowers has alternative explanations, including an explanation in terms of natural selection. She may go on to wonder whether it makes sense to think of natural selection as the vehicle for creation and, if so, how this would work. Again, someone meets another who comes to play an important and enriching role in his life, perhaps enabling him to deal with some of the stresses and strains of life. A nontentative theist would at once understand himself to see the hand of God at work in his life. A tentative theist would be more likely to combine an awareness of that possibility with the possibility that he just had good luck. In the case of the tentative believer, the religious picture has a looser grip than in the case of the nontentative believer. But it can nevertheless be part of a picture of reality that plays a central role in his life, at times admonishing, or giving hope or confidence or direction to, the believer.

To summarize, tentative belief that p is belief that p is true that involves an awareness that p may need revision, and may even be false, and that there may be viable alternatives to p. It involves openness to inquiry and openness to change, and it may involve ongoing inquiry and experimentation. Since it is not wedded irrevocably to any particular stance, someone who adopts it need not be apprehensive about advances in other areas of knowledge that call the relevant beliefs into question. He can be open to letting the chips fall where they may, being perfectly happy to plead uncertainty or ignorance on numerous matters of doctrine. However, one of the many possibilities to which he is open is the possibility that belief that is more than tentative may at some point be found to be appropriate.

One can hold a belief in this tentative way without having its tentativeness, or what it is about it that makes it a case of tentative belief, in mind. Just as I do not need to think about a belief in order to hold it, I do not need to think about, or be aware of, the tentativeness with which a belief is held in order for me to hold it tentatively. Indeed, I might not even understand what it would be for a belief to be tentative. That the belief is held tentatively will, however, be manifested in, for instance, my being disposed to consider alternatives or in the absence of dogmatism in my assertion of my beliefs.

In spite of the many respects in which tentative belief is weaker than full, nontentative belief, tentative belief can be a serious matter for a person who holds it and may play a significant role in his life. (So it is quite different from the minimal belief discussed in chapter 3.) I give more substance to these remarks later in this chapter when I explore some respects in which this sort of belief is compatible with thoroughgoing commitment of certain sorts. In doing so I attempt to address the complaint that to embrace this sort of belief is to abandon much, or what is important, or even everything, that is distinctive of religious belief. The tentative believer approaches his experiences, or many of them at any rate, within the framework provided by his tradition. But he does not do so solely in the mode of entertaining that framework or toying with it or adopting it as a thought experiment; to some extent he lives through it.

Finally, to believe p, even if only tentatively, is—as you would expect—to believe p. And to believe p is to believe that p is true: you cannot believe p and also believe that, for instance, the truth of p remains to be settled. Furthermore, if you believe p, even tentatively, you cannot consistently hold that you see no reason that anyone else should do so. Your view entails that someone who denies p is going wrong with respect to this belief. But tentative belief involves a disposition to be tolerant and respectful of belief that is inconsistent with it. In admitting that it could be wrong, you recognize that the opposition could be right. Your view is that they are not right; but your view is also that you may be wrong about this and that they may be right. Further, since someone who holds tentative religious beliefs will view his own religious beliefs as open to revision, and as concerning matters about which it is easy to be wrong, he will therefore not be surprised by the fact that many sincere, intelligent, reflective people *are* wrong about religious matters.

In virtue of this tolerant and respectful attitude toward alternatives—a matter of no minor significance—tentative belief has excellent prospects for being at the heart of a tolerant and open society, a society that will permit and even encourage a diversity of opinion, including opinions on religious matters, although this is not to say that tentative belief alone is capable of delivering these benefits. (The link with tolerance is discussed further in the last section of this chapter.)

2. But Can Religious Belief Be Tentative?

So far in part II of this book, I have attempted to treat various beliefs about religion, whether they be theistic, atheistic, or distinctive of a nontheistic religious tradition, as on a par. Next I want to explore a problem for the position I am defending that is especially likely to be presented by members of various religious traditions, especially the theistic traditions.

The problem is just this. The sort of belief that religions typically recommend, and in some cases require, is more than tentative in nature. Tentative belief is therefore unlikely to satisfy most members of most traditions: it seems to lack many of the distinctive features of religious belief. Thus Gary Gutting says that "a belief is religious not only in virtue of its content . . . but also in virtue of the way it functions in the life of one who holds it".[6] He thinks there are at least three reasons that the ways in which religious beliefs typically function require that they be more than tentative. (In his terms these are reasons that religious belief must involve "decisive rather than interim assent" [106].) Gutting's view, therefore, is that if belief is tentative, then it does not count as religious belief.

Alasdair MacIntyre expresses more or less the same view when he says that a "provisional and tentative adherence is completely uncharacteristic of religious belief. A God who could be believed in this way would not be the God of Christian theism. For part of the content of Christian belief is that a decisive adherence has to be given to God. So that to hold Christian belief as a hypothesis would be to render it no longer Christian belief."[7] I assume that MacIntyre would think the corresponding claim to be applicable in the case of the other theistic traditions.

This claim from Gutting and MacIntyre is echoed by many other authors: that religious belief cannot be tentative is even something of a commonplace among scholars of religion. Rather, such belief is said to involve believing with every fiber of your being. "Religion," writes Pierre Bayle, "ought to be based on certainty. Its aim, its effects, its usages collapse as soon as the firm conviction of its truths is erased from the mind."[8]

Terence Penelhum puts it thus:

> It has often been pointed out that the adherence which the man of faith has to the doctrines that he proclaims is quite different from the adherence, if that is the word, which someone may have to some explanatory hypothesis, for example in the sciences. In the lat-

ter case some proposition is tentatively adopted, and our confidence in it is in proportion to the amount of confirmation that it receives. If the evidence seems predominantly against it, it is abandoned. Religious belief is not tentative in this way. . . . The basic reason for this total commitment is, as religious thinkers have always insisted, that faith is not only a state in which someone considers himself to know certain things about God, but is also a personal acceptance of and commitment to the God about whom these things are considered to be known.[9]

Intimately linked to these points is the Pascalian and Jamesian line of thought according to which one has to commit oneself, one way or the other, or that we confront, in James's terms, a forced option.

The view that religious beliefs cannot be tentative is also held by some scholars who think that since any beliefs we hold about religious matters *ought* to be tentative, it therefore follows that we ought not to hold religious beliefs. The late Ernest Gellner took just such a view. In *Postmodernism, Reason and Religion*, Gellner defends what he calls "Enlightenment Rationalist Fundamentalism."[10] In matters of faith, modern societies have, he believes, three main options: the rationalism that Gellner himself espouses, the sort of religious fundamentalism that is conspicuous today in some parts of the Islamic world, and relativism such as is embraced by postmodernists. (Gellner has a thing or two, all of it both highly critical and altogether convincing, to say about the postmodernists.)

Gellner's own Enlightenment Rationalist Fundamentalism (which I will refer to as "rationalism" while discussing his views) is best understood by contrasting it with the alternatives of religious fundamentalism and relativism. Unlike religious fundamentalism, rationalism eschews any privileged source of information: *all* such sources are to be queried. Our "world-pictures" are constantly to be subject to critical reevaluation. A rationalist repudiates the religious fundamentalist's idea of "a unique and final Message, delivered at one place and one time, exempt from scrutiny, from the disaggregation into its constituent claims, and from the need to subject those claims to question" (84). But rationalism shares with fundamentalism the idea that there is a uniquely true way to describe the world. Unlike postmodernists and other relativists, rationalists claim that there is a correct procedure for arriving at the truth, which is roughly the procedure of modern science. What it shares with relativism is skepticism about all of the various claims to have discovered the truth.

It is Gellner's next move that is interesting for my purposes. He moves with alacrity from endorsing rationalism to rejecting all religion. He says that the fact that "there are no privileged or a priori *substantive* truths . . . at one fell swoop . . . eliminates the sacred from the world" (80). Since all world-pictures are scrutinized, all are destabilized. This vision "desacralizes, disestablishes, disenchants everything substantive: *no* privileged facts, occasions, individuals, institutions or associations, . . . no miracles, no divine interventions and conjuring conferences and press conferences, no saviours, no sacred churches or sacramental communities" (81). The only thing that is absolutized and exempt from criticism is the method itself.

The general idea is clear, and Gellner is hardly bashful in his defense of it. (But what on earth is wrong with press conferences?) However, some of Gellner's claims are very questionable. The two most obvious flaws are these. First, if there really are no privileged facts, then presumably among the unprivileged claims—the claims that are subject to inquiry, revision, and so forth—the claim that God does not exist must figure as prominently as the claim that God exists. Consistency seems to require that Gellner should accept that it could turn out that some distinctively religious claims are true. Indeed, he should accept that it may turn out to be true that, for instance, many of the uniquely Islamic claims (e.g., that there is no God but Allah, or that Muhammad is the seal of the prophets) are true, even though it could not turn out, for instance, that the Islamic appeal to the Qu'ran should have the authority that Muslims believe it to have. On what basis does Gellner privilege non-religious viewpoints? He needs to give us arguments at this point.

Second, we certainly should agree with Gellner that religions typically expect, and sometimes demand, of their adherents—and, if they can get away with it, of everyone else too—a type of belief that is not thought of as being subject to inquiry and revision. And it may be reasonable to make the historical claim that the *effect* of opening a tradition to criticism and inquiry has generally been a desacralizing one. But of course Gellner wishes to go much further than this, for he baldly asserts that to adopt the rationalist stance is in effect to reject all religion. He assumes that religious beliefs cannot be held in such a way that they are open to change and to rejection. But he does not give us any arguments to this effect. Since I believe there to be room for a serious sort of religious involvement that is open in these respects, I am not convinced by this part of his argument.

So let us turn to Gutting, who provides us with three arguments as to why religious beliefs cannot be held in such a way that they are open to change and to rejection. Gutting's first reason is that

> religious belief represents the (relative) end of a quest for emotional and intellectual satisfaction. . . . [Any] religious belief worthy of the name must surely call for and legitimate a longing for God as the all-dominating longing of the believer's life, the believer's "master passion." By contrast, the life of a believer who gave only interim assent to God's reality . . . could be rightly dominated not by the longing for God but, at best, only by the longing to *know* whether or not God exists.[11]

First, in response to the point that religious belief is the outcome of a search for emotional and intellectual satisfaction, it is worth pointing out that it is deeply intellectually unsatisfying to neglect the important facts of religious ambiguity and religious diversity and their implications, or to use inappropriately a discrediting mechanism to remove inappropriately the challenge provided by other traditions. Correspondingly, there is great intellectual satisfaction to be found in taking adequate cognizance of other traditions and perspectives and in making appropriate changes in one's beliefs. For the awareness of other traditions constitutes a challenge that people in many traditions feel at some level of awareness; this awareness is disquieting; it is often banished in the to-and-fro of day-to-day religious life, but it is likely to occur again and again, especially in modern societies in which diverse faith communities live together and develop some understanding of each other. So even if it is true that belief would not count as religious belief unless it is a source of emotional and intellectual satisfaction, this is not an insurmountable obstacle to tentative religious belief.

Gutting also says that "any religious belief worthy of the name must surely call for and legitimate a longing for God as the all-dominating longing of the believer's life, the believer's 'master passion.'" I take it that a longing is all-dominating only if it is both a very consuming preoccupation in one's life and one's greatest or strongest longing: a longing would not qualify as "all-dominating" if it were merely, say, one of two or more equally strong longings. In addition to being the strongest longing, in order to qualify as "all-dominating" it must, I think, be the concern that provides the setting for one's other concerns: thus it might serve as a test for which other concerns should be given priority. Gutting may be right that religious belief calls for and legitimates such an all-dominating longing for God. But it hardly requires or presupposes it. For one thing, it is doubtful that most religious believers have a longing for God that is all-dominating, even if they might agree that they *ought* to have it. There seem to be plenty of people who count themselves, and whom it is right to count, as religious believers but who do not satisfy this very demanding description. Perhaps this is an ideal toward which religious traditions urge their practitioners to aim rather than a requirement that must be satisfied before their beliefs may properly be classified as religious. This is to set the standard for what is to count as religious belief much too high.

More to the point, a longing for God, however dominant, seems compatible with tentative belief. Indeed, tentative theistic belief and a longing for God eminently suit each other: both have about them the air of a quest, of something incomplete.

Part of Gutting's thinking here seems to be that the character of the longing would be different in the two cases—that at most a longing to know whether God exists would be warranted by tentative belief, whereas a longing for God would be warranted by full belief. But the contrast here is a bit unclear. The tentative believer is not an agnostic: he believes that God exists, albeit in a way that involves a recognition that he may be wrong, and this seems to provide the basis for some degree of longing for God. The tentative believer may long to know whether God exists; but then the full believer may also long to know this and may in general long for the ambiguity that surrounds religious matters to be dissipated. Both sorts of believer find themselves in circumstances in which God is hidden, if God exists, and the way in which they believe and how they react ought to take account of this. Presumably part of what longing for God consists in is a wish for a fuller understanding of God and a wish for communion with God: but there is no reason that the tentative believer should be barred from these aspirations. He can long to know more about, and to be more fully aware of, the being in whom he tentatively believes.

But perhaps we are still missing part of Gutting's point. Perhaps part of Gutting's point is that what is characteristic of religious belief is that it is *adhered to* religiously. Belief is religious belief not only because it is *about* certain things, such as the path to enlightenment or the curative powers of the waters of the Ganges: it must in addition be adhered to religiously; one must be passionately committed, altogether gung-ho, and not at all tentative about it. There is indeed a use of "religious belief" that fits with this suggestion and in accordance with which to have religious belief or to believe religiously is to believe in a wholehearted and thoroughly passionate manner. The theistic traditions have often expected this sort of belief from their adherents; and many strands within those traditions would consider tentative belief to be worthless. But insofar as this is what Gutting has in mind, it is clear how we should respond. This point would provide no reason for thinking that beliefs that are held in virtue of membership in a religious tradition (such as the uniquely Islamic beliefs that Muhammad is the seal of the prophets, that Allah communicated the Qu'ran to the prophet Muhammad, and so forth) must be held religiously (in this sense). All that is involved is the statement of a stipulative, or at least selective, definition to the effect that to hold a belief religiously is to hold it nontentatively. But this provides us with little reason to think that the beliefs that are associated with the various religious traditions must be held religiously (in this sense). And that is what is at issue.

Gutting's second reason is as follows. He says that religious belief must involve decisive assent because

> what is believed religiously requires a total commitment to its implications for action that is incompatible with continuing reflection on its truth. Thus, at least as far as the fundamental content of their faith is concerned, believers should be prepared to forego any earthly goods and to run any temporal risk for the sake of what they believe. . . . The very fact that I act so decisively on a belief requires that my assent be decisive. (107–8)

Gutting's central point here concerns the need to be decisive in how one acts on one's religious belief. And decisive action requires decisive belief. Or at least it requires something more than tentative ("interim") assent.

First, a couple of preliminary points. I am sure that Gutting would agree that many actions that many religious believers have thought to be required by their beliefs are such that a less than total commitment to doing them would be desirable. On the other hand, actions that are manifestations of tentative belief can be very decisive. If I know tentative belief to be appropriate, for instance, I can be very decisive in attempting to refute those who disagree. I can also be decisive in my opposition to those who insist on non-tentative belief, and in persuading others of the appropriateness of tentative belief. And so on.[12] But we need to go beyond these preliminary and rather unimpressive points.

There is a part of Gutting's case here that is right. Consider this case. Suppose that I have been a devout Muslim who has held the usual core beliefs associated with Islam, and who has tried to live the life of a good Muslim. Suppose that, among other things, I have believed that I ought to try to convert as many non-Muslims as possible to Islam. It seems likely that if I were to become tentative in my Muslim beliefs, this would have an effect on the way in which I perceive the importance of the project of converting others. Presumably my sense of the importance of the project, and my sense that I have the obligation in question, would be diminished. It would be peculiar if this were not to occur. In cases of this sort, which involve actions whose perceived rightness or appropriateness or wrongness (etc.) is intimately linked to particular religious beliefs, it seems that when the assent ceases to be decisive and becomes tentative, actions too will be less decisive. To borrow from a remark in William James, martyrs would hardly sing in the flames for the sake of such belief.

In general, if beliefs that are associated with a tradition become tentative, some parts of the way of life associated with that tradition probably will become less viable: they may lose an underpinning in the absence of which they make less sense, or perhaps they may become psychologically more difficult or even out of the question. Thus some of the more radical biblical injunctions, such as the injunction to care not for the morrow or to love your neighbor as yourself, may fall into one of these categories: in the absence of a more than tentative belief in the love of God, such very demanding injunctions, whose primary justification is provided by various religious beliefs with which they are associated, simply make less sense. A way of life that is associated with a tradition might even, in its entirety, require an anchoring in something more than tentative belief.

However, the radical injunctions may, in the context of tentative belief, be cashed in in a somewhat different form, perhaps as ideals for which one should aim as far as possible rather than as standards that one is expected to meet fully. And much of the less radical moral content of many traditions may stand on its own, not needing the support of the religious claims with which this moral content has historically been associated. Consequently, even if the religious beliefs with which certain standards have been associated were not merely to become tentative, but were instead to be entirely abandoned, this need not undermine the sense that one ought to adhere to the relevant norms, or deprive one of the motivation to do so. It is also worth mentioning the possibility that people may vary with respect to the extent to which tentativeness in belief would bear on what is possible for them and on their behavior.

Gutting also says that "as far as the fundamental content of their faith is concerned, believers should be prepared to forego any earthly goods and to run any temporal risk for the sake of what they believe" (107). But suppose the loss or weakening of a fundamental belief, such as the belief that God exists, were (somehow or other) to achieve a great earthly good, perhaps a good that benefits many people. Is it obvious that it would be wrong to lose or weaken such a belief under such circumstances? Why should preserving our beliefs, even our fundamental beliefs, be that important? Perhaps the assumption is that the religious person will believe that (a) to abandon the fundamental content of her beliefs is to forgo otherworldly goods which depend for their availability on not abandoning those beliefs, and that (b) no loss of those otherworldly goods can be compensated for by any amount of earthly goods. But why believe (a) or (b)?

Or perhaps the idea, or part of it, is that the content of the relevant beliefs is (usually?) such that they require you to forgo any earthly goods for their sake: that is, the beliefs in question include one or more that expressly rule out changes in the fundamental content of the beliefs in question irrespective of what goods may thereby be achieved. But if it seems to you that in virtue of the fundamental content of your beliefs you are required to forgo some great earthly good, perhaps you should devote more energy to considering the possibility that there is something wrong with these beliefs or your understanding of them than you do to making sure that you forgo the goods in question. If the tentative believer is more flexible in this regard, that seems to be a mark in her favor.[13]

Or perhaps the idea is that one ought to forgo any earthly goods for oneself if acquiring those goods would result in a change in the fundamental content of one's beliefs, and that one ought to risk losing (for oneself) any such earthly goods, if this is necessary to avoid changing the fundamental content of one's beliefs. Cases in which people have had to declare that they have changed their religion in order to avoid death or torture may illustrate the point. Of course in such cases what is usually required is a declaration or explicit indication of some sort that one holds a certain belief, or a public renunciation of certain beliefs, and it is of course possible to make such a declaration or renunciation without meaning it: so perhaps such cases are not really cases in which one is changing a belief in order to achieve an earthly good or to avoid an earthly harm. Still, there probably is a relevant difference here between the tentative and the full believer: the tentative believer probably will be more willing to abandon her position for the sake of some worthwhile and important earthly good for herself and to think it appropriate to do so if this sort of situation were to arise. This is, in effect, just to repeat the point about martyrs being less willing to sing in the flames for the sake of such beliefs. But why think this to be an objection?

Gutting's third reason is that

> a merely interim assent is inconsistent with the typically religious attitude toward nonbelief . . . [Believers] must . . . assert the superiority of their belief and see even justified nonbelief as an unfortunate fact. (108)

It may well be true that certain typical attitudes to nonbelief would be abandoned if religious belief were tentative. But perhaps some of the changes in attitudes to nonbelief would be for the better. In fact, the attitude toward nonbelief that is a concomitant of the Critical Stance is one of its strengths rather than one of its weaknesses. The last section of this chapter, in which I explore the connections with tolerance, amplifies this theme.

If I believe p, I believe that p is the superior belief in that I believe that p, rather than not-p, is true, and that those who believe not-p are in an inferior state with respect to this particular belief. But all of this can be held tentatively. I can believe tentatively, say, both that God cares about human beings and that those who believe otherwise are mistaken. If I believe tentatively that God cares about human beings, then I must believe that it is unfortunate that some people believe otherwise in this very limited respect: it is better, in general, for people to have true beliefs, and I believe (tentatively) that on this issue others hold a belief that is false. If I am, say, a tentative Presbyterian, then I must believe, however tentatively, that those who deny my Presbyterian Christian beliefs—at least the core beliefs among them—are mistaken. But once you recognize the integrity of those who hold the opposing belief and the fact that this integrity has been deployed even in the articulation of the opposing belief, and the further fact that part (at least) of the explanation of disagreement is the fact that the relevant issues are ambiguous, much of the point of regarding their holding their beliefs as unfortunate is lost. People of integrity are likely to disagree in areas of ambiguity.[14]

Another way to respond to all of Gutting's points, and indeed to any other arguments for his claim that religious belief cannot be tentative, is to explore some types of commitment that are compatible with tentative belief. An exploration in this area will actually yield the result that tentative belief is compatible with much that matters about religious belief to those who hold it. I devote the next three sections of this chapter to this topic.

By way of introduction, consider this further point from Alasdair MacIntyre: he says that the acceptance involved in religious belief "must be of a kind compatible with the practice of worship. Thus it cannot be in any sense a conditional or provisional acceptance, for this would perhaps make it possible to say 'O God, if there is a God, save my soul, if I have one'; but it would not make it possible to worship."[15] Elaborating on what is involved in worship, MacIntyre says that

> [to] believe in God resembles not so much believing that something is the case as being engrossed by a passion: Kierkegaard compares the believer to a madman; he might equally have compared him to a lover. . . . The inability of the believer to adopt an abstract, neutral, speculative attitude to his belief resembles the lover's lack of objectivity. There is the

same total engagement. But if we compare belief to love it must be not so much to romantic love as to that married love which Kierkegaard distinguishes from romantic love by re-
ferring to the resolution and decision that underlies it." (194)

But the passion that MacIntyre considers essential to worship may be compatible with a
great deal of reticence about, for example, the object of worship. Actually MacIntyre's
emphasis seems to be on a certain type of passionate commitment *rather* than on an in-
sistence on being right. On this note I turn to some extended reflection about the sorts
of commitment that are compatible with tentative belief.

3. Tentative Belief and the Prospects for Commitment

I will not waste time on the trivial point that a sort of commitment that is compatible
with tentative belief is commitment to the appropriateness of tentative belief, although
certainly one might be deeply committed to the pursuit of, and advocacy of, this approach. Let us consider instead what it is (or at any rate was) to be committed to Marxism. Suppose I am a committed Marxist, dedicated to the overthrow of capitalism, public ownership of the means of production, the dictatorship of the proletariat, and so
forth. And suppose that my confidence in Marxism is shaken when I realize that many
of the tenets of Marxism are false.[16] Clearly I can become tentative about *many* distinctively Marxist beliefs, and even deny some of them, and still be committed to Marxism.
I may simply accept that it is not important for me to be right about all the details, or I
may be confident that a way of working them out will be found. I can continue to be
committed to Marxism in that I rely upon the truth of *much* of it. I can also put much of
my hope and trust in Marxism: I can look toward the glorious human future that Marxists believe will eventually come. The commitment that remains possible has at least two
dimensions: it involves a commitment to its being the case that certain states of affairs
obtain and will obtain, and it involves an investment of oneself in a cause.

   But can there be thoroughgoing commitment to Marxism if *all* of the distinctively
Marxist beliefs are tentatively held? The natural question to ask is *to what* would one be
committed if the entire content of your beliefs has become something about which you
are tentative? Actually there is much to be said about the sorts of commitment that remain viable. Let us try to set it forth systematically.

   Marxism may continue to provide you with an interpretation, or partial interpretation, of many phenomena even if all of your distinctively Marxist beliefs were to become tentative. For instance, it might continue to inform your interpretation of various
events, past or present. Thus you might find the notion of class interests particularly insightful in attempting to understand the reasons that a particular group accepts religious views that legitimate their privileged social or economic status. The texture of the
interpretation will be different just because the relevant beliefs are tentatively held. The
interpretation will feel more optional, more like one possibility among many; it too
will be affected by the awareness that there may be a need for revision. But this is
no barrier to its playing an important role in the interpretation of events. The total
picture can retain considerable liveliness and vigor, informing one's worldview to a
considerable extent. Corresponding points can be made in the case of the religious traditions. Thus the conception of oneself as a sinner can serve as a useful tool for under-

standing the tendency to self-aggrandizement or greediness that one sees in oneself or in others.

You might also *trust in* or *believe in* Marxism, and it may be the focus of many of your hopes, even if all the relevant beliefs are held tentatively. Whether or not there can be *thoroughgoing* belief in Marxism if all of the distinctively Marxist beliefs are held in a tentative way is, however, questionable. It seems that trust (or belief in) will, under these circumstances, have something of the character of longing or of hope.

Another obvious possibility is that you might be thoroughly committed to a certain way of life or to certain ways of behaving that have been associated, and that you and others associate, with your beliefs. In the case of the religious traditions these practical commitments may usefully be divided into, on the one hand, practice in accordance with the ethical implications of the tradition, as specified, for example, in the injunction to care for the poor that is common to many religious traditions and, on the other hand, practice of the distinctively religious rituals that are associated with a tradition, such as, for example, genuflecting in a certain fashion. (This distinction is not altogether clear. For example, a member of a tradition may feel morally obligated to take part in the rituals associated with the tradition. And there may be cases of behavior that are not clearly in one category rather than the other. But the distinction is still a useful one.) In both of these areas there is room for commitment, although we need to keep in mind the qualifications, mentioned earlier in the discussion of Gutting's reasoning. Thus some parts of a moral code that is associated with a tradition may lose their rationale, or may be more difficult to comply with, or may be harder to discern, once belief is tentative.

In the case of some religions, the relationship between, on the one hand, various practices and rituals, including for example those that are involved with worship, prayer (etc.) and, on the other hand, the cognitive aspect of religion, is such that people can change many of their relevant beliefs, either with respect to their content or with respect to the way in which they are held, while continuing with much the same practices and rituals and while thereby continuing to participate fully in the life of the tradition. Different traditions, and different strands in different traditions, vary with respect to the extent to which they permit this sort of disconnection of practice from belief. Some groups probably set out to make room for people to continue with the practices, whatever may be their beliefs, although in the case of many traditions there are changes in belief such that if they occurred one would be within the tradition only in name. The important point is that the tentative believer may be able to continue to participate in the life of his tradition even while he explores the question of how much of it he can maintain.

So tentative belief is compatible with thoroughgoing commitment to various practical implications of your tradition. We need to avoid thinking of this practical commitment in a one-dimensional way. It may not amount solely to commitment to certain ways of behaving. It may also involve, for instance, a commitment to grasping more thoroughly the implications for behavior of one's religious position, even if it is a position that is held tentatively. So we can see here an interweaving of practical with what we might think of as cognitive points.

There are cases that clearly fall into one category or the other, the cognitive or the practical: thus a commitment to loving your neighbor is a practical commitment, whereas a commitment to believing the tenets of your tradition if at all possible is a case of cognitive commitment. A commitment to the belief that you ought to love your neighbor seems to belong in both categories. But, once again, the fact that there are cases that fall into both categories and perhaps other unclear cases does not call into question the fact that there is a distinction here to be drawn.

Some further aspects of practical commitment that are worth considering in this context are discussed in an article by John King-Farlow and William Christensen, who advocate a "tentative-and-exploratory or 'hypothetical' approach" to theological claims.[17] Their article was a contribution to the debate of a few decades ago about the theological implications of theories of meaning that focus on verifiability and falsifiability, and their point is in part that the particular approach to religious belief that they endorse fits best with an acceptance of the falsifiability of theological claims. In the course of presenting their position, they consider the objection that "no beliefs held in [a tentative and exploratory] way may be held in matters of faith as matters of faith. For . . . faith requires a kind of serious commitment which excludes contemplation of any possible revision as a form of unfaithfulness or 'backsliding'" (119). King-Farlow and Christensen respond to this objection as follows:

> We answer that the relevant criteria of genuine faithfulness, seriousness, commitedness, etc. in matters of faith should be matters like willingness to make sacrifices for one's belief, to risk one's comforts, affections, and even one's life, willingness to re-examine and criticise oneself often in the light of faith's demands and sometimes to try forcing oneself to change a great deal to meet those demands. (120)

But none of this, King-Farlow and Christensen suggest, requires "total unwillingness to change one's mind."

In considering these remarks, it is important to keep in mind their historical context. Falsifiability requires only something as modest as a willingness to change one's mind under certain imaginary circumstances. And when King-Farlow and Christensen talk about the tentative approach to theological claims, they seem to understand beliefs to be tentative merely in virtue of the fact that they fall short of involving a total unwillingness to change one's mind about them.[18] But the less total we think the unwillingness to change one's mind to be—that is, the more openness to change, flexibility, (etc.) we think particular beliefs to involve—the less plausible is the claim that belief of this sort would not involve a diminution of the sorts of "genuine . . . committedness" referred to in the preceding quotation. As I have indicated earlier in response to Gutting's second point, it is hard to see how, for instance, your willingness to make sacrifices for your beliefs and your willingness to risk other things that matter to you would not be affected by the degree to which your beliefs are open to change.

In spite of the need for this qualification, part of what King-Farlow and Christensen propose can be appropriated for my purposes. Tentative belief (in my sense, and not only in their apparently narrower sense) can be accompanied by, for instance, a willingness to reexamine and criticize oneself, to try forcing oneself to change to meet the demands of faith, and to implementing the faith in practice to the extent that one can do so. Presumably the following is roughly true: to the extent that your beliefs come to be held tentatively (whether this be a matter of various beliefs being held more tentatively or a matter of more beliefs being held tentatively), the extent to which you are willing to make sacrifices for your beliefs, to risk your comforts, affections, or life, will be accordingly diminished. However, this is consistent with holding that belief that is fairly tentative can still be accompanied by a good deal of commitment to making sacrifices for your beliefs, to risking your comforts, and so forth.

Even if (as I have conceded in the preceding section and have mentioned here) some parts of the way of life associated with a tradition, or some of its ethical ideals or required practices, become less viable if the relevant beliefs are tentative, there are interesting and important respects in which tentativeness in belief may actually be accompanied by a heightened degree of appreciation of, and commitment to, the way of life or ideals or practices in question. In some cases such a heightened commitment may be necessary if tentative belief is to be sustained. In this way the commitment to behave in accordance with the tenets of the tradition may in fact be deepened for the tentative believer. If it runs a risk of lapsing into indifference, tentative belief may require more in this area than its nontentative counterpart.

The practical responses under discussion may be easier, and may occur more readily, if beliefs are decisive rather than tentative. One reason for this is that if everything is certain, it may just be obvious how one ought to react, and this very obviousness may propel one in the direction of certain attitudinal and behavioral responses. If, on the other hand, your beliefs are tentative, more concentration on and exploration of, for instance, their practical implications may be necessary. To pursue their implications for practice may therefore be more difficult and hence more impressive. Even maintaining the influence of the concepts, ideals, (etc.) of the tradition over your life may take effort and persistence. Hence even if tentative belief is less likely to be accompanied by, for instance, various practical manifestations, it may open opportunities for efforts in this area that are particularly laudable in virtue of the fact that they are more demanding. Values that seem less deeply embedded in the structure of things may need more persistent attention. This is all worth pointing out because the criticism may be forthcoming that tentative belief is easier and less demanding in its practical implications.

There is an additional sort of commitment that is somewhat practical in nature and that may consistently be felt by a tentative believer, namely, a commitment to the community in which one has acquired one's religious position. This may take the form of a commitment to protecting what is valuable in one's religious culture from being submerged by a hostile secular culture, if there happens to be such a threat, or indeed, in the case of a minority tradition, from being swamped by the majority. Since I am restricting discussion to groups that meet a high standard, we can assume that there is a lot about them that is worthwhile and worthy of preservation.[19]

Yet the character of the commitment that the tentative believer has to his community is complex. The tentative believer is poised in something of a no-man's-land between (a) a community of like-minded people who share a perspective and identity and who agree ("of course"!) that they have the right position on religious matters and (b) having no connection with any religious tradition, so that there is an absence of religion and all of its trappings from his life. Along another dimension too, the tentative believer, at least when conceived of as being motivated in part by the fact of religious diversity, is in a no-man's-land in that his beliefs are the product of a process of reaching across the religious traditions, of paying attention to the integrity of people in other traditions, and so forth. There are joys and comforts that come with a shared understanding and that are characteristic of a thriving and well-defined religious tradition which provides a sense of belonging: to all of this, too, the tentative believer has a somewhat detached exploratory attitude.

4. Tentative Belief and Cognitive Commitment

When we move from the practical to the cognitive sphere, other interesting possibilities emerge. The tentative believer is one who holds, in a tentative way, the core beliefs that are associated with his tradition. By way of considering the prospects for commitment in this area, consider the sorts of hope that such a person may have. Certainly you can hope that, say, God exists, that there will be an afterlife, that your enemies will fare well in the afterlife, and so forth. There are various sorts of hope that need to be considered, in addition to the obvious sort of hope that certain propositions will turn out to be true and that certain states of affairs will obtain. For instance, imagine that you have held certain beliefs but now find that they are at odds with beliefs whose pedigree is such that you feel that you ought to accept them or at least take them very seriously. You can hope that a way of reconciling your beliefs with what you have found to be at odds with them can be found. Hope of any of these sorts may be very intense, having the character of strong desire.

It would be natural for hope of the last sort mentioned, which is hope that a certain problem will be solved, to issue in a further sort of practical commitment, namely, a commitment to a search for a way to solve the problem in question, which might be a matter of reconciling the apparently incompatible beliefs. Such a search might involve, for example, thinking about the relevant issues, discussing them, not allowing them to fade from your attention, and not allowing yourself to become distracted by less important issues. And all of this in turn might be thought of as involving a commitment to providing some useful direction on these matters for others.

Another possibility for commitment in this area is probably the most interesting of all. This is the possibility that you may be committed to keeping as many as possible of your beliefs intact. This sort of perseverance, or attempt to keep one's faith, may involve an attempt to make as much of it as possible important to you: this might take the form of an effort to live as if the beliefs in question are true. It may also involve wanting the relevant beliefs to be true. The latter is to be contrasted with indifference to how many of one's beliefs one holds on to, and with a willingness to abandon them at the first sign of trouble. Actually it is more likely that someone would have a hierarchy among her beliefs such that there are some that she will abandon easily, some she will abandon only if pressed, and some she is committed to holding almost at all costs. Connected to this, there is likely to be an acceptance of the belief that it would be much better if your antecedently held beliefs, or many of them, turned out to be true.

5. Audi's Proposals

Although it is not his purpose to focus on this issue, some of Robert Audi's recent work raises the possibility that faith might be altogether thoroughgoing even if belief is less than thoroughgoing.[20] In order to get at the themes from Audi that are especially important for my purposes, we need first to get a sense of his general position.

Audi suggests that religious *faith* can be rational under circumstances in which religious *belief* is not rational. His aim is to redirect some of the discussion of the rationality of belief in the direction of the rationality of faith. He argues for

> a conception of faith which is both psychologically strong enough to enable it to play a central part in the cognitive dimension of religious commitment and evidentially modest enough to be rational on the basis of substantially less grounding than is required for the rationality of belief with the same content. (234)

Audi distinguishes attitudinal faith from propositional faith. Attitudinal faith is *faith in*: so examples of attitudinal faith include faith in God and faith in another person. Propositional faith, on the other hand, is faith *that* a certain proposition is true, such as the proposition that a certain person will recover from an illness. Audi's main concern is with propositional faith. Propositional faith (henceforth, while discussing Audi, I refer to this just as "faith" unless the context indicates otherwise) may or may not involve belief (216), and Audi limits his discussion, for the most part, to a type of faith that, he says, does not involve belief; he refers to this as "non-doxastic faith." He says that one can have faith that one will complete some very difficult assignment without believing that one will do so. Or one can have faith that a friend will prove to be reliable in some respect without believing this to be so.

> One might have strong faith in God and accompanying propositional faith that God is, say, sovereign, without having a belief that this is so, yet also without in any way doubting it. (223)

> [A] whole dimension of conviction is possible without beliefs of existential propositions about God: one can, for instance, grant that one does not know or believe that God exists, and that only one's faith is justified, without lacking a sense of surety, even a kind of certainty, about God, say about God's sovereignty over life and death. (227)

Yet belief and faith have a lot in common: "both are cognitive; both admit of rationality; both influence behavior, and both vary in many of the same dimensions, such as strength and centrality to the person's outlook on the world" (217).

On the other hand, belief and faith also differ in important ways. In particular, a greater degree of doubt about p is compatible with faith that p than is compatible with belief that p. Audi points out that if p turns out to be false, someone who believes that p is more likely to be surprised than someone who has faith that p. And he points out that if p turns out to be false, a belief that p would then be found to be mistaken, whereas faith that p would be misplaced.

I am doubtful that the sort of propositional faith that Audi discusses is best characterized as nondoxastic. It seems to me to be better understood as a sort of belief or as belief held under particular circumstances.[21] Nevertheless, there are important lessons to be learned from his analysis.

Audi says that

> the criteria for rational faith . . . are less stringent than the criteria for rational belief. I can have rational faith . . . that a friend is leading a constructive life, even though I know

I have little evidence for this. . . . [Rational] faith still requires a lesser degree of positive grounding than does rational belief." (219)

Audi says that even if we are evidentialists in our account of the rationality of belief, we need not be evidentialists in our account of the rationality of faith. Yet this sort of faith, Audi believes, can be the basis of a strong religious commitment. The strength of the commitment is manifested in, among other things, "the depth of one's resolution to try to quell doubts one may have about God's love and goodness, and the extent of one's determination to make one's religious outlook central in one's life" (223). It is also manifested in "its resistance to being forgotten or given up too readily upon discovery of counterevidence." He says that "[wholehearted] devotion to God is possible through such faith" (224).

In clarifying the sort of faith that Audi has in mind, it is useful to consider the respects in which he attempts to distinguish faith of the sort he has in mind from hope and also from belief. (The hope under discussion here is propositional hope, or hope that something or other is the case, and not hope of a more general sort, where this is a mood or an outlook on life.) Audi says that faith differs from hope on at least two counts.

First, faith involves a positive evaluative attitude that may be absent in the case of hope. His reason for thinking that this difference exists appears to be that "the positive attitudinal component in hope may be only desire" (219). But I doubt that this is correct, at least not when hope is discussed in religious contexts. For one thing, to hope for X, or at any rate to have hope that is associated with involvement in a religious tradition, is not only to desire X but also to regard X as something good. It is true that in nonreligious contexts we sometimes use the term "hope" in a more trivial, more neutral, and less serious way. ("I hope that I will win my racquetball game this afternoon." "I hope that we have not missed the highway exit.") But even in such trivial contexts there normally would be something which the person who hopes believes to be good about the hoped-for outcome. We would not count a person's attitude to X as one of hope unless he thought that X was good, although there need not be anything objectively good about something for which someone hopes. In any case, it obviously is hope as an attitude in a religious context that Audi has in mind. And in this context hope involves a positive evaluation of what is hoped for. It is hope for something that has been endorsed by the tradition. Perhaps Audi means that the positive evaluation involved in faith is different from that involved in hope, but it is not clear to me what the difference here is supposed to be.

The second respect in which hope differs from faith, according to Audi, is that "hope is . . . a cognitively weaker attitude than faith, as indicated by its compatibility with a higher degree of doubt" (219). Here Audi is on firmer ground. For it seems that one respect in which hope and faith differ is that faith involves more confidence than hope. Thus if I have faith that I will survive death I have more confidence that I will survive death, than if I merely hope that I will do so.

For this reason hope does not operate under the same restrictions as faith. Thus in spite of what I know about the probability that I will win the Illinois Lottery, I might reasonably hope that I will win it, but only under very unusual conditions would it be reasonable for me to have faith that I will do so. For this reason, situations in which it is wrong or unreasonable to have hope seem fewer than situations in which it is wrong or unreasonable to have faith.

I think that Audi implicitly recognizes another important respect in which hope and faith differ, although he never spells it out. Suppose that I hope that I will survive death. What more would need to be added to this hope in order to transmute it into faith? Certainly an infusion of confidence that I will survive death would propel me in that direction. But would the result be faith? I do not think that it would. For faith (and with Audi I continue to restrict discussion to propositional faith) has about it the suggestion of *reliance* on some person or being (or perhaps process or force). If I have faith that someone will recover from his illness, it seems that I am relying on some being or other to bring this about. In short, to use Audi's terms, propositional faith involves an element of attitudinal faith. Audi is, I think, recognizing this connection when he says that "at least when . . . faith is well developed, it implies . . . an attitude of trust in God, by which I mean in part a sense that God has seen to it, or will see to it, that ultimately things turn out as they should" (224), and again when he says that "where it is rational to have certain kinds of propositional faith, for instance that God is sovereign, it is rational to describe oneself as having faith in God" (228). His recognition of this connection between propositional and attitudinal faith is also implicit in a remark he makes early in his essay, in the course of clarifying the distinction between belief and faith: he says that if p turns out to be false, then one's belief that p will have been mistaken, whereas one's faith that p "might be shown to be *misplaced*, and it would be *disappointed*" (217). This talk of misplacing faith signifies that to have faith is to place it in some being or other. Again, when he is distinguishing faith from belief he says that faith has a positive attitudinal component (225).

As mentioned, Audi also discusses the relationship between faith and *belief*. For it is central to his position that what he is endorsing is not a form of belief. He says that both faith and belief come in weak and strong forms. But weakness and strength in the one area are not the same as weakness and strength in the other. Weakness in belief would involve a lack of "a sense of surety" (223); weak belief "is not strongly entrenched or highly resistant to dissipation through forgetting, or to being chipped away by time, or crushed by confrontation with counterevidence" (223) Weakness in faith, on the other hand, "is more a matter of a lack of sustaining force in the agent's behavior, emotion, and cognition" (223).

But it seems that the features that are said to characterize weakness in faith will also be features of weakness in belief: for if weak belief lacks a sense of surety and "is not strongly entrenched or highly resistant to dissipation through forgetting, or to being chipped away by time, or crushed by confrontation with counterevidence" (223) it is likely that these features of it would manifest themselves in "a lack of sustaining force in the agent's behavior, emotion, and cognition." And, correspondingly, weak faith, that is, faith that lacks "sustaining force in the agent's behavior, emotion, and cognition" is also very likely to manifest those features that Audi takes to characterize weak belief: it probably will involve a lack of a sense of surety; and of it too it can be said that it "is not strongly entrenched or highly resistant to dissipation through forgetting, or to being chipped away by time, or crushed by confrontation with counterevidence." It is natural to think of the two sorts of weakness as going hand in hand. So far, then, the contrast with belief is unclear.

Although it is not clear to what extent Audi is willing to go along with this claim, it seems that the sort of faith that he has in mind ought to be responsive to the available relevant evidence. And in this respect, too, it resembles belief. Consider a simple example. John is a friend who has something of a drinking problem, and as a result sometimes fails to keep appointments and is often unreliable in this and in other ways. Suppose that I make an appointment to meet him at a certain time and suppose that I have faith that he will show up. It seems that the reasonableness of this faith will be in large part a function of his earlier track record, and it seems that the strength of my faith ought to reflect this record. If John has *never* kept our appointments, or has done so only on the rarest of occasions, then at most all that it is reasonable for me to have is very weak faith that he will show up on some particular occasion, assuming of course that there is nothing that distinguishes this particular occasion from all the others. (For example, his promises to be there without fail lack any special tone of sincerity that would persuade me that this time he *really* means it, and he shows no signs of having recently undergone a dramatic reformation of character.) Strong faith that he will come through on this occasion would not be rational. And it would not be rational because of the available evidence, and for much the same reason that strong belief would not be rational.

Faith that John will show up on some occasion differs from strong belief in that, among other things, faith—even strong faith—involves a lack of psychological certainty; or at least one is not psychologically certain of its cognitive content (230). But then faith is no different from weak belief in this regard. So how does faith differ from weak belief? I suggest that faith that John will keep an appointment is best distinguished from weak belief that he will do so in the following four respects.

(a) To have faith that John will show up as arranged involves wanting him to show up or at least being well disposed to the possibility in question. This need not be the case for there to be weak belief. I could have weak (or even strong) belief that he will show up without wanting him to show up, indeed even if I were to dread his showing up.

(b) To have faith that John will show up as arranged also involves thinking that it is right that he should do so and wrong for him not to do so. Again, this need not be the case for there to be weak belief. So there is a normative component here that is distinct from my being favorably disposed toward, or wanting, the state of affairs in question and that may be absent in the case of weak (or strong) belief. This is particularly likely to be prominent in the case of religious faith.

(c) Faith also involves a component of the following sort. Whether or not John shows up is up to John. To have faith that he will show up is to place one's confidence in him and to view him in a favorable light to some extent: this is the attitudinal element. Again, this need not be so for weak belief. Audi says that the faith that he has in mind can provide the *basis* for faith in the attitudinal sense; maybe there is some truth in this, but it also seems to *involve* attitudinal faith.

(d) Finally, there is the role of the will in faith. Audi says that "whatever psychological certainty there is in [faith] comes from the contribution of the will rather than from demonstration. We might compare that certainty to the strength of faith in the sense of its resistance to erosion and degree of influence on the subject's life *rather* than the doxastic confidence level of its cognitive component; and this kind of certainty seems consistent with non-doxastic faith" (231). Although the degree of psychological certainty involved in faith ought to be calibrated to some extent to the evidence and to the apparent reliability of the person in whom faith is put, there is a special role for the will that is a function of the attitudinal dimension to faith. For example, whether or not I have faith that John will appear as arranged will depend on whether or not I place my confidence in him. And this is something over which I am able to exercise some control. For example, I may decide to give him yet another chance to prove himself even if he has often let me down.

Actually I am inclined to think that propositional faith is *the same thing* as weak belief that involves, or is combined with, ingredients (a) to (d).[22] Audi thinks that this is not so. One of his reasons is that "at least in non-religious contexts the closer one comes to . . . belief, the less natural it is to speak of faith rather than simply belief." (He seems to offer this by way of an explanation of why "propositional faith does not entail having the corresponding belief" [216].) But the fact that it is less natural to talk of faith in a certain context and more natural to talk of belief provides neither reason to think that faith does not involve belief nor reason to think that faith is not a type of belief just as, in another context, the fact that it is less natural to talk of knowledge in some circumstances and more natural to talk of belief does not provide reason to think either that knowledge does not involve belief or that knowledge is not a type of belief.

Another difference that Audi thinks there to be between faith and belief is that if p turns out to be false, belief that p is *mistaken* whereas faith that p is *misplaced* rather than mistaken; or at least faith *need not* be mistaken. But I am not persuaded by this point either. If I have faith that John will show up at some place and time that we have arranged, and he does not do so, then I am mistaken. My faith that he would show up on this occasion is indeed also misplaced. This dimension of faith is present in virtue of the fact that my belief that he will show up involves reliance on John. And the source or genesis of the mistake has a particular character in the case of faith: it arises from an investment of my confidence in someone. I see no reason being offered here to deny, or even to doubt, that propositional faith *involves* belief.

Audi considers the possibility that propositional faith is reducible to "a complex of beliefs and attitudes, for example to some degree of belief that p and a positive attitude to p's being the case." He responds as follows:

> It is true that faith implies some degree of positive attitude toward the state of affairs in question; but adding such an attitude to belief is still not sufficient for propositional faith. Far from salvaging a reductionist strategy of analyzing faith in terms of belief, this move shows that in addition to finding an appropriate belief component, the reductionist would have to show this belief to imply an appropriate attitude. I doubt that either of these conditions can be met. (218)

But, as I have suggested above, it is a complex along the lines of (a) to (d) that would need to be added to belief: so the important question to ask is whether an account of faith that includes those components in it, as well as belief, would work.[23]

I have suggested that Audi underestimates the place of evidence in supporting faith. Consider the case mentioned in a passage quoted earlier. Audi says that he can have rational faith that a friend is leading a constructive life *even though he knows that he has very little evidence for this* (219). This seems wrong. Presumably there are numerous propositions pertaining to his friend for which Audi has very little evidence. These include, let us suppose, the propositions that his friend is fighting poverty in Africa, is leading a constructive life as a salesman, and has died and has gone to heaven. Surely not all of these propositions are suitable candidates for rational faith. What would it take to make it rational for him to have faith that one such proposition rather than another is true? It seems that the evidence must play a role here: the fact that the friend always showed considerable promise of leading a constructive life would provide some evidence for his leading a constructive life now; an interest in Africa and in combating the ravages of poverty would provide evidence for his acting on the basis of those interests; and so forth. This is so even if faith differs from belief in that it involves *more* than a certain reaction to the evidence. It seems that in order for faith that p to be rational, there must be some basis to conclude (and probably one must actually conclude on that basis) that a case can be made for p.

Furthermore, since the faith in question admits of degrees, it is possible for us to go wrong not only by investing our faith in the wrong places but also by investing it to too great or too little an extent. How much is the right amount, it seems, will be in large part a function of the track record of the person in question. Faith can be seriously misplaced. The perils in this area seem at least as serious as they are in the area of belief. So faith can go wrong in being invested in the wrong place and in being invested to the wrong extent. And these are related, since what the right extent is will be determined in large part by features of the being in whom it is invested.

But in spite of these various objections Audi is right, I think, that there is a sort of faith that need only meet a lower standard for rationality than must be met by belief, or, as I think of it, by belief of other sorts. Just because faith involves investing your confidence in someone, you have something additional that may provide the basis for your going out on a limb to some extent. But then this attitudinal element is warranted only if, for example, the track record of the being in whom you put your confidence is of the right sort, and is known by you to be so. My faith that John will show up on a particular occasion involves and relies upon faith in him, and my attitude to the proposition that he will do so can derive support from this faith in him. Again, compare the belief of a nonreligious person that her child will get well, which is backed up only by a knowledge of the statistics that tell you what percentage of children with such an illness will recover, and the faith of a religious person which is backed up by the belief that God will look after his child. The faith in question derives a lot of its support from the trust in, or reliance on, God that underpins it. It seems that we have here something that obeys somewhat different rules from other sorts of belief. Faith of this sort requires less evidence and always involves a certain amount of risk.

However, the prospects for *religious* faith (of this sort) are somewhat limited. Think of it this way. Propositional faith is underpinned by belief in, or trust in, a certain being. As I have said, even if all the beliefs that we have about such a being are tentative, there is still room for trust. But it will be trust of a more hesitant, uncertain, and exploratory character. And the fact that it has this nature is bound to have an influence on the character of the propositional faith that is underpinned by it. For a start, it seems that the nature of one's faith that a certain being in whom one trusts will do such-and-such is bound to be affected if one is tentative even in one's beliefs about the existence of such a being and if one's trust reflects this tentativeness. (Imagine the implications for my faith that John will meet me at the appointed hour if it somehow or other turns out not to be completely clear even that John exists. Perhaps even in the belief that he exists I have been the victim of an elaborate deception. Or it might be unclear that John still exists: maybe we made the appointment some years ago.) Nevertheless, tentativeness in belief does not altogether exclude the possibility of faith of the sorts under discussion. Because such faith involves a sense of reliance on someone or some being, it can cope with a certain amount of risk. A considerable amount of faith, therefore, may be compatible with tentative belief. It will not have the certainty that Audi takes to characterize nondoxastic faith. But it may nevertheless play a role in the life of the tentative believer.

So, to conclude this discussion, it is clear that there are a number of respects in which commitment is compatible with tentative belief. This is so even though the more tentative one is—that is, the more openness to change, flexibility (etc.) certain beliefs involve—the less plausible is the claim that belief of this sort would not involve a diminution of the sorts of commitment I have discussed. *How* wholehearted commitment of any of the sorts I have discussed is will be a function of, among other things, how prominent it is in someone's thinking, how seriously it is taken, how often it comes to mind, and, in general, how important it is to the person who holds it.

6. Tentative Belief and Tolerance

Next I turn briefly to the topic of tolerance. I understand tolerance to be a constituent of tentative belief so that belief would not count as tentative unless it involved (even if only dispositionally) tolerance of alternative beliefs. However, the view that tolerance is something that would inevitably accompany tentative belief, or would generally accompany it, even though it is not part of it, would be equally useful for my purposes. What I want to focus on is the *sort* of tolerance that is relevant. By doing so I understand myself to be displaying the appeal of tentative belief. In the next chapter I introduce a series of arguments in its defense and, more broadly, in defense of the Critical Stance.

What is tolerated may be, for instance, a culture or a person or an ideology or a type of music, but my concern here is of course primarily with tolerance of beliefs. It is useful to distinguish two different notions of tolerance, or at least two different things that people may have in mind when they think of tolerance, for it may be that one of them is more accurately described as tolerance than is the other. There is what I shall call *weak* tolerance. You weakly tolerate something when you live with it, accept it, endure it, or put up with it, and when you refrain from reacting negatively to it in spite of the fact that there is something wrong with it, or that it is not as you would wish it to be. *Deep* tolerance, on the other hand, involves taking the object of tolerance more seriously, and it involves something like *respect*. It is likely to be accompanied by a willingness to protect and preserve what is tolerated, whereas weak tolerance is likely to be accompanied by a mere willingness not to attack it. As an attitude to another group deep tolerance would involve, for example, a willingness to interact extensively with them in a variety of social contexts and a willingness to form friendships with them.

Both sorts of tolerance, weak and deep, are possible only if you have a particular point of view or position; what you tolerate is a significant challenge to that point of view or position. Both involve the assumption that your view is better than the view of which you are tolerant: what is tolerated has something wrong with it, at least in your view. Yet you refrain from reacting negatively to it.

But deep tolerance (of the beliefs of others) is to be understood as allowing that there is some significant likelihood that the others with whom you disagree may be right and you may be wrong. To have deep tolerance is also, in effect, to acknowledge that you can see how a reasonable person could hold the view in question. It involves a recognition that those with whom you disagree are people whom it is worthwhile to approach with rational arguments. Since we assume that those whose views we are deeply tolerating are people with whom we disagree (as defined), we are in effect assuming that the views in question are in fact held by reasonable people. Respect for the person who disagrees is part of what is involved in this sort of tolerance—even though there is no avoiding thinking that they are wrong on the matters about which you and they disagree.

Another respect in which deep tolerance differs from weak tolerance is that it need not be reluctant. If you endure or put up with something, there is always reluctance involved: presumably it would be better in your view if you did not need to put up with it. Deep tolerance, on the other hand, values the other position to some extent for its own sake and sees it as worthy of preservation, and perhaps as worthy of exploration. Actually weak and deep tolerance are two points on a continuum that extends from, at one extreme, the utter rejection of other perspectives (complete intolerance) to, at the other extreme, regarding them all as equally good (complete neutrality). Deep tolerance is farther along on the continuum in the direction of neutrality than is weak tolerance.

Even weak tolerance involves a recognition that the other point of view is not *altogether* unacceptable: this is signified by the fact that you are willing to live with it and with its adherents. And in the area of religion, even weak tolerance can be quite an accomplishment. The standard argument against allowing others to proselytize or preach is that if they do so they will lead people astray, and why shouldn't we do everything we can to prevent *that*? Isn't preventing that our first and deepest duty? I think it is clear that to move from intolerance to even weak tolerance on such a matter as this is to go through a very significant shift. But while it is an accomplishment, in the area of religion weak tolerance does not go far enough, assuming that we are dealing with groups among whom there is disagreement of the sort we have discussed. Instead we should aim for deep tolerance; but deep tolerance, and in general the Critical Stance with which it is closely associated, has revolutionary implications.

There is an important respect in which what I call weak tolerance may not be so weak and a respect in which what I call deep tolerance may not be so deep. For sometimes, at any rate, weak tolerance is an attitude that you might take to what you have previously regarded as alien or even repulsive, and certainly wrong, and in such cases it may be very difficult to be (even) weakly tolerant. Deep tolerance, on the other hand, may sometimes be plainer sailing. Thus if you view the traditions toward which you have deep tolerance as worthy of respect, exploration (etc.), having deep tolerance of them will not be such a difficult task: it will come more naturally. You see others and their views as less of a threat, and you have less need to endure them. So weak tolerance can be demanding, while deep tolerance can be easier to feel and display.[24]

However, in thinking about the ease with which either type of tolerance can be achieved, we need to be clear about where one is starting from when it is achieved. It is clear that a move from intolerance to deep tolerance would demand far more from one than a move from intolerance to weak tolerance. The claim that deep tolerance would be easier to achieve than weak tolerance is plausible only if we assume that the attitudes to the beliefs of others that are associated with deep tolerance are already more or less in place. Thus if you see the views of others as worthy of respect, exploration, and preservation, and as having a very good chance of being true, then deep tolerance will come easily. In fact, the ingredients of deep tolerance are already in place. But then the corresponding point holds in the case of weak tolerance: it too is hardly an accomplishment if you have already adopted a live-and-let-live attitude to the views of others, if you have already decided that although those who hold certain views are wrong, they are not, for example, so dangerous that they should not be allowed to practice their religion, or so repulsive that you must wipe them out at the first opportunity. In that case you already are in a position from which weak tolerance would come naturally. The element of truth here, then, is just this: weak tolerance of what is regarded as wrong but also as repugnant is more difficult and demanding than deep tolerance of what is regarded as wrong but not repugnant and instead worthy of respect.

The arguments for deep tolerance toward the religious views of others with whom there is disagreement include the following pragmatic argument: although (mere) weak tolerance in the area of religion will help you to get along with each other to some extent, it will probably always make for unstable relations. For it is very likely to become clear that your tolerance of others is *only* weak: a comment here, a raised eyebrow there, will give the game away. Deep tolerance, on the other hand, signifies that you are more or less happy with other religious groups as they are. If they know this, they will feel that they are accepted by you and find it a lot easier to get along with you.

A simple appeal to intuitions is also in order here. In the community in which I live in the American Midwest, as in almost all communities in the United States, the majority of people are Christians of one or another denomination. But there are also various minority religious groups: Jews, Muslims, Hindus, Bahai, Buddhists, Jains, Sikhs, and so forth. An absence of even weak tolerance on the part of any one group toward the others would be very unfortunate. But it is not enough for one group to *put up with*, or *endure*, the others and their beliefs and practices. Each group needs to go further than that, although it cannot give up the belief that it is right, unless it is to cease altogether to be what it is. I would say the same about the community in which I grew up in the west of Ireland, in which Catholics and Protestants live side by side: the notion that it would be enough for members of my community to put up with or endure the other community, or vice versa, is simply a deeply repulsive one. In such cases more than weak tolerance is needed. The reason is that in these cases there is disagreement of the sort under discussion, which involves the groups in question meeting a high standard.

It is very difficult to separate tolerance of the religious beliefs of others from tolerance of their behavior, and to separate tolerance of their beliefs and behavior from tolerance of them. After all, it is not beliefs in the sense of propositions that we tolerate, but rather people's acceptance of beliefs, and what matters most about their acceptance of their beliefs is in large part a function of their related behavior and of the way of life and type of person that go with the beliefs in question. I do not suggest that there is no distinction to be drawn between, on the one hand, tolerating the beliefs of others and, on the other hand, tolerating their behavior, or tolerating them. Nor do I mean to imply that it is out of the question that we would tolerate certain beliefs and yet not tolerate certain behavior that we associate with those beliefs. But, in practice, the main reason that it is difficult for us to tolerate certain beliefs has everything to do with the behavior that we associate with the beliefs and with the people who accept them. That weak tolerance of the religious beliefs of others is not enough is connected to the fact that, in general, weak tolerance *of others*, in particular of people of integrity, is not enough. There has to be something really wrong with others for you to want to settle for a mere weak tolerance of them. Deep tolerance of the religious beliefs of people of integrity is appropriate partly because they *are* people of integrity and their religious beliefs probably are precious to them, and probably are central to their conception of themselves, and to their way of life. To merely put up with their beliefs is to merely put up with them; and that usually is not good enough. Tolerance of the deep sort is a natural ingredient in the Critical Stance, given its openness to others who meet a certain standard.

9

THE CRITICAL STANCE II

Arguments and Objections

In this chapter I provide further arguments for the Critical Stance and respond to some arguments against it. I take the case presented thus far to have at least helped to display its appeal. Also, I have already responded to some objections, such as the claim that religious belief cannot be tentative. And by showing that the Critical Stance leaves room for types of commitment that typically are thought to characterize, or to be associated with, religious belief, I have shown that it can serve as the basis for some important aspects of what it is to be a religious believer, and that it therefore cannot fairly be rejected by religious people on the grounds that it simply involves an abandonment of their faith. I return to this theme in section 5 of this chapter, in the course of responding to various objections to my position. As was the case in chapters 7 and 8, my main concern is with privileged people and with the reactions that may reasonably be expected from them.

I take it to be *obvious* that the presence of disagreement of the sort I have been discussing (and as defined at the end of section 4 of chapter 7) provides reason to believe that one's relevant beliefs may be mistaken and hence deserve examination. But, fortunately, we need not leave it at that. I will discuss three main reasons that disagreement provides reason for us to adopt the Critical Stance. These reasons are relevant to beliefs in other areas, but as I proceed I will make some comments specifically about beliefs about religion. I assume that beliefs in this area do not have such a distinctive character that the general rules pertaining to beliefs that I discuss here do not apply to them.

1. The Appeal to Ambiguity

First I want to return to the topic of ambiguity. The presence of disagreement suggests that the matters about which there is disagreement are ambiguous. In particular, disagreement in the area of religion suggests that this is an area in which the available evidence does not point clearly in one direction rather than another, and it suggests that the matters about which religions purport to speak are matters about which it is unclear what we ought to believe. The case developed in chapters 1 to 6 is also a partial defense of the claim that many issues that are central to the religions are ambiguous. My discussion of religious experience in chapters 10 and 11 will further buttress this position. Although many people have religious experiences and those experiences provide them with much justification for holding their religious beliefs, they do not suffice to show that the beliefs in question are correct—or so I shall argue. In general, many of the phenomena to which appeal is made by those who accept a particular religious position have their counterparts in the case of the other traditions. Two small pieces of evidence that this is so: the basic belief apologetic, as developed by Alvin Plantinga, can be deployed as readily by members of non-Christian traditions as by Christians. And the same goes for the doxastic practice apologetic of William P. Alston, as Alston acknowledges. These are two of the best games in town; and many teams are equally capable of playing them. These considerations provide additional support for the claim that the world is religiously ambiguous.

If there is ambiguity in a certain area, our beliefs, and our attitude toward our beliefs, ought to reflect this fact. For one thing, when there is ambiguity in a certain area, it is more likely than it otherwise would be that people may be mistaken in what they believe in that area. The more likely it is that our beliefs in a certain area are mistaken, the greater is our obligation to examine those beliefs, ceteris paribus. The reason is that, in general, it is a bad thing for us to have mistaken beliefs and, correspondingly, it is a good thing for us to have true beliefs.[1] The latter is good from a practical point of view and good in itself. So we ought to take steps to achieve it.

I assume that, in general, scrutiny of beliefs, particularly by people with integrity, makes for believing truths rather than falsehoods. If it is, or typically is, good and worthwhile that we should believe truths rather than falsehoods, then presumably believing truths rather than falsehoods on matters of importance is particularly good and worthwhile. Hence it must typically be particularly good that we should examine our beliefs about matters of importance. (I discuss some exceptional cases later.) I will call this first consideration *the appeal to ambiguity*.

The presence of disagreement is a warning sign, an indication that there may be something wrong with our beliefs in a certain area. It is also a sign that the relevant area is one in which the procedure of relying on our intuitions may be unreliable. After all, many people with integrity are going wrong in the beliefs they hold about it.

Beliefs about which there is disagreement, particularly since by definition these are beliefs about matters of importance, and since by definition the disagreeing parties include people of integrity, are especially deserving of scrutiny. The argument that begins from the fact of disagreement and appeals to ambiguity is basically an embellishment of this reasoning. It goes as follows:

(Premise 1) Disagreement about an issue or area of inquiry provides reason to think that that issue or area of inquiry is an ambiguous one.

(Premise 2) If an issue or area of inquiry is ambiguous, it is more likely than it otherwise would be that our views on it are mistaken.

(Premise 3) The more likely it is that our views on an issue are mistaken, the more likely it is that we have an obligation to examine our own beliefs and the beliefs of the other groups with whom there is disagreement about that issue.

(Premise 4) If an issue or area of inquiry is ambiguous, it is more likely than it otherwise would be that we have an obligation to examine our own beliefs and the beliefs of other groups about that issue.

(Conclusion) Disagreement about an issue or area of inquiry provides reason to think that each side has an obligation to examine beliefs about that issue.

Premise 4 follows from premises 2 and 3. And the conclusion—the E-principle—follows from premises 1 and 4. For if we have reason to think that an issue or area of inquiry suffers from ambiguity, and if that would make it more likely than it otherwise would be that we have an obligation to examine our relevant views, then we have reason to think that we ought to examine our views about that issue. So the crucial premises here are 1, 2, and 3.

Premise 1 says that disagreement provides reason to think that an issue is ambiguous. When there is disagreement (as that notion is understood here), the explanation of it cannot be, for instance, that one side has thought carefully while the others have not. The best way to explain its occurrence would seem to be to appeal to the ambiguous nature of the relevant topic. Or if this is too strong, ambiguity ought at least to have a central place in the best explanation. At least this is so in areas in which relativism is not a plausible option. If relativism were a plausible option, we would have an explanation of why there is at least an appearance of disagreement, although the disagreement would in that case be *only* apparent. I take it that relativism is not a plausible option in the area of religion.[2] Thus, either God spoke to Moses out of the burning bush or God did not do so; either we are reincarnated or we are not; either Jesus was born of a virgin or Jesus was not born of a virgin; either Jesus was resurrected or Jesus was not resurrected; and so forth. The notion that it is true for one group but false for another that such events occurred is unintelligible.

Premise 2 seems clearly correct. Presumably we are more likely to go astray in forming beliefs about ambiguous issues, and less likely to do so in the case of issues that are straightforward.

Premise 3 is particularly plausible in the case of important beliefs, and beliefs that are the subject of disagreement are, by definition, important. To the extent that we have reason to think that we may be wrong about important beliefs, we have reason to think that such beliefs ought to be examined.

Perhaps the extent to which we have reason to think that we may be wrong about an important belief should bear on the strength of the relevant obligation rather than on the extent to which we have reason to believe that we have such an obligation, but while there is a distinction here—between, for instance, having reason to believe that we have a very strong obligation and having very strong reason to believe that we have an obligation—it is one that makes little practical difference. Both seem to bear in more or less the same way on the need to examine and on how extensive the process of examination should be.

Another feature of premise 3 that is worthy of comment is that it assumes that it is important that our beliefs should be true: for the fact that a process of examination will help to make it more likely than it otherwise would be that a belief is true partly gives rise to this obligation. This does not require that the person in question cares about having true beliefs: the importance may arise from a person's social role, irrespective of whether she recognizes that it does so.

The preceding argument, if sound, is far from being a proof that there is an obligation to examine beliefs about which there is widespread disagreement. All that the conclusion says is that the fact that there is widespread disagreement provides reason to think that it is also a fact that we have such an obligation. I say more about what this amounts to later.

The appeal to ambiguity also provides support for the T-principle. The T-principle says that a certain response is appropriate when there is disagreement of the sort under discussion. In accordance with premise 1 of the argument for the E-principle presented earlier, there is reason to think that a subject about which there is disagreement is ambiguous, and hence that it is a subject about which it is easy to go wrong. One strategy for coping with an awareness that your beliefs in an area may be wrong is to hold them in a tentative way, a way that involves openness to change and openness to alternatives.

Finally, my aim here has been to argue for both the E-principle and the T-principle by starting from the fact of disagreement and suggesting that this, in turn, supports the idea that the world is religiously ambiguous. But, as indicated in earlier chapters, there are many other reasons, in addition to the fact of disagreement, to believe that the world is religiously ambiguous. That this is so further strengthens the case for the Critical Stance.

2. The Appeal to the Integrity of Others and to Respect for Others

A second reason that disagreement contributes to a case for the Critical Stance is this: among the procedures and strategies we normally and properly use in acquiring and testing beliefs in numerous areas is the strategy of relying on the relevant views of those who seem to have integrity. We need to know who can be relied upon. We seem constantly to assess the credibility of others, screening—much of the time fairly unconsciously—those with whom we interact. And what we find is that some people can be relied upon to a great extent. They know a great deal, avoid exaggeration, confabulation, and distortion, are intelligent and reflective, and admit ignorance when it is appropriate to do so; they think carefully and judiciously, and in general display what I have called integrity. These are the sorts of people about whom we would say that the fact that they accept a belief speaks for that belief.

It seems obvious that those who can best lay claim to integrity are deeply divided on religious matters. Such people include many religious thinkers in the various religious communities. This fact, too, should be reflected in our beliefs in the area of religion. Whereas widespread agreement among those whom it is reasonable to consider as having integrity, or reasonable to consider as people upon whom we can rely, gives reason to hold a belief, widespread disagreement among people of that caliber gives reason to question whether a belief we hold (and about which there is disagreement) is correct, to examine the available alternatives, and to be tentative in our relevant beliefs.

I realize that it is always possible that an opponent may argue that the conditions of disagreement are not met with respect to the particular area of inquiry under discussion. Just as others may seem to us to be competent as acquirers of beliefs in, say, the areas of history and chemistry but not, say, in their beliefs about child rearing, so some may claim that only their own religious group has competence in the area of religion, and that all other religious groups lack competence. As I have indicated, there is no way to show that the advocates of such a view are wrong. And because of the lack of connections between the subject matter of beliefs about religion and the subject matter in other areas, we are unable to rely on such connections with a view to establishing competence in the area of religion. Perhaps the best we can do here is point out that people of integrity are to be found in the various traditions, and to suggest that this is about as good an indicator as we can have that competence is not restricted to one group.

A related point concerns respect and may be put as follows. We have an obligation to respect the rationality and seriousness of other groups. A recognition that other groups have a history of reflection and of refinement and development of their views, and a recognition that members of those groups are just as intelligent as members of our own group, that their interest in the truth is as great as ours, and their need to find plausible explanations in crucial areas of human life as urgent as ours, is a strong reason to subject our beliefs to examination, just as it is a strong reason to be tentative in our relevant beliefs. The fact that views which are opposed to ours have had a central place in enduring and rich cultures strongly suggests that there must be something valuable or worthwhile about them. Not to recognize this is uncharitable and parochial.

The respect for others in question is not the sort of respect for rational agents that Kantians urge upon us. It is rather a matter of appreciating others as responsible acquirers and holders of beliefs. Respect for them as persons is compatible with thinking that their beliefs are not worthy of serious consideration, and with thinking that the fact that they hold certain beliefs gives those beliefs no claim whatsoever on our attention.

Respect for others as acquirers of beliefs, while not incompatible with thinking that they are wrong on any particular issue, suggests that their beliefs in an area in which we disagree with them are at least worthy of some attention. There is likely to be a close connection in practice between this sort of respect for others and an awareness that we ought to subject our own beliefs to scrutiny. We might think of having this sort of respect for others as a matter of having epistemological good manners: we display such an attitude when we consider the fact that others disagree with us to warrant an examination, both of our own beliefs and of their beliefs on the matters on which we disagree.

Further, its connection with respect for others is one of the attractive features of tentative belief. For this sort of belief involves considering those who disagree with you as peers, or as close to peers, with respect to the integrity they display in the acquisition and maintenance of their beliefs. This provides reason to take their beliefs seriously. To disregard the point of view of others is to assume that they are very far from being your peers. And tentative belief has the further connected virtue of seeing the beliefs of others as providing rich terrain that is worthy of exploration. Let us call this second set of considerations *the appeal to the integrity of others and to respect for others.*

What are essentially the same issues may also be approached by considering what I shall call the appeal to conservatism. In order to explain this point I need to comment briefly on methodological conservatism, or conservatism as I shall call it. The various formulations of conservatism share the idea that the fact that someone holds a belief actually is a reason for that person to hold it.[3] This topic of conservatism is a large and complicated one; here I will just point out some respects in which versions of conservatism differ, and then draw out some implications for my discussion.

First, the fact that S holds a belief may be understood to justify S in holding that belief; or it may be understood to contribute something to the justification for S's holding that belief. Obviously the weaker reading is more plausible and easier to defend.

Second, conservatism may be understood to come into play only when there is epistemic indeterminacy. On this reading the fact that someone holds a belief would provide a reason to hold that belief only if the belief is epistemically indeterminate. In deploying the notion of epistemic indeterminacy I will follow Gary Gutting, according to whom p is epistemically indeterminate if "the evidence of which [S] is aware relevant to the truth or falsity of p does not entitle [S] to believe p and does not entitle [S] to believe not-p."[4] However, it seems counterintuitive to think of conservatism as applicable only if there is epistemic indeterminacy. For instance, if the fact that S believes p justifies S in believing p when p is epistemically indeterminate, then it seems that the fact that S believes p ought at least to bear favorably on whether S is justified in believing p when p is *not* epistemically indeterminate, perhaps providing a prima facie and defeasible reason for S to believe p. Even if the fact that S believes p does not justify S in believing p but merely counts in favor of the rationality of S's believing p, or contributes in some other way to p's having a positive epistemic status for S, when the evidence balances out, it seems that it ought also to do so—even if to a lesser extent—when the evidence does not balance out. If, for instance, there is just a little more evidence against p than there is for p, perhaps in that case the fact that S believes p can help to balance things out. So it seems best not to think conservatism to be restricted to situations in which there is epistemic indeterminacy.

Third, versions of conservatism may differ with respect to their understanding of what it is about S's belief that p that is relevant. The *mere* fact that we accept a belief p may be understood to give us reason to continue to accept it.[5] Alternatively, the fact that we hold a belief may be understood to indicate that that belief possesses some further feature or quality in virtue of which it deserves to be held, or which at least contributes to a case for its rationality. Thus we might be confident that we are justified in holding most of our beliefs, or that most of our beliefs are true, or that since our beliefs have enabled us to survive, as a whole they must have a lot to recommend them.

Obviously there is a lot to say about each of these possibilities. I will simply make the weak and vague assumption that there is something to be said for some version of conservatism. If so, it is likely that the fact that there is a consensus about a belief within one's group, in particular a consensus among people of integrity in the group, would provide further support for that belief. That is, if S's holding a belief provides some justification for S to continue to hold that belief, then the fact that there is an entire group, to which S belongs, and which shares that belief, provides further justification for S to hold it. And the deeper the reflection there has been within the group about the relevant issues, and the more numerous are members with integrity, the more this is likely to be so.

If—and this is the important point—there is anything to conservatism either at the individual level or at the group level, then the fact that people with integrity who have reflected deeply on a belief still deny it or do not hold it should also have some significance for belief. But what significance? At the very least, I suggest, it should lead us to examine the relevant alternatives and to have some doubts about our own alternative. Indeed, the more compelling is the case for conservatism—of whatever stripe—the more compelling also is the case for taking seriously the views of other groups. For if we should be conservative in the relevant respect, so should they. But if they should be conservative there may well be something about their beliefs that makes those beliefs worthy of acceptance. If so, we ought to explore what that might be. This is the appeal to conservatism.[6]

It may be that once a situation is recognized to be ambiguous, the appeal to conservatism is nugatory. But not everyone accepts that the world is religiously ambiguous. We can think of the appeal to conservatism as an argument that should have some weight with those who do not accept that the world is religiously ambiguous.

3. The Appeal to the Possibility of a Compromise

Here is another reason that disagreement gives reason to examine our beliefs. If there is disagreement, it is likely that each party to the dispute has a well-worked-out line of thought, with arguments of some power to bring to bear in support of its position. The views of each side probably reflect important concerns and considerations.

We could have defined the notion of disagreement in such a way that there is disagreement between two groups only if each has a well-worked-out line of thought and relevant considerations of some power, just as we defined disagreement as involving a number of groups with people of integrity. In that case, deciding that there is disagreement in some particular case would require investigating whether each side has well-worked-out lines of thought and arguments of some power in support of its position; and it would of course be harder to tell whether there is disagreement in any particular case. The notion of disagreement which I am assuming is closer to the everyday notion.

If a number of positions reflect important concerns and considerations, there may be some way to reconcile them with each other. There may be a position that includes and accommodates components taken from a number of alternatives, and which is preferable to each of them in virtue of that fact. It might be a synthesis of much of what has been important to each side, or it might involve each side giving up part of what it has believed. The possibility of arriving at a perspective that takes account of a richer set of concerns, preserving much of what is important to one or more other groups, in addition to your own, provides reason for you to examine the relevant alternatives and to be tentative in whatever position you hold. For it suggests that the beliefs of each side may be incomplete; it may be that there is some way to combine the best of each of them. (Some of John Hick's work in philosophy of religion, in particular his work on conceptions of an afterlife in *Death and Eternal Life*, provides an impressive example of an attempt to combine part of what matters to different traditions on central religious issues.) Let us call this *the appeal to the possibility of compromise.*

4. The Import of These Considerations

The case for the Critical Stance has both moral and epistemic dimensions. The moral dimension springs in part from the personal and social importance of the belief. It is also a function of the need to respect members of other groups as responsible acquirers and holders of beliefs. The epistemic dimension springs in part, for example, from the cognitive importance of these beliefs. It springs, too, from the fact that the process of examination increases the likelihood that our beliefs will be true.

The fact of disagreement constitutes a powerful reason to subject your beliefs to examination and to be tentative. So the E-principle specifies a very powerful reason to think that those to whom it applies—who, first and foremost, are privileged people—ought to examine their beliefs: so only a *very* weighty body of evidence would suffice to make it the case that the obligation was no longer binding. And the same goes for the T-principle. (All of the points in the remainder of this section bear on the T-principle as well as the E-principle, but I will avoid constant repetition of this fact.) However, this talk of "powerful reasons," of "weighty body of evidence," and of evidence that is "somewhat more supportive of one side than it is of the others" is vague, as is talk of "providing reason to think" something to be the case. I can have reason to think that p is true, even powerful reason to think this to be so, and at the same time have yet more compelling reason to believe that p is not true or is questionable (etc.). It is useful at this point to consider some exceptions and to consider their significance.

Exceptions to the E-principle are cases of beliefs about which there is disagreement but which, because of special circumstances, there is no obligation to examine. For instance, scrutiny of some important beliefs for some people may be dangerous or self-destructive. They may crack up or lose their peace of mind; life may lose its meaning or its joy or its richness or its zest for them. It may be clear to them, or they may sense, that such changes would occur as a result of going through the process of examination. They may derive security or comfort from beliefs that are held dogmatically. Some people may urgently need unexamined and nontentative religious belief.[7] Their way of life or culture may revolve around it and to some extent depend on it. Or their moral system may collapse without it, whereas as it is, as the possessors of unexamined and nontentative beliefs, they are very impressive and admirable people. Scrutiny of beliefs may also lead to social conflict, perhaps bringing to the surface tensions best left undiscussed.

Well, if it *is* harmful or dangerous for someone to subject his beliefs to critical scrutiny, for that reason alone there is a lot to be said against the idea that he has an obligation to do so. Perhaps considerations of well-being can sometimes outweigh the case for the E-principle. Some such exceptional cases may involve an appeal to other obligations, such as an obligation to oneself to maintain one's own happiness, or an obligation not to undermine the necessary supports for an admirable moral stance.

Of course people's fears about the harmful consequences of subjecting their beliefs to examination may be misplaced: they may think that the process of examination would undermine their beliefs when it would not do so, or they may think that the effects of their beliefs being undermined would be harmful when it would be harmless or even beneficial. And there are cases in which considerations of well-being may actually support the case for an obligation to examine. This would be so, for example, if continuing to hold a belief were damaging. In that case, proper consideration of the possibility of harm *adds* to the strength of the case for scrutiny of one's beliefs.

Moreover, not every case in which examination would involve a risk to well-being or comfort is an exception to the E-principle. (So in addition to exceptions to the E-principle, there are also exceptions to the exceptions.) This would be so if the risks were very slight, for example.

Consider also the following sort of case. Imagine that someone believes that receiving the Sacraments of the Catholic Church is necessary for salvation. She believes that *extra ecclesiam nulla salus,* and she interprets this claim in a traditional and exclusivist way. Suppose that she finds great comfort in a deeply held conviction that she herself will achieve salvation, partly on account of her participation in the Sacraments. (And since this is supposed to be a case that bears on the E-principle, let us keep in mind the fact that the beliefs in which this person takes comfort are the subject of disagreement, as defined.) Surely such a person—assuming she has the resources, opportunities, and so forth—needs to consider how dreadful for many other people are these circumstances in which she takes comfort. For in her view all of those who do not participate in the Sacraments face an awful future. Reflection on the plight of those whose future prospects appear to be bleak should surely be a source of *discomfort* to her. She may also want to consider the psychological and social costs of taking this attitude to others, of thinking of the people whom she encounters as consisting of an in-group who will achieve salvation and an out-group who will not do so. Maybe such matters really *are* bothering her, perhaps at an unconscious level. (Let us hope so.) In any case the point is that if it were true that following the E-principle would undermine a sense of comfort that is established on such a problematic foundation, this would be a consideration that counts for rather than against the E-principle.

Still, it remains the case that there are various exceptions to the E-principle. Considerations of well-being should sometimes take priority over the obligation specified in the E-principle, although not just any appeal to harmful consequences suffices to undermine the case for there being an obligation to subject your beliefs to examination when there is disagreement. Whatever exceptional cases there are arise in virtue of the interplay between the various considerations that are relevant, both epistemic and moral. It would be handy to have a procedure for measuring the relative importance of all such considerations. But there is no such procedure to be had. Not only do we lack one at present, but a procedure that assigned particular weights to particular considerations would be arbitrary. We have to settle for saying that the obligation specified in the E-principle is both a moral and an epistemic one, and is generally binding, but may in exceptional circumstances be suspended. But neither the fact that there are exceptions to the E-principle nor the fact that it is impossible to give a full account of the relevant exceptional circumstances undermines the claim that the obligation in question is generally binding.

Suppose that we recognize that under certain conditions an exception to the E-principle will occur. Let us say that this will be so if condition C holds. (Condition C might be the fact that the process of examination will be very damaging to someone, or the fact that it will lead to social conflict, for example.) We could modify the E-principle and specify that it holds only if C is not met. (One way to do this, although it probably would not always be the best way, would be to modify slightly the definition of disagreement in chapter 7 and to say that disagreement of the relevant sort occurs only if C is not met.) If we were to do this a number of times, adding further conditions to cope with exceptions, we would come closer to specifying an *ultima facie* or all-things-considered obligation to examine our beliefs. But how would we know that we had turned up all of the exceptions? More important, there is no need for a watertight case. It is enough to specify a prima facie obligation that is generally binding.

The E-principle states sufficient conditions for the presence of the prima facie obligation in question. There is no suggestion that these are necessary conditions. It is easy to imagine other cases in which someone might have an obligation to examine some of her beliefs, such as cases in which someone holds a belief p but then has experiences (other than the experience of encountering others with integrity who deny p) that call p into question, and cases in which there is ambiguity that has not given rise to disagreement.

There is another respect in which the conditions specified in the E-principle are sufficient rather than necessary conditions for the presence of an obligation to examine. My main concern is with the area of religious belief, and this is an area in which there obviously is disagreement about matters of importance among many communities and groups. But that there should be *many* communities is not necessary. It would suffice for there to be *two* such communities. But when there are many such communities, it seems that it must be especially easy to go wrong on the matters about which there is disagreement—since so many groups (that include conscientious, reflective, and intelligent individuals) *are* going wrong on such matters—and for the further claim that some reappraisal is appropriate. We might also consider the case where one *individual* encounters another who appears to have integrity but whose views are very different: is such a person obligated to subject her beliefs to some scrutiny? Someone who is committed to the E-principle, which operates at the level of large cultural groups, need not make any particular response to this question. But if there is anything to the idea that in cases in which there is disagreement among individuals there is reason to subject your beliefs to scrutiny, then there is yet more to be said for the E-principle.

It might be suggested that it is wrong to think that the E-principle has application only when there is disagreement. Is there not, it may be asked, a more general obligation to try to ensure that *all* of one's beliefs are true? And does that not require us to examine *all* of our beliefs about religion, or perhaps all of our beliefs irrespective of what they are about, and not merely those about which there is disagreement? But we are hardly in a position to examine all of our beliefs: time is scarce and opportunities are limited. Since probing all of them obviously is an impossible task, and "'ought' implies 'can,'" at most what we ought to do is probe some of them. We have no choice but to be selective. So we need a procedure for deciding which among our beliefs are especially worthy of examination. The presence of disagreement is a useful indicator that examination is especially appropriate.

5. Objections

I have, in effect, already considered some objections, such as the objection that adoption of the Critical Stance may be psychologically harmful. Next I want to respond to some additional objections. Doing so will help both to clarify and to strengthen my case.

A. The Critical Stance Is Unsatisfactory from a Religious Point of View

In chapter 8, I responded to the objection that to take the Critical Stance is to empty religious belief of the sort of commitment that is distinctive of it. But there is also an intertwined set of related objections to consider.

The demand that there should be critical reflection and the demand that belief should be tentative will be seen as a nuisance from the point of view of traditions that call for one's entire loyalty, devotion, trust, and obedience. Many theists, in particular, see their theism as something precious around which one should build one's life, and into which one should throw oneself unreservedly.

Some would argue, too, that to take the Critical Stance with respect to the beliefs of a religion is to adopt a perspective that is so alien to the tradition within which the beliefs in question are embedded that it will be difficult even to get a clear view of what it is to be religious in the relevant way, and even in effect involves an abandonment of religious belief. Or at any rate to accept the case for the Critical Stance is already to accept the beliefs in a quite different way, and in a detached way. Religion, it is said, is not so much a matter of finding a theory that is intellectually satisfying; it is more a matter of a man who feels he is drowning finding a lifeline and holding on to it for all he is worth, and now finding that he can breathe again; and its seeming to him that the lifeline will keep him afloat only if he holds on for all he is worth—holds on "for dear life." Laura Bernhardt has put it thus in correspondence: "If the whole meaning of my life depends upon the understanding that I was born in a certain condition relative to God, was generally opened to salvation by the sacrifice of Jesus, and may only achieve salvation . . . through him, then questioning these things may necessarily entail ceasing to be a Christian. This sort of examination . . . [involves] the changing of a person's life."[8] Also, for a member of a tradition to acknowledge that one or more other traditions are close to being as likely to be right as one's own tradition is to call into question the point of one's own tradition.

Others will object that I am assuming that there is an independent point of view from which you can assess claims about religious matters, whereas much religion wants to be the point of view from which you assess everything else. And to belong to a tradition is to accept that your tradition dictates the boundaries of inquiry, specifying which questions may be asked and which may not be asked. Someone might put it as follows: "Admittedly there is an opposition between the Critical Stance and orthodox religion; but what makes you think that the Critical Stance should take priority?" Someone who is advancing this objection may also be questioning the whole process of giving arguments and of approaching religion in this way. Such a person may say that if you approach these issues as an exercise in detached reflection, and while presupposing a Western, post-Enlightenment epistemology, there may be something to be said for my views. But there are many other perspectives and "voices."

These are serious objections that require a response. One might begin by asking why it matters how people in the various traditions will respond: if a strong case can be made for the Critical Stance, why should we be concerned about the fact that it will be found to be unsatisfactory from many religious points of view? The line of objection under discussion, or at least one strand in it, consists in pointing out that the Critical Stance is alien to, and would be opposed by, many religious groups. *But of course;* what else would you expect?

The isolationist suggestion that a tradition should dictate the boundaries of inquiry, specifying which questions may be asked, what sort of reasoning may be engaged in, and so forth, is one that it is not easy to show to be mistaken. After all, it calls into question the relevance of reasoning that is not restricted within the confines specified by the tradition; so any attempt to question these limitations is automatically disqualified from serious consideration to the satisfaction of the insiders who adopt this view. Yet in a world in which there is growing recognition that there is disagreement among many traditions, this sort of isolationism is not likely to be successful. It is also ahistorical: it ignores the fact that the history of the relationship between faith and reason is one of engagement, of victories and losses, of compromise, and of rapprochement. The Critical Stance represents an attempt to combine faith and reason, giving appropriate weight to each of them, as distinct from an attempt to batten down the hatches and withdraw from the fray.

It is also important at this point to reiterate the various forms of religious commitment that are compatible with tentative belief. Doing so helps to mitigate the charge that to adopt the Critical Stance is to abandon religious belief and all that is involved in it.

Also, the objection is, in part, that the Critical Stance ought not to be adopted with respect to the claims of the religions because it will fail to satisfy people in many of the traditions. Baptists will not approve of it, Catholics will reject it, Jews will disapprove of it, Muslims will repudiate it, and so forth. And since orthodox members of so many religious traditions agree that there is something wrong with it, there really must be something wrong with it. But if this objection has any weight, it must be because it matters what people in the different traditions say. Their views have some authority. But it is largely in virtue of the fact that *many* traditions have views that matter that the Critical Stance ought to be adopted! Moreover, those who put forward the objection under discussion disagree radically about the beliefs that they take to be sacrosanct and not to be subject to assessment and criticism. In the absence of further argument, there is no reason to trust any one such group rather than another. In effect their objections cancel each other out.

But—and here the voice of the objector is heard again—don't members of a tradition have an obligation to keep the faith? Why should the E-principle or the T-principle take priority over that religious obligation? Moreover, the obligations involved in the E-principle and the T-principle are said to fall especially heavily on people of influence—people whose views are interpersonally important. But those are often the people who have, and feel, a special responsibility to serve as exemplars of their faith—to serve as shining examples of what a faithful follower of the tradition ought to be.

I propose that many members of many religious traditions ought to live with what we might think of as a tension or conflict between two pressures. On the one hand, there is the appeal of keeping the faith and of maintaining one's own traditions. Religious commitment, when sincerely adhered to, is a sort of love, a passion, a form of idealism; it usually seems to serious adherents to be the highest form of idealism. It is also partially definitive of one's identity; someone who is a serious member of a tradition does not come *from nowhere* to the issues under discussion: rather, one comes as a person who already belongs and whose belonging is partly constitutive of his identity. There is the good of a sense of comfortable belonging: it involves a shared understanding with other members of a tradition, with all of the meaningfulness that that provides for one's experience. But all of this—the appeal of keeping the faith, this love and idealism, and so forth—has somehow to be combined with a cosmopolitan respect for other traditions and with a recognition of the religiously ambiguous character of the world. Doing so involves an attempt to balance two sets of worthwhile goods. The life, outlook, and experience, of a believer who feels the appeal of both sets of goods, and who therefore lives with conflicting loyalties, will be different from the life of a believer who does not do so. And in response to the point about the special responsibility of leaders, leadership can also be displayed in redirecting the tradition in a way that enables it to take account of all of the relevant obligations and considerations.

Yet another reason might be offered as to why the Critical Stance is unsatisfactory from a religious point of view. Religions help people to cope with difficult aspects of life, including tragedy and loss. How can a religion play this important role if its assurances are subject to scrutiny and held tentatively? The Critical Stance, and especially tentative belief, is likely to be resisted precisely because religious beliefs satisfy deep human needs, including a need for explanation in difficult areas of human life. In coping with bereavement or tragedy, the assurance of happiness in heaven, or in any other such happy state that is posited by a tradition, is of great value for many people. Many also find great comfort and assurance in a system of thought that provides—with no hint of tentativeness—an interpretation and a guide in most areas of life.

I do not deny that there may be a price to be paid in these areas for loss of certitude; we should concede that tentative belief will not be capable of playing the same role as untentative belief. On the other hand, one should not underestimate the extent to which tentative religious belief may fulfill the important social and psychological roles that have usually been played by nontentative beliefs. It would be useful to explore this fully. And to turn matters somewhat on their head, the very fact that certain beliefs play a profound and important role in our lives, and perhaps even are central to our happiness, should lead us to countenance the possibility that it may be what they do for us that gives them the appearance of being inescapable and clearly correct. Their important role may tend to conceal the fact that we ought to adopt the Critical Stance with respect to them.

Finally, it might also be objected that to begin by characterizing the fact that there are many competing positions on religious matters, as I do, as a matter of disagreement—with all that that implies, such as the integrity of the advocates of each position—is already to be launched away from traditional orthodoxy. It is not surprising, so this charge continues, that we find ourselves concluding that the alternative positions ought to be scrutinized and that if one accepts one of the available positions, one should entertain seriously the possibility that the others might be right. My response to this charge is just that I happily confess to what it alleges: but I think of this objection as, in effect, a recognition that the various themes and ideas I have explored fit well together.

B. To Ask People to Adopt the Critical Stance Is to Ask Too Much

Most people, according to this objection, are not capable of going out as far on the limb of independent inquiry as is required. People need to have firm beliefs in order to get on with their lives. (Their need to have a firm position on the basis of which to live, it may be said, is a lot more pressing than their need to be right.) Also, it may be suggested that just as we cannot suddenly adopt outlandish or even patently false beliefs, or give up certain obvious beliefs, likewise we are unable to change suddenly to holding tentatively many beliefs that we previously held nontentatively. (For instance, I seem to be unable to change suddenly to holding tentatively the belief that I have two arms or the belief that there are other people.) And some people may be incapable of adopting tentative beliefs in certain areas, including the area of religious belief.

There is indeed some reason to believe that people find it hard to continue to hold their beliefs in a tentative way, that they are disposed to convert tentative belief into full belief.[9] Hume makes some relevant observations.

> The greater part of mankind are naturally apt to be affirmative and dogmatical in their opinions, and while they see objects only on one side and have no idea of any counterpoising argument, they throw themselves precipitately into the principles to which they are inclined. . . . To hesitate or balance perplexes their understanding, checks their passion, and suspends their action. They are, therefore, impatient till they escape from a state which to them is so uneasy, and they think that they can never remove themselves far enough from it by the violence of their affirmations and obstinacy of their belief."[10]

Peter Berger makes this closely related point: "[It] is precisely the groups that exude certainty, insist on strict doctrines, and make difficult behavioral demands to which people flock in large numbers. By contrast, religious groups that admit uncertainty and are lax in doctrine as well as codes of behavior have difficulty retaining their members let alone acquiring new ones" (FG, 19).

If Hume's analysis is correct and we have the tendency he mentions, the upshot is just that it will take more of an effort than would otherwise be the case to achieve the Critical Stance. However, people are obliged to do only what they are able to do, and it is indeed advisable not to expect more of people than they are able to deliver. If some people are currently incapable of adopting the Critical Stance in areas in which it would otherwise be appropriate, perhaps this should in such cases be thought of as a goal toward which they should strive rather than as a standard that they should be expected to meet. Also, various peripheral beliefs may be easily shifted into the tentative mode, whereas core beliefs would be less easily so shifted.

One reason that many beliefs are such that we are unable to adopt the Critical Stance with respect to them appears to be that everything speaks for them, and nothing against them. The situation is otherwise when there are sizable bodies of evidence against a belief, or when there are plausible alternatives. It seems that in order for tentativeness with respect to some belief to be an option, there must be something about the belief that provides a foothold for that tentativeness. It must be that it is not the case that everything speaks for the belief. Perhaps there has to be a sizable amount of evidence against the belief. If so, the fact that it is psychologically possible to hold certain beliefs tentatively suggests that they are beliefs about an area of some ambiguity. I take it that many people are able to exercise some control over whether or not some of their beliefs in the area of religion are held tentatively. This supports strongly the claim that the world is religiously ambiguous.

There is a different construction that might be put on the claim that the Critical Stance demands too much. The T-principle says, roughly, that disagreement is a powerful reason to hold tentatively beliefs about which there is disagreement. Consider the following situation. We find there to be disagreement on some matter between my group and yours. My group modifies its beliefs somewhat: let us assume that we become somewhat tentative. Thus, for instance, we might change from being conservative and devout Mormons to being tentative Mormons so that it still seems to us that the Church of Jesus Christ of Latter-Day Saints is the one true religion but we now recognize that we could be wrong. Whether or not your group does likewise, however, disagreement between our groups persists. To be sure, the new disagreement will not have quite the same character as it had heretofore, for the groups involved will not be as far apart. Yet there still is disagreement. The objection is this: in the face of this new disagreement, does the Critical Stance require both sides to undergo the same process again, noting the nature of the disagreement, and reflecting that disagreement in the character of their beliefs, perhaps by becoming *more* tentative? And if such further changes *are* made, should the maneuver be repeated yet again?[11]

There are two responses that can be offered here by a defender of the T-principle. The first is to say that we should take the T-principle to say that the beliefs of other groups should be taken into account *once*. Once they have been taken into account, perhaps by modifying our beliefs, there is no need to *keep* taking them into account. If this were our response, we would have to accept the following outcome. Consider two believers, one of whom takes the beliefs of others into account and in accordance with the T-principle modifies certain beliefs, with the result that she now holds those beliefs in a tentative way. The second person starts from the point at which the first person ends and then confronts the fact that there are disagreements. In virtue of the T-principle, let us suppose, she has reason to change her beliefs. On this approach what is an appropriate stopping point for one is an inappropriate stopping point for another.

An alternative response is to say that in some cases the new disagreement—the disagreement that remains after one or more sides has, for example, become tentative in belief—*may* constitute a reason for further examination and for additional tentativeness. We might simply be unsure about how far we need to go, about how many times you should allow the fact of disagreement to make a difference. In any case, my general response to this objection is to say that the absence of a general formula for how many times the principles involved in the Critical Stance are to be applied is no reason to reject the Critical Stance.

A related question. Suppose once again that my group and your group start from very different positions. And suppose that the facts about us are such that in virtue of the T-principle we both ought to become tentative in our beliefs. Now suppose that my group responds by becoming tentative but that yours fails to do so. Does this mean that your group now has less reason to be tentative than it would have had, had my group not already become somewhat tentative in our beliefs? The beliefs of my group, after all, constitute a serious challenge to those of your group to the extent that they are different from those of your group. If we have shifted to a more tentative position, then the gap between us is not so great.

I suppose that we might reasonably demand that our beliefs, held in their original nontentative way, should be taken into account. ("After all," we might say, "*we* have taken *yours* into account. Fair is fair; you have to do the same.") Yet why should our beliefs in the form in which we no longer hold them now be taken into account? So although it may seem curious to concede that your group has less reason to be tentative if we become more tentative, this seems to be the best position to take.

Finally, the issue of the feasibility of adopting the Critical Stance requires for its proper investigation a recognition that under current circumstances we lack institutions that would nourish this sort of endeavor. Consequently, to adopt the Critical Stance is to step out into something of a no-man's-land where who knows what dangers may lurk, and it requires doing this alone. Belief in accordance with the Critical Stance does not currently have what Peter Berger calls "plausibility structures." ("Human beings, due to their intrinsically and inexorably social nature, require social support for whatever they believe about the world" [FG, 125].)

But the Critical Stance could have such supporting structures. In order to address this issue properly we would need to consider the sorts of institutions and structures that might be put in place and that would facilitate the attitudes to religion for which I argue. I will just make a remark or two on this topic here.[12] An obvious possibility would be for a group of people who believe that this stance is the correct one to devote time to exploring it together. Groups that involve people from many traditions (each of which is recognized by the participants to satisfy a fairly high standard) are another possibility. (It might even be suggested that the correct position to take on religious matters is the one that would emerge when consensus is achieved in a group of some such sort. But I have my doubts about this pragmatic suggestion.) In any case the ideal institutions will have little emphasis on the parroting of credal statements. We might think of them as societies for the investigation of religious reality—informed by one or more religious traditions, and by the relevant sciences and social sciences.

There is another group of people with respect to whom it might be said that the Critical Stance asks too much. Here I have in mind people who have little interest in religious matters and to whom the subject matter of religion does not seem important. Is it really true that such a person ought to examine whatever views she may have in this area and the relevant views of others? I have in mind here both cases in which someone has beliefs in this area but those beliefs lack personal importance for him and cases in which someone has few, or has very undeveloped, beliefs in the area of religion.[13]

In general, in the case of numerous disagreements—of the sort under discussion—there are many people to whom none of the positions that are taken matter. They may not even have a relevant view or be aware of what the relevant alternatives are. Thus anyone who has not had training in philosophy is unlikely to have a view about whether the rationalists and empiricists were really as different as historians of philosophy used to think. Anyone who is not a serious student of politics is unlikely to have a view of the extent to which the methodology deployed in political science should be quantitatively based. And yet there are disagreements about all of these matters, and of course about numerous matters in other areas of knowledge about which people tend not to have an opinion unless they have specialized training. Does the position for which I am arguing imply that everyone has an obligation to examine the options in each of *these* areas? Some of these issues are such that even the people who have the relevant beliefs would concede that there is no reason that everyone ought to have a position on them. (Only someone who is out of touch with reality to an exceptional degree would argue that *everyone* ought to have a position on the extent to which the rationalists and empiricists differ.)

One strategy that we could adopt here would simply be to restrict discussion to groups for whom certain beliefs *are* important and to leave the question of what to say about other cases as a matter for further discussion. We might also hope that a person who has no relevant position or who has not considered such matters to be important would be given pause by the fact that so many others hold opinions with such conviction on such matters and often build their lives around those convictions: perhaps this should stimulate the opinionless person to *acquire* a position. But a better response is to recall that the importance of beliefs is to some extent a function of their content: there are beliefs such that in virtue of their content it is hard to imagine how they would not be important, in all of the ways in which beliefs are important, to someone who holds them. The interpersonal importance of a belief is also to some extent a function of the social roles that are actually occupied by the person who holds it. If the fact that someone holds certain beliefs makes a difference to others, then those beliefs are important just in virtue of that fact. Hence beliefs about religion that are held by someone to whom the entire question of religion is neither cognitively nor personally important may nevertheless be interpersonally important. So the obligation to examine the relevant beliefs may be binding even on someone who does not care about and is not interested in the entire topic of religion. However, if an area of belief actually had little or no importance for someone in *all* of the relevant senses of importance, namely, personal, impersonal, and cognitive importance, we can simply say that in such a case the obligation to examine a particular belief or set of beliefs is weaker than it otherwise would be and is therefore more easily overridden.

C. Disagreement Per Se Is Not What Matters

It might be objected that if someone with a particular position on religious matters encounters others who disagree, what gives her reason to examine her beliefs and the various alternatives to her beliefs, and what gives her reason to hold her beliefs tentatively, is the *evidence* on which the others rely or the reasons they have for holding their beliefs rather than the mere fact that they disagree. In short, if there is evidence against her beliefs on religious matters, isn't *that* what does the work here? And if there isn't evidence against them, who cares who disagrees? If there really is religious ambiguity, isn't *that* the fact that should be reflected in people's beliefs?

But recall that disagreement, as defined in this discussion, occurs only if all parties to it are people of integrity who have engaged in reflection. This strongly suggests that our opponents have reasons for the positions they take. If I have reason to think your group to be responsible and to think that you hold opinions that have been thought out and reflected upon, then I have every reason to think that you have reasons for your beliefs.

My main reaction to this objection, however, is that it does not matter greatly how we conceive of the connections here. We can think of disagreement, which in turn suggests that there is ambiguity, as the source of the obligation specified by the E-principle and the reason to be tentative that is specified by the T-principle. Or we can think of dis-

agreement as suggesting that there is ambiguity and, in turn, of the obligation to examine and the reason to be tentative as arising, at least in part, from this further (suggested) fact. If what actually does the work here is the fact of ambiguity, then the significance of the fact that others disagree with us—that is, the reason this gives us reason
to examine our beliefs and to be tentative in the way we hold them—may be, or may
largely be, that it provides reason to think there is ambiguity. However, I think that there
is good reason not to take this approach: to do so is to underestimate radically the
proper role of testimony per se in the acquisition and maintenance of our beliefs. In addition, a reason for starting from the fact of disagreement is that it is easier to secure
agreement that there is disagreement—which requires that the different sides meet certain standards, and so forth—than that there is ambiguity.

D. *The Significance of Disagreement is Outweighed by Other Considerations*

What about cases in which there is disagreement about some issue, but in which some
individual or group of individuals has clear and decisive evidence for a certain position?
Suppose, in the case of the tale with which I began chapter 7, that there is disagreement
within my isolated group about what is "on the other side" beyond the mountains, but
suppose too that I alone have crossed the mountains, and have done so without the
knowledge of others. Why should the fact that there are others who disagree provide
any reason for me to examine my beliefs or to be tentative about them? It may be entirely apparent to me that I am in a uniquely privileged situation with respect to this
issue. The challenge to the T-principle might go as follows: "All right, you have made
your point. The fact of diversity constitutes a reason for tentativeness. But it is far outweighed by other considerations." In general, the response will be forthcoming from a
number of quarters that while the considerations I have identified may provide some
reason to think that the T-principle and the E-principle have application in the area of
religion, the collective force of these considerations is outweighed by others.

My response has a number of parts. First, since I have not tried to *prove* that people
who confront disagreement ought to adopt the Critical Stance, and have merely attempted to point out strong and powerful reasons to believe this to be so, reasons that
can be overridden only by weighty considerations, I readily concede that the case that I
have derived from the fact of disagreement, while it is important, is just one of many
relevant considerations. I recognize that there are other factors that are relevant to
which beliefs one should hold and to how one should hold them, and which need to
be taken into account. For instance, it could be that one religious group enjoys religious
experiences that provide decisive support for the correctness of its beliefs and that others do not. If the probability that the claims of some particular religious position, such
as Buddhism or Islam, or that associated with Jehovah's Witnesses or Mormonism, or
atheism, is correct were very high on such grounds, then the force of the overall case
for the Critical Stance would be diminished. Whether or not one ought, say, to be a theist, and if so whether or not one ought to hold one's theistic beliefs tentatively, all
things considered, are questions that it is beyond my purposes to try to answer conclusively. As I have indicated, I think the available evidence *not* to point decisively in any
particular direction: there is considerable evidence that the world is religiously ambiguous. If I am right, this suggests that tentative belief, at most, is appropriate when all

things are considered. I suggest that the burden of proof lies with those who would say that other considerations outweigh the case that I have made for tentativeness. Still, it may be that once certain additional evidence is examined or certain additional considerations are taken into account, and a full assessment is made, more—or less—than tentative belief will be seen to be appropriate. Cases in which one group has special access to evidence that suffices to resolve the disagreement should be included among the exceptions both to the E-principle and to the T-principle.

Second, my concern is with the significance of disagreement for people who take some particular position on religious matters. I assume that people who accept a position of the sort that goes with being a member of a religious tradition find that their relevant beliefs fit with, and enable them to interpret, their day-to-day experience. Also they typically are part of a like-minded community, and often have access to arguments and evidence that they take to support their position. The facts that a belief is central to your entire system of belief and even to the sort of person you are, and has been found valuable by you throughout your life, also have to be taken into account. While anything I say about the collective force of such considerations would have to be at such a level of generality that it would be well-nigh useless, I take such considerations to provide a good deal of support for a variety of religious positions. They provide reason for someone who has held a particular position to believe it to be correct and to go on holding it. I am exploring the significance of disagreement for people who are so situated.

Often the hard job will be to determine whether a particular case in which different positions are held adds up to a case of disagreement, with all that that involves and entails. It seems best to acknowledge that there are marginal cases and that there are unclear cases: that is, there are cases in which the relevant conditions (integrity on the part of the advocates of each position, long traditions of reflection, apparent competence, important subject matter, and so forth) are only partly satisfied and cases in which it is unclear whether they are satisfied. There seem to be principles that are weaker than the E-principle and the T-principle that bear on such cases. Thus in some such cases there might be an obligation to engage in examination that is not as extensive as the examination that is required by the E-principle. There may be cases in which it is sufficiently uncertain whether there is full-blown disagreement that there is merely an obligation to take account in some weaker way of the fact that there are so many different views, or perhaps an obligation to come up with some account of why others hold their views. Or perhaps in some such cases one should settle for saying that one's own group ought to learn from other groups and ought to try to pay attention to their distinctive insights, or for saying that it is conceivable that one's own system of beliefs may need to be revised. In all such cases the appropriate beliefs will be less tentative than they would be in the case of full-blown disagreement of the sort that is to be found among the main religious traditions.

E. *There Is Disagreement in Many Areas: Surely We Do Not Have an*
   Obligation to Examine Our Beliefs in Every Such Area and to
   Hold Our Beliefs Tentatively in All Such Areas

If people have such obligations in the area of religion, in what other areas do they have them? There are disagreements of the relevant sort with respect to many ethical and aesthetic issues, in political theory, on matters of public policy, and of course in theology and philosophy. Almost every academic discipline outside of the natural sciences has competing schools of thought. And within the natural sciences too there are disagreements, such as disagreement about whether a unified field theory is possible or about the causes of the destruction of the dinosaurs. Consider someone who understands himself to have made a new discovery in science, for instance, and in the process has acquired views that are at odds with the received views. Does he thereby acquire an obligation to adopt the Critical Stance vis-à-vis his new position in virtue of the fact that it is at odds with the received view?

First, there are areas in which it would be unusual for people to take a position without first having actually gone through a process of inquiry and investigation. Certainly this is likely to be so for disagreements in philosophy or theology or literary criticism, for example. In the course of acquiring beliefs in such areas, people will frequently consider, and be exposed to the merits of, a variety of points of view: this is just a function of the nature of the training in the course of which people acquire beliefs in such areas. Typically one would not even be in a position to form an opinion in these areas unless one had considered various alternatives. So someone who takes a relevant position will typically have fulfilled the E-principle at any rate.

Second, on some moral issues on which there is apparent disagreement, one or more party to the dispute may not have reflected adequately, or may not have attempted to inform themselves about the issue in question, or may be in the grip of palpably mistaken beliefs. An apologist for slavery who denies that an enslaved population is fully human, for instance, is a simple example of someone in the grip of a palpably mistaken belief. In disputes over the distribution of scarce resources, for instance, the views of some of the parties to the dispute may largely be reflections of, or may be greatly influenced by, an attempt by those parties to protect their interests. To the extent that a point of view is an expression of a wish to protect interests, or of a failure to have reflected adequately, it does not have the same significance. More to the point, to the extent that parties to a dispute are thus flawed, it does not even count as an instance of disagreement, as I use that term; hence my remarks do not bear on such cases.

Third, there are other reasons that the disagreement may be apparent only: thus on some moral, political, and public policy matters, it may be that there is no correct position, and that subjectivism or relativism of some sort provides the best analysis: in that case different groups who appear to disagree with each other can be right, and the disagreement is only apparent. However, in the case of religious matters relativism seems implausible.

Fourth, in the case of many disagreements it behooves us to expose the precise nature of the disagreement. This may not be apparent at first glance. Consider, for instance, the ongoing debate in the United States about the availability of handguns. There are people who believe that handguns ought to be widely available, and there are people who deny this. But precisely how different are the positions? Presumably no one who has integrity thinks that it is appropriate for guns to be in the hands of criminals. (And it is only disagreements between people of that sort that have the significance under discussion.) So what are the issues on which there is disagreement? Presumably there is disagreement, for example, about whether it should be permissible for a law-abiding citizen to have a gun in his house for his protection. But this surely is an issue with respect to which each side deserves to have its views taken seriously by the opposition. The general point is that once the conditions that need to be satisfied for there to be disagreement in my sense of the term are satisfied, the case for adopting the Critical Stance with respect to such an issue is more compelling.

It is clear from the foregoing points that *some* apparent disagreements may be disposed of in one or another way so that the T-principle and the E-principle do not apply to them: thus it may be that all but one party to the dispute is in the grip of manifestly mistaken beliefs, or that a relativistic analysis of the apparent disagreement is appropriate. But obviously there are numerous genuine disagreements that cannot be disposed of in ways such as those just suggested.

Consider a disagreement in philosophy. Here, as mentioned, the E-principle is likely to be satisfied just in virtue of how beliefs are acquired in this field; but what about the T-principle? In philosophy of mind, for example, there are numerous competing theories, such as dualism, functionalism, identity theory, eliminativism, epiphenomenalism, and so forth. Ought one therefore to be tentative in, say, one's eliminativism? I think that one ought to be. In saying this, however, it is important to keep in mind that here too there are various sorts of commitment that are compatible with tentative belief. And the Critical Stance is not inconsistent with going as far as you can with your analysis of what you believe, and with presenting whatever arguments for it are available.

But it might be pointed out that there are advantages to positions in philosophy being taken nontentatively: advances in this field seem to come in part as a result of the fact that well-defined positions are defended wholeheartedly. And since constant inquiry, mutual criticism, and so forth, are institutionalized in this field, adoption of a nontentative position in this context has a different significance from what it has in many other contexts: it is part of an ongoing process in the course of which it is very likely that it will be subjected to analysis and criticism. Because of the nature of this field and of the sort of discourse that it embodies, even a dogmatic assertion of a position is a move in a process in which criticism and scrutiny are inevitable, and will typically be understood as such. Also, wholehearted defense may in this context serve to enable people to see more clearly what is at issue between the various sides. So there are, in this case, institutional reasons for parties to the discussion to put forward positions in a more than tentative way.

Some of the same points apply in the case of moral and political issues. If on some moral issue there *has* been deep reflection on all sides, if relativism is not an option, and if tentative belief is feasible, the presence of disagreement is a reason that tentative belief is appropriate. This is partly because it is likely that when there is disagreement each party has a well-worked-out line of thought, with arguments of some power to bring to bear. If flourishing and enduring communities have adopted the conflicting moral positions, then there is some reason to think that each side reflects important values that have a claim on our allegiance. Consider a political example: take the conflict between Irish nationalists and Irish unionists about the political future of the territory that currently constitutes Northern Ireland, restricting attention as we do so to people who have integrity. The Critical Stance requires a recognition that one has reason to take both sides seriously, and reason to hold whatever relevant beliefs one holds in such a way that one takes account of what the other side believes. This is particularly the case if you have reason to think that the views of both sides in related areas are impressive.

Since there are many cases of disagreement, we will have to be selective in choosing which disagreements should be the focus of our attention. So what should be the principle of selection? If there are many disagreements and many attendant prima facie obligations, among the considerations that bear on which of these obligations ought to be fulfilled, and which disagreements ought first to be responded to, are the following two. First, there is the importance of the relevant beliefs, where all three types of importance are taken into account, including the likelihood that one will be expressing one's views about the disputed matter. Second, the more reason there is to believe that a certain subject matter is ambiguous, the more reason there is to adopt the Critical Stance with respect to it. As indicated, the very fact of disagreement provides reason to believe that there is ambiguity, but—as I have argued in earlier chapters to be the case—there may of course also be independent reasons for believing there to be ambiguity.

At the end of the discussion of the last objection, I mentioned the possibility that there might be principles that are weaker than the T-principle and the E-principle, as stated. This possibility is also relevant here. Consider, by way of an illustration, the different positions that are adopted concerning the role of reason in deciding about religious matters. Fideists think that reason should have no role here. Natural theologians and numerous others, including both proponents and opponents of religious belief, deny this. There are many fideists, and some of them, presumably, are people of integrity. And while there may not exactly be long traditions of fideist reflection, this position has reappeared often enough in the history of reflection about religion that we might count it as a tradition. So should I therefore hold my relevant belief (namely, that reason has an important role in settling religious disputes) tentatively in virtue of the fact that there are fideists? There are at least two reasons for thinking that while I have an obligation to take account somehow of the fact that there are fideists, less is required here than is required in the case of full-blown disagreement. First, like other disagreements in philosophy, what we have here is a move in an ongoing process of give-and-take in philosophical reflection, a process in which there is even something to be gained from presenting a well-defined view that is different from the views of others. Second, and this is a closely related point, what we do not have here is disagreement between communities whose views have been fashioned on the anvil of life experience. Weaker conditions have been met, and weaker principles are therefore applicable.

F. If Disagreement Provides a Reason for Tentativeness, Is It Not Also a Reason for Skepticism, for Suspension of Judgment, and for Agnosticism?

Why, for instance, don't we endorse something as strong as agnosticism or skepticism, or as weak as an openness to a slight possibility or even a mere logical possibility, that one may be wrong? If we weigh up the significance of arguments such as those I have mentioned, including the appeal to ambiguity, to respect for others, and so on, what reason is there for thinking that their cumulative effect is such that we should end up where I think we should end up?

My view is that the case for the Critical Stance is also a reason for skepticism, but a considerably weaker, and hence more easily overridden, reason. A change from non-tentative belief to tentative belief is a minor change in comparison with a change from nontentative belief to skepticism; so it is not surprising that a strong reason for the former should be a weak reason for the latter. Further, if someone is able to show that the appeal to disagreement requires more than I think it to require, at least we agree that it requires as much as I think it to require.

I do not presume that I have presented a set of arguments that are powerful enough that they require of anyone that they give up their religious position. I do not feel that I am in a position to judge what it is like to be a member of a tradition, or to possess a viewpoint, of which I have no personal experience, or to consider all of the relevant evidence at once, or even seriatim. As far as I know, there are numerous positions that may reasonably be held on religious matters, including the positions that go with being a member of any of the main world religions. My contention is that it is reasonable, nevertheless, to make some recommendations about how one should hold whatever beliefs one holds in virtue of membership in such a tradition.

G. The Critical Stance Ought to Be Taken toward My Own Claims

The final objection is that the E-principle and the T-principle ought themselves to be accepted tentatively; we ought to adopt the Critical Stance with respect to them. (For this objection to be applicable we must of course assume that these claims are themselves the subject of disagreement, as defined; so let us assume that.) Of course if someone who advances this objection thinks that the Critical Stance is appropriate in this context because there is disagreement, then she, too, is committed to both the E-principle and the T-principle: we agree on a great deal, and there is just one detail here to resolve.

But the objection may not reflect an acceptance of the Critical Stance but may rather be that anyone who accepts the case for the Critical Stance ought to adopt that stance with respect to their own claims, including the E-principle and the T-principle, whether or not the Critical Stance is itself plausible. I am inclined to think that there is something to this objection, and that I ought to allow that in accordance with my central claims, I ought to take a critical position with respect to those very claims. (But as I have gone to some trouble to indicate in the course of the discussion of tentative religious belief, this is compatible both with believing them and with taking them very seriously.) So while I think that what I have provided adds up to a strong case for the two principles, I am open to the possibility that someone may provide arguments that refute that case. If they do so, well and good; but I have given reason to think that it will not be so easy.

6. Conclusion

As I have made clear throughout, I do not claim to have made a decisive case for the Critical Stance. I think that it is not possible to prove much in this area. The best that one can do is paint a certain picture, highlight as many of its attractive features as possible, show its consistency with other beliefs that are widely shared, and hope that it will be found to have appeal. It might be asked why anyone should concern themselves with a case which, I allow, I cannot make in a decisive way. My response is just that no one else can do any better, and my view has the great virtue of taking into account the views of many different groups. The respect for others that the Critical Stance encapsulates is one of its virtues. Another is its capacity to cope with the loss of innocence that occurs when the phenomenon of disagreement, with all that it involves, is recognized for what it is.

Generally speaking, it is irresponsible for a privileged person to be, for example, a Muslim or Buddhist or Jew and not to consider the implications of the presence of other traditions, and in particular to fail to act in accordance with both the E-principle and the T-principle. This would not be so if belonging to a religious tradition were merely a matter of following a certain way of life or identifying with a certain community. But belonging to a religious tradition is normally, at least in part, a matter of holding beliefs, including beliefs about what sort of world we live in and beliefs about other people.

Roughly the same point applies to those who do not belong to a religious tradition. The fact that there is disagreement between those who reject all religious beliefs and the defenders of one or another religious system suggests that the beliefs of those who reject all religion should also be held tentatively. Religious belief, in all its diversity, is a challenge to those who reject it in all its forms, just as that diversity is a challenge also to orthodoxy. Partly for reasons of economy I have sometimes characterized the issue of religious disagreement as a matter of disagreement between different religious groups.

An implication of my position is that most martyrs who have died for their faith have been misled. Of course most orthodox members of most traditions agree that many martyrs have been misled, since martyrs have suffered for the sake of traditions other than their own and for causes that are not theirs. But even the martyrs in *our own* tradition have been misguided insofar as they have died in the name of *certainty* about their beliefs. At least, if they were privileged they should have accepted that the beliefs they held, while they seemed to them to be right, might actually be wrong.

Finally, religious traditions should be ranked by their capacity and willingness to accommodate the Critical Stance, just as they may be ranked in some other respects. Thus they may be ranked in virtue of their ability to respond to the currently most pressing human problems. (The latter is tricky of course because some of the problems may be visible only when seen through the eyes of a member of the tradition. Yet there is no need to descend into complete mystery here; a lot is objectively recognizable, such as the fact that environmental destruction is a currently pressing problem globally: some traditions may have more resources to cope with it.) Again, a tradition that cultivates charity and generosity of spirit or that emphasizes the value of learning comes out ahead of those that do not. Traditions may also be ranked with respect to whether their history of reflection seems more sustained or their interest in the truth seems greater, for instance.

The process of ranking the traditions is fraught with difficulties. Needless to say, it is all too easy to dismiss a tradition that is unfamiliar, or with which one has little contact. It is all too easy for one's personal predilections or the fact that one is most familiar with, or comfortable with, one's own tradition to have improper weight. There is a natural and ubiquitous tendency to think that one's own tradition has actually gone the farthest in reflection, self-scrutiny (etc.): all of the traditions claim that theirs is the tradition that scores most highly in this regard. Consequently, such thoughts are not reliable.

Still, the more a tradition, or a strand within a tradition, is open to the Critical Stance, the more worthy it is of our loyalty, all other things being equal. There is a grave and serious error that traditions sometimes make, and in virtue of which they are almost automatically disqualified from being worthy of loyalty: this is the mistake of punishing or ostracizing those who decide not to believe, or who believe tentatively, or who change to another religion. (It is especially important to make tentative belief possible if membership in a tradition is essential for full membership in a larger society.) A tradition that does not permit "answering back" is less worthy of allegiance. An admirable tradition admits what it does not know and is "up front" about the questionable character of its competence in various areas that the traditions once thought to be their special preserve, such as cosmology or the nature of human beings. Worship services and religious observations as currently constituted do not permit dissent, and this is their deepest flaw. This defect bespeaks a sort of immaturity; and it encourages immaturity on the part of its adherents.

Religions protect themselves from these conclusions by attempting to engender in and elicit from their adherents a sense of fear or of failure or of guilt, in the event of a failure to believe or to believe "in the right way." This seems to be a mechanism whose function is to fill the gap that results from the fact of religious ambiguity.

10

⊱────◦────⊰

RELIGIOUS EXPERIENCE AND
RELIGIOUS BELIEF

There is no doubt that deeply felt experiences are at the very heart of the religious life. Presumably the religious traditions would not even have come into existence were it not that their first members had experiences that led them to hold their beliefs. The idea is well expressed by William James when he remarks that "feeling is the deeper source of religion, and . . . philosophical and theological formulas are secondary products. . . . [In] a world in which no religious feeling had ever existed, I doubt whether any philosophic theology could ever have been framed."[1] And in the absence of all relevant experiences on the part of subsequent generations, it is unlikely that membership in a tradition would be sustained.

One aspect of this link with experience is that all of the major religions have a capacity to be integrated with the experience of their followers: that is, the concepts, symbols, and so forth, of each tradition provide a framework within which its adherents are able to interpret and explain their experience, including both their ordinary daily experience and less ordinary and particularly noteworthy events. A tradition that was not integrated with experience in this fashion probably would not survive. It would devolve into empty formulas that have less and less meaning for those who subscribe to them, and into practices whose point would increasingly be called into question; and over a generation or two they might well disappear entirely.

I take it for granted that, generally speaking, people have the religious experiences that they claim to have. At least this is so insofar as a report on an experience is a report on a phenomenal state that a person experiences. Thus I take it for granted that those who report on religious experiences are not engaging in widespread deception. Rather, they have experiences that, it seems to them, are correctly to be described as they describe them.

So the notion of religious experience deployed here is such that we can accept that people have religious experiences and yet leave it as an open question whether there is any external reality (of the sort that religions uniquely posit) that is encountered in such experience. The contrast is with a construal of religious experience such that someone has a religious experience only if the reality they believe themselves to encounter really is encountered.

If someone feels that, for example, she is aware of a being who provides her with guidance in her life, or if she follows guidance that she believes herself to have received from such a being and then seems to herself to find this guidance to be reliable, then it seems reasonable to think that her belief that that being exists receives some justification from this experience. And if such a person ever wonders whether her religious beliefs are correct, or if others ask her what reason she has to think that her religious beliefs are correct, it would be reasonable for her to include the fact that she has had those experiences in her account of why it is reasonable for her to hold those beliefs. In general, if someone has experiences that it seems reasonable to her to interpret as experiences of God, perhaps because she has been led to expect that such experiences will occur in the course of interaction with God, then it seems to be rational for her to base her theistic beliefs to some extent on those experiences. This is especially likely to be so if, for example, the experiences in question are part of a pattern that seems to her to be apparent in her life, and if others also report on the same or similar experiences and interpret them in the same way. Such claims seem *obviously* correct.

Yet the procedure of relying on one's experiences in the area of religion with a view to deciding what to believe, or with a view to seeing which beliefs are supported by experience, is one whose reliability is suspect. For it is plain that people in a number of religious traditions, whom we have every reason to believe to have integrity, and who seem to have as much right as anyone else to claim relevant expertise, enjoy experiences that they understand to support the particular religious beliefs associated with their tradition. Yet the beliefs of the traditions are, to a great extent, mutually exclusive. It is as if we were to find that people are typically wrong in what they think they are observing in a certain area or in using a certain procedure. Consequently, if religious experience provides evidence for religious beliefs, it is evidence that appears equally supportive of a bewildering array of traditions. That this is so has significance both for the person who actually enjoys the experience and for the outsider whose sole acquaintance with religious experience is through the reports of others.

In this and the next chapter I consider some aspects of this topic of religious experience. I ask whether the very possibility of experiences providing epistemic support for religious beliefs is undermined by the fact that there is disagreement about religious matters. That is, does the presence of disagreement (of the sort that I have been discussing) serve to neutralize, or to reduce, whatever support would otherwise be provided for religious belief by religious experience? And what are the implications of the connected but distinct fact that people report on experiences that appear to them to be consistent with, and to support, a variety of religious positions? In general, can appeals to what may be known or reasonably believed on the basis of religious experience suffice to undermine or weaken the case for the E-principle or the T-principle?

My case in the foregoing chapters has been in part that the combined facts of religious ambiguity and religious diversity provide the basis for a case for tentativeness in beliefs about religious matters. A response to this case that will be forthcoming from various quarters is that this case is fine as far as it goes, but that there is a firm basis on which the claims of one tradition can be established, and by appeal to which a case for belief that is more than tentative can be made. An appeal to the experiences of the adherents of a tradition is one obvious candidate for such a basis. It will be contended that in virtue of their experiences the adherents of some tradition know (or reasonably believe [etc.]) that they are right. Hence belief that is more than tentative is warranted after all, at least for them, and perhaps for others too. It is the force of claims of this sort that I want to assess. My contention will be that while the force of such claims is not negligible, it is fairly limited.

The topic of religious experience is a vast one. Its vastness is a function of, among other things, the variety of experiences that are reported and the diversity of traditions within which they are reported and for whose tenets they are thought to provide support. So of necessity I will be selective in dealing with this enormous topic. My intention is to say enough to indicate how we should respond to appeals that will be made to experience in an attempt to undermine the arguments of the foregoing chapters.

It is now widely recognized that there are two distinct ways in which religious experiences might support religious beliefs. One possibility is that experiences might provide evidence for beliefs. Thus it may seem to the person who has certain experiences, or to other people, that the best explanation of the occurrence of various experiences is that God is involved in their production. The other possibility is that the experiences might involve perceiving, or seeming to oneself to perceive, that certain beliefs are true: thus the experience might involve someone seeming to herself to perceive that God is guiding her or forgiving her. This chapter bears on both possibilities, and chapter 11 deals exclusively with the latter possibility.

It may well be that many, or even most, people who have religious experiences do not think of them as providing support for any of their religious beliefs. If this is so, the reason—or a reason—may be that they do not feel any need to consider where support for their religious beliefs is to be found. That is, they simply assume a certain picture of things and interpret their experiences, their lives, and so forth, in accordance with that picture. They are therefore unaccustomed to classifying their experiences, or phenomena of any sort, as supporting their religious beliefs. However, this fact, if it is a fact, is quite beside the point when we ask what support is provided for any particular set of religious beliefs by experiences that the adherents of those beliefs associate with them. And that is what I wish to consider.

1. Experience and Initial Justification

In his book *Return to Reason*, Kelly James Clark contends that at least with respect to beliefs that are based directly on experience, the fact that there is widespread disagreement about such beliefs does not diminish the support that the beliefs in question receive from the relevant experiences. I use Clark's remarks as a starting point for the discussion of this chapter. He asks us to consider the following tale:

> Suppose a person, say Theodore, is alone on a mountain and acquires the belief that he has seen a timber wolf. Surely he is initially justified in the belief that there is a timber wolf before him. Suppose further that when he descends and tells his intellectual peers that he

saw a timber wolf, they disagree with his claim and roundly denounce his credulity. . . . Does the mere fact of disagreement constitute a reason against his belief that he saw a timber wolf? Presumably it would be difficult for him to produce a good argument for his belief. Furthermore, timber wolves aren't the sorts of things that sit around waiting to provide irrefragable evidence to convince one's peers. Granted, the reasons for which Theodore's intellectual peers disagree—suppose they know that timber wolves are extinct or that they don't live above a certain altitude—*may* constitute reasons against his belief. But the simple disagreement of his intellectual peers is not detrimental to his belief that he saw a timber wolf.[2]

Is this really so? Clark is making a number of claims here. Let us set aside the issue of disagreement for a moment and consider first the claim that if Theodore is alone on a mountain and acquires the belief that he has seen a timber wolf, he is initially justified in the belief that there is a timber wolf before him. Is this so? Consider Theodore. Who is he? Is he a forester or a naturalist who is familiar with wolves, or is he a city dweller who does not know the first thing about wolves? (For example, does he mistakenly believe that *all* wolves are timber wolves?) Is it reasonable for him to be confident that he can tell the difference between a timber wolf and a red wolf, or even the difference between a timber wolf and a coyote? The more qualified he is to tell the difference, the more reason he has to take what he understands himself to perceive at face value. If Theodore has at his disposal the concepts that are necessary to describe what he observed, this increases the support provided by his experience of seeming to see a timber wolf for his belief that he saw a timber wolf. On the other hand, if he lacks the requisite concepts, he would be ill equipped to describe what he has seen. Thus someone who has never heard of wolves may not know what to say about what he experiences on the mountain even if he actually encounters a timber wolf: he may say that he saw an unusually shaped German shepherd. So Theodore's relevant competence and conceptual equipment matter greatly.

How did Theodore acquire the belief that he saw a timber wolf? Did it suddenly pop into his head, for example? (Has his doctor told him that he is prone to this sort of thing? Does he see timber wolves everywhere he goes? Do people say: "There goes poor Theodore; what will he 'see' next?" Has he been crying "timber wolf" so often that everyone is sick and tired of his nonsense?) Is there reason to believe, and does Theodore have reason to believe, that the process through which he acquired the belief is a reliable one? Was what he saw ambiguous and hard to interpret? Was there bright sunshine or a heavy mist? The nature and circumstances of the experience also bear on the degree of support that his experience provides for the relevant belief.

Then there is the question of the relevant background beliefs that Theodore had when he had the experience For example, did he previously believe that there were no timber wolves for thousands of miles? Was he aware, for example, that there are some who claim that when the sun shines in a particular way on a coyote that is regularly seen just where he thinks he saw a timber wolf, the coyote greatly resembles a timber wolf, so that even experienced naturalists have been deceived by this phenomenon? On the other hand, at the time that he had the experience Theodore may have known, or may have had every reason to believe, that there *are* wolves in the area. He might have had access to satellite reports that show timber wolves migrating in this direction for the first time in known history. The latter beliefs seem to provide support for his interpretation of his experience. They give him more reason to take at face value what he takes himself to observe.

However, whatever background beliefs may have been in place, Theodore's belief that he has seen a timber wolf will typically be at least partly based on his experience. In this it differs from, for example, the belief that there are timber wolves on the mountain.

I think it is clear that whether or not Theodore is initially justified in believing that he has seen a timber wolf, and—if he is—the extent to which he is, depend on conditions such as those I have mentioned. The amount of support provided by the experience for the belief depends, among other things, on the nature of the experience and the competence and background beliefs of the person who enjoys it.

2. The Principle of Credulity

Implicit in the claim that Theodore is initially justified in his belief that he has seen a timber wolf is a principle along the lines of Richard Swinburne's Principle of Credulity, according to which

> we ought to believe that things are as they seem to be (in the epistemic sense) unless and until we have evidence that we are mistaken.[3]

To say that things seem *in the epistemic sense* to be a certain way is just to say that things appear really to be that way. The contrast is with the comparative notion of seeming, where to say that something seems to be a certain way is to say that it appears as it would appear if it were that way.

Swinburne believes a principle of this sort to apply both to the person who has the experience and to others. Hence he accepts both (a) if it seems to S that he is seeing x, then S ought to believe that he is seeing x until he has evidence to the contrary and (b) if it seems to S that he is seeing x, then everyone else ought also to believe that S is seeing x, in the absence of evidence to the contrary. (Swinburne refers to (a) as the Principle of Credulity and to (b) as the Principle of Testimony.) The situation of the person having the experience is what is relevant here.

In the course of expositing the Principle of Credulity, Swinburne actually characterizes such a person's situation in a number of ways. The important question to ask is this. Assuming that S lacks evidence to the contrary, if it seems to S that x is present, what follows? Is it, as the passage quoted here entails, that S ought to believe that x is present? Or is S provided with significant evidence that x is present (136), or with "substantial grounds for belief" that x is present? (*The Existence of God*, 254). Or "good grounds" for supposing or believing that x is present? (255, 260). Or just "grounds" for so supposing? (260). Or, again, is it merely right or permissible for S to take it that x is present? (*The Existence of God*, 254). These claims differ considerably in their force; some are weaker than others and hence easier to defend.

Let us consider the claim that if S lacks evidence to the contrary, then if it seems to S that x is present, S is *justified* in the belief that x is present. In its force, this seems to be roughly in the middle of the various formulations that I just noted in Swinburne: thus it is weaker than the claim that if it seems to S that x is present, then S *ought* to believe that x is present, unless and until S has evidence that he is mistaken; but it is stronger than the claim that if it seems to S that x is present, then S *has grounds* for supposing that x is present, unless and until S has evidence that he is mistaken. The latter is consistent with S's having even better grounds for supposing otherwise. Exactly what being justified in a belief amounts to is itself a difficult issue. Let us assume the following: S is justified in believing p provided that S has good reason to believe p, no (or much less) reason not to believe p, and S is not blameworthy in any respect in virtue of believing p.

Swinburne considers a number of types of contrary evidence. First, we may have evidence that the conditions in which the experience occurred are such that the experience is unreliable (*Is There a God?* 134). The problem might be with the perceiver. She might lack the conceptual equipment or the prior experience that is required for a certain type of perception. Or the problem might be the conditions in a more general sense: thus the experience might be a visual one that is made in circumstances in which our vision has been found to be unreliable. Second, there may be independent evidence that what S believed himself to perceive is in fact not the case. Third, there may be independent evidence that S's experience was not caused in the way that S understands it to have been caused. In each case, Swinburne says, "the onus is on the sceptic to give reason for not believing what seems to be the case" (136).

The picture, then, is this. S is justified in believing that x is present if it seems to S that x is present—unless one or more of the defeating conditions obtain. And it is up to someone who is skeptical that x is present to *show* that some such condition obtains. Until the skeptic does so, S is justified in the belief that x is present. If, however, the skeptic shows that some such defeating condition holds, then the burden of proof shifts, and S will continue to be justified in believing that x is present on the basis of its seeming to S that x is present only if the skeptic's challenge is met.

It is true that the burden of proof shifts to S if the skeptic shows that a defeating condition holds. In fact, it probably does so if the skeptic does something weaker, such as provide reason to believe that a defeating condition holds. But we should reject the idea that if it seems to S that x is present, S is justified in the belief that x is present until such times as the skeptic shows, or provides reason to believe, that a defeating condition holds. For example, if Theodore is himself aware that his belief that he has seen a timber wolf was formed in circumstances in which it was hard to tell what was before him, or that his grasp of what distinguishes different types of wolves is shaky, or if Theodore has hitherto believed that it is very unlikely that there are timber wolves on the mountain, then—in any of these situations or any combination of them—his initial justification for believing that he has seen a timber wolf on the mountain may be very much reduced, so much so that he may not be justified at all in so believing. The suggestion that prima facie justification is conferred by the experience and that the defeating conditions come into play only if someone else makes a compelling case for their applicability seems mistaken. Theodore might be initially justified in forming the belief that he has seen a timber wolf in virtue of seeming to see a timber wolf. Or he might be completely unjustified. Or he might be something in between. It all depends on the details of the situation.

3. Disagreement and Justification

So far I have focused on the claim that Theodore is *initially justified* in believing that he has seen a timber wolf. Let us now turn to what is actually the main focus of the tale of Theodore, namely, the significance of disagreement.[4] As Clark puts it

> Suppose . . . that when [Theodore] descends and tells his intellectual peers that he saw a timber wolf, they disagree with his claim and roundly denounce his credulity. . . . Does the mere fact of disagreement constitute a reason against his belief that he saw a timber wolf? . . . Granted, the reasons for which Theodore's intellectual peers disagree—suppose they know that timber wolves are extinct or that they don't live above a certain altitude—may constitute reasons against his belief. But the simple disagreement of his intellectual peers is not detrimental to his belief that he saw a timber wolf.[5]

Clark's intuition here is not an unreasonable one. After all, Theodore was there; he was the one who had the experience. Those who disagree were not there and did not have the experience. Why should the fact that they disagree diminish the support provided for his belief by his experience?

Nevertheless, in considering the significance of the fact that others disagree, there are many factors to take into account. Clark says that what he has in mind is disagreement among Theodore's "intellectual peers." The implication seems to be that if those who disagree are *less* than peers, there would be no question but that their disagreement would give Theodore no reason to question his beliefs. So it matters *who* is disagreeing. But what if they were *more* than peers? Perhaps it is apparent that they are, for example, forest rangers or zoologists or local experts on the flora and fauna of the mountain. Or what if he had some reason to believe that they were more than peers? At any rate, it matters greatly who they are.

It also matters what they say. Clark is discussing the implications of the mere fact that people disagree with beliefs one acquires on the basis of experience. But it is not so clear what *mere disagreement* consists in. Those who disagree may merely say to Theodore that he is wrong. But their disagreement may involve their saying: "Surely you did not fall for that old stunt, Theodore!" Or they may declare with an air of conviction or with great authority: "Well, we *know* that you are wrong!" Normally more can generally be said than just that there is disagreement. What is said, who says it, and even how it is said, may make a difference to how Theodore ought to react when there is disagreement. So while Clark is right to draw a distinction between the mere fact of disagreement and the reasons other people have for disagreeing, "the mere fact of disagreement" seems to dissolve somewhat under scrutiny: the reality will always have a particular texture, and its import will be in part a function of that texture.

However, if an experience "scores" very well in all of the areas mentioned, then it does seem that the fact of disagreement would not diminish significantly the support that that experience provides for the relevant belief. That is, if Theodore is an expert on timber wolves and had ample opportunity to observe and even to study in bright sunlight the animal he saw on the mountain, and if those who disagree do not come close to Theodore's level of expertise, then it may be that the fact that there is disagreement should not reduce at all the support that Theodore derives for his belief that he saw a timberwolf from the experience in which he seemed to himself to do so. Clark is certainly right to this extent: there is nothing at all to be said for the view that whenever there is disagreement, Theodore ought not to believe that he saw a timber wolf in all such cases.

It is plain that there is a lot to take into account. And the story of Theodore hardly suffices to show that disagreement does not reduce the support that a belief derives from an experience on which it is based.[6] As we have seen, to say that the fact that there is disagreement does not diminish the support that is provided for Theodore's belief that he saw a timber wolf by his experience of seeming to see a timber wolf is to fail to consider many possibilities and to treat extremely different cases in an unduly monolithic way.[7]

Clark's main purpose, of course, does not have to do with wolves. Rather, his purpose is to suggest that the following two cases ought to be treated in the same way. First, there is the case of Theodore. The fact that Theodore encounters people who disagree with him does not give him reason not to base his belief that he saw a timber wolf on his experience. Then there is the case of someone—let's call him Franklin— who is on a mountain on a starry night and who is "overcome with the conviction" that God has created everything around him. In his case, too, the fact that he encounters people who disagree with him does not provide reason for him not to base his belief that God has created everything around him on the experience in question.

But much the same questions need to be asked in both cases, and the same criticisms apply. And the case of Theodore provides little support for the case of Franklin. Here, too, it all depends: it depends on Franklin's competence, the competence of those who disagree, the character and circumstances of Franklin's experience, and so forth. Only if Franklin's experience of being overwhelmed with the conviction that God has created everything around him gets high marks in those areas that we have seen to bear on the case of Theodore, would it be reasonable for Franklin to base his belief that God has created everything around him on this experience.

4. Differences between the Two Cases

There are in fact some reasons to think that the two cases differ in ways that weaken any attempt to extrapolate from the case of Theodore to the theistic case. Here are three such reasons.

First, there is a difference between these two cases with respect to how various background beliefs are likely to function. The relevant background beliefs include whatever other reasons or evidence the person who has the experience has for believing whatever it is that he takes his experience to be telling him to be the case. Thus in the case of Franklin, who is overcome with the conviction that God has created everything around him, the relevant background beliefs would include whatever independent reasons Franklin has for thinking that God exists and for thinking that God has created the world around him.

The difference here between these two cases is this. If (a) Theodore knows a lot about wolves, about their habitat, variety, markings, behavior, footprints, and so on, and (b) he reasonably believes that there are timber wolves on the mountain and if (c) other favorable conditions that I have explored obtain—so that Theodore had a good look at the animal on the mountain, and so forth—then it is reasonable to think that Theodore would be justified in believing that he has seen a timber wolf on the basis of his experience. However, Franklin's case is different. It is natural to think of the relevant background beliefs providing part of the basis on which Franklin believes that God has created everything, *whatever* experiences he may have on a mountaintop on a starry night. It is to be expected that experiences can do more by way of providing support in cases of the former sort, all other things being equal. The belief that God has created everything goes far beyond anything that could be yielded by any experience. Theodore's belief that he saw a timber wolf is, after all, partly about Theodore, or at any rate about a particular item in Theodore's experience, whereas the belief that God has created everything is entirely about God and about God's relation to everything else that exists. This difference cuts against the claim that really matters to Clark, for it suggests that the support that Theodore's experience on the mountain provides for his belief that he sees a timber wolf will be greater than the amount of support provided by any theistic experience on a mountaintop for the belief that God has created the world. It suggests that the experience itself is capable of doing less work in the theistic case, that it is less likely in the theistic case that the relevant belief may reasonably be based on the experience alone.

Also, the fact that it is indisputable that there *are* timber wolves, whereas it is less clear that God exists (so that intelligent and well-informed people have different views) is relevant. Since there are known to be timber wolves, the sighting of one, even in a very unusual setting, is less remarkable than it otherwise would be. The belief that there is such a thing need not be at all dependent on an experience.

Yet it remains the case that the degree of justification in either case will largely be a function of the actual character, circumstances (etc.) of the experience. And this brings us to a second difference between the two cases. Theodore is justified in believing that he saw a timber wolf only if what he saw was clear and unambiguous; and we can easily imagine that condition being satisfied in the case of Theodore. On the other hand, it seems natural to think that whatever may be seen by someone who, while on a mountaintop, forms the belief that God has created everything, will not be clear and unambiguous—at least in terms of its support for the belief that God has created everything. He may see the outline of valleys, towns, trees, and so forth, far below him. And above him he may be able to pick out various constellations and stars. All this may fill him with a general sense that God has created everything, combined with a sense of wonder and awe. But the support provided in the religious case for the relevant belief seems to be diminished on account of the looser connection in this case between the experience and the belief.

Third, the issue of whether special expertise is required to interpret the experience correctly bears on the attempt to extrapolate from the one case to the other. There are cases in which no special expertise is needed and almost anyone can be relied upon to give an accurate report. Thus almost anyone would be able to tell whether it was raining or the sun was shining on the mountaintop. On the other hand, both in the case of Theodore and in the case of Franklin, some fairly specialized expertise is needed in order to interpret the experience correctly. This is clear in the case of Theodore in that one can easily imagine someone without much expertise mistaking, say, a red wolf for a timber wolf. (I, for one, am incapable of distinguishing them.) The same holds in the religious case: for there are many people from many backgrounds from whom the experience of being on a mountain on a starry night will not elicit the thought that God has created everything. Yet in this area, too, there seems to be a difference between the two cases. For in Theodore's case we can easily imagine its being uncontroversial that he has the requisite expertise to recognize a timber wolf. This is because it is clear what this expertise consists in. Hence, it is clear whether or not someone has it. But in the religious case there will be no such agreement about what the required expertise amounts to, and hence about who has it. Nor is there agreement about what procedure is best suited to discerning the facts of the matter, whereas everyone agrees on the best procedure for deciding whether there was a timber wolf on the mountain. (The lack of a clear procedure in the case of God is itself indicative of its being hard to discern the facts of the situation.) Uncertainty in these areas reduces the support provided by experience for belief.

Another feature of the case is worthy of comment. Franklin is said to be *overcome* with the conviction that God has created everything around him, whereas nothing of this sort was claimed in the case of Theodore. Nor are we inclined to read the story of Theodore in this way. We have no reason to exclude the possibility that Theodore may have had difficulty identifying an animal of which he only caught a glimpse. In fact it would be strange for Theodore to be overcome with the conviction that he saw a timber wolf: it is not the sort of belief that normally would occur with that sort of force. One would have to make up a story to make sense of it doing so, such as a story about how Theodore has worked for years against all odds to restore timber wolves to the mountain and now at last has seen his first wild timber wolf. And even in that case he is more likely to be overcome on account of having seen a timber wolf than he is to be overcome with the belief that he has seen a timber wolf: that is, the state of being overcome is more likely to be a consequence of the experience of seeing the wolf rather than the mode in which the experience occurs. This difference between the two cases may seem to provide some support for the cause that matters to Clark, for if Franklin is overcome with the belief that God has created the world around him, he must find that belief unavoidable, whereas this feature may be absent in the case of Theodore. But while this feature that is present in Franklin's case, but may be absent in Theodore's case, would bear, for example, on whether either is to be praised or blamed for acquiring the relevant belief in the circumstances in which it is acquired, it has little bearing on the question of what support was provided by the experience for the belief. The important question is whether Franklin was overcome with the belief that God has created everything around him in virtue of the content of that belief being delivered with great clarity to him by the experience. What matters is not whether he was overcome with the belief; rather, it is whether the nature and circumstances of Franklin's experience make it appropriate for him to be overcome with the belief.

So far, in discussing the case of Theodore, I have considered the significance of the diversity of beliefs. Let us briefly consider another topic, namely, the significance of a diversity of reported experiences. Suppose that some of Theodore's peers were with him on the mountain, and suppose they report on experiences that appear to them to support beliefs that are at odds with the belief that Theodore bases on his experience. What would be the significance of *that* for the capacity of his experiences to support his beliefs? Suppose, for instance, that *you* are there looking at whatever Theodore is looking at. He exclaims, "My word, it's a timber wolf," whereas you are of the opinion that it is something else, such as a coyote or an oddly shaped piece of timber. ("Well, Theodore," you say, "it may or may not be a timber wolf, but at least it's timber.") Suppose that it is clear that you and Theodore are indeed looking at the same thing and that it is not, for example, that you are both merely looking in the same general direction while the focus of your vision is different. In that case the support provided for your reading of what you observe by what you each believe yourself to experience seems to be diminished by awareness that a peer interprets the same thing in a different way. And if it simply isn't clear whether you are both interpreting the same thing, then to the extent that there is reason to believe that you are doing so, to that extent also the fact that you interpret it differently gives reason to believe that it must be something that is hard to interpret and is easily misread. The support that you derive for your reading of it should be reduced accordingly.

Moreover, if two observers interpret the same thing in such different ways, there must be some explanation of this occurrence. Although this is not the only possible explanation, a natural explanation in such a case is that what you are both observing is difficult to interpret and is open to being read by reasonable people in a number of ways.

Suppose that when Theodore reports on seeing a timber wolf, you cannot see anything there that he might even be talking about. He might say: "Look, it's just in front of us, about 10 feet away" and yet you are puzzled as to what he might even be talking about. In this bizarre and puzzling case, things have gone dreadfully wrong, for at least one of you. If you are peers, then it seems that both of you have good reason to question your ability to see what is right before you, and hence good reason to doubt that what you think yourself to perceive is actually the case.

It is not clear which of these cases is closest to the situation we find in the area of religion. Each of us certainly is faced with a plethora of traditions, the adherents of each of which report on experiences that appear to them to provide reason to believe what they believe. If we do not ourselves enjoy any such experiences, we seem to lack much justification for believing what any one of these parties believe on the basis of experience.

If, on the other hand, we ourselves enjoy some such experiences, the amount of justification provided by those experiences for our beliefs seems to be reduced by the diversity of reported experiences to some extent, with the extent in question being a function of, for example, the clarity of one's experiences, and the apparent competence of the opposition. Yet there is no reason to think that the fact that there is disagreement[8] reduces the justificatory force of such experiences to zero.

5. Some Varieties of Religious Experience

It is important to keep in mind the many types of religious experience. What follows is a list of nine such types. What they have in common is the fact that they are among the phenomena that will be mentioned if religious people are asked what in their experience gives them reason to think that their religious position is correct. In addition to not being exhaustive of the types of religious experience that have been reported, the list includes types that are not mutually exclusive. My list also excessively emphasizes theistic religious experiences and neglects various experiences that are associated with nontheistic traditions, although I am discussing in general terms the significance of the fact that there are religious experiences that are taken to confirm the beliefs associated with many traditions, including nontheistic ones.

(a) Normal sense experience of events or phenomena that are understood to have a special religious significance and that are extraordinary in the sense that they are highly unusual and are understood by those who experience them to have been brought about in a special way, such as by divine intervention. In such experience one's sensory modes such as sight, hearing, smell (etc.) are working in the usual way, and these processes are directed toward the normal sorts of objects that those sensory processes enable us to perceive, such as apples, stones, trees, books, and so forth. But what is perceived is understood to have a special and unusual significance. Examples of what I have in mind include experiences such as those reported on by early Christians who claimed to see and touch the resurrected Jesus, as well as claims to have observed various miracles such as water being turned into wine or a blind man receiving the ability to see. I take it that early Christians who are said to have encountered the resurrected Jesus are represented in the New Testament as having perceived him by their senses while those senses were working normally, just as we normally perceive ordinary folk and the objects around us. And observing water become wine, I take it, would involve observing what is water and therefore actually looks like and tastes like (etc.) water, and then observing, in its place, what is wine and actually looks like and tastes like (etc.) wine. Even if there were transitional phases during which the liquid in question was partly water and partly wine, what is there during the transitional phases would itself be observed in the normal way.

Since I want to focus on the implications of experiences that clearly occur, we need to restrict attention here to experiences in which it *seems* to people that they are having experiences of this sort. Obviously, it is highly controversial whether events of the sort alluded to in the last paragraph actually occur. For one can experience a miracle only if a miracle occurs, just as one can experience getting married only if one gets married. So (a)-type experience, therefore, is sense experience that seems to the person who has it to be of extraordinary events of the sorts mentioned in the preceding paragraph.

(b) "Seeing" visions and "hearing" voices, where this does not involve normal sense experience. Many cases in which someone understands himself to have perceived an angel or an apparition or a ghost, for example, would belong in this category. Although (b)-type experiences involve something other than normal sense perception, they share with normal sense perception a content with many of the same phenomenal properties: thus to see in a vision someone who is wearing a red coat would involve an awareness of something that looks red. That is, it would involve having an experience that is close in its content to the experience of seeing something red. *What* is observed is just whatever objects (if there are any) this sort of experience would enable one to observe. Here, too, the experience needs to be characterized as experience that seems to someone who has it to be of the sort under discussion. (This rider is to be assumed, when appropriate, in the case of all of the remaining types of experience too.) So (b)-type experience includes, for example, experience in which it seems to someone that she is "seeing" a vision.[9]

(a)-type and (b)-type experiences are distinguished in terms of the sort of perception that they seem to involve. This is less complicated than distinguishing them on the basis of the sorts of the objects whose perception they seem to involve.

There may be experiences about which it is hard to know whether it is category (a) or category (b) they are in. For instance, if someone were to seem to see an apparition, perhaps it would not be clear, even to him, whether sense perception was involved.

Presumably in the case of (b)-type experiences, just as in the case of (a)-type experiences, (and, for that matter, in the case of religious experiences of all sorts), various brain states and certain brain activity would be involved. Presumably someone could not have a vision of a person with a red coat standing before her unless she had brain states of much the same sort as is normally involved when she sees that there is a person with a red coat before her. (This is, of course, a matter that could be settled decisively only by appeal to empirical data.) However, if the construal of what is occurring that is proposed by those who report on the experiences in question is correct, the brain states involved will of course have been brought about in a way that differs markedly from normal sense perception.

(c) A sense or awareness of God doing something in relation to oneself, such as communicating with you or guiding you, or a sense or awareness of God as having some property such as benevolence or sternness. In the case of God talking to you, this might be a matter of (a)-type experience in which you actually hear a voice, or it might be a matter of feeling or "sensing" (a term that, interestingly, conveys the idea of a sort of awareness that does not involve the senses and is really in no way sensory) that you are being told something without hearing any such voice.

Some experiences of this sort involve clear propositional content. The content might include, for instance, information about what God is like, or about what you ought to do. A voice might be heard saying "I am the Lord your God who has brought you out of the land of Egypt." But propositional content might be conveyed in other ways. For instance, someone might have an experience that it was difficult for her to articulate, even to herself, but which she felt was best interpreted as involving some message or other being transmitted to her.

(d) Awareness of the presence of God or of some God-like being or entity that involves no sensory content. A sense of companionship may be felt. Here are two examples of the sort of thing I have in mind:

> Then in a very gentle and gradual way, not with a shock at all, it began to dawn on me that I was not alone in the room. Someone else was there, located fairly precisely about two yards to my right front. Yet there was no sort of sensory hallucination. I neither saw him nor heard him in any sense of the word "see" and "hear," but there he was; I had no doubt about it. He seemed to be very good and very wise, full of sympathetic understanding, and most kindly disposed towards me. . . . There was no sensible vision, but the room was filled by a Presence which in a strange way was both about me and within me. I was overwhelmingly possessed by Someone who was not myself, and yet I felt I was more myself than I had ever been before.[10]

The second example of this type of experience is from Saint Teresa. She refers to this experience as a vision, but it seems to fall into the category of experience under discussion because it involves none of the phenomenal content shared by (a)-type and (b)-type experiences.

I was at prayer on a festival of the glorious Saint Peter when I saw Christ at my side—or, to put it better, I was conscious of Him, for neither with the eyes of the body nor with those of the soul did I see anything. I thought He was quite close to me and I saw that it was He Who, as I thought, was speaking to me. . . . Jesus Christ seemed to be beside me, but as this was not an imaginary vision, I could not discern in what form: what I felt very clearly was that all the time He was at my right hand, and a witness of everything that I was doing, and that, whenever I became slightly recollected or was not greatly distracted, I could not but be aware of His nearness to me.[11]

(e) Mystical experiences. People report on various types of mystical experience, including theistic ones that involve a sense of union with God, nontheistic ones that involve a sense of absorption into some larger whole such as some sort of religious reality that is impersonally conceived, or into nature as a whole, and an experience of pure empty consciousness from which all thoughts, perceptions, and other mental content has been removed.

(f) Numinous experience. This is experience of contact with a holy being, involving all or some of these attitudes: awe, fear, dread, a sense of the presence of God as a living, personal being, and a sense of individual unworthiness, dependency, powerlessness, and insignificance.

(g) A sense of deep contentment and assurance, or calm and tranquillity, or of being at peace with oneself, or a reduction in anxiety, when this occurs in a context that is understood to have religious significance, such as during, or after, meditation or prayer.

(h) A sense of having hit on what really matters, or of having your life transformed, or of having solved important problems in your life. It may involve a sense of having found salvation or liberation or of being free from sin, or the closest equivalent to sin in the tradition in question.

(i) Experience of events or phenomena that can be construed in a purely secular way (and about whose occurrence, so construed, there can be no question) and that are given a religious interpretation. For example, you might experience an event or sequence of events in your life, such as recovery from an illness or the kindness of a stranger, as involving guidance by, and interaction with, God, or as displaying the effects of the operation of the law of Karma or the effects of the agency of some local deity. The events in question might be events in your own life but they may also be events in other people's lives, in the life of your whole religious group, or in the history of a nation.

In this category it is also reasonable to include, for example, cases in which someone is overwhelmed religiously at the sight of a beautiful sunset or a cluster of wild flowers, or at the sight of other splendors of nature: I have in mind in particular cases in which someone sees, say, a cluster of wildflowers as manifesting the hand of God. Such a case resembles (a)-type experience in that it involves sensory modes, such as sight, hearing, or smell, working in the usual way. And these processes are directed toward the normal sorts of objects that those sensory processes enable us to perceive, such as apples, trees, houses, and so forth. But while (a)-type experience is taken by those who enjoy it to be of extraordinary events, what I have in mind here are ordinary events (a stunning sunset over central Illinois, for example) that are perceived to have a religious significance.

It might be said that we should not think of the practice of interpreting everyday events and everyday life religiously as religious experience at all, but rather as ordinary experience that is interpreted in a religious way or as ordinary experience to which an additional layer of interpretation has been added. It does not matter what we call it, but there are good reasons to think of it as a type of religious experience. In fact, it is one of the most important respects in which the religious beliefs and religious worldview of the typical member of the typical tradition bear on his or her experience. An interesting feature of such experience is that the depth of a person's religious commitment will bear on the extent to which it colors his experience.

Actually this category, the previous two categories ((g)-type and (h)-type experiences), and (c)-type experiences of the less dramatic sorts, are the most common forms of religious experience. For it is unclear to what extent the typical member of a religious tradition has experiences that are dramatic and out of the ordinary, as are many of the experiences in the other categories.

The fact that these (less dramatic (c)-type, (g)-type, (h)-type and (i)-type experiences) are the types of religious experience that are most frequently enjoyed squares with the proposal that our world is religiously ambiguous. For example, the fact that certain patterns are discernible in one's own life, or in the lives of others (etc.) may be something that is not obvious and that is easy to miss. It may require a certain type of focus and approach if it is to be noticed at all.

There is some overlap between the types of experience I have distinguished: that is, there are experiences that are in more than one of these categories. Thus if you were to interpret some event in your life, such as a serious illness, as involving divine guidance, this would be an instance both of (c)-type and of (i)-type experience. Also (d)-type and (f)-type experiences, for example, are very similar, and many experiences would be in both of these categories.

There are various ways to sort out these types of religious experience. Some are exclusively theistic, while others are not. Some (e.g., (d)) are private to each perceiver, in the same way that a person's sensations of pain and other sensations are private, whereas others (e.g., (a)) involve something public, in the sense in which the external world is public. But some at least of those that are private, such as the experience of having contact with God, are normally understood by those who have them to involve contact with an external being, and hence to be, in this respect at least, unlike other private experiences. Some (e.g., (b) and (d)) seem to involve direct, unmediated, or face-to-face experience of some person or being, whereas others (e.g., (i)) involve experiences that are taken to point in the direction of some such being, but in an indirect and mediated way. Some ((b)–(f), but not (a) or (g)) typically are usually understood to involve an awareness of a supernatural being or state. Some have propositional content, while others do not.

My usage of the term *religious experience* is a broad and inclusive one.[12] As indicated, it is intended to encompass anything in a believer's experience to which she might point in support of her religious position. To remind ourselves of the considerable variety of such phenomena is to remind ourselves of the variety of sources of epistemic support that are available to the believer. For obvious reasons I am concentrating on experiences that can be characterized in such a way that it is clear and uncontroversial that they occur: thus that people seem to themselves to be guided by God, or to feel the presence of God, is entirely clear.

6. The Possibility of Indubitable Experiences

Now that we have before us a variety of types of religious experience, let us return to the question of their force. Some people say that they have experiences of a religiously significant sort that are so clear in their content and so unquestionable in their nature that in virtue of those experiences they can no more doubt the various beliefs that they consider to be supported by those experiences than they can doubt, say, their belief that there are other people or that there is an external world. In such a case the person who has the experience cannot see how he could be wrong; and this is because of the character of the experience and not just because he lacks imagination, for example. Let us say that someone who is in this position has an *indubitable experience.* Thus if someone has experiences that seem clearly and unquestionably to involve God talking to her, or to involve visions of the Virgin Mary, and if those experiences have all of the clarity and the unquestionableness of character that is typical of, say, the sense experience that we rely on in our perception of physical objects in our immediate vicinity, this person is enjoying an indubitable experience. The idea is that the experience has such a degree of clarity that it carries over to the belief, rendering it indubitable. So strictly speaking it is a belief that is rendered indubitable in virtue of its association with an experience. And the point is not just that one has, say, an overwhelming sense of the truth of the belief in the course of the experience. Rather, the content of the belief is presented or delivered clearly by the experience. We need to consider the possibility that experiences with such a character might occur, even if they are less common than their tamer cousins.

What I have in mind may be illustrated as follows. Consider first an ordinary everyday experience. Suppose that a colleague is in his office. I go into his office, see him, and speak with him, and immediately form the belief that he is there. But now suppose that a tragedy has occurred and that he has died. Sometime after he has died I go into the same room and there, it seems to me, he is once again. It is not just a matter of having a vague sense that he is there or of my thought of him having a particular immediacy or vividness. I *see* him; or it is as if I see him, and I do so with all of the clarity with which I used to see him, and that is typical of sense perception in conditions in which it is working at its best. He appears to be in his favorite chair, sitting as he used to sit. It is not just a matter of my seeming to myself to catch a fleeting glimpse of him. Rather, it appears to me for some time that he is there and that I am seeing him. He even speaks to me, perhaps continuing a conversation from the past. I find that I am in circumstances in which it is unthinkable for me to deny, or even to doubt, that he is there. Part of what would make these experiences indubitable is the fact that not only does it seem to me that I could not deny or doubt that he is there: it is also the case that it would not be sensible for me to do so, or only insofar as it would be sensible for me to doubt almost *any* beliefs I hold, including the most obviously true beliefs. Such experiences are not open to any interpretation other than the obvious one: there is no room here for saying that the experience is one thing, whereas the interpretation of it is another.

But how could I be *sure* that I am not imposing a particular interpretation on something that could be interpreted differently? My first reaction might be to think that he must all the while have had an identical twin of whom I was unaware and who has now made an appearance, or that I was dreaming or hallucinating or had become deranged, and perhaps to say something like this: "But it can't be you. You are dead. I was at your funeral and I saw your coffin being lowered into the ground. . . ." But suppose that he replies that it is he; suppose he gives me an account of his adventures since he died; suppose we compare notes about numerous events in our shared past and I find that his memories are just as they used to be; suppose, too, that his appearance and behavior are just as they used to be. My reasons for being sure that it is he are not *as* good as they were before he died. After all, he has died, and I have never come across anything like this before. Nevertheless, it seems that it could be utterly obvious to me that it is he, however baffling that may be to me. The clarity of the experience could compensate for my lack of an explanation.

Presumably *how* baffling it is would be largely a function of whether or not I had any idea how this extraordinary state of affairs had come about. And here my colleague might be able to help me. There are in fact some interpretations of how this remarkable state of affairs has come about that are such that if we were to adopt them, the experience of encountering my friend again might not even be properly described as a religious experience. (Perhaps his story is that he did not die, even though everything led us to believe that he did, and that the coffin that we saw buried contained another body.) But let us assume that we are dealing with a case that is so mysterious that there is no plausible nonreligious way to interpret it, so that it seems that it just *has* to involve the supernatural as part of its explanation. (Perhaps I was there when he died and had occasion to watch over the body until it was interred . . .) Assume, too, that there is an available religious interpretation that is confirmed by my friend.

If there are cases of this sort, they are most likely to be cases that involve someone *seeing* something and especially cases, such as the case of my departed colleague, in which a visual experience is supported by experiences through other sensory modes. Consider an auditory experience. If, for example, you were to hear a voice in the night clearly telling you to mend your ways, it could be that your friends are playing a trick on you: perhaps a small speaker has been hidden in your bedroom. (Even if it sounds like Charlton Heston—well, it could *be* Charlton Heston.) While in such cases there may be a clearer propositional content than in the visual case, there nevertheless seems more room for a nonreligious interpretation.

(g)-type, (h)-type, and (i)-type experiences seem unlikely to be indubitable. (So we can see that this is another way in which religious experiences can be categorized, namely, into those that we can imagine being indubitable and those that seem unlikely to have this sort of import; or we can at least see that some are less likely to be indubitable than others.) Consider (i)-type experiences, which involve the events that people encounter in their lives and observe in the lives of others being religiously interpreted. Perhaps the world *could* be such that it would be hard for us to avoid interpreting various phenomena in a certain religious way. Thus we could, even though we obviously do not, live in a world in which good things always happen to good people whereas bad things happen, and happen quickly, dramatically, and painfully, to bad people. In that case we would have good reason to posit some mechanism that brings this about. But even if no nonreligious interpretation of all that would be involved in that being the case were plausible, there might be a number of equally plausible religious interpretations.

Are there people who have indubitable religious experiences? I have no idea. Nor do I know how to settle the question whether or not there are. But there may be. It would be unwise to rule out the possibility that, say, a Christian might have experiences that indicate to her with a great degree of clarity and convincingness that, say, Jesus is talking to her or, in the Islamic case, to rule out the possibility that the prophet Muhammad had experience of the indubitable sort in the course of receiving the revelations recorded in the Qu'ran. And so on for the other religious traditions.

I think it is reasonable to believe that people who have indubitable religious experiences are not too numerous and that most believers do not have experiences of this sort. For what it is worth, I, for one, do not have experiences that are even remotely like anything of this character; anything I can report on is much more a matter of hints and intimations and of feelings that seem open to various interpretations. But, fortunately, we can go beyond autobiographical declarations, which may after all merely reflect the limitations of their author: here are three reasons for thinking that most believers do not have experiences of the indubitable sort.

First, if there is religious ambiguity, as defined and discussed in earlier chapters, then there is no indubitable experience; rather, all religious experience, however intense, is ambiguous, even at the very moment of its occurrence. The observation that (g)-type, (h)-type, and (i)-type experiences are among the types of religious experience that are most frequently enjoyed is relevant here. For example, the fact that certain patterns are discernible in one's own life, or in the lives of others (etc.) might be something that is not obvious and is easy to miss: it might require a certain type of focus and approach if it is to be noticed at all. If there is ambiguity, then there is always room to question and to wonder about what is going on.

Second, and relatedly, the various reasons to believe that the world is religiously ambiguous are relevant here. Thus, consider the fact that believers typically view loss of belief as something to be avoided and resisted, something that it is often necessary to struggle against. Exhortations to keep the faith are commonplace in religious circles. Yet for those who enjoy indubitable experiences, loss of belief would be well nigh impossible. If indubitable experiences were common, exhortations to believe would be less common than they are. This does not *show* that most believers do not enjoy indubitable experiences, since exhortations to believe might, say, be necessary only at times at which people are not having such experiences, or they might be necessary for some but not for others. It is conceivable that people would have such experiences at some point in their lives and later forget or doubt that they ever occurred, so that the exhortations in question would become necessary for them. The relevant experiences might be rather different from the rest of one's experience, and hence it may be hard to feel their force and to connect up with them when you are not having them. Or the experiences may require for their intelligibility a certain way of looking at things, so that if you no longer hold various relevant beliefs that you had when the experiences occurred, this may make it difficult to recapture your sense of the content of the experiences. All of this is rather speculative, to be sure, but it provides some reason to qualify the claim that the frequency of urgings to keep the faith *shows* that few, if any, people have indubitable experiences. Still, there is much reason to think this to be so.

In this context it is interesting to note that even those who seem to have enjoyed much religious experience have wondered at times if even their most intense experiences were genuine. This concern is expressed over and over in *The Autobiography of St. Teresa* of *Avila*. And consider these remarks from the contemporary philosopher of religion Robert Merrihew Adams:

> I would like to reflect on a religious experience of my own adolescence. I wanted to feel God's presence in prayer. After a time of looking for it, I noticed a certain feeling that I commonly had when I prayed. It was in some ways rather like a sensation. I wondered whether this could be the experience of the presence of God. I think I sometimes took it to be so. But was it really so? Did I perceive God in that experience? I had my doubts then, and I have them now. The experience certainly did have a content that went beyond anything I could convey discursively. One who had not had a similar experience could not know exactly what I felt. . . . I do remember some of my misgivings about it, however. One main misgiving I would express . . . by a question about what I felt that went beyond anything I could grasp or express discursively. Was it something about *God*, or only something about *me*? Of course, in those moments when I believed the experience to be genuine I took myself to be feeling the presence of a God who had all the attributes I believed God to have—but that's discursive content. . . . A more disturbing doubt about my adolescent feeling of God's presence in prayer has to do with its causes. Was it something I was doing to myself? Was it perhaps a distinctive complex bodily sensation caused by squeezing my eyelids shut very hard and unconsciously controlling my breathing in a certain way? Or was it simply begotten of my imagination by my desire to feel God's presence?[13]

Third, bearing in mind the point that indubitable experience is likely to involve visual experience, it is important to notice that the phenomenal qualities of a vision will never themselves be such that only one interpretation of them will be feasible. For example, a vision of the Virgin Mary, however clear it may be, is always of a person with a certain shape. Even if the being that appeared to one were to declare herself to be the Virgin Mary, and to engage in activities and to make pronouncements of the sort that you would expect from such a personage, it seems that the experience in question would always fall short of being indubitable.

But, in spite of these reasons for thinking that indubitable experiences are not very common, I know of no reason to be certain that they never occur. (As far as I know, no one else does either.) It is clear that there are people in a number of traditions who claim that they do occur, and that they have them. Of course the very diversity of such appeals provides us, once again, with reason to be suspicious of all such claims, but it is still *possible* that there is one such group that is getting it right, some of whose experiences are indubitable in the sense I have in mind, and whose reports uniquely describe correctly the content of what is experienced.

In any case, if there are such experiences, a good case can be made for the claim that they provide a considerable measure of justification for certain beliefs for those who have them. Such experiences could, I assume, outweigh the considerations which, I have argued, make for the Critical Stance. Such experiences might suffice to make it reasonable to believe in a more than tentative way. The situation, however, is that the types of experience that we have every reason to believe to occur, such as sensing that one is being guided or supported or comforted by God, are subtle and could easily be missed, and are such that we have little reason to think them to be indubitable. Again, experiences that are open to a variety of readings, that can correctly be interpreted religiously, and that require that you be in a certain frame of mind in order to interpret them correctly are unlikely to have this force. So there is a general formula that has application here: the more dramatic the experience, the greater the cognitive content that it would yield, and the more capacity it would have to override the Critical Stance, the more doubtful it is that it occurs. The experiences of the tamer sorts that clearly occur lack this sort of yield and provide justification for tentative belief, at most.

7. The Gap between Experience and Doctrine

Next I raise some questions about aspects of the relation between the cognitive, or belief, part of religion and the religious experiences that are had by people who hold those beliefs. In this section I argue that religious experiences have, at most, a capacity to support only some of the beliefs that one has in virtue of membership in a religious tradition. They provide little support for most of those beliefs.

Suppose, for instance, that a devout Muslim feels that God is guiding her in a particular way. Perhaps she believes that God is guiding her to struggle to achieve freedom to criticize Islam, freedom to dissent, and to subject to critical scrutiny the teachings of various recognized religious authorities in Muslim countries. The question is this: What is the significance of this experience of feeling that she is being guided by God for the bulk of her Muslim beliefs? How much of the teachings of her tradition do such experiences support?

To be a member of any one of the world's religions is typically to subscribe to a large interconnected set of beliefs. Thus to be a Muslim is to believe that God has revealed the Qu'ran to the prophet Muhammad, that Muhammad was the seal of the prophets, that one should pray five times a day, and so forth. The traditions differ with respect to the extent to which they emphasize beliefs, but they all include a large array of beliefs, such as beliefs about the origins and nature of the universe, human nature, survival of death, how we should live, and numerous other matters; in the case of the theistic traditions these include beliefs about God's nature, purposes, and activities. Needless to say, belonging to a tradition involves much more than holding a set of beliefs: there is also a way of life and a rich array of feelings, hopes, and longings, and all of this often feels to the believers to be part of a seamless web along with the relevant beliefs. The way of life feels as though it is the right one, just as the beliefs feel correct.

Experiences such as a sense that one is being guided by God in some particular respect have a very limited capacity to support the entire array of beliefs that is involved in being a member of a religious tradition. Thus a Muslim who feels that God is guiding her in some particular respect probably derives little support from this particular experience for the belief that Muhammad was the sole recipient of the Qu'ran. It seems that this sort of religious experience, at any rate, will support only some of the large interconnected set of beliefs that are accepted in virtue of membership in a tradition.

Let us call beliefs that are supported by experiences "experientially supported beliefs." If someone feels that God is guiding her in some respect, then this experience provides some support for her belief that God is guiding her, just as it provides some support for her belief that God is the sort of being that guides people, and indeed for the belief that God is guiding her to do whatever it is that her experience leads her to believe God is guiding her to do.[14] These directly supported beliefs may in turn provide support for various other religious beliefs that this person holds: the belief that God exists, the belief that God is good, and the belief that God has an interest in her behavior are good candidates for inclusion in this category of indirectly supported beliefs, since each of these further beliefs seems to receive epistemic support from the belief that God is guiding one, although it also seems natural to think such beliefs to get some of their support directly from the experience that appears to the person having it to involve God guiding her. But there may be other cases in which it is natural to think indirectly supported beliefs to get all of their support from directly supported beliefs. In any case, let us think of a belief that receives support in any of these ways (directly or indirectly or in a mixed fashion) as an experientially supported belief. If the support in question is very extensive, one will be justified in holding the belief in question; if not, the experience can at least contribute to the justification.

But then, in addition, there typically are numerous other beliefs that a person holds in virtue of membership in a tradition but that are supported in *neither* of these ways. In the sort of case mentioned in the previous paragraph, for instance, this would seem to be so for the uniquely Muslim beliefs that Muhammad is the seal of the prophets and that the Qur'an was revealed solely to the prophet Muhammad, for the uniquely Christian belief that Jesus rose from the dead, and for the uniquely Catholic belief that Mary, the mother of Jesus, was immaculately conceived. This is no small point, since it bears on the inability of a very frequently reported sort of religious experience to contribute to the justification for the majority of the beliefs that are held in virtue of membership in a tradition. The experiences that religious people commonly report on do not support many of the religious beliefs that they accept. I have made the point specifically about the sense of being guided by God, but corresponding points can of course be made about other types of religious experience.

Here it is useful to imagine systems of beliefs that include whatever beliefs among one's system of beliefs are supported by experiences (assuming that there are such) along with other beliefs that are not among one's system of beliefs. Thus a Muslim might be otherwise orthodox except for the fact that she believes that the Qur'an was not revealed solely to the prophet Muhammad, believing instead that the revelation was shared by, say, Muhammad and one of his wives. Or a Christian might be otherwise orthodox but believe that Jesus was not born of the Virgin Mary but was instead an adopted illegitimate orphan—a belief that, incidentally, would fit nicely with the belief that is prominent in some strands of the Christian tradition, that Jesus is on the side of the outsider and the disadvantaged. These are just examples, and it is not difficult to multiply them. In the case of each tradition it is easy to imagine experientially supported beliefs coexisting with sets of unsupported beliefs that are quite different from those with which they currently coexist; it seems that there typically are many beliefs that could be either dropped or added or altered without any alteration in the amount of support provided by experiences for the various supported beliefs. This fact appears to diminish any support that trickles down to unsupported beliefs.

But could, say, the Muslim belief that the Qur'an was given solely to the prophet Muhammad be supported in some other, yet more indirect, way by a Muslim's sense that God is guiding him in some fashion? Perhaps it is reasonable to think of the experiences in question as supporting the set of Islamic beliefs, taken as a package, where the package includes the belief that the Qur'an was given solely to the prophet Muhammad. Correspondingly, the Christian system of beliefs or the Hindu system of beliefs, considered as a package, might be thought to be supported by the experiences that a Christian or a Hindu enjoys, even though on face value experiences that are enjoyed by members of the tradition seem to support only a limited subset of the whole set of relevant beliefs. This possibility requires analysis. There are a number of relevant considerations that pull in conflicting directions.

Suppose you have received all or most of the beliefs that constitute your system of religious beliefs from a certain source. The source might be your family, or your religious tradition, or authoritative voices within that tradition, or the sacred scriptures of your tradition, for example. Assume that your system of beliefs includes two categories of belief: those that receive support from experiences either directly or indirectly in the various ways I have mentioned, and those that are not supported in those ways. So some parts of the system of beliefs that you have received from this source are supported by experiences. Perhaps your tradition has told you that God exists, that God is good, and that God has some interest in your behavior. And your own experience of being guided by God has provided you with some support for these beliefs. This, in turn, seems to give you reason to believe that the source from which you have received these beliefs is reliable; and this in turn appears to provide some support for *all* other beliefs received from the same source.

Let us call this the "common origin argument." The import of the common origin argument in any particular case will of course depend on the extent to which one reasonably believes that one's beliefs *have* a common origin. Naturally, if one has reason to think that numerous independent sources were involved, so that the association of the beliefs with each other is somewhat accidental, the common origin argument has little purchase.

Also, not every instance of a common origin confers the right sort of unity on the relevant beliefs. Thus it could be that the beliefs associated with a tradition have in the past had a number of independent sources (with some, say, being the product of revelation, others arising from the influence of some historical movement, others the product of certain economic conditions, others the product of wishful thinking, and so forth) and yet some group may at some later point transmit those beliefs as a unit on to some other group. The group at the receiving end of this process is indeed receiving the beliefs in question from a single source but not in such a way that the common origin argument comes into play; the beliefs lack the requisite sort of ancestry.

Obviously the source of the beliefs associated with a religious tradition, or of many of them, is often a controversial matter, with competing schools of thought defending different interpretations. And there is a related relevant issue that is almost guaranteed to be a matter of dispute, namely, which beliefs are to be understood to belong to the set of beliefs that are received from a particular source. Clearly in the case of all of the religious traditions there are branches or sects or subgroups that differ on numerous matters of doctrine. So the question will be: Whose version of the beliefs that are associated with a tradition is to be taken as definitive? Which beliefs exactly are to be traced to the relevant source? It will often be unclear which beliefs are to receive the support that arises from the apparent reliability of the source in question. Unclarity of this sort diminishes the epistemic support that carries over to unsupported beliefs when the source of all of one's beliefs, supported and unsupported, has been shown to be reliable.

Furthermore, particular beliefs that are experientially supported may be associated with a number of traditions. For example, someone in any one of the theistic traditions may feel that God is guiding her. The reasonableness of concluding that a certain source—namely, the source from which one believes one has acquired whatever beliefs one has about God—is reliable on this basis seems to be diminished if one is aware that others have the same, or much the same, experience or corresponding experiences, and that they think them to signify the reliability of a completely different source, with support thereby accruing to a different set of beliefs.

Still, there is no reason to think that these points undermine completely the proposal that some indirect support is provided in the way under discussion. So far, then, the picture appears to be this. There are beliefs that are supported either directly or indirectly by, say, a sense that one is being guided by God. And there are other beliefs to which some support might trickle down from those that are directly supported, although this trickle-down sort of support seems slight compared with, for instance, the support provided for the belief that God is guiding one by the sense that God is guiding one.

But are there not other, so far undiscussed, ways in which "unsupported" beliefs might receive some support from experience? Suppose, for example, that entertainment of a certain belief is correlated temporarily with various experiences. Thus it might be that while a Christian is contemplating the resurrection of Jesus or the Trinity, she has a sense of being guided by God or a sense of inner joy or of freedom from anxiety. Maybe some slight support could sometimes be provided for beliefs in this way. However, it seems that if believers find comfort, contentment, or joy in accepting certain beliefs, living by them, worshiping in accordance with them, and so on, what this entitles them to assert, first and foremost, is not that those beliefs are true or that this is the correct way to worship, but rather that this is a way to find comfort, contentment, and joy.

Another possibility that at least deserves mention is that one might be entertaining a certain belief, such as belief in the Trinity, or the Roman Catholic belief in the immaculate conception of Mary, or the Muslim belief that Muhammad is the seal of the prophets, and have at that very moment a heightened sense that the belief in question is true. This might be experienced during worship or during a time of religious exaltation. Perhaps it is a deep assurance that one is right in one's religious beliefs, an assurance that is integrated with much of one's experience, so that the events in one's life are experienced as falling into a certain pattern that squares with one's religious orientation.

Obviously a person has to take account of the fact that certain beliefs seem right to her. If it feels completely obvious to you that, say, Jesus rose from the dead, why should you not take that into account? The feeling that some belief that we hold is obviously correct is something that we rely on in many contexts, so why not here? And this is not a matter of support trickling down from experientially supported beliefs. Yet one has to keep in mind the doubtful reliability of such a feeling: it is shared by too many people who are mistaken.

It seems that experiences are unlikely to suffice to undermine the case for tentativeness with respect to "unsupported" beliefs, even though some support may accrue to them in ways such as those I have identified; the case for tentativeness is likely to be undermined only in the case of experientially supported beliefs, if at all.

The point about experiences having a very limited capacity to support the full array of beliefs that are typically accepted in virtue of membership in a religious tradition applies both to experiences that are of a rather "generic" sort and to "tradition-specific" experiences. A generic experience is one that might be reported on by people in a number of religious traditions: a sense that God is present to one and a feeling that one is guided by God belong in this category, since clearly these experiences might be enjoyed by a member of any of the theistic traditions. Tradition-specific experiences, on the other hand, are experiences that you would not expect someone outside a particular tradition to report: thus visions of the Virgin Mary are specific to the Catholic tradition, and the sense that God is guiding one to be a good Muslim is specific to the Islamic tradition. Thus—to illustrate again the point under discussion—if a first-century Christian were to have an experience that, he believed, was of the risen Jesus, this would provide him with reason to believe that Jesus had risen but would provide little, if any, support for, say, his beliefs about the origins of life on earth.

Finally, I do not mean to imply that the mistake I am criticizing (which involves an exaggerated reading of the support provided for one's beliefs by the experiences one enjoys) is one that religious traditions will inevitably make. Some traditions may agree that the experiences enjoyed by their adherents take you only as far as I have suggested. Or theologians or intellectuals within the ranks may agree that this is so. But it seems to be the case that the mistake of jumping to the conclusion that one's entire system of belief is supported, or even shown to be correct, in virtue of experiences of the sort discussed, is made by many believers in many traditions.

8. The Two Sources of Religious Experience

Next I want to examine an issue that it is natural to consider once one recognizes that religious experiences are reported within a number of religious traditions. My contention will be that here we will find reason to doubt that religious experiences may justify even experientially supported beliefs being held in more than a tentative way.

Since religious experiences are reported in many religious traditions, it is natural to consider the possibility that there might be an external input that is received in religious experience and an internal input that is contributed by the person having the experience, as well as the associated possibility that the same input is received, or is sometimes received, by people in different traditions, and that their reports of what they experience are different because the people in question come from different traditions of interpretation.

Presumably one's religious experiences are typically cashed in in terms of the concepts provided by one's own tradition. As James nicely puts it, "our ideas . . . form the background for all our facts, the fountain-head of all the possibilities we conceive of."[15] If because of, say, his cultural context or their lack of the requisite mental ability someone lacks the concept of God, then there is an important sense in which he will not have the experience of being guided by God. He may have an experience such that, if *he had* the requisite abilities, concepts (etc.), he would interpret that experience as a matter of God guiding him. And if God is guiding him in that, for instance, he feels drawn in one direction rather than another on this account, then he is being guided by God. But he does not experience what is occurring as a matter of his being guided by God. He does not see what he is encountering for what it is.

It is difficult to address the question of what is external input and what is internal while keeping in mind the variety of types of religious experience. What is externally given and what we contribute might vary across different types of experience. There might be experiences whose content would be a function, or almost entirely a function, of the external input. One good candidate for an experience of this sort would be one that results in the overturning of a previously accepted set of religious beliefs: in such a case there is some reason to think that the experience is altogether, or largely, the product of external contributions.[16] And there may be experiences in which there is little or no external input.

Rather than trying to keep different types of experience before our minds at once, let us focus once again, by way of example, on experiences of type-(c), and more specifically on the experience of feeling guided by God to pursue a particular course of action. Suppose, too, that this is not also a case of type-(a) experiences, so it does not involve hearing any voices in the normal way; rather, it is a more subtle matter of feeling or sensing that one is being guided by God in a certain direction. Once again, it seems especially appropriate to focus on this frequently reported type of experience rather than on one of the more exotic and less frequently reported varieties. So the question is this: How are you to tell where the external input leaves off and your own input begins? How are you to tell what you have contributed to the experience? Let us call this the internal-external question.

This is not the same as asking whether there are any uninterpreted religious experiences. Steven T. Katz has answered this latter question in the negative:

> There are NO pure (i.e. unmediated) experiences. Neither mystical experience nor more ordinary forms of experience give any indication, or any grounds for believing, that they are unmediated. That is to say, all experience is processed through, organized by, and makes itself available to us in extremely complex epistemological ways. The notion of unmediated experience seems, if not self-contradictory, at best empty. . . . [The] forms of consciousness which the mystic brings to experience set structured and limiting parameters on what the experience will be, i.e. on what will be experienced.[17]

It follows from Katz's analysis that the experiences enjoyed in the different traditions are very different. As he puts it:

> There is no intelligible way that anyone can legitimately argue that a "no-self" experience of "empty" calm is the same experience as the experience of intense, loving, intimate relationship between two substantial selves, one of whom is conceived of as the personal God of western religion and all that this entails. (40)

The alternative view is that there are raw, uninterpreted, experiences that are had by members of a number of religious traditions and that the members of those traditions supplement the experiences in question with interpretive content that is supplied by their own tradition. What a Christian describes as being guided by Jesus might be described by a member of another theistic religion as a matter of being guided by God. But they would both have the same basic experience; they just interpret it quite differently.

If the view that people in different traditions share the same raw experience and then impose different interpretations on it were clearly correct, this would help to answer the internal-external question. For if different religious groups all have the same basic experience and then variously interpret it, there is some reason to believe that that basic experience at any rate is mostly a matter of external input, although this would not, strictly speaking, follow, since the homogeneity of basic experience might be accounted for in terms of, say, the structure of the human brain. On the other hand, if there are no uninterpreted experiences and the entire experience of people in different traditions is structured by their concepts, and so forth, this would leave the internal-external question unanswered. It would not help us to discern to what extent what is experienced is a product of the interpretation of the person enjoying the experience, what fraction of the content of the experience comes from each source, the internal and the external. I find the arguments on neither side compelling in the debate about whether there are raw, uninterpreted experiences; I do not see that I have an adequate basis on which to make up my mind about it. Likewise, I think it is unclear how the internal-external question is to be answered.

At least these issues cannot reasonably be settled on the basis of a priori considerations. In the case of *both* issues (i.e., to what extent the same "raw" experience is had in different traditions, and to what extent what is experienced is contributed by the experiencer) there are types of cross-cultural study that would help to resolve it. Inquiry that would illuminate these issues would include an attempt to get reflective religious people who are acquainted with traditions other than their own to consider whether they can conceive of experiences they interpret in one way being reasonably interpreted in another way; perhaps too they could probe whether they are contributing anything to their experience. In the absence of such inquiry there is no way to tell to what extent a person who claims to be experiencing being guided by God is actually having experiences that clearly indicate that she is doing so, and to what extent she is instead imposing a theistic interpretation on experiences that could reasonably be described in another way. There is no way to tell how much is being contributed to the content of the experience by the person having it. It is not clear, in the case of the sort of (c)-type experience under discussion, where experience ends and interpretation begins.

I am inclined to think that religious experience typically involves the two components, and hence should be understood as the confluence of two streams, one internal and one external, and that this is so in spite of the fact that it may feel to a believer as if it is all being externally received: for our own contribution may often be invisible to us, or visible only after probing and comparison. But it is difficult to show this to be so; and, if it is so, it is difficult to show to what extent it is so.

I take the fact that the internal-external issue is unresolved to call into question the capacity of appeals to religious experience to defeat the case for the Critical Stance—even in the case of experientially supported beliefs.

9. More on the Significance of Appeals to Experience

Nevertheless, religious experiences provide those who have them with some reason to hold some of their religious beliefs. This is especially clearly so in the case of someone (a) who has reflected on her experiences in a conscientious way (in the way in which you would expect someone with integrity to reflect), (b) whose experiences are what she has been led by her tradition to expect in the course of her religious life, (c) whose experiences form a pattern that is apparent in her life in an ongoing way, and (d) who has no compelling reason to deny that the being that she believes herself to experience exists.

That some individuals see more deeply than others is a commonplace in many other areas of human experience. A simple example. Someone walks through an Illinois prairie and sees merely an assortment of flowers, grasses, bushes, trees, and so forth; someone else knows the names of the plants, knows which are indigenous and which are invaders, knows which are expanding their range and which are threatened, and knows in each season what to expect to find growing. Here, as elsewhere, ignorance does not announce itself to those who suffer from it.

Some people may be receptive to certain religious experiences, while others are not. Some may know what to look for and know how to interpret what is occurring, while others do not. It is something of a cliché to mention in this context the inability of a blind person to understand talk of color. Again, the ability to have and appreciate the experience might be thought similar to an ability to appreciate music, or to be aware of the subtleties of human interaction. Such abilities may require a certain sort of disposition and training and a certain sort of exposure, and may be out of the question for some people. It may typically take a long hard road to get to where you see what is to be seen, and it may be unintelligible to a person who is not receptive to it. A whole range of feelings and responses and perceptions may be out of the range of the nonreligious person, or be likely to be misinterpreted. There seems also to be something to the idea that in order for you to have an awareness that God is forgiving you, you would have to have a sense of needing to be forgiven. A sense of needing guidance would be necessary for feeling that one is guided by God. Probably it is also true that in order for you to have a sense of God sustaining you, you would need to have a sense of needing to be sustained. In general, you cannot have a sense of a need being satisfied unless you have a sense that you have an unsatisfied need. To summarize the contents of this paragraph, it would not be surprising for people to vary in their receptivity.

If people vary in their receptivity, it would be unsurprising that the religious experiences of some would be unintelligible or inaccessible to others. There certainly are numerous other human experiences about which those who have them are uniquely qualified to talk—such as the experience of being in battle or of giving birth. A familiar claim among those who report on certain types of religious experience is that "you do not know what it is like until you get there."

> The spiritual life . . . justifies itself to those who live by it; but what can we say to those who do not understand? This, at least, we can say, that it is a life whose experiences are proved real to their possessor, because they remain with him when brought closest into contact with the objective realities of life. . . . These highest experiences I have had of God's presence have been rare and brief—flashes of consciousness which have compelled me to exclaim with surprise—God is here!—or conditions of exaltation and insight, less intense, and only gradually passing away. I have severely tested the worth of these moments. . . . But I find that, after real questioning and test, they stand out today as the most real experiences of my life, and experiences which have explained and justified and unified all past experiences and all past growth.[18]

> Whosoever has had no experience of the transport knows of the true nature of prophetism nothing but the name. . . . As there are men endowed only with the sensitive faculty who reject what is offered them in the way of objects of the pure understanding, so there are intellectual men who reject and avoid the things perceived by the prophetic faculty. A blind man can understand nothing of colours save what he has learned by narration and

hearsay. . . . The chief properties of prophetism are perceptible only during the transport, by those who embrace the Sufi life. The prophet is endowed with qualities to which
you possess nothing analogous, and which consequently you cannot possibly understand.
How should you know their true nature, since one knows only what one can comprehend? But the transport which one attains by the method of the Sufis is like an immediate
perception, as if one touched the objects with one's hand.[19]

Of course the mere introduction of these two passages, representing two religious
traditions, is a reminder of the familiar phenomenon of the diversity of religious experiences and of the diversity of associated beliefs. Charles Darwin nicely makes some of
the relevant points about the import of this familiar phenomenon:

Formerly I was led by . . . deep inward conviction and feelings . . . (although I do not
think that the religious sentiment was ever strongly developed in me), to the firm conviction of the existence of God and of the immortality of the soul. In my Journal I wrote that
whilst standing in the midst of the grandeur of a Brazilian forest, "it is not possible to give
an adequate idea of the higher feelings of wonder, admiration, and devotion which fill and
elevate the mind." . . . but now the grandest scenes would not cause any such convictions and feelings to rise up in my mind. It may be truly said that I am like a man who has
become colour-blind, and the universal belief by men of the existence of redness makes
my present loss of perception of not the least value as evidence. This argument would be a
valid one if all men of all races had the same inward conviction of the existence of one
God; and we know that this is very far from being the case. Therefore I cannot see that
such inward convictions and feelings are of any weight as evidence of what really exists.
The state of mind which grand scenes formerly excited in me, and which was intimately
connected with a belief in God, did not essentially differ from that which is often called
the sense of sublimity; and however difficult it may be to explain the genesis of this sense,
it can hardly be advanced as an argument for the existence of God, any more than the
powerful though vague and similar feelings excited by music.[20]

Yet Darwin overstates the case when he suggests that in virtue of the diversity of the
beliefs about God that people base on, or at least connect with, their experience, inward
convictions and feelings are of no weight as evidence of what really exists. For one
thing, this is to fail to recognize that people may vary in their receptivity.

While people should take into account how things seem to them to be, an interpretation of the significance of such experiences requires attention to the various considerations I discuss. These include the fact that different groups report on experiences that they
believe to support their own religious position, the fact that experiences seem at best to
be capable of providing epistemic support for only a subset of the total set of beliefs associated with a tradition, and the fact that some uncertainty concerning the sources of
experience is appropriate. It may even be possible to give utterance to much of what is
counted as religious experience without accepting the tenets of any religious tradition.

Although there is no way to measure precisely its significance, the inconclusiveness
of the results in the various areas I have probed suffices to call into question attempts to
undermine the Critical Stance by appeal to religious experience. In fact there is much to
be said for the idea that the character of religious experience *supports* the Critical Stance,
in which case this road, too, leads to our destination.

11

⊳━◆⊷━○━⊶◆━⊲

ALSTON ON RELIGIOUS EXPERIENCE

In this final chapter I support my conclusions by showing that they are not undermined by William P. Alston's influential and important recent work on religious experience. In particular I argue that the case that Alston makes is a weaker one than he recognizes; I also argue for modifications of it that render it sympathetic to the Critical Stance. I begin by outlining and critically examining some central moves in his book *Perceiving God: The Epistemology of Religious Experience* (PG for short).

1. Alston's Theory

Alston's approach to religious experience is rather different from what was generally assumed in the previous chapter. His concern is with what he calls "direct perceptual support," which he considers to be a sometimes neglected source of support for theism. He restricts his attention to a very specific sort of religious experience, which he calls *mystical perception*, and to the support that it can provide for theistic beliefs. This is perception of God as having certain properties, such as being good or loving, or as doing certain things in relation to the perceiver, such as forgiving or comforting or supporting him. To say that mystical experience occurs is not to imply that God exists; rather, it is to say that people have experiences in the course of which it appears to them that they are perceiving God as loving or as forgiving or as comforting them, for example. Alston is not taking God's existence for granted.

Alston argues that the relationship between mystical perception and the beliefs that we form on the basis of it resembles in important respects the relationship between, on the one hand, our sense experience of the world and, on the other hand, the beliefs about the world that we form on the basis of sense experience. The relationship has the same basic structure in each case. In particular sense perception and mystical perception share the character of givenness or presentation, which is common to all perception. Alston says that "a person can become justified in holding certain kinds of beliefs about God by virtue of perceiving God as being or doing so-and-so" (PG, 1). These are "beliefs to the effect that God is doing something currently vis-à-vis the subject—comforting, strengthening, guiding, communicating a message, sustaining the subject in being—or to the effect that God has some (allegedly) perceivable property—goodness, power, lovingness" (PG, 1).

The sort of perception on which Alston focuses is direct and noninferential. When I see (in this direct and noninferential way) the cat on the mat before me, I do not infer that there is a cat on the mat. I do not infer this from, say, my belief that I am having certain experiences or from any other proposition such as the proposition that there seems to be a cat on the mat, or the proposition that I seem to see a cat on the mat. Rather, I directly perceive that there is a cat on the mat. Various background beliefs need to be in place in order for this perceptual process to occur, but the process can nevertheless be direct and noninferential. Thus in this case I would need to have certain beliefs about cats and about mats, and yet my perception that there is a cat on the mat may be direct and noninferential. And I am justified in believing that there is a cat on the mat in virtue of its appearing to me that this is so.

So, too, there is direct and noninferential perception of God. People are aware of God as forgiving them or as being just or good. Such perceptual experiences have the character of appearance or presentation. And people are justified in believing that God is forgiving them or that God is just or good, on the basis of such experiences. Here, too, there is extensive reliance on the background system of beliefs, including, for example, beliefs about when it is likely that God's forgiveness will be experienced. But among the important differences is the fact that the perception of God on which Alston focuses is nonsensory.

Drawing from Reid and Wittgenstein, Alston observes that there are a number of doxastic practices that are established socially and psychologically. "[A] doxastic practice . . . [is] the exercise of a system or constellation of belief-forming habits or mechanisms, each realizing a function that yields beliefs with a certain kind of content from inputs of a certain type" (PG, 155). It involves "a family of ways of going from grounds—doxastic and experiential, and perhaps others—to a belief with a certain content" (PG, 100; also PG, 153). Thus in the case of the practice of forming beliefs on the basis of sensory experience, which Alston calls "sense-perceptual practice" ('SP' for short), the inputs are various sensations, and the outputs include beliefs that there are various particular external objects with certain qualities. Alston notes that some doxastic practices, such as SP, memory, the practice of forming beliefs on the basis of the testimony of others, inference, and rational intuition, are almost universally engaged in. Others are specific to some group. Thus what Alston calls "mystical perceptual practice" ('MP' for short) which is the practice of forming beliefs about what God is doing in relation to oneself, and about God's nature, on the basis of what God is perceived to be doing, or on the basis of its appearing to one that God has a certain nature, is specific to theists. Doxastic practices also differ in other ways. As mentioned, SP involves the senses, whereas MPs are nonsensory. And the properties perceived in SP have a well-defined phenomenal content, whereas this is not so for the properties perceived through mystical practices.

Alston says that "all our established doxastic practices . . . deserve to be regarded as prima facie rationally engaged in . . . pending a consideration of possible reasons for disqualification" (PG, 153). They should be considered innocent until proven guilty. Any doxastic practice that is well established socially and psychologically provides prima facie justification for its outputs; and unless such a practice is disqualified in virtue of, for example, internal inconsistency (that is, it generates beliefs that are inconsistent with each other) or external inconsistency (that is, it generates beliefs that are inconsistent with beliefs that are the outputs of doxastic practices that are recognized as very reliable), it is reasonable to conclude that that doxastic practice is reliable. (A doxastic practice is reliable if most of the beliefs that are its outputs are true.)

Alston sensibly says that it would be unrealistic to expect complete reliability from our doxastic practices. We live happily with a certain amount of inconsistency in the case of SP, as is evidenced by, for example, the fact that conflicting accounts of a car accident are often provided by witnesses (PG, 235). Alston also argues that our basic doxastic practices suffer from a benign sort of circularity in that all attempts to show that a person is justified in continuing with these practices rely on the practice itself. For example, there is no noncircular way to show that SP is reliable: any attempt to show its reliability has to rely on SP.

Each doxastic practice has associated with it an overrider system, or a regulating mechanism for deciding whether or not a belief that has been generated by the practice, and hence is prima facie acceptable, ought to be accepted, all things considered. An overrider system can handle a considerable amount of inconsistency, enabling those who engage in the practice with which it is associated to decide which among inconsistent pairs of beliefs they ought to accept. Overriders come in two forms: rebutters and underminers. A rebutter provides sufficient reason to think that a certain belief is false, whereas an underminer provides sufficient reason to think that the ground of the belief in this case does not have its usual justificatory force. Since the system of overriders that is associated with a doxastic practice may involve background beliefs and procedures that have no special relation to the practice (and may have been acquired through other practices) but that may be useful for testing the beliefs that are its outputs, the overriders are best thought of as attached to the practice rather than as internal to it.

Overriders are an important part of Alston's theory. Thus he says that the concept of prima facie justification has application only if there is a system of belief about the subject matter, against which a particular prima facie justified belief can be checked (PG, 262). And once the outputs of a well-functioning doxastic practice have been so checked, they are not only justified prima facie; rather, they are unqualifiedly justified.[1]

A central thesis of Alston's book is that each doxastic practice "carries its own distinctive modes of justification, its own distinctive principles that lay down sufficient conditions for justification, not only prima facie justification but also, through its overrider system unqualified justification as well. These conditions differ markedly from one practice to another" (PG, 162).

He aims to show, in particular, that various attempts to disqualify what he calls the *Christian Mystical Practice* (CMP), "the practice of forming perceptual beliefs about God that is standard in . . . mainline Christianity" (PG, 193), are unsuccessful. He argues, for instance, that the outputs of CMP are free of massive internal and external contradiction (PG, 170–71). What follows is that CMP is not only prima facie rational: it is also unqualifiedly rational. So "CMP is rationally engaged in since it is a socially established doxastic practice that is not demonstrably unreliable or otherwise disqualified for rational acceptance" (PG, 194).

Alston is not suggesting that the whole edifice of Christian belief can be founded on CMP. His claim is rather that *some* Christian beliefs can be so established, including, for example, beliefs such as the belief that God is forgiving one and the belief that God is good. So CMP can make a contribution to the justification of Christian belief; there is no suggestion that it alone can do all the work of justification or that it should be expected to do so. Many Christian beliefs, including, for example, the belief that Jesus was resurrected three days after being crucified, are not supported in this way.

Other sources of justification for Christian beliefs include appeals to religious experience that are inferential in character: thus someone may pray to God for strength to face some obstacle and afterward may feel better able to face that obstacle, and she may be justified in reasoning her way to the conclusion that God has strengthened her. It is just such an inferential appeal to religious experience that most people who have appealed to an argument for religious experience have had in mind. Then there is the entire tradition of natural theology, about which Alston says that he finds "certain of the arguments to be not wholly lacking in cogency." One can, in addition, to some extent reasonably rely on one's tradition as a source of beliefs. Finally, there is revelation of various sorts, which may also reasonably be relied upon to some extent. And these various sources of beliefs can support each other in various ways: for example, some of the other sources mentioned may provide the background beliefs that provide the overrider system for the operation of CMP.

Alston allows that the individuation of practices is a difficult business. There will be borderline cases in which it is not clear whether we are dealing with two practices or with two versions of one practice (PG, 193; also PG, 165f.). He sensibly wonders, for example, if the Roman Catholic and Christian Pentecostal traditions involve distinct belief-forming practices. He suggests that part of what settles the question of whether we are dealing with a single doxastic practice or with more than one is whether there is a shared set of overriders. And he characterizes CMP as the practice of forming beliefs about God on the basis of perception of God that takes as sources of its overrider system "the Bible, the ecumenical councils of the undivided church, Christian experience through the ages, Christian thought, and more generally the Christian tradition" (PG, 193). These are what a follower of CMP relies upon to decide whether to accept or reject a belief that is produced via CMP. So there is a single mainline Christian tradition that includes both the Roman Catholic and the Christian Pentecostal traditions and of course numerous other Christian denominations and sects. However, even this is something of a construction:

> There is no uniquely right way to group mechanisms into practices. A doxastic practice has only "conceptual" reality. It proves convenient for one or another theoretical purpose to group particular mechanisms into larger aggregations, but a practice is not something with an objective reality that constrains us to do the grouping in a certain way. One way

of cutting the pie will be best for some purposes and other ways for other purposes. (PG, 165)²

The result of dividing practices as Alston does, so that there is a single mainline Christian doxastic practice, is that this doxastic practice generates quite a lot of inconsistent beliefs (PG, 236). Consider, for example, the differences between Catholics and Baptists on transubstantiation or on the authority of the Papacy. But contradictions are less surprising, Alston says, in the case of CMP than they are in the case of SP, since in CMP our grasp of the subject matter is shaky and incomplete, whereas in the case of SP we have a much more structured and detailed knowledge of the physical world. Also, CMP can cope with many of the contradictions among its outputs through the use of its overrider system. Thus outlandish beliefs that a group or individual may develop about God, and that are at odds with traditional beliefs about God, may be overridden. Still, CMP generates more contradictions than SP. Hence

> the degree of reliability it is reasonable to assign to CMP is less than it is reasonable to assign to SP and other basic secular practices. Is that degree too low for us to be rational in engaging in it? . . . I can't say anything very definitive, both because we have no usable metric for degrees of reliability . . . and because there is no determinate answer to how much reliability is required for rational participation. . . . If we had sufficient reason to judge that the degree of reliability is quite low, say 50-50 or less, that would show that the practice is not rationally engaged in. But I see no grounds for any such judgment. (PG, 237–38)

Alston also says that CMP is "less firmly established, can lay claim to a weaker degree of epistemic status, [gives] rise to more critical questions, and [is] subject to more doubt, than, for example, SP" (PG, 283). So the presence of internal contradictions has the result that it is less reasonable to consider CMP to be reliable than it is to consider SP to be reliable. But Alston's view is that there is no reason to think that the contradictions that CMP generates require the conclusion that CMP is unreliable.

Alston's project is a conservative one in its espousal of the rationality of continuing with familiar practices that are firmly established psychologically and socially, provided that they satisfy certain conditions. And it is a community-focused view in its emphasis on socially established doxastic practices.

2. External Contradiction

What about external contradiction? The first question is whether there is a doxastic practice that is more firmly established than CMP and whose outputs are massively inconsistent with CMP; and it is Alston's view that there is no such practice. There are, however, many religious traditions with mystical practices whose outputs are inconsistent with the outputs of CMP to a very considerable extent.

Alston's analysis of the character of the inconsistency in question has a number of strands. Basically there are two options, each of which is associated with a certain conception of reference. On a descriptivist account of reference, the various background beliefs about what is understood to be the object of perception that are held within the various traditions "leak through" in perception so that what we believe about the perceived object is made use of when we perceptually identify it. "[One's] conception of God . . .

enters, to a greater or lesser degree, into a particular subject's identification of the perceived object as God" (PG, 258). A Christian and a Muslim, for example, will agree that God guides people, but the Christian is committed to its being the case that God *who is identical with Jesus Christ, who wishes all people to be Christians, whose fullest revelation was through Jesus, who created the world, who cares about individual beings (human and other)*, and so forth, guides people, whereas the Muslim is committed to its being the case that God *whose fullest revelation is to be found in the Qu'ran and was through the prophet Muhammad, who wishes all people to be Muslims, who expects all believers who can do so to visit Mecca at least once in their lifetime, who created the world, who cares about individual beings (human and other)*, and so forth, guides people. In each case one's commitments "enter into the identification of the subject of attribution" (PG, 259). If reference is construed in this way, there is "no alternative to construing each of our religious perceptual doxastic practices as including within it at least the main lines of the body of beliefs of the religion within which it flourishes." The reason is that on this account of reference, "God" is an abbreviation for a conjunction of discriptions.

However, Alston says that it is doubtful that the descriptivist account of reference is correct. It is more likely, he suggests, that at least in the case of proper names, a "direct" account of reference is correct, so that "God" and other proper names function as labels "for something perceived, described, or taken from the talk of others" (PG, 260). If so, when a Christian asserts that God has created the world, she is not explicitly asserting that, for example, God who is identical with Jesus Christ, and who in general satisfies the standard Christian descriptions, has done so. And likewise for the Muslim and for theists of other persuasions. Consequently, when a Christian and a Muslim both assert that God has created the world, they may not be disagreeing, in spite of their different beliefs about God.

What you have instead, in that case, is large-scale disagreement at the level of the main body of beliefs that are associated with the tradition.[3] The reason is that if an MP is to provide even prima facie justification, it must have an associated overrider system. In the case of CMP this consists in various basic beliefs of the Christian tradition. So a whole array of Christian beliefs must be in place as part of the background to the perceptual experience. And at this more general level, there is no escaping large-scale incompatibility. The best efforts of John Hick and others notwithstanding, there is no escaping the inconsistency between the claims of the traditions about God, human nature, human destiny, and so forth.

As in the case of internal contradictions, the large-scale inconsistency that there is among the religious traditions reduces the rationality of relying on the perceptual doxastic practice of any one of them, at any rate for those who are aware of the fact that there are many such religions.

> Thus it can hardly be denied that the fact of religious diversity reduces the rationality of engaging in CMP (for one who is aware of the diversity) below what it would be if this problem did not exist. Just how much it is reduced I cannot say. We do not have the conceptual resources to quantify degrees of rationality or justification in this area (and perhaps in any area). (PG, 275)

However, Alston's view, once again, is that there is no reason to think that the rationality of engaging in CMP is reduced to such an extent that it is not a source of justification. I return to this issue in section 4 of this chapter.

3. The Force of Alston's Claims

In attempting to get clearer about the character of Alston's case, there are two areas that I want to probe. First, in this section I want to consider what he understands himself to have established about the justification of beliefs that are the outputs of CMP. In the next section and in most of the remainder of this chapter, I discuss his treatment of the phenomenon of religious diversity.

Alston's notion of justification is an externalist one that involves truth-conducivity. He opts for a nondeontological conception of justification, according to which "to be justified in believing p is to be in a *strong position* for realizing the epistemic aim of getting the truth" (PG, 73). The contrast is with deontological conceptions, according to which being justified in believing that p requires, for instance, "being free of blame for believing that p or having satisfied one's intellectual obligations in doing so" (PG, 72–73). To be in an epistemically strong position of the sort that is required for justification in Alston's sense is to have an adequate ground or basis for believing that p. The theory is externalist in that what is required is that the ground in question actually renders it objectively likely that the belief be true: there is no internalist requirement that the subject must be aware that the ground in question has this significance. A doxastic practice must actually be reliable (which is to say that it yields, or would yield, mostly true beliefs) in order for it to provide justification (PG, 178; also PG, 75).

However, Alston is not arguing that CMP is reliable; nor is he arguing that the outputs of CMP are prima facie justified. Rather, his claim is the weaker one that it is rational for those who engage in CMP to regard CMP as reliable. And it is rational for those who engage in CMP to suppose that the products of CMP are prima facie justified. This is so in spite of the fact that we are unable to show that any of our basic practices are reliable.

Actually what the last paragraph offers is a *weak* reading of Alston's project. According to this weak reading, the best we can come up with is a two-part case of the following sort. First, we can make a case for its being practically rational to rely on our established doxastic practices: "where doxastic practices are firmly rooted in our lives, it would be folly to cease practicing them without very strong reasons for doing so" (PG, 178). And we have no such reason, either in the case of SP or in the case of CMP. So people should "sit tight" with the MP with which they are familiar provided that it is free of massive contradictions and has a functioning overrider system.

Second, CMP exhibits "significant self-support." That is, various outputs of CMP can be used to test CMP. Alston says that this process involves using CMP to test itself, but that CMP is no worse off in this regard than practices such as SP. We use SP (along with memory and reasoning) to predict and control the future, but then when we test to see whether our predictions have been accurate and our attempts to control have been successful, we have no choice but to rely on SP itself. We can also use SP to investigate how SP operates, for example, by observing how the human brain functions. Much the same situation obtains for CMP, although in each case the sort of self-support that is available is a function of the character of the practice in question and of the sort of reality with which it puts us in contact. Thus in the case of CMP the self-support that is available is not a matter of predicting and attempting to control the future, and then observing whether the future conforms to what we had predicted or planned; rather, the self-support includes the enjoyment by those who pursue CMP of "the fruits of the spirit—love, joy, peace, and so on" (PG, 251) and "a transformation into the kind of nonpossessive, nondefensive, loving, caring, and serene persons God has destined us to become" (PG, 252); there is also the conformity that can be observed between perceptual experiences of God and the expectations about what will be perceived that are shared within the tradition.[4] In both cases, however, the effort is circular.[5] And because of its circular character, this self-support does not provide reason to believe that the practice in question is reliable. Rather, it strengthens the case for practical rationality that arises from being an established doxastic practice that is free of extensive contradiction.

Nevertheless, to engage in a practice is to be willing to agree that the practice is reliable. The reason is that to engage in a doxastic practice is to accept that the beliefs that are its outputs, or most of them, are true; and to think that the outputs of a doxastic practice, or most of them, are true is just to think the practice to be reliable. In order to engage in a practice one need not ever have the thought that the practice is reliable; but if the question were to arise, one would agree that this is so. One is committed to agreeing that this is so just by engaging in the practice. But then if it is practically rational to engage in a doxastic practice, it is also practically rational to agree (should the question arise) that that doxastic practice is reliable. It is in this sense, Alston believes, that it is rational for those who follow a doxastic practice to take it to be reliable, and hence as a source of justification. It would be nice if we could *show* SP or CMP or any other doxastic practice to be reliable. But we cannot. We have to settle for showing it to be practically rational to continue with such a practice. The upshot is that

> [CMP] . . . is prima facie worthy of rational participation. And this means that it is prima facie rational to regard it as reliable, sufficiently reliable to be a source of prima facie justification for the beliefs it engenders. And if, furthermore, it is not discredited by being shown to be unreliable or deficient in some other way that will cancel its prima facie rationality, then we may conclude that it is unqualifiedly rational to regard it as sufficiently reliable to use in belief formation. (PG, 194; see also PG, 278)

Since CMP has not been shown to be unreliable or deficient, Alston concludes that it is unqualifiedly rational to engage in it, and to take it to be reliable and a source of justification. However, it can be practically rational to engage in a certain practice even if it is not reliable. Indeed, Alston says that the practical rationality of engaging in a practice *is not even evidence* for its reliability (PG, 179).

So much for the weak reading. Sometimes Alston does not limit himself to saying that the best we can provide is a case for the practical rationality of continued adherence to established practices and for the practical rationality of supposing that the outputs of such a practice are prima facie justified. Thus at one point he says that "[it] is a reasonable supposition that a practice would not have persisted over large segments of the population unless it was putting people into effective touch with some aspect(s) of reality and proving itself as such by its fruits" (PG, 170). This seems to imply, or at least to suggest strongly, that well-established and long-standing practices *are* reliable. He says, in remarks that are echoed in many passages throughout his book, that "one to whom God is apparently presenting himself as [X] is thereby prima facie justified in believing God to be [X]" (PG, 279). There are many other passages in which he says, or implies or suggests, that his purpose is to argue that "mystical perception *is a source of* justification for M-beliefs" (PG, 69; my emphasis). He says that "the main aim" of his book is "to show that putative perceptions of God can provide justification for certain beliefs about God" (PG, 69; also PG, 70). And he says that "a Christian is epistemically justified (at least prima facie) on the basis of mystical perception in holding certain Christian beliefs about God" (PG, 278). Let us refer to passages of this sort, which support a strong reading of what Alston means to accomplish, as *J-passages*. Such passages suggest that Alston believes himself to show that people *are justified* in holding various beliefs about God on the basis of mystical experiences.

However—to return to the weak reading—there are also numerous passages that suggest that Alston understands himself to show only that it is practically rational for people to believe that they are justified in holding various beliefs about God on the basis of mystical experiences. I take this to be the import of his remark that what he is offering is "a weak defense of justification in a strong sense" (PG, 76). Again, he says that what he has shown is that "it is *reasonable* to take SP to be reliable, and hence reasonable to suppose that its products are prima facie justified [in the strong sense that involves likelihood of truth]" (PG, 182); and he says, in a passage that is all italicized for emphasis, that he has made a case for thinking that *"for any established doxastic practice it is rational to suppose that it is reliable, and hence rational to suppose that its doxastic outputs are prima facie justified"* (PG, 183; see also PG, 184, 194). Let us refer to passages of this sort as *PR-passages*, on account of their emphasis on what it is practically rational to believe about justification. Sometimes passages of these two different sorts are intertwined, as in these remarks at the end of chapter 5:

> CMP is a functioning, socially established, perceptual doxastic practice with distinctive experiential inputs, distinctive input-output functions, a distinctive conceptual scheme, and a rich, internally justified overrider system. As such, it possesses a prima facie title to being rationally engaged in, and its outputs are thereby prima facie justified, *provided we have no sufficient reason to regard it as unreliable or otherwise disqualified for rational acceptance*. (PG, 225)

This seems to say that if it is prima facie rational for S to engage in a doxastic practice, and there is no sufficient reason to believe the practice to be unreliable or disqualified for any reason, then S is prima facie justified in accepting the outputs of that doxastic practice. But if the rationality in question is practical, why think that this suffices for justification in the strong, externalist sense under discussion? (How is the blood of strong justification to be extracted from the turnip of practical rationality?) Maybe the PR-passages provide the correct way to read the J-passages. This would make for coherence, although in that case the J-passages are misleading. I take it that the PR-passages express Alston's considered view, which is that at most we can make a practical case both for the reliability of a practice and for the outputs of a practice being justified.

The following important passage suggests that while acknowledging that his case for the rationality of a large-scale perceptual doxastic practice such as SP or CMP is a practical one, with the result that the case for its outputs being justified is also practical, he means to *assert* that the outputs in question are justified:

> The lower epistemic status we have settled for attaches to the *higher-level* claim that SP is reliable, not [to] the particular perceptual beliefs that issue from that practice. As for the latter, what we are claiming is still the full-blooded (prima facie) justification . . . that involves likelihood of truth. . . . At the higher level we have settled for showing that it is

(practically) *rational* to take SP to confer justification in the full-blooded sense. But it would be a level-confusion to suppose that this implies that perceptual beliefs themselves are not justified in the stronger sense. [According] to our account of justification, the justification of perceptual beliefs requires that it is *true* that SP is reliable, not that we are truth-conducively justified in believing this. Moreover, though I do not claim to have shown that SP is reliable, and that its products are prima facie justified in my strong sense, I do claim to have shown that it is reasonable to take SP to be reliable, and hence reasonable to suppose that its products are prima facie justified in that strong sense (PG, 181–82).

If, as Alston says at the end of this passage, his aim is to show that it is reasonable to suppose that SP is reliable and (hence) reasonable to suppose that the outputs of SP are prima facie justified in the strong sense that requires SP to be reliable, it seems misleading to say that the lower epistemic status in question—which arises from our inability to go beyond showing that it is practically rational to continue with the practice—attaches only to the higher-level claim that SP is reliable and not to the outputs of SP. He says that he has "shown that it is . . . *reasonable to suppose* that [the] products [of SP] are justified in the [strong] sense" (PG, 182; my emphasis)—which is to say that he means to make a practical case for the outputs in question being justified in the strong sense. Yet he also says that "for the latter" he is still claiming "the full-blooded (prima facie) justification . . . that involves likelihood of truth." But he is not providing a case for believing that the outputs of SP *are* justified in this strong sense. And a weak case for reliability will not suffice for a strong case for full-blooded prima facie justification. (In fact it is, it seems, reasonable only for those who pursue the practice under discussion to believe that the outputs of SP are justified in the strong sense. Thus far it seems that an outsider to a practice that it is practically rational for its followers to continue to pursue, to believe to be reliable, and so forth, may not have any reason whatsoever to believe the practice to be reliable or to think that its outputs are justified. I address this issue in section 6.) So Alston is not really making a weak case for justification in the strong sense: what he is providing is rather a weak case for believing that there is justification in the strong sense, and for believing that some beliefs are so justified. As Alston correctly points out, it would be confused to think that because the case for the reliability of a practice is practical in character, it follows that the outputs of the practice are *not* justified in the strong sense (that requires reliability). It would also be mistaken to think that the justification of any beliefs requires that one should be truth-conducively justified in believing that the doxastic practice of which they are outputs is reliable. (What it requires is rather that the doxastic practice in question *be* reliable.) But there is no confusion—either level-confusion or other—involved in thinking that if the case for the reliability of a practice is practical, then so, too, is the case for its outputs being justified.

4. Religious Diversity

Alston addresses the topic of religious diversity in a forthright fashion. He nicely presents the problem that arises on this account as follows:

Since each form of MP is, to a considerable extent, incompatible with all the others, not more than one such form can be (sufficiently) reliable as a way of forming beliefs about the Ultimate. For if one is reliable, then most of the beliefs that issue from it are true; and hence, because of the incompatibility, a large proportion of the beliefs issuing from each of the others must be false; and so none of those others is a reliable practice. Now why should I suppose that CMP is the one that is reliable (if any are)? (PG, 268–69)

Alston's answer to the question he has posed is that it remains practically rational for a practitioner of any of the "internally validated" forms of MP to engage in his or her own religious doxastic practice "despite the inability to show that it is epistemically superior to the competition." (An "internally validated" practice is one that is free of large-scale internal and external inconsistency and has a well-functioning overrider system.) There are competing MPs (with incompatible outputs), and there is no independent way to show one of these practices to be more reliable than the others; the rational thing to do is to "sit tight" with the practice that is familiar. This applies to CMP and to the MPs of other religious traditions. (In taking this approach he is assuming for the sake of argument that natural theology will not help to show that one tradition is better off than the competition.) The result is that it can be, and often is, rational to stick with a doxastic practice that is not reliable.

Alston concedes that the phenomenon of religious diversity is something of a challenge to the rationality of believing any particular MP to be reliable. He concedes that the existence of a plurality of traditions reduces somewhat the rationality of relying on one's own MP, and also reduces the rationality of believing one's own MP to be reliable. His honest acknowledgment of the difficulties that arise for his views in this and in other areas, but especially in this area, is refreshing and part of what makes his an inspiring book.

While delineating the precise implications of religious diversity, Alston compares the disagreement among the various MPs with disagreement within SP. In doing so he asks us to consider the fact that sometimes witnesses offer conflicting accounts of an automobile accident that they have observed (PG, 270f.). Suppose that in the case of some such accident there is no independent way to discern what occurred and which witness was better placed to discern what occurred, and suppose that a particular witness lacks sufficient reason to believe that she is more reliable than the other witnesses. Here Alston makes two points about a person who finds herself so situated, and these points seem to differ in their force. He says that the confidence of a particular witness in her account of what she observed should be *drastically reduced*; and he says that the other reports *nullify* whatever justification she otherwise would have had for believing that the accident occurred as she believed it did. Perhaps he means that the confidence of the witness should be *so* drastically reduced that it will be nonexistent, in which case the point about nullification and the point about drastic reduction amount to the same thing. But it is hard to see why the significance of disagreement should be *that* great. After all, the witness in question saw the accident. Why should she take what others say to undermine utterly the justification she would otherwise have had for her belief that the accident occurred in the way in which she thought it to occur, given of how it appeared to her to occur?

Of course this is a case of disagreement about a particular belief rather than a case of large-scale incompatibility among doxastic practices. But a more crucial further difference, according to Alston, arises from this fact, and is as follows. Because the disagreement in the car accident case is an intrapractice one in that all of the witnesses are operating within the same doxastic practice, namely SP,[6] there is agreement about what would disqualify an observer and about what would resolve the disagreement. For example, "it is clear what would constitute non-circular grounds for supposing one of the contestants to be superior to the others, even if we do not have such grounds" (PG, 271). It is for this reason that any particular account of the accident is undermined by the fact of disagreement. On the other hand, we have no idea how to resolve the disagreement between the various competing MPs. Hence the rationality of relying on any of them is not reduced (or at least not greatly reduced) by the presence of the others. ("Hence the sting is taken out of the inability of each of us to show that he is in an epistemically superior position. The lack does not have the deleterious consequences found in the intra-practice case. Or, at the very least, it is not clear that it has those consequences. . . . The lack of a common ground alters drastically the epistemic bearings of an unresolved incompatibility" [PG, 272].)

Nevertheless, "the existence of a plurality of unelimated interpractice competitors . . . [has] significant adverse consequences for the epistemic status of CMP and other forms of MP . . . [and] reduces the rationality of engaging in CMP . . . below what it would be if this problem did not exist" (PG, 275). In fact, Alston says, what saves the day for the practitioners of CMP—saving them from a drastic reduction in justification—is the significant self-support provided by enjoyment of the "payoffs" of the Christian life. This self-support "rightfully [shores] up the participants' confidence that the practice gives them at least a good approximation to the truth." Yet he acknowledges that the practitioners of other MPs can also point to their own forms of self-support. Thus he says that the self-support in question is available "[for] both secular and religious practices" (PG, 276). And he says concerning his point about the self-support provided by the "payoffs" of the Christian life that the same point applies to other forms of MP "[assuming] that comparable modes of self-support are enjoyed" therein (PG, 276 n. 20). He rightly does not presume that such self-support is available in all traditions. But he is—equally rightly—far from assuming that it is available only to practitioners of CMP.

5. Reduced Justification

There is no doubt that it appears to many people that God is guiding them or forgiving them or that they are perceiving God as having certain qualities. So it is clear that people have the experiences that Alston is talking about. But whether such experiences have the significance that Alston thinks them to have is another matter. My contention is that he overstates his case and that more modest conclusions are in order. I have already argued that at most what we have here is a weak practical case for believing there to be justification of the strong truth-conducive sort that is important to Alston. Next I want to take a closer look at the notion of prima facie justification.

Let us consider first the claim that if parties that disagree share the same doxastic practice, as in the car accident case, the conflicting reports of the witnesses nullify each other, but that, on the other hand, when there is interpractice disagreement and hence no agreement on a procedure that will resolve the conflict, disagreement does not reduce much the justification that each side has for its beliefs.[7] Why should the absence of agreement on a conflict-resolving procedure have exactly this significance? Why not conclude, for example, that the fact that we are unable to agree on a procedure for resolving the dispute shows how hopelessly out of our depth we must be, and shows that we ought not to trust our judgments in this area, and hence gives reason to doubt the outputs of our own MP?

Moreover, the fact that "[our] knowledge of the physical world is much more detailed, precise, structured, and extensive than our knowledge of . . . God" and the further fact that "our cognitive grasp of the subject matter [in the case of CMP is] . . . incomplete and shaky" (PG, 237) may serve to explain, for example, why it is hard for us to make predictions in the religious arena and why the different religions have different conceptual schemes. But it ought also to influence our confidence about the outputs of CMP and other MPs.

Imagine that someone tries to persuade you that seeing underwater is as reliable as seeing in broad daylight. You object that this is not true: you say that our eyes do not work as well underwater as they do in broad daylight, with the result that objects are not as clear to us and are difficult to make out. Imagine that you receive the following response: "You have not given a reason for thinking that seeing in broad daylight and seeing underwater are not epistemically on a par. Because it is murky, objects are hard to make out underwater, and our eyes are not as well adjusted to that environment. We should therefore expect that there will be differences between the deliverances of the procedure of seeing in broad daylight and the deliverances of the procedure of seeing underwater. For example, we should expect there to be more disagreement about what is to be seen underwater, and we should expect that some people will have difficulty seeing much, or at all, underwater. "

But what is being proposed by way of an explanation of why the deliverances of the two procedures differ amounts to giving, or to specifying the basis for giving, the procedure of seeing underwater a lower epistemic status. It may still have a status that is respectable, and we may see fairly well underwater, but it is wrong to think that seeing underwater is epistemically on a par with seeing in broad daylight. The fact that in this case both procedures involve SP seems beside the point.

Alston concedes that CMP has a lower status than SP, both because CMP generates more contradictions than SP and because of the existence of other MPs whose outputs massively contradict those of CMP. CMP is "less firmly established, can lay claim to a weaker degree of epistemic status, [gives] rise to more critical questions, and [is] subject to more doubt, than, for example, SP" (PG, 283). But how can he be sure that in spite of these weaknesses "it is unqualifiedly rational to regard [CMP] as sufficiently reliable to use in belief-formation"? (PG, 194). He responds to the worry that the reliability of CMP may be too low for it to be rational for us to engage in it by saying that he "can't say anything very definitive, both because we have no usable metric for degrees of reliability . . . and because there is no determinate answer to how much reliability is required for rational participation" (PG, 238). At crucial points (e.g., PG, 274, 5), he concentrates on showing that *diversity does not suffice to render it irrational* to engage in CMP. But that is to leave other important possibilities untouched, including, for example, the possibility that diversity reduces the rationality of engaging in CMP to such an extent that it is *unclear* whether it is irrational to engage in it.

Alston thinks that beliefs that are the outputs of functioning, socially established, perceptual doxastic practices, each of which has distinctive inputs and outputs, associated overrider systems, and so forth, receive the same degree of prima facie justification. Although justification is a matter of degree (PG, 72), he writes that "in suggesting that a belief may be prima facie justified solely by experience, I am suggesting that this mode of justification can suffice for rational acceptance, in the absence of sufficient overriders" (PG, 81).

I suggest that we should think of prima facie justification as something that admits of degrees. (At one point Alston indicates that he is not unfavorably disposed to so thinking, but he does not pursue the topic [PG, 105].) There seem to be cases in which a belief has what we might think of as first-class prima facie justification and cases in which it just barely meets the necessary conditions for prima facie justification. If prima facie justification is a matter of degree, and some degrees are low enough that they are easily defeated, to say that a belief is prima facie justified is in some cases not to confer on it a very high status; it is sometimes a shaky and precarious condition. Then, too, there are cases in which a belief just barely falls short of meeting the necessary conditions for prima facie justification, and cases in which it falls far short of doing so. In the latter two types of cases, the fact that some belief is among the outputs of a practice in which it is practically rational to engage may merely provide *some reason* for people who follow the doxastic practice in question, and who have the relevant experience, to believe the relevant proposition. That is, the fact that a belief is the output of a generally reliable doxastic practice may merely provide some reason to accept it, and may not suffice to provide full-blown prima facie justification. Of course there are also many gradations between those mentioned.

Here are some simple cases that illustrate the point that we should think in terms of degrees of prima facie justification. (These cases involve particular beliefs rather than entire doxastic practices; and the beliefs in question are all, in Alston's terms, outputs of SP.) Suppose that we are hiking on a remote trail in the Canadian Rockies. And suppose that you think you see a bear, although what you think to be a bear is far away, hard to see, and open to interpretation. In fact I think that it is not a bear: I suspect strongly that it is a tree stump that from a distance resembles a bear. Compare that with the following case. I look out my window and believe that I see a person in a red coat walking past. The day is bright, and the person passes within a few feet and in full view. Now if there is prima facie justification in both cases in virtue of how things appear, and in virtue of the generally reliable character of SP, it differs with respect to what it is natural to think of as the *degree* of prima facie justification. (And along with this, it seems, goes a difference in inherent capacity to resist overriders.) It seems to you that you see a bear. And you may be justified in believing that you see a bear. It seems to me that I see a person in a red coat. And I am justified in believing that I see a person in a red coat. But you do not have the same degree of prima facie justification for believing that you see a bear as I have for believing that I see a person in a red coat. This is so after I have given my opinion about what we were both seeing. But it seems reasonable to think that it was also the case before I had done so. Presumably this is partly because we ought to know that there are objects other than bears that at a distance can resemble bears, and because it is easy to misinterpret what you see at a distance, whereas there is not the same room for misinterpretation in the case of seeing the person with the red coat. It is also because what you saw in the distance on the trail did not have the sort of clear and over-

whelming character that is possessed by, say, what I now see before me in broad daylight. Perhaps it is also because we know that we are prone to mistaking bearlike shapes
for bears when we are out on the trail in bear country and are mindful of the dangers
that are sometimes involved in encountering bears. I suggest that for these reasons your
belief had what we might think of as second-class prima facie status even when you
were seeing what you took to be a bear, and prior to my giving my opinion. That its
status is second-class is especially clear after we had discussed what we both thought
we had seen. For at that point you knew (or so I like to believe) that an otherwise sane
and fairly reliable perceiver had interpreted in a quite different way what we had both
perceived.

Now your belief that you saw a bear was formed under circumstances in which it
was hard to be sure about what you were observing. That seems to be the central feature
of the case that reduces the degree of prima facie justification that is provided by your
experience for your belief that you saw a bear, although my disagreement may further
reduce the justification provided in this case.

So let us consider a case in which disagreement is the main relevant factor. Suppose
that three of us are lost in the desert. We see a speck far to the east on the horizon. We
set up a telescope on a tripod, focus it on the speck, and one by one look through it at
what had appeared as a speck to the naked eye. It seems to you, let us suppose, that
there is a tent with some bedouin beside it. It seems to our other companion that it is
an oasis. I hear both of your reports. And then it is my turn to look through the telescope. I think that I see a man riding on a camel. At least I have sensations to which
under normal circumstances I would respond by forming at once the belief that I see a
man riding on a camel. But the circumstances in the desert are highly abnormal. What
is the right way to respond to them? It is clear that whatever prima facie justification
may arise for my belief that I see a man riding on a camel from my seeming to myself
to do so, it is a greatly diminished degree of justification.

Given the other reports that I receive before I even make my own observation, the
beliefs I base on what I see have a second-class status. Indeed, it would not be surprising if we went farther than this and concluded that the situation we are in is such that
our usual method for deciding what we are observing is not reliable, and that the reasonable thing to say is that we do not know what is out there in the desert. (I might say:
"Gosh, it seems to me that I am seeing a man riding on a camel, but there obviously is
something strange afoot, and I am not sure that I can trust what my own eyes seem to
be telling me.")

In such a situation there is a lot of other information that will be relevant to deciding how to react. For instance, there is the question of how likely, on other grounds, is
each of the various claims about what is seen through the telescope. It may be quite
likely that there should be a camel there: that partly depends, for instance, on whether
we are in a desert in California or in Saudi Arabia, for instance. Another piece of information that is relevant is the plausibility of possible explanations of the fact that our reports are so different. Perhaps the heat has affected our thinking, or perhaps this is not a
real telescope, or perhaps someone is playing an extraordinary and elaborate practical
joke. We might have heard from a reliable source that there is a group of bedouin who
amuse themselves by creating illusions of camels and of oases in order to fool the inexperienced traveler. If any one of us were to look again and find our original perception

to be confirmed, the fact that what he had thought to be there still appears to be there would have to be taken into account. And so forth. But, to repeat, at the very least, under the circumstances my belief that it is a man on a camel will either have a very low level of prima facie justification or fail even to have that much going for it.

Because it seems clear to me that I am perceiving a camel in spite of the fact that others disagree, it would be natural for us to think that in this situation our normal perceptual procedures have broken down. Things must have gone terribly wrong in such a case for us to be so far apart in our accounts of what we perceive. If, on the other hand, the facts seem murky, as in the bear case, it is less surprising that people interpret them differently, and there is less reason to infer from the fact that different interpretations are offered that there is a malfunction of our normal perceiving processes. In areas in which some considerable measure of discernment is necessary in order to tell what is going on, a variety of interpretations is just what you would expect. Moreover, the camel case is set up so that the possibility that we are actually seeing two different things has been excluded, whereas in the bear case there is always the possibility that we were not looking in exactly the same direction. The elimination of that possibility gives additional reason to believe that somehow things have gone terribly wrong, with the result that a normally reliable practice is failing us in this case. The clearer it is that the same object is being perceived, the lower is the status of any of the conflicting observations of it.

The moral of the story, or rather a moral of the stories, is that Alston views a doxastic practice such as SP in an unduly monolithic way. We may agree that SP is

> a functioning, socially established, perceptual doxastic practice with distinctive experiential inputs, distinctive input-output functions, a distinctive conceptual scheme, and a rich, internally justified overrider system. As such, it possesses a prima facie title to being rationally engaged in, and its outputs are thereby prima facie justified, *provided we have no sufficient reason to regard it as unreliable or otherwise disqualified for rational acceptance.* (PG, 225; emphasis in original)

But this is consistent with its being the case that the degree of prima facie justification possessed by different beliefs that are outputs of SP varies greatly.

The case of testimony is similar. It is widely recognized that people vary greatly in the extent to which their testimony is believable. It seems doubtful that testimony should be considered to confer a set amount of justification for all of its outputs. And examples can be multiplied. In fact the whole idea of a unified practice that provides a certain amount of justification for its outputs seems dubious. Rather, what we seem to have is an array of subpractices that differ greatly in their reliability, or a single practice whose different applications vary widely in their reliability. So it is also with the perceptual practices, including the various MPs. It is not difficult to accommodate this thought in Alston's scheme, since he characterizes a doxastic practice as a family of ways of going from inputs to outputs; that such a family would vary in its justification-conferring capabilities is in fact what you would expect.

If we think of the prima facie justification that is conferred by our doxastic practices as a matter of degree, and if, for instance, the amount of ambiguity or uncertainty in what is perceived is one of the considerations that is relevant to whether or not, and to what extent, the belief in question is justified, then there must be some degree of ambiguity or uncertainty (etc.) below which there is no prima facie justification at all. In some such cases a person may nevertheless be provided with *some reason* to believe, which is a possibility mentioned by Alston at (PG, 81). So how can we tell whether we are dealing with a case in which there is weak prima facie justification for belief rather than a case in which we merely have a reason to believe, but a reason which would not itself suffice for the belief to be (even prima facie) justified? (Perhaps in the Rocky Mountain case my friend was not prima facie justified [at all] in believing that there was a bear. Perhaps she was justified in thinking that what she was seeing *might* be a bear.)

To say that there are degrees of prima facie justification is to say, for instance, that although two propositions p1 and p2 are prima facie justified, and innocent until proven guilty, it would take less by way of defeaters to override the one than it takes to override the other. It is also to say something about the degree of confidence that it is proper to have in each of them, even in the absence of defeaters.

We might consider trying to cash in what I am thinking of as degrees of prima facie justification in terms of degrees of defeasibility. To say that a belief p is more defeasible than a belief q is just to say that it is easier to make a case for p not being justified *simpliciter* than it is to do so in the case of q. On that approach we would think of being prima facie justified as an all-or-nothing affair, but then we would think there to be degrees of defeasibility. However, I think that there is good reason not to opt for this analysis. For example, the fact that a belief is acquired in circumstances that are recognized to be ambiguous, and in which there is known to be disagreement, should affect the extent to which one is initially justified in holding it and not just the ease with which it should be given up.

6. Reduced Rationality

There is a general principle that accounts for our intuitions in the cases discussed in the last section. I will call this the "DAM principle" on account of its focus on the implications of disagreement, ambiguity, and the fact that a belief-forming mechanism may be malfunctioning or out of its depth:

> Beliefs with respect to which (a) there is disagreement, that are (b) about matters that are ambiguous and hence difficult to interpret, and that are (c) generated by a doxastic practice that we have reason to suspect may be at its limit or out of its depth or malfunctioning (such as when we are in the desert and the sun has been baking down on our heads) are less justified on that account.

Obviously, there are a number of other principles that are closely related to this one. These include one that says that there is less justification when condition (a) is met, another that says that this is so when condition (b) is met, another that says that this is so when condition (c) is met, another that says that this is so when both (b) and (c) are met, and so forth. The most plausible of those mentioned, however, has application when all three conditions are met and I will restrict discussion to that case.

If we assume that Alston does not propose to establish that the outputs of CMP are justified, but rather that it is rational to suppose this to be so, the DAM principle would take the following form:

The practical rationality of judging to be reliable any doxastic practice that issues to a very considerable extent in beliefs that satisfy conditions (a) and (b) above, and that (d) we have reason to suspect may be at its limit or out of its depth or malfunctioning (such as when we are in the desert and the sun has been baking down on our heads) is considerably reduced.

How the DAM principle is to be stated will depend on how we individuate doxastic practices. Consider, say, the operation of SP in conditions in which there is disagreement, the subject area is ambiguous and hence difficult to interpret, and in which we have reason to suspect that SP may be at its limit or out of its depth or malfunctioning (such as when we are in the desert and the sun has been baking down on our heads or when we are seeing deep underwater), so that we may easily go wrong. We might think of this as a separate practice from SP under normal conditions so that there would be the doxastic practice of seeing in broad daylight and the doxastic practice of seeing underwater. In that case two practices would deal with somewhat similar subject matter, share much of the same physiological underpinnings and many of the same overriders, and so forth. An alternative is that we think in terms of a larger doxastic practice that includes various subpractices that vary with respect to the degree to which it is rational to rely on them.

So there are various ways to go here. Alston's view is that there are various factors that bear on how doxastic practices are to be individuated, including the following: homogeneity with respect to reliability, "similarity in causal genesis, similarity in psychological function, and similarity in physiological underpinnings" (PG, 167). Since it is unclear how much weight each of these (or other) considerations that bear on the individuation of practices is to have, it is also unclear which of the options mentioned at the end of the previous paragraph best fits with Alston's theory.

I propose that the best approach is to think of the conditions specified in the DAM principle as together constituting an underminer for a practice, or perhaps as what I shall call a "restrainer," which is a weaker version of an underminer. An underminer provides "sufficient reasons to think that in this instance the ground of the belief does not wield its usual justificatory force" (PG, 79; see also PG, 72). Alston later says, in remarks that clarify further how he understands an underminer to operate, that in the case of perceptual justification "this would involve reasons for supposing the situation of perception to be abnormal in some way that would prevent the perceptual experience from functioning as a reliable sign of what is believed" (PG, 191). I take Alston to mean to say in the latter part of this sentence that an underminer would prevent a perceptual experience from functioning as a reliable sign of what is to be believed. And I take it to be clear from this last quoted remark from Alston, therefore, that an underminer has the result that justification, which otherwise would have been provided, is not provided. That is, an underminer does not exactly have the effect that a practice does not have its usual justificatory force: rather its effect is that the practice lacks all justificatory force. There is, in any case, another possibility here, namely, that one or more factors might reduce somewhat the prima facie justification provided for the outputs of a practice. And this is what I am calling a "restrainer." When a restrainer is operative, the doxastic practice in question may still be relied upon, but only with caution and in awareness that one may be out of one's depth. The justification that is conferred in such conditions is reduced.

The DAM principle applies to *all* practices. In particular, there is no reason to think of this as a rule of SP. (We are not making the "imperialistic" assumption "that reports of perception of God are properly treated the same way as reports of perception of the physical environment" (PG, 216; PG, 220). We are not adopting the rules of SP and then applying these rules to practices to which they are not appropriate.) The DAM principle seems to apply to numerous other practices such as the practice of accepting beliefs on the basis of testimony. It is best thought of as a commonsense background belief we bring to whatever doxastic practice we engage in.[8] It is part of what we have learned through using numerous doxastic practices in numerous situations. Beliefs such as this have been built up through trial and error and by observing the operation of our doxastic practices.

The DAM principle bears on the case of religious belief and on the doxastic practices, including the various MPs, that are deployed within religious traditions. Interestingly, Alston more or less states that conditions (a), (b), and (d) are met in the case of CMP. He believes that the outputs of each MP massively contradict those of other MPs. The outputs of CMP, he says, are "usually but dim, meager and obscure" (PG, 208). And he talks of the "incomplete and shaky character of our cognitive grasp of the subject matter" (PG, 237).

What I am proposing can be fairly easily accommodated within the Alstonian scheme. In certain conditions a practice comes to be somewhat suspect or to be such that one ought to rely upon it less confidently, even if it is still rational to rely upon it. The rationality of believing the practice to confer prima facie justification is diminished. The justification that it is rational to believe the practice to confer on its outputs is of a lower quality. There is a case to be made for being somewhat disconnected from a doxastic practice under certain conditions and for being cautious in one's reliance on it. One relevant consideration is whether there is any alternative to "business as usual": that is, to continuing with doxastic practices upon which one has relied provided that they are internally validated. And in the religious case there are such options. One such option is to continue to accept the outputs of an MP (or other doxastic practice that is established within a religious tradition) that is internally validated and to continue to take it seriously as a source of beliefs, but to do all this in the tentative mode. There are alternatives to either "sitting tight" with your practice or abandoning it: one can sit loosely with it, or at any rate one can do so in the case of religiously based MPs. It is not practically rational to carry on with business as usual under the DAM conditions. Finally, I see no way to measure exactly the extent to which the rationality of continuing with a practice is diminished under these conditions. Nor—if this is the relevant issue—do I see any way to measure the extent to which justification is reduced under these conditions.

7. Third-Person Justification

Finally, a word or two on the third-person case. Alston contends that the justification that a person who follows CMP has for believing on the basis of perceptual experience that, say, God is kind or just may also transfer to a third party who is not a practitioner of CMP. He makes a number of claims in this area that seem correct, or at least on one reading seem correct. Thus he says that he believes "that [his] arguments . . . provide anyone, participant in CMP or not, with sufficient reasons for taking CMP to be rationally engaged in" (PG, 283). If, in the third-person case, this means merely that a non-practitioner of CMP has reason to agree that it is practically rational for a practitioner of CMP to adhere to CMP, it is unexceptionable. But Alston also holds that third parties may be justified in accepting the outputs of CMP, although they are justified to a lesser extent than is the case for practitioners. His claims in this area are more problematic.

The transfer of justification in question is to occur via testimony, which is the source of much of what we justifiably believe. Alston points out that in secular contexts if (a) someone else is justified in believing that p, (b) he tells me that p, and (c) I am justified in believing that he is justified in believing p, we generally suppose that I am justified in believing p (PG, 280). Why, he asks, should the same reasoning not apply in religious contexts? He says that there is no sound reason for denying this to be so.

He allows that the justification that the outsider has for the outputs of CMP will be somewhat diminished, however. For the outsider in this case "not only has the task of determining whether the testifier is justified in his belief according to the standards of the practice that generated the belief, but also the task of determining whether that practice is reliable or rational" (PG, 283).

Two serious problems arise for Alston's reasoning in the third-party case. First, the fact that the best case that those who follow CMP can make for its reliability is practical in character is once again relevant. This sort of case—which arises from the impossibility of evaluating doxastic practices from the outside and from our having no choice but to continue with our socially established doxastic practices—does not carry over to an outsider. An outsider may have reason to believe that an insider ought to continue with a doxastic practice, and yet have little reason to adopt that doxastic practice.

Second, the familiar issue of the presence of diverse traditions is relevant once more. In an important set of remarks on this topic Alston says the following:

> It goes without saying, I hope, that the conclusions I have been drawing concerning the epistemic situation of practitioners of CMP hold, *pari passu*, for practitioners of other internally validated forms of MP. In each case the person who is in the kind of position I have been describing will be able to rationally engage in his/her own religious doxastic practice despite the inability to show that it is epistemically superior to the competition. (PG, 274–75)

These claims seem correct. But is justification to carry over from the first person to the third person in the case of every MP? We are all outsiders to many MPs whose outputs contradict each other: Why should we consider it rational to accept the outputs of one rather than another? Does the outsider have any reason to subscribe to anything stronger than the view that one of the conflicting MPs may be reliable? I doubt it.[9] So I do not see that we should go along with what Alston says about the third-party case. If I am right, this reduces greatly the significance of his conclusions.

NOTES

1. If the personal and somewhat anthropomorphic conception of God mentioned in my opening paragraph is off the mark and an impersonal conception or the conception proposed by Process Theology, for example, is accurate, then of course the situation is different. Thus a changing and developing deity after the fashion proposed by Process Theology may not be able to do more than is currently done to make the facts about its nature and existence clear to us.

2. This may have been Calvin's attitude toward nonbelief. For a brief discussion, see Nicholas Wolterstorff, "Is Reason Enough," in *Contemporary Perspectives on Religious Epistemology*, edited by R. Douglas Geivett and Brendan Sweetnam (New York: Oxford University Press, 1992).

3. Thomas V. Morris makes more or less the same point in "The Hidden God," *Philosophical Topics* 16, no. 2 (Fall 1988): 8. See also James A. Keller, "The Hiddenness of God and the Problem of Evil," *International Journal for Philosophy of Religion* 37 (1995): 13–24.

4. For an extended treatment of such motifs, see Samuel E. Balentine, *The Hidden God: The Hiding of the Face of God in the Old Testament* (Oxford: Oxford University Press, 1983).

5. Robert Mesle, "Does God Hide from Us? John Hick and Process Theology on Faith, Freedom and Theodicy," *International Journal for Philosophy of Religion* 24 (1988): 94–95. This essay has also appeared as chapter 5 of C. Robert Mesle's *John Hick's Theodicy: A Process Humanist Critique* (New York: St. Martin's Press, 1991).

6. Alvin Plantinga is a representative of the it's-all-obvious school: he says that beliefs that entail God's existence do not require evidence in order for them to be justified, which is one reason that these candid remarks in an autobiographical essay are interesting:

> For me as, I suppose, for most others, spiritual life is an up and down proposition, with what one hopes are the consolidation of small but genuine gains. Sometimes I wake in the wee hours of the morning and find myself wondering: Can all this really be true? Can this whole wonderful Christian story really be more than a wonderful fairy tale? At other times

I find myself as convinced of its main lineaments as that I live in South Bend. (Alvin Plantinga "A Christian Life Partly Lived," in *Philosophers Who Believe: The Spiritual Journeys of 11 Leading Thinkers* edited by Kelly James Clark (Downer's Grove, Ill.: InterVarsity Press, 1993), 67.

7. Blaise Pascal, *Pensées*, translated with an introduction by A. J. Krailsheimer (New York: Penguin, 1966), 103.

8. Clark H. Pinnock, *Reason Enough: A Case for the Christian Faith* (Downers Grove, Ill.: InterVarsity Press, 1980), 18; quoted in Nicholas Wolterstorff, "Is Reason Enough?" in *Contemporary Perspectives on Religious Epistemology*, edited by R. Douglas Geivett and Brendan Sweetman

9. William P. Alston, *Perceiving God: The Epistemology of Religious Experience* (Ithaca, N.Y.: Cornell University Press, 1991), 208.

10. In *Divine Hiddenness and Human Reason* (Ithaca, N.Y.: Cornell University Press, 1993) J. L. Schellenberg attempts to make a case for atheism on the grounds that if God were to exist, God would want to be in loving communion with us and would take steps to ensure that we would be in such communion. Schellenberg contends that since these steps are not currently being taken, God does not exist. I discuss Schellenberg's arguments in chapter 5.

11. Blaise Pascal, *Pensées*, 101.

12. D. Z. Phillips, "Faith, Scepticism, and Religious Understanding," in *Contemporary Perspectives on Religious Epistemology*, edited by R. Douglas Geivett and Brendan Sweetman; reprinted from D. Z. Phillips, *Faith and Philosophical Enquiry* (London: Routledge and Kegan Paul, 1970), 85.

13. George Berkeley, *Principles of Human Knowledge* in vol. 2 of *The Works of George Berkeley, Bishop of Cloyne*, edited by A. A. Luce and T. E. Jessop (London: Thomas Nelson and Sons, 1949) secs. 148–51.

14. *Methodist Hymn Book* (London: Methodist Conference Office, 1993).

15. The Christian Gnostics are among the many groups who have appealed to God's transcendence in an attempt to account for God's incomprehensibility to us. For some discussion of their views, and of what they took to be the theological implications of those views, see Francis M. Young "The God of the Greeks and the Nature of Religious Language" in *Early Christian Literature and the Classical Intellectual Tradition*, edited by W. R. Schoedel and Robert L. Wilken (Paris: Beauchesne, 1979), 45–74, esp. 50ff.

16. Rudolf Otto, *The Idea of the Holy*, translated by John Harvey (London: Oxford University Press, 1958), 179, 28.

17. Joseph Butler, *Fifteen Sermons Preached at the Rolls Chapel*, with introduction, analyses, and notes by the Very Rev. W. R. Matthews (London: G. Bell and Sons, 1969), 240.

18. Søren Kierkegaard, *Concluding Unscientific Postscript*, translated by David Swenson (Princeton, N.J.: Princeton University Press, 1944), 182.

19. Butler, *Fifteen Sermons*, 235.

20. John Hick, *An Interpretation of Religion: Human Responses to the Transcendent* (New Haven, Conn.: Yale University Press, 1989), 12. What I have to say on this topic of ambiguity owes much to the work of Terence Penelhum and John Hick. See Terence Penelhum, "Parity Is Not Enough," in *Faith, Reason, and Skepticism*, edited by Marcus Hester (Philadelphia: Temple University Press, 1992), 111ff.; "Reflections on the Ambiguity of the World," in *God, Truth and Reality*, edited by Arvind Sharma (New York: St. Martin's Press, 1993), 165–75; and the final chapter ("Faith and Ambiguity") of *Reason and Religious Faith* (Boulder, Colo.: Westview Press, 1995). See, too, J. Hick, *An Interpretation of Religion*, 122–24, and passim. William Wainwright makes some useful observations in his review of Hick's book in *Faith and Philosophy* 9, (April 1992): 259–65.

21. Hick, *An Interpretation of Religion*, 123.

CHAPTER 2

1. Eliezer Berkovits, *Faith after the Holocaust* (New York: KTAV Publishing House, 1973), 64.

2. Furthermore, the loss-of-responsibility proposal reflects a very limited perspective on the

very diverse connections that may obtain between theistic belief and our responses to moral and social concerns. A good book to read while reflecting on this topic is H. Richard Niebuhr's *Christ and Culture* (New York: Harper, 1956). Niebuhr explores the many ways in which faith has been understood to have ramifications for social life. The different strands, or many of them, which Niebuhr identifies in the case of Christendom, can also be found in other theistic traditions, and I expect that analogues to them can be found in the nontheistic traditions. The suggestion that theism, of whatever variety, and irrespective of the degree of certainty with which it may be adhered to, and however obvious its claims might be thought to be, would elicit in its adherents just one reaction, such as leaving them with no alternative but to regard social problems as no longer requiring their attention, is one that would require a lot of further argument, and has a lot of evidence against it.

3. There are other aspects of the loss-of-responsibility proposal that are worth exploring. What attitude we take to this proposal will be in part a function of the extent to which we think that what morality requires of us is something that *could* be accomplished better by God. If, for instance, it is very central to our conception of morality both that we ought to cultivate within ourselves various moral virtues and that part of what is valuable about our possession of such virtues is that we ourselves have cultivated them, at least *this* part of morality is unlikely to be undermined (in the way discussed earlier) by the facts about God being clear to us. The same goes for any other morally significant area in which our own efforts are regarded as especially important. I will not try to address here the question of the extent to which morality is of this nature and is therefore such that God could not sensibly be understood to take over from us with respect to its fulfillment. On any plausible conception of morality, we also have a duty to ensure that our actions will bring about certain consequences—and it is in such areas that (it is alleged by the point of view under discussion) our sense of responsibility would be diminished.

4. Immanuel Kant, *Lectures on Philosophical Theology,* translated by Allen W. Wood and Gertrude M. Clark (Ithaca, N.Y.: Cornell University Press, 1978), 123; my emphasis (henceforth LPT).

5. Immanuel Kant, *Critique of Practical Reason,* translated by Lewis White Beck (Indianapolis: Bobbs-Merrill, 1956), 152; my emphasis (henceforth CPR).

6. On this theme see also LPT, 162. A somewhat different reading of the main thrust of Kant's thinking on this topic is proposed by Douglas Drabkin in "The Moralist's Fear of Knowledge of God," *Faith and Philosophy* 11, no.1 (January 1994): 88–89.

7. Drabkin, "The Moralist's Fear of Knowledge of God," 86.

8. Exactly what Kant thought to be involved in postulating the existence of God is a difficult topic. For example, must it involve believing that God exists, or might it merely involve believing that it is possible that God exists? For some discussion see M. Jamie Ferreira, "Kant's Postulate: The Possibility or the Existence of God?" *Kant-Studien* 74 (1983): 75–80.

9. I should add that the puzzles under discussion in this and the two previous paragraphs emerge from consideration of the relevant parts of *Lectures on Philosophical Theology* and the *Critique of Practical Reason.* Although I do not know this to be so, it may be that a solution to these puzzles is to be found in other writings by Kant in which these themes are pursued; and it may be that Kant's views on these matters evolved in ways that I am not recognizing.

10. Richard Swinburne, *The Existence of God* (Oxford: Clarendon Press, 1979), 211ff.

11. My main interest is of course in what Swinburne says about the unfortunate consequences of our knowing for certain there was a God. But there is reason to question Swinburne's assumption that if God were to give us directly information about what consequences our actions would have if they were to occur, this would result in certain facts about God becoming clear. For example, couldn't God plant information in us without letting us know its source?

12. J. L. Schellenberg makes some further criticisms of Swinburne on this point in his *Divine Hiddenness and Human Reason,* 119f.

13. My thinking about this point has benefited from reading Schellenberg's account of the relation between the different parts of Swinburne's views.

14. An interesting feature of Swinburne's position is that he assumes, in effect, that we suffer from limited depravity. The temptation to do wrong that we experience has a force such that it would be overridden by certainty that God exists. But it could have had a greater force: it could have had a force such that we would continue to be tempted and wrong options would retain their appeal even if we were certain that God exists. However, Swinburne says, it would be a great evil for us to be depraved to that degree (Richard Swinburne, "Knowledge from Experience, and the Problem of Evil," in *The Rationality of Religious Belief*, edited by William J. Abraham and Steve W. Holtzer [Oxford: Clarendon Press, 1987], 157). A related thought is that the inhibiting effects of a permanent and intimate sense of the presence of God might be felt by some people to a greater extent than they would be felt by others. Some people might not feel them at all, while others might feel them strongly: perhaps the behavior and choices of saintly individuals would be influenced hardly at all whereas people of more mixed character would be influenced to a considerable extent. Some such differences would be what you would expect. Again, the inhibiting effects might be greater (or less) in the case of very wrong actions than they would be in the case of marginally wrong actions, even in the case of the same individual.

15. John Hick, *Faith and Knowledge* (London: Macmillan, 1987), 27.

16. Incidentally, Swinburne's view, I take it, is not that ongoing intimate communication with God would have the result that people would no longer be sinners. I assume that his view would be that sin would in that case take another form. Perhaps, instead of leading to wrong actions, it would result in right actions being done for the wrong reasons. Or the idea might be that an ongoing inner drama of selfish inclinations warring with other inclinations—with tendencies to hatred, malice, contempt, indifference, and so forth warring with altruistic and benevolent tendencies—would still occur even though wrongful actions would no longer be on the cards.

17. Butler, *Fifteen Sermons*, 235.

18. C. Robert Mesle, *John Hick's Theodicy: A Process Humanist Critique*, 31ff.

19. Schellenberg mentions this possibility in *Divine Hiddenness and Human Reason*, 130.

20. John Hick, *Evil and the God of Love* (San Francisco: Harper and Row, 1977), 255–56; Hick, "An Irenaean Theodicy," reprinted in Mesle, *John Hick's Theodicy*, xxii.

21. Mesle, *John Hick's Theodicy*, 34.

22. Schellenberg, *Divine Hiddenness and Human Reason*, 122ff.

23. Swinburne mentions this idea in *Is There a God?* (Oxford, Oxford University Press, 1996) 108.

CHAPTER 3

1. I borrow the term from Louis Pojman, whose book *Religious Belief and the Will* (London: Routledge, 1986) explores, both historically and conceptually, the relation between belief and the will, with particular reference to religious belief.

2. John Hick, *Christianity at the Centre* (London: Macmillan, 1970), 55–56; Alasdair MacIntyre, "The Logical Status of Religious Belief," in *Metaphysical Beliefs*, edited by Stephen Toulmin, Ronald Hepburn, and Alasdair MacIntyre (1957; London: SCM Press, 1970), 186–87; see also 199. I take it that MacIntyre is exploring here what he takes to be the ill effects of the existence of God being demonstrated, rather than the ill effects of the existence of God being demonstrable. It may be that the existence of God is provable but that the proof is currently (or even permanently) beyond the capacity of the human mind to grasp.

3. While I think that it is reasonable to read Hick as espousing cryptovolitionalism in the preceding passage, in other parts of the work from which it is excerpted, and in other works such as *Evil and the God of Love* (New York: Harper and Row, 1966), he is less sympathetic to it in other writings. See *Arguments for the Existence of God* (New York: Herder and Herder, 1971), 104–7. For a good discussion of how best to interpret Hick's many remarks on this topic, see chapter 5 of

J. L. Schellenberg's *Divine Hiddenness and Human Reason*. Schellenberg says that Hick's concern is not really with freedom with respect to the belief that God exists, and that it is more a matter of its being important that we engage in a search for God before experiencing God's presence. There would be no need and no place for such a search if God's presence were obvious to us. (98f.) Schellenberg thinks that Hick "is primarily concerned not with the belief *that* there is a God, but with belief *in* God (i.e. religious commitment, involving love and trust) and with the preservation of our freedom in respect of it" (98). Schellenberg may be right about all this, but the ideas that I impute to Hick also represent a strand in his thinking. I will return to the additional points that he imputes to Hick, including the point about the value of a search, the value of trust, and the value of commitment in later chapters.

4. It probably is also true that (a) we are unable to bring it about, just by willing it, that we hold a belief in a full or in a minimal way, where previously we held it in another way and (b) we are unable to bring it about, just by willing it, that we believe in some being, in whom we did not previously believe. (In section 4 of this chapter I explain what I mean by "full" and "minimal" belief and by "belief in": however, my usage is not out of the ordinary and is as one would expect it to be.) Incidentally, if I am wrong in what I say and direct volitionalism is viable after all, the result is just that instead of the two ways in which we can exercise control over our beliefs that I go on to discuss, there actually are three ways in which we can do so.

5. Not everyone agrees that people are unable to bring it about directly by an act of will that they believe a proposition. I suspect that those who claim to be able to do so are misdescribing cases in which they wish to believe some proposition and then find that they believe it.

6. Some of the literature relevant to this issue is discussed by Pojman, *Religious Belief and the Will*, passim. The two arguments against direct volitionalism that I mention in this paragraph roughly correspond to Pojman's phenomenological argument (157f.) and logic of belief argument (170f.).

7. William P. Alston, "Belief, Acceptance and Religious Faith," in *Faith, Freedom, and Rationality*, edited by Jeff Jordan and Daniel Howard-Snyder (Lanham, Md.: Rowman and Littlefield, 1996), 7.

8. That we should acquire a belief as a nonbasic act that is achieved through one or very few basic acts seems not to be something that is out of the question as a matter of principle. One can imagine it being possible to take a drug that will result in a change of beliefs. (Let us assume that it also results in the eradication of the memory that it is consumption of the drug that has resulted in this change of beliefs.) It might be a drug that induces paranoia, including the belief that others are out to get you. Such a case would involve acquiring a belief as a nonbasic act that is engaged in by pursuing a strategy that, at least, includes some basic acts.

9. Terence Penelhum, *Problems of Religious Knowledge* (New York: Herder and Herder, 1971) (henceforth PRK); Penelhum, *God and Skepticism* (Dordrecht: Reidel, 1983) (henceforth GS).

10. In quite a different context George Berkeley goes farther than Penelhum and suggests that there are cases in which even after we have encountered a proof of a proposition p, we may be unable to accept p. Here Philonous, Berkeley's spokesman, is speaking:

> [Though] a demonstration be never so well grounded and fairly proposed, yet if there is withal a stain of prejudice, or a wrong bias on the understanding, can it be expected on a sudden to perceive clearly and adhere firmly to the truth? No, there is need of time and pains: the attention must be awakened and detained by a frequent repetition of the same thing placed oft in the same, oft in different lights. (*Three Dialogues between Hylas and Philonous*, in *The Works of George Berkeley Bishop of Cloyne*, edited by A. A. Luce and T. E. Jessop [London: Thomas Nelson and Sons, 1949], vol. 2, 223.)

Penelhum's point is that even if you have a proof of p, you may be able to reject p. Berkeley's point is that even if you have a proof of p, you may not be able to accept p. Both seem right.

11. Someone who is so situated seems trapped in a certain respect. He sees that p follows

from premises that he accepts; hence he is in an important sense committed to p. Yet he refuses to believe p, being committed to not doing so. It is hard to imagine someone staying long in this precarious condition. It seems likely that such a person will either stick with denying the conclusion and start to doubt either one or more premises or the validity of the argument, or move in the direction of accepting the conclusion.

12. In cases of this sort control of even the second, effortless, sort seems absent. The reason is that one's particular attitudes, interests, character (etc.) do not contribute to one's acceptance of the belief.

13. Rationality of the sort that I have in mind is possessed by a belief p in virtue of the relation between p and the evidence for p that is currently available. There are of course other conceptions of rationality. For example, the belief that p could be irrational in the sense indicated, and yet S might be rational in believing p in the sense that S has not failed to take any steps to discern whether p is true, or to consider evidence which is relevant to the truth of p, which it would be reasonable to expect S to take. Or S might be rational in the sense that S has not violated any relevant norms of rationality, or in the sense that S nonculpably knows of no evidence that provides reason for S to give up p. Rationality of these latter sorts is a matter of what may be expected of a person.

14. Revised cryptovolitionalism must also be understood to involve the idea that it is a good and valuable thing that we are able to exercise control over what we believe in the area of religion under conditions in which the various options for belief are rational.

15. It might be thought that we should think of nominal belief as an extreme form of minimal belief rather than as belief merely in name. After all, if you are willing to *say* that you believe, this may have some implications for your conduct, even if this is so only under counterfactual conditions. If this is right, there is no such thing as purely verbal assent, and the distinction here is best thought of as between belief that matters little to someone and belief that does not matter at all to him. However, I am inclined to think that there are those who are best understood as believers "only in name."

16. Hick makes remarks that are at least suggestive of this objection. "Could a verbal proof of divine existence compel a consciousness of God comparable in coerciveness with a direct manifestation of his divine majesty and power? Could anyone be moved and shaken in their whole being by the demonstration of a proposition as men have been by a numinous experience of overpowering impressiveness? . . . [A] verbal proof of God's existence cannot by itself break down our human freedom" (*Arguments for the Existence of God*, 106–107).

17. But what about belief in God? Could it be rational not to believe in God even if it is irrational not to believe that God exists? This question is unanswerable in the absence of an account of rationality with respect to trust or *belief in*. The notion of what it is for a belief to be rational that was sketched in section 3 does not have any clear implications for the rationality of trust.

18. Mesle, *John Hick's Theodicy*, 77.

19. Mesle raises questions of this sort in ibid., 75.

20. William P. Alston, "Experience as a Ground of Belief," in *Religious Experience and Religious Belief: Essays in the Epistemology of Religion*, edited by Joseph Runzo and Craig K. Ihara (Lanham, Md.: University Press of America, 1986), 48.

21. Alston, *Perceiving God*, 199.

CHAPTER 4

1. For discussion of some relevant issues, see chapter 4 of Richard Swinburne, *Faith and Reason* (Oxford: Clarendon Press, 1981).

2. Marilyn McCord Adams, "Redemptive Suffering," in *Rationality, Religious Belief and Moral Commitment*, edited by Robert Audi and William Wainwright (Ithaca, N.Y.: Cornell University Press, 1986), 251.

3. However, I do not propose to provide a comprehensive analysis of the notion of trust. For one thing, the only accounts of trust that are relevant are those that appear to have a capacity to explain, or to help to explain, God's hiddenness. By way of a gesture in the direction of other theories, I will just mention one proposed by Richard Swinburne.

> To trust a man is to act on the assumption that he will do for you what he knows that you want or need, when the evidence gives some reason for supposing that he may not and where there will be bad consequences if the assumption is false. (*Faith and Reason*, 111)

Swinburne's account is somewhat similar to Adams's. But while her view is that trusting S to do an action *a* requires some uncertainty about whether or not S will do *a*, Swinburne's view is that trusting S to do *a* requires having evidence that gives some reason to suppose that S will *not* do *a*. (Whether this requires that the evidence, on balance, gives reason to suppose that S will not do *a*, or merely requires that there be some evidence that S will not do *a*—where this evidence can, for example, coexist with weightier evidence that S *will* do *a*—is unclear. But in either case this goes beyond what Adams requires.) It is beyond my present purposes to discuss Swinburne's proposal, but it seems to me to have some flaws in it. First, I take trust to be an attitude that may underpin action of the sort mentioned by Swinburne, but the trusting is one thing and acting on the basis of it is another. Second, it is not clear that in order for there to be trust that S will do something that you want or need, it needs to be true that there will be bad consequences if S does not do what he is being trusted to do. Third, as I argue in opposition to Adams, trusting S to do *a* does not require uncertainty about whether S will do *a*, and a fortiori does not require having reason to suppose that S will not do *a*.

4. Some theists may find it problematic to think of God as a person but all that is meant is that God has a personal nature and personal qualities. Thus God is understood by all theists to know, want, respond, act, remember, interact with human beings and perhaps with other beings, and so forth. And this is what is meant by saying that God is a person.

5. Incidentally, if it were incorrect to think that there is room for trust in S if it is certain (or close to certain) how S is going to act, there certainly would still be ample room for a great measure of dependency and reliance. And the question, in that case, would be: Why is trust more important than such dependency and reliance?

6. Drabkin makes much the same point ("The Moralist's Fear of Knowledge of God," 84), as does Keller ("The Hiddenness of God and the Problem of Evil," 7). A similar point needs to be made in response to a related argument discussed by Schellenberg (*Divine Hiddenness and Human Reason*, 139f.). According to this argument, which Schellenberg calls the "Presumption Argument" and which he traces to Pascal, human beings would relate to greater knowledge of God in arrogant and presumptuous ways. It is hard to see why this claim is any more plausible than the claim that an awareness of God's majesty, greatness, justice (etc.) and in general a more intimate awareness of a being in comparison with whom we are as dust, would restrain us from such attitudes. Perhaps it is a sense that we are the most developed, most knowledgeable (etc.) beings in existence that is more likely to lead to presumption on our part.

7. Robert Merrihew Adams, "The Virtue of Faith," in *The Virtue of Faith and Other Essays in Philosophical Theology* (New York: Oxford University Press, 1987) 9–24).

8. This raises questions about the meaning of Job's remark that "[though] he slay me, yet will I trust in him" (Job 13:15). Does Job merely mean that if God were to slay Job, this would be part of God's plan? If Job knows this much, he has enough knowledge of God's nature to know that even if he is slain, it must be for the best. But perhaps this remark from Job is sheer hyperbole, amounting merely to a declaration of the depth of Job's trust in God.

9. Schellenberg, *Divine Hiddenness and Human Reason*, 181ff.

10. Schellenberg has some discussion of this (ibid., 171ff.). Drabkin also indicates that he thinks there may be something to this idea ("The Moralist's Fear of Knowledge of God," 90).

11. John Wesley, "A Plain Account of Genuine Christianity," in *Selections from the Writings of the Rev. John Wesley, M.A.* (New York: Eaton & Mains, 1901), 246.

12. Schellenberg, *Divine Hiddenness and Human Reason*, 184f.

13. Otto, *The Idea of the Holy*, 28; Paul Ricoeur, *The Symbolism of Evil* (Boston: Beacon Press, 1967), 33.

14. Hilary Putnam, *The Many Faces of Realism* (La Salle, Ill: Open Court, 1987), 49.

15. There is a large literature on the theme of the hidden God in Luther. See, for example, the extensive footnotes in B. A. Gerrish, "'To the Unknown God': Luther and Calvin on the Hiddenness of God," *Journal of Religion* 53 (1973): 263–92.

16. *Martin Luther: Selections from His Writings*, edited with an introduction by John Dillenberger (New York: Doubleday, Anchor Books, 1961), 190.

17. Gerrish's article "'To the Unknown God': Luther and Calvin on the Hiddenness of God" includes a good discussion of Luther's terror in the face of what he regarded as the inscrutable will of God, and of its significance for Luther's views of God.

18. Gerrish, "'To the Unknown God,'" 273–74.

19. Martin Luther, *Lectures on Romans* in *Works*, Volume 25 (St. Louis, Mo.: Concordia Publishing House, 1972), 375.

20. Martin Luther to Melanchthon, 13 January 1522, in *Luther's Correspondence and Other Contemporary Letters*, translated and edited by Preserved Smith, Ph.D., and Charles M. Jacobs, D.D., vol. 2 (1521–30) (Philadelphia: Lutheran Publication Society, 1918), 85.

21. A discussion of unknown goods of mystery might be expanded to include discussion of the possibility that there are other relevant considerations other than goods that are unknown to us. Since I think it likely that the explanation of God's hiddenness will appeal to goods of mystery rather than to any such additional considerations, I will not broach this topic.

22. William L. Rowe, "The Empirical Argument from Evil," in *Rationality, Religious Belief and Moral Commitment: New Essays in the Philosophy of Religion*, ed. Robert Audi and William Wainwright (Ithaca, N.Y.: Cornell University Press, 1986); Stephen Wykstra, "The Humean Obstacle to Evidential Arguments from Suffering: On Avoiding the Evils of 'Appearance,'" *International Journal for Philosophy of Religion* 16, no. 2 (1984): 73–94; Rowe, "Evil and the Theistic Hypothesis: A Response to Wykstra," *International Journal for Philosophy of Religion* 16, no. 2 (1984): 95–100; Rowe "The Problem of Evil and Some Varieties of Atheism," *American Philosophical Quarterly* 16 (1979): 335–41. Schellenberg's discussion is at *Divine Hiddenness and Human Reason*, 88–91.

23. As I have noted, the point under discussion seems to have a significance for our chances of knowing of goods of mystery that it lacks in the case of goods of clarity. For the same reason, it is also less likely to contribute to an explanation of the problem of evil—or other evils, if God's hiddenness is to be classified as an evil. Perhaps this is the, or a, reason that the appeal to unknown goods seems intuitively somewhat more promising in the case of God's hiddenness than it appears in the case of the problem of evil. That is, it seems somewhat less satisfactory to say that God has good reason to permit evils, but we do not know what those reasons are, than to say that God has good reasons to leave it unclear to us whether God exists, but we do not know what those reasons are.

24. For example, I have barely mentioned the idea of the Fall of man. This might be thought to contribute to the hiddenness of God. Among the various obvious problems this proposal confronts is that it would be unjust that anyone should suffer because of the wrongdoing of their ancestors just as, more generally, it is unjust that anyone should ever be punished or suffer grave ill effects on account of the wrongdoing of others. In fact the entire idea of the Fall seems to boil down to a recognition that the world, including human nature, is not as we would wish it to be, combined with an attempt to blame human beings for the fact that this is so.

There are two other themes mentioned by Schellenberg that I have not discussed: the idea, found in Pascal, that "[by] withdrawing, God hopes to awaken us to the wretchedness of life on our own" (*Divine Hiddenness and Human Reason*, 138), and the idea that God's hiddenness requires that human beings pass on information about God from generation to generation, and that this greatly increases the responsibility that we have for each other and the extent to which people are dependent on each other, with the result that some are entrusted with a treasure which they are responsible for passing on intact to others (191–96). I have not discussed these ideas because they do not seem to have much promise.

CHAPTER 5

1. Thomas V. Morris, "The Hidden God," *Philosophical Topics* 16, no. 2 (Fall 1988): 5–21. See also Morris, "Agnosticism," *Analysis* 45 (1985): 219–24.

2. Schellenberg's view is that one is unable to add to one's beliefs by choosing to do so (30). On being presented with sufficient evidence one will believe unless one chooses not to believe, which will involve ignoring or overriding evidence (112) or looking at the evidence selectively (110). Thus if God were to provide us with experiential evidence that renders nonbelief irrational, we could choose not to notice it (27). However, if we can choose to avoid belief, we can also choose to stop avoiding it, which gives us at least some limited ability to add to our beliefs.

3. Marilyn McCord Adams, "Forgiveness: A Christian Model," *Faith and Philosophy* 8 (1991): 291; quoted at Schellenberg, *Divine Hiddenness and Human Reason*, 25.

4. Schellenberg quite appropriately draws on contemporary renderings of the notion of a loving God. As he construes it, it comes to the idea of a being who is interested in helping us, whose intentions are therapeutic, and whose treatment of us is gentle and kind. All in all, what this amounts to is the idea of a wonderful friend. Yet many believers in a loving God readily accept that, for example, God intentionally drowned all human beings except for Noah and his family as well as almost all nonhuman animals, and allowed Job to be ruined in an attempt to test him. I do not mean to offer this as a criticism of Schellenberg, however, as he is responding to a widely accepted set of views.

5. For some discussion that bears on this topic see Daniel Howard-Snyder, "The Argument from Divine Hiddenness" *Canadian Journal of Philosophy* 26, no. 3 (September 1996): 433–53. In this essay, which is a critical response to Schellenberg's book, Howard-Snyder's strategy is to consider a number of different types of people. These are classified in accordance with the extent to which they are disposed to respond favorably to God's overtures and the extent to which they are responsible for being so disposed. In the case of each type he proposes a reason, that in each case has to do with their current state of development, as to why God might currently permit inculpable nonbelief.

CHAPTER 6

1. For relevant discussion see Robert Merrihew Adams, "Must God Create the Best?" in *The Virtue of Faith and Other Essays in Philosophical Theology*, 51–64.

2. If (H4) is correct, what is needed to explain God's hiddenness is an account of why it is not disastrous for God to be hidden, and hidden to the extent to which God is hidden. So what we have here is yet another reading of what it is to explain God's hiddenness.

CHAPTER 7

1. I do not mean to suggest that the diversity of *beliefs* that is to be found in the various traditions constitutes the only difficulty for the traditions that is presented by the more general phenomenon of religious diversity. By way of a token gesture in the direction of other aspects of the situation that merit mention, consider for example the case of a group that feels that its beliefs,

way of life, rituals, celebrations, moral standards, and so forth, are the correct ones, and that also feels that it has been uniquely blessed by God with economic prosperity. But then it finds that people with other beliefs, other ways of life, other rituals, other celebrations, and so forth, are also prospering economically, and are even enjoying a higher level of economic prosperity. Not only that, but their community is vibrant, their celebrations are observed with gusto, and so forth. To the ordinary member of a tradition that purports to have found the answer to all of life's religious perplexities, this often seems genuinely puzzling.

2. I explore this possibility in "Could God Have More Than One Nature?" *Faith and Philosophy* 5 (October 1988): 378–98.

3. I mean to oppose a number of positions that have enjoyed some currency in philosophy of religion in the last few decades, including what is often known as the "Wittgensteinian" approach, which is associated with D. Z. Phillips, Peter Winch, and others. For convincing critical discussion of that approach, see chapter 1 of Gary Gutting's *Religious Belief and Religious Skepticism* (Notre Dame, Ind.: University of Notre Dame Press, 1982); also Richard Gale, *On the Nature and Existence of God* (Cambridge: Cambridge University Press, 1991), 291f.

4. There is quite a lot that needs to be said about what is unfortunate in this area. It all depends on what conditions obtain. Thus, if there is no afterlife, there is something unfortunate about people of many creeds investing themselves in and taking comfort from a hope that will not be fulfilled. If, on the other hand, there is an afterlife, then either there is salvation for people of all creeds or there isn't. (I use "salvation" here as shorthand for all conceptions of the desirable future state that the various religions posit—such as heaven, nirvana, moksha, and the like.) If salvation is not universal, and one group alone (ultra-Orthodox Jews, for example) achieve it, then the situation of all those whose hopes are invested elsewhere, and whose hopes will be unfulfilled, is unfortunate. However, if there is salvation for people of all creeds (perhaps because there is universal salvation), the situation of those whose hopes are inappropriately invested— such as those who have a false conception of what it takes to do well in the afterlife or who are mistakenly convinced that the particular beliefs they hold or practices they pursue or rituals they partake of (etc.) are necessary for salvation—is clearly much less unfortunate.

5. It is no accident that discrediting mechanisms have a place in large-scale systems of beliefs, such as those associated with the religions. It could hardly be otherwise, for this probably is something which is necessary for the survival of a system of beliefs, that is, for its continuing to be a system of beliefs which is tremendously important to people, and by which they define themselves. For if the relevant beliefs of others are not discredited, and if their beliefs are instead seen as just as good as (or, horror of horrors, better than) ours, why bother to continue to hold on to ours and to propagate them and transmit them to the next generation? Why not, for example, accept theirs or accept some compromise position?

6. In suggesting that there are various processes through which people acquire beliefs, I follow Reid, Wolterstorff, Alston, and others. I assume that we acquire beliefs from hearsay, from recognized experts, through the operation of psychological processes over which we have little control, from consideration of the evidence, as well as in other ways. For a discussion of this topic, which owes much to the work of Reid, see section V of Nicholas Wolterstorff's essay "Can Belief in God Be Rational?" in *Faith and Rationality*, ed. Alvin Plantinga and Nicholas Wolterstorff (Notre Dame, Ind.: University of Notre Dame Press, 1983), 148–55. This is also a central theme in Alston's *Perceiving God*, which I discuss at length in chapter 11.

7. I have now used this term "system of beliefs" in two different ways, but its meaning is clear in each case from the context. I have used the term to refer to the set of beliefs that is associated with a religious tradition: in virtue of the various relations that obtain among them, it seems reasonable to think of such beliefs as a system rather than just as a set of beliefs. In the occurrence to which this note is attached, I use the term "system of beliefs" to refer to the set of beliefs which a person has, and I also think of this as a system for much the same reason. Thus, on

this usage, there is my system of beliefs, yours, my brother's, and so forth. The term "system" is used in a loose way in this second context. For instance, I do not mean to imply that the beliefs that someone has are connected with each other in any particular way or display any particular structure, although I assume that there is always an immensely complicated story to be told about the network of relations that occur among a person's beliefs.

8. It might be thought that there is a tension of some sort, or even an inconsistency, between my claim here that theistic belief is important in the respects distinguished and the claim in chapter 6 that—for various reasons, each of which invokes in one way or another the hiddenness of God—theistic belief is not important. But the claim in chapter 6 is a normative one and concerns a conclusion that theists ought to come to concerning whether our currently holding theistic beliefs is part of the purpose of our lives and central to our flourishing in the ways that matter most for beings of our sort. The claim here is a descriptive one and concerns the role that theistic beliefs, and other beliefs about religious matters, actually play in the lives of believers.

9. The case for the E-principle and the T-principle is strongest when there is disagreement, with all that that involves. The import of another tradition diminishes if, for example, it has been careless in its maintenance of its beliefs, perhaps passing them on routinely from generation to generation without engaging in any serious reflection about them. It increases, on the other hand, if the tradition in question has gone through a process of refining and developing its views, if it has wrestled with alternatives and with secular interpretations. The more integrity there is on a particular side, the more ought their views to be taken seriously. And so forth. There is no need to be committed to the view that all traditions are on a par. In fact I do not think that this is so. For example, if people cannot be trusted in certain other areas—perhaps they seem very inclined to cheating or lying or stealing or corruption—then they may not be honest in the area of religion: perhaps they will not face up to beliefs that would cause them difficulty; perhaps they are therefore unreliable across the board. How can we be sure that they are even telling us what they really believe?

10. Reinhold Niebuhr, *The Children of Light and the Children of Darkness* (New York: Scribner's, 1944), 134, 135, 137.

11. This sense of the importance of avoiding the assumption that the current formulations of one's tradition are definitive is shared by a leading contemporary Iranian Islamic thinker, Dr. Abdolkarim Soroush. At some risk to himself in the current Iranian political climate, Dr. Soroush has argued against accepting any single understanding of Islam as definitive and in favor of openness to change. For an introduction to the thinking of Dr. Soroush, see Valla Vakili, "Debating Religion and Politics in Iran: The Political Thought of Abdolkarim Soroush," (New York: Council on Foreign Relations, Inc., 1996).

12. Peter Berger, *The Heretical Imperative: Contemporary Possibilities of Religious Affirmation* (New York: Anchor Books, 1980) (henceforth HI); Berger, *A Far Glory: The Quest for Faith in an Age of Credulity* (New York: Free Press, 1992) (henceforth FG).

13. Berger also says that "one's own faith and the experiences brought on by this faith will actually constitute 'data' or 'evidence' upon which inductive reasoning can take place." (HI, 128–29) I understand the idea that experiences encountered in the process of living a life of faith are to be taken into account. But in what sense is "one's own faith" also to be taken into account? Whatever may be involved here, it appears to be something other than a return to experience.

14. This raises another question about Berger's approach. If experiences are to be tested at the bar of reason (whatever exactly this may amount to), why restrict reason to this subsidiary role, so that its sole function is to enable those who have various experiences to screen and assess them in a certain way? Why may not reason serve as an independent source of information about what is to be believed? If reason can test experiences, why can it not test beliefs?

15. Ian Barbour, *Religion and Science: Historical and Contemporary Issues* (San Francisco: HarperSanFrancisco, 1997), 160, 161.

16. Alvin Plantinga, *Warrant and Proper Function* (New York: Oxford University Press, 1993), 19; see also 216.

17. Here and throughout, I mean not to commit myself on the extent to which our beliefs are under our control except on those occasions, such as in a brief discussion in chapter 2, when I address this question. I see this as, at least in large part, an empirical issue, one that does not lend itself to being resolved on a priori grounds. But whatever results an empirical inquiry would yield in this area, it does seem that we are able to subject our beliefs to scrutiny, and that doing so will probably result in certain changes, including changes in the way in which our beliefs are held.

18. For some thoughts about how the nonprivileged should conduct themselves, see Basil Mitchell, "The Layman's Predicament," in *How to Play Theological Ping-Pong: And Other Essays on Faith and Reason*, ed. William J. Abraham and Robert W. Prevost (Grand Rapids, Mich.: William B. Eerdmans, 1990). Although examination may more reasonably be expected of the privileged, being unprivileged may actually sometimes force one into a process of examination. For example, hardships (such as confronting, or suffering, a dreadful evil) in virtue of which one might not have the opportunity to engage in a lot of reflection on religious matters, and in virtue of which therefore there would be no, or less, obligation to examine the relevant beliefs, might also force one to examine those beliefs.

19. For one account of rationality that includes a requirement of this sort, see Swinburne, *Faith and Reason*, chap. 2.

CHAPTER 8

1. Gutting, *Religious Belief and Religious Skepticism*, 105. In this book Gutting advances a position similar to that which I take in defense of tentative belief. But he does so in the context of discussing Plantinga's case for the proper basicality of various theistic beliefs. Gutting argues, roughly, that if there is disagreement about some issue, then a belief about it is not likely to be properly basic. ("[When] there is widespread disagreement about a claim, with apparently competent judges on both sides, those who assert or deny the claim need to justify their positions" (83f.). The fact of disagreement makes for an obligation to justify. It seems to me that Gutting is right about this.

2. Gilbert Harman, *Change in View: Principles of Reasoning* (Cambridge, Mass.: MIT Press, 1986), 46.

3. Ibid., 49.

4. The distinction between the "big picture" and the details is, as I say, imprecise. How are we to tell what is to count as a detail that is relatively unimportant? There will be disagreement about this across traditions and even among individuals within a tradition. This is as one would expect: it reflects, among other things, the fact that particular beliefs have a different significance for different individuals within a tradition. Conceivably there are members of different traditions who will actually find themselves with more or less the same tentatively held core beliefs once the details are taken less seriously, so that, say, a tentative Jew and a tentative Muslim would have a tremendous lot in common.

5. In addition to the distinction between core beliefs and matters of detail, the following distinction also merits comment. On the one hand there are beliefs that are unique to a particular tradition in the way that the belief that Jesus rose from the dead is unique to Christianity, the belief that God revealed the Qu'ran to Muhammad is unique to Islam, the belief that atman is Brahman is unique to Hinduism, the belief in the immaculate conception of Mary, the mother of Jesus, is unique to Roman Catholicism, and so forth. But then there are, say, Buddhist beliefs that are reasonably counted among those that are definitive of the tradition—they are among the beliefs that you would expect someone who is a Buddhist to accept and may therefore reasonably be counted among the core Buddhist beliefs—but that are not unique to Buddhism; for example, in this category is the belief that human beings are driven by desire and experience suffering as a

consequence. This belief is associated with, but is not unique to, the tradition; and it may not be the subject of disagreement at all; if it is, it is so to a lesser extent; clearly it is shared by many people who are not Buddhists. Hence there is less reason to adopt the Critical Stance with respect to such a belief. The upshot is that the outcome of adopting the Critical Stance with respect to the tenets of a tradition will probably be that they will be held with varying degrees of tentativeness. This is, incidentally, a reason that the system of beliefs can retain its vigor as an interpretive framework: for a system of beliefs that is held in accordance with the Critical Stance probably will not all be held tentatively.

6. Gutting, *Religious Belief and Religious Skepticism*, 106. Incidentally in Gutting's case there is just one belief that qualifies for this status, namely, the belief that there is a good and powerful being who is present to us: Gutting says that "we know almost nothing of God beyond his presence to us" (179).

7. Alasdair MacIntyre, "The Logical Status of Religious Belief," in *Metaphysical Beliefs*, Stephen E. Toulmin, Ronald W. Hepburn, and Alasdair MacIntyre, 171; see also 187, 197.

8. Pierre Bayle, *Historical and Critical Dictionary: Selections*, translated by Richard H. Popkin (Indianapolis and Cambridge: Hackett, 1991), 195.

9. Penelhum, *Problems of Religious Knowledge*, 133.

10. Ernest Gellner, *Postmodernism, Reason and Religion* (London: Routledge, 1992).

11. Gutting, *Religious Belief and Religious Skepticism*, 106–7.

12. In chapter 16 of *Religious Belief and the Will*, Louis P. Pojman makes some similar remarks about Gutting; see pp. 230–34.

13. Here there is also a related position to consider, one that does not figure in Gutting's discussion but that is closely related to his concerns. This is the contention that a reason tentative Christian belief is out of the question, and why such belief must involve decisive assent, is that among the beliefs that Christians hold is the very belief that belief must involve decisive assent. (And again, the same point obviously can just as readily be made with respect to the other theistic traditions.) But then one wonders why Christians could not shed this particular belief and yet keep all or most of their other beliefs intact. And if the point were not that the particular belief that assent must be decisive rather than tentative is a central part of Christian belief but rather were that the appropriateness of decisive rather than tentative belief is, so to speak, woven into the fabric of Christian belief, the question of how much of that belief can survive if belief becomes tentative remains open.

14. There is something unfortunate about so many people investing their deepest hopes in beliefs that are not true. However, the tentative believer is one who recognizes that *he* may himself be such a person.

15. MacIntyre, "The Logical Status of Religious Belief," 184.

16. For instance, in many advanced capitalist societies the working class has not slipped ever deeper into destitution and powerlessness, contrary to what Marx predicted. There is also much truth to Sir Michael Howard's observation that "so far from development in means of production enabling the proletariat to eliminate the bourgeoisie, they have enabled the bourgeoisie very effectively to eliminate the proletariat" ("Cold War, Chill Peace," Ditchley Foundation Lecture 30, Supplement to the Ditchley Conference Reports, 1992–93, 4).

17. John King-Farlow and William Christensen, "Faith—And Faith in Hypotheses," *Religious Studies* 7 (1971): 113–24.

18. In general this seems to be what King-Farlow and Christensen have in mind. But remarks such as the following suggest that they have in mind something stronger than a mere awareness that it is possible that there might be a need for revision, and suggest instead something closer to the Critical Stance:

Consider the following questions. Is the man who holds the view willing to discuss it seriously? Is he willing to try to clarify it for himself and for others? Is he willing to accept the serious possibility of having made an error? Is he willing to listen to criticism, to give objections to his view a fair hearing? Is he willing to give the critics of his view what he himself considers good reasons or grounds for retaining his view and for rejecting the arguments and proposals of those critics? Does he show tolerance and respect for others? Is he willing to entertain the possibility that he can learn from the beliefs of others? (119)

To be willing to accept the serious possibility of having made an error seems to involve more than viewing a belief "as conceivably worthy of revision" (120). It may be that King-Farlow and Christensen feel that what they need to establish is the fairly weak position that religious beliefs may be held in such a way that those who hold them can conceive of their being wrong under imaginary circumstances while their own view is the stronger one that such beliefs, or perhaps some such beliefs, should be held in a way that involves a recognition that there is a serious chance that one may be wrong about them, and that others who disagree with one may be right. Or perhaps they are thinking of tentative and exploratory belief in a fairly loose way and mean it to include both belief that involves, or is accompanied by, an awareness that it could conceivably be wrong, as well as belief that includes, or is accompanied by, something stronger such as an awareness that there is a very good chance that one is wrong.

19. Here is another point that bears on practical issues. It might be suggested that the Critical Stance will be insufficiently critical in the social sphere. Here I have in mind a distinction between religion as a critical and prophetic force and religion as a sanctifier of the social status quo, however much in need of reform it may be. The criticism is that because of its tentative and self-critical character, belief of the proposed sort will be incapable of serving as a force for social reform but will rather tend to reinforce existing arrangements and outlooks. This is a complex matter, and I will not go into it further here. It is, however, a familiar point that nontentative religious belief can and does function in both of these ways in different conditions. So tentativeness, or the lack thereof, is certainly not the only factor that bears on whether religion will serve to operate as a reforming or as a stabilizing force.

20. I have in mind, in particular, Audi's essay "Faith, Belief, and Rationality," *Philosophical Perspectives*, 5, Philosophy of Religion (Atascadero, Calif.: Ridgeview Publishing Company, 1991): 213–39; references to Audi's work are to this article, an expanded version of which appears as "Rationality and Religious Commitment," in *Faith, Reason and Scepticism*, edited by Marcus Hester (Philadelphia: Temple University Press, 1992).

21. In his article "Nondoxastic Faith: Audi on Religious Commitment," *International Journal for Philosophy of Religion* 37 (1995): 73–86. Dana Radcliffe also criticizes Audi on this point.

22. Here I disagree with Radcliffe, who says that "[the] use of the word 'faith' implies, not an absence of belief, but an acknowledgment by the speaker that there are reasons for doubting the truth of the proposition, which he nonetheless believes—perhaps confidently," ("Nondoxastic Faith," 76). The attitudinal dimension to faith also needs to be included.

23. Further, I am unsure what Audi considers to be the problem with thinking of belief of the relevant sort as something that involves a certain attitude. He says that "it is in part because faith has a positive attitudinal component that I have resisted assimilating propositional faith to belief." But, for one thing, it may be best to think of propositional faith as involving both a type of belief and certain attitudes so that the belief part is not itself understood to involve the attitudes in question.

24. I owe this observation to Ed Langerak.

CHAPTER 9

1. Perhaps it is not merely *better* that we should believe truths rather than falsehoods. Perhaps we have an *obligation* to do so or to try to do so. If so, the case for examining beliefs is all the more

compelling. For discussion of the possibility that we have an obligation to believe truths rather than falsehoods, and of relevant views of Locke and Chisholm, see Nicholas Wolterstorff "Can Belief in God Be Rational?" For discussion of how an intellectual obligation might be morally based, see Roberta Cutler Klein, "Are We Morally Obligated to Be Intellectually Responsible?" *Philosophy and Phenomenological Research* 48 (September 1987), 79–92. There is also some relevant discussion in Lorraine Code, *Epistemic Responsibility* (Hanover, N.H.: Published for Brown University Press by University Press of New England, 1987), passim; and in Richard Swinburne, *Faith and Reason*, chap. 3.

2. A serious, though in my view unconvincing, case for the contrary view is offered in Joseph Runzo, "God, Commitment, and Other Faiths: Pluralism vs. Relativism," *Faith and Philosophy* 5, no. 4 (October 1988), 343–64.

3. For some discussion of methodological conservatism see, e.g., Daniel Goldstick, "Methodological Conservatism," *American Philosophical Quarterly* 8 (1971): 186–91; Lawrence Sklar, "Methodological Conservatism," *Philosophical Review* 84 (1975): 374–400; Gutting *Religious Belief and Religious Skepticism*, 92–108; Gilbert Harman, *Change in View: Principles of Reasoning*, 30ff.; Jonathan Vogel, "Sklar on Methodological Conservatism," *Philosophy and Phenomenological Research* 52, no. 1 (March 1992), 125–31.

4. Gutting, *Religious Belief and Religious Skepticism*, 100. This condition would, I take it, be met if S is aware of no, or little, evidence relevant to the truth or falsity of p; it would also be met if S is aware of a significant body of evidence relevant to p but this evidence does not entitle S to believe either p or not-p. Gutting also says that on many controversial subjects, such as various issues in economics, politics, or psychology, he himself bases his beliefs on scanty and inaccurate information (101), and he says that even if he were to be as thorough as it would be practical for him to be, his reasoning would still be an easy target for experts. "So," he concludes, "I have very good reason to think that my beliefs on these subjects are epistemically indeterminate" (101). However, this is to introduce a rather different notion of epistemic indeterminacy. It suggests that p is epistemically indeterminate for S if the evidence that S has that is relevant to p is incomplete and there is additional evidence that is known to others. (Or maybe the idea is that p is epistemically indeterminate for S if S is aware both that the evidence that S has that is relevant to p is incomplete and that there is additional evidence that is known to others.) So perhaps Gutting means that there is epistemic indeterminacy if *either* of the following conditions is met: (a) the evidence of which S is aware entitles S to believe neither p nor not-p, or (b) the evidence of which S is aware is incomplete and others are aware of additional evidence. Both conditions may be satisfied simultaneously, but sometimes one will be satisfied while the other is not.

5. See, e.g., Harman, *Change in View*, 31–32, 46. Harman says that this is so provided that S's acceptance of p is full and not tentative. Harman suggests that this way of looking at conservatism fits with a coherentist notion of justification; and he contrasts this with foundations theories of justification, according to which no justification is provided for a belief merely in virtue of the fact that one accepts it. Conservatism, on this construal, is an innocent-until-proven-guilty doctrine for beliefs. As long as S has no reason to think that p, a proposition that S fully accepts, does not cohere with other beliefs that S holds, S is justified in holding p.

6. In situations in which there is disagreement about p and S believes p whereas other groups deny p, should we think—in accordance with conservatism—of S's acceptance of p as still giving S reason to accept p in spite of the fact that the denial of p by other groups gives S reason to call p into question? Perhaps the import of the fact that S believes p is reduced so that it continues to provide some justification for S's acceptance of p but not as much as it otherwise would have. Another possibility is that the fact that S believes p no longer has much significance once there is disagreement, or at least once S knows that there is disagreement, so that conservatism would be more or less irrelevant when there is disagreement. I am not sure which of these views is best.

7. The case of William Cowper illustrates this well. As one of his biographers remarks, "to his

temperament . . . [a] soul-absorbing passion . . . was a necessary condition of happiness. . . . [What] he wanted was a doctrine that would demand the absolute surrender of every energy of his mind and body. . . . [The] religion he wanted . . . [was] a creed that spoke to the heart, that commanded the undivided allegiance of the whole personality, that fired the imagination and gave scope to the desire for action" (Lord David Cecil, *The Stricken Deer: The Life of Cowper* [London: Constable and Company, 1929], 117). To such a person a switch to tentative belief and to the attitude of examination might be damaging. Of course we have to bear in mind that there may also be cases of the opposite sort: cases in which the *avoidance* of the sort of all-consuming allegiance and surrender of the mind that Cowper needed is a prerequisite of happiness.

8. Laura Bernhardt, unpublished note to author.

9. See Richard Nisbet and Lee Ross, *Human Inference: Strategies and Shortcomings of Social Judgment* (Englewood Cliffs, N.J.: Prentice Hall, 1980), especially chap. 8, "Theory Maintenance and Theory Change."

10. David Hume, *An Inquiry Concerning Human Understanding* (Indianapolis: Bobbs-Merrill, 1955), sec. 12, pt 3, 169.

11. I am grateful to Alan Weir for some comments on these issues.

12. We might also consider the forms that worship, trust, faith, spiritual states, religious longings, and much more that is central to being a serious member of a religious tradition can take for the tentative believer. I have focused largely on the *critical* aspect of the Critical Stance. It has to be admitted that tentative belief will not serve to allay various fears and anxieties as effectively as its nontentative counterpart; but how effective it can be in this regard also remains an open question.

13. In section 3 of chapter 7, I defined the notion of disagreement broadly enough that it includes the case in which there is someone to whom the entire area of religion seems unimportant and others to whom this area seems important.

CHAPTER 10

1. William James, *The Varieties of Religious Experience* (London: Fontana, 1960), 414–15.

2. Kelly James Clark, *Return to Reason* (Grand Rapids, Mich.: Eerdmans, 1990), 152.

3. Richard Swinburne *Is There a God?* 132; also 132–34. In chapter 13 of *The Existence of God*, Swinburne provides a more detailed discussion of the Principle of Credulity.

4. In this discussion of the case of Theodore I take it that there is disagreement if someone merely says that Theodore is wrong. So I do not just have in mind disagreement of the sort discussed in the previous three chapters. Later in the chapter I revert to that more carefully defined notion.

5. Clark, *Return to Reason*, 152.

6. Clark is actually a little unclear about what he takes the story of Theodore to show, or— if this is the intended import of the story—what points he takes it to illustrate. He says (or implies) variously that the fact of disagreement "is not detrimental" to Theodore's belief, does not undermine Theodore's right to believe, does not contradict the justification that Theodore has for the belief, "does not carry sufficient evidential weight for him not to take belief in God as basic," and does not constitute a reason against his belief that he saw a timber wolf. Some of these claims are easier to defend than others. Most implausible is the claim that Theodore's encountering people who disagree never diminishes (to any extent) the support that what Theodore experiences provides for his belief that he saw a timber wolf.

7. It might be thought that disagreement does not reduce the amount of support provided by Theodore's experiences for his belief but rather that it leaves that unaffected and instead diminishes the (total) amount of support he has for the belief in question. But the net effect in that case would be about the same. In any case I have given reason to believe that the capacity of the expe-

rience to support belief may itself be reduced. Thus, for example, if Theodore is aware that he is not a great judge of wolves and that the people who disagree do so vehemently and are leading experts on wolves, he has reason to take less seriously what he thought at first to be an experience of seeing a timber wolf.

8. Here I am reverting to using this term as it has been defined in earlier chapters. So there is disagreement only if, for example, people of integrity have different positions on a matter of importance.

9. Here are some examples from the *Autobiography* of St. Teresa of Avila, a work in which numerous remarkable experiences are reported:

> Once, when I was holding in my hand the cross of a rosary, [the Lord] put out His hand and took it from me, and when He gave it back to me, it had become four large stones, much more precious than diamonds. (*The Autobiography of St. Teresa of Avila*, translated and edited by E. Allison Peers (New York: Image Books, 1960), 270)

> It pleased the Lord that I should sometimes see the following vision. I would see beside me, on my left hand, an angel in bodily form. . . . He was not tall, but short, and very beautiful, his face so aflame that he appeared to be one of the highest types of angels who seem to be all afire. . . . In his hands I saw a long golden spear and at the end of the iron tip I seemed to see a point of fire. With this he seemed to pierce my heart several times so that it penetrated to my entrails. . . . The pain was so sharp that it made me utter several moans. . . . It is not bodily pain, but spiritual, though the body has a share in it—indeed, a great share. (273–74)

> One Trinity Sunday, I was in the choir of a certain convent, and, while in a rapture, I saw a great battle between devils and angels. . . . On other occasions I saw around me a great multitude of devils, and yet I seemed to be enveloped by a great light, which prevented them from coming nearer. I realized that God was guarding me so that they should not come near me and thus make me offend Him. From what I sometimes saw in myself, I knew the vision was a genuine one. (291)

10. Timothy Beardsworth, *A Sense of Presence* (Oxford:Religious Experience Research Unit, 1977), 122; quoted in William P. Alston, *Perceiving God*, 17.

11. *Autobiography*, 248.

12. However, as mentioned earlier, what I have provided is not an exhaustive list of the types of religious experience. For example, I have not mentioned a sense of contingency or dependency, nor have I mentioned a sense of being aware of an evil presence; moreover, there undoubtedly are numerous experiences that are associated with, say, the polytheistic traditions or with animism in its numerous forms, and these have not been mentioned. Nor has there been a mention of experiences of a sort discussed by John Hick: he writes of how, for example, contemporary Jews "dwell upon, 'remember,' 'experience,' 'participate in' the exodus as a great act of divine deliverance," thereby seeing themselves as part of a group that has been delivered by God, and from whom trust in God is an appropriate response" (*An Interpretation of Religion*, 100). This sort of experience, in which real or mythical events in a tradition's past are appropriated in some fashion by people in the present, is an important feature of the lives of many people in many traditions.

13. Originally unpublished remarks by Robert M. Adams, quoted in Alston, *Perceiving God*, 204.

14. This support will be provided given that some of the conditions mentioned in the discussion of the case of Theodore and the timber wolf are met. For example, the person in question must not have reason to believe that she is likely to make mistakes in this area. Let us assume that the relevant conditions are met.

15. James, *Varieties of Religious Experience*, 71.

16. I am grateful to Philip Barnes for observations that bear on this topic.

17. Steven T. Katz, "Language, Epistemology, and Mysticism," in *Mysticism and Philosophical Analysis*, edited by Steven T. Katz (New York: Oxford University Press, 1978), 26.

18. J. Trevor, *My Quest for God* (London, 1897), 256–57; quoted in James, *Varieties of Religious Experience*, 383.

19. Al-Ghazzali, in his autobiography; quoted in James *Varieties of Religious Experience*, 390–91, where it is translated from A. Schmolders, *Essai sur les écoles philosophiques chez les Arabes* (Paris, 1842).

20. Charles Darwin, *The Autobiography of Charles Darwin* (New York: Harcourt, Brace, 1959), 91–92.

CHAPTER 11

1. In broad outline the idea here is clear but Alston acknowledges that his notion of an overrider has not been fully developed (PG, 159, n. 26). Here is a question that is unresolved. It is unclear whether numerous commonsense beliefs that people generally share—beliefs about how the world works, about human history, about the reliability of other people, and about the human condition, for example—are part of the overrider system for all of our doxastic practices. If so, the overrider systems for different practices have a lot in common. Commonsense beliefs about such matters have implications for so many doxastic practices that it seems natural to think of them as permanent fixtures—as a background system of beliefs that stays in place, whatever doxastic practices we may engage in—rather than as an attachment to particular doxastic practices.

2. Not only is this something of a construction. It is in addition one that many Christians will themselves find problematic. Thus many evangelical Protestant Christians obviously conceive of what it is to be a Christian in such a way that Roman Catholics are not included. They may be willing to concede that there is a broadly defined "Christian tradition" that includes Catholics, High Church Anglicans, members of the Eastern Orthodox tradition, and so forth. But then they are unlikely to think of that broad tradition, taken as a whole, as a reliable source of overriders.

3. As mentioned, Alston eschews the descriptivist account of reference and prefers the direct account, at least in the case of proper names. It seems to me that it is a good thing from the point of view of defending his own theory that he does so. As indicated, Alston characterizes CMP as the practice of forming beliefs about God on the basis of perception of God that takes as sources of its overrider system "the Bible, the ecumenical councils of the undivided church, Christian experience through the ages, Christian thought, and more generally the Christian tradition" (PG, 193). But if the beliefs of a group about God are to enter into their perceptual reports in the fashion suggested by the descriptive account of reference, this seems to make for the fragmentation of CMP. For instance, a devout Catholic's beliefs about the role of the Sacraments, as administered by her church, in securing reconciliation between individual believers and God, may enter her perceptual experience of God, with the result that she does not share an MP with non-Catholic Christians. That is, it may be God-who-has-provided-the-Sacraments-as-a-vehicle-for-salvation that she understands herself to perceive. Clearly, numerous examples of the same general sort can be given. (The relevant question to ask each group when attempting to tease out what sort of being they understand themselves to perceive is: Who is this God that you understand yourself to perceive?) This puts additional pressure on the idea that CMP should be thought of as a single practice. It is doubtful that there is a way to think of the penetration of perceptual beliefs in such a way that the differences between, say, Christian and Muslim beliefs would issue in distinct perceptual practices whereas the differences between, say, High Church Anglican and Baptist beliefs will not do so. (For discussion of the related objection that if we attend to the mechanisms and institutional authorities involved in an effective system of overriders, we will see that the situation is much more fragmented than Alston acknowledges, see Terrence W. Tilley, "Religious Pluralism as a Problem for 'Practical' Religious Epistemology," *Religious Studies* 30 [1994]: 161–69.)

4. This is just a detail, but, contrary to what Alston suggests, a conformity between perceptual experiences of God and the tradition's expectations about what will be perceived seems to make room for some prediction and maybe even an element of control.

5. Many of the "fruits of the spirit" to which Alston alludes are not appropriate objects of CMP. Thus if I found myself to be more loving or caring or nonpossessive or serene, this is something that I would know by introspection, or by observing changes in my behavior via SP, or because of what others tell me about myself, or because of how others react to me, for example; I would not know these things by CMP. Alston's view, I think, is that there are other "fruits of the spirit," including some he mentions in this context, such as a sense that one is "living one's life in the presence of God," awareness of which is possible only through CMP. Still, there does seem to be a considerable amount of external support available here, so I do not see why the support provided in this way should be thought merely to strengthen the case for the *practical* rationality of continuing with one's practices. What exactly is the import of the support that is provided in this way for CMP is another matter: one obviously relevant consideration is that other MPs undoubtedly have their own spiritual fruits or corresponding beneficial effects for their adherents, as Alston notes at PG, 276 n. 20.

6. Incidentally, while it is true that in the car accident case "the competitors confront each other within the same doxastic practice," a particular witness who encounters a discrepancy between what she thought she observed and what others in the same situation claim to have observed is also relying on other doxastic practices, including the practice of relying on testimony—as Alston notes, in effect, at PG, 279.

7. As I see it, the issue that we should be discussing here is whether interpractice disagreement reduces the practical rationality of believing there to be justification. But I will follow Alston in posing the question as one concerning justification.

8. Alston recognizes that there are some such transpractice truths. For example, he says that "massive and persistent inconsistency between the outputs of two practices is a good reason for regarding at least one of them as unreliable" (PG, 171). I take him to understand this to be so whether or not those who follow either of the practices in question recognize, or would be willing to accept, that it is so. Another such truth about the operation of doxastic practices arises from my discussion in chapters 7 to 9. I have argued that privileged people should subject beliefs about which there is disagreement to examination, in the process subjecting their own beliefs and the competing beliefs to critical scrutiny. At the very least, a failure to engage in such a practice of examination when it is appropriate to do so diminishes the extent to which it is rational to believe the practice to be reliable. So we should think of the E-principle as also among the background truths that bear on all doxastic practices. If this is right, what it signifies is that there is a maneuver that is required in the case of CMP in virtue of the presence of disagreement between its outputs and the outputs of various other practices including various MPs, a maneuver that is unnecessary, say, in the case of SP. The T-principle is another such transpractice truth.

9. This is especially clear if significant self-support is apparent only to the insider. I have already suggested that Alston sells himself short in this regard and that the self-support in question should not be thought to be apparent only to the insider; but there remains the problem that significant self-support will be apparent in a number of traditions.

INDEX

Adams, Marilyn McCord, 73–76, 100–01, 260
    n.2, 263 n.3
Adams, Robert Merrihew, 77, 224, 261 n.7,
    263 n.1, 271 n.13
Allah, 124, 161, 162
Alston, William P., 11, 51, 66, 68, 182, 234–53,
    256 n.9, 259 n.7, 260 n. 20, 260 n.21,
    264 n.6, 271 n.10, 271 n.13, 272 n.1,
    272 n.3, 273 n.4, 273 n.5, 273 n.6,
    273 n.7, 273 n.8, 273 n.9
  on Christian Mystical Practice, 237–53
  on doxastic practices, 235–53
  on justification, 240–50
  on overriders, 236–39
  on reference, 238–39
  on religious diversity, 243–53
  on religious experience, 234–53
  on significant self-support, 240
  on third-person justification, 252–53
American Midwest, 179
attentiveness, 67
Audi, Robert, 170–77, 268 n.20, 268 n.21, 268
    n.23

Bahai, 179
Balentine, Samuel E., 255 n.4

Baptists, 238
Baptist beliefs, 272 n.3
Barbour, Ian, 145, 265 n. 15
Barnes, Philip, xi, 272 n.16
Barth, Karl, 144
Bayle, Pierre, 159, 267 n.8
Beardsworth, Timothy, 271 n.10
beatific vision, 97
belief
  autonomous, 54, 55
  basic, 139
  belief that vs. belief in, 58–60, 64,
      260 n.17
  examination of, 146–49
  exercising control over, 49–57, 60–65, 69,
      70, 266 n.17
  experientially supported, 225–29
  importance of, 137, 150, 197, 265 n.8
    cognitive, 137, 197
    interpersonal, 137, 197
    personal, 137, 197
  importance of theistic belief, 113–23
  management, 139
  said to be unimportant to some religious
      traditions, 132–33
  strong vs. weak, 101–02, 173–75

belief (*continued*)
  tentative belief, 141, 142, 154–59, 184, 185,
    187, 193, 201, 202
  tentative religious belief, 123, 124, 157–80,
    193–95, 198–99, 203, 205
Berger, Peter, 134, 142–45, 194, 196,
    265 n. 12, 265 n. 13, 265 n. 14
Berkeley, George, 17, 68, 256 n.13, 259 n.10
Berkovits, Eliezer, 26, 27, 29, 256 n.1
Berman, David, xi
Bernhardt, Laura, 191, 270 n.8
Bible, 139
Brahman, 23
Buddhism, 198
Buddhist claims, 134
Buddhist monks, 134
Buddhists, 129, 134, 151, 179, 204
Butler, Joseph, 18, 19, 39, 256 n.17,
    256 n.19, 258 n.17

California, 248
Callas, Maria, 121
Calvin, John, 255 n.2
Canadian Rockies, 247
Catholicism, 51, 229
Catholic beliefs, 226, 228
Catholic priests, 134
Catholic Sacraments, 189, 272 n.3
Catholics, 129, 157, 179, 238, 272 n.2
Chandler, Hugh, xi
Chisholm, Roderick, 268–69 n.1
Christensen, William, 168, 267 n.17, 267–
    68 n.18
Christianity, 51, 77, 312, 272 n.3
Christian beliefs, 124, 226, 226, 237,
    272 n.3
Christian Gnostics, 256
Christians, 129, 130, 134, 144, 150, 179, 191,
    217, 223, 228, 230, 239,
    267 n.13, 272 n.2
Chrysostom, St. John, 18
Church of Jesus Christ of Latter-Day Saints,
    195
Clark, Kelly James, 208–15, 256 n.6, 270 n. 2,
    270 n.5, 270 n.6
Clayton, Philip, xi
Code, Lorraine, 268–9 n.1
common origin argument, 227
competence, 136, 140
compromise, 187

conservatism, 186–87
Cowper, William, 269–70 n.7
credulity, principle of, 210–11
cryptovolitionalism, 50, 54, 56–72
  extended, 65–72, 110, 115
  revised, 58, 62, 63, 65, 260 n.14
  unrevised, 58

DAM principle, 250–52
Darwin, Charles, 233, 272 n.20
Davidson, Matt, xi
disagreement, 129–31, 133–36, 138, 140, 141,
    142, 154, 181–84, 195, 197–203
  deep, 133
  widespread, 133
discrediting mechanisms, 135–37, 140–41,
    152
dinosaurs, 63, 93
disaster avoidance principle, 116, 120, 123
Diversity Argument, 80–81, 110
divine transcendence theories, 17, 18, 109
Drabkin, Douglas, 257 n.6, 257 n.7, 261 n.6

Eastern Orthodox tradition, 272 n.2
Eliot, T. S., 128
enlightenment, 162
epistemic atheism, 92–97
E-principle, 138, 140, 141, 142, 146–53, 184,
    185, 188–90, 192, 197–204, 207,
    265 n.9
ethical egoism, 141
ethics of belief, 139
ethics of enquiry, 139
evil, problem of, 6, 73, 88, 90, 111, 117–18,
    262 n.23

facilitators 66–72
fallenness of human nature, 85, 86, 262 n.24
falsifiability, 168
faith, 73, 123, 124, 170–77
Ferreira, M. Jamie, 257 n.8
fideists, 202
fine-tuning of the universe, 100
Freud, Sigmund, 134
Freyfogle, Eric, xi

Gale, Richard, 264 n.3
Ganges, 162
Geertz, Clifford, 134
Gellner, Ernest, 160–61, 267 n.10

Gerrish, B. A., 86, 262 n.15, 262 n.17,
    262 n.18
Ghazzali, al-, 272 n.19
God, 3, 23
    goodness of, 73–74
    human ignorance of, 3
    as a person, 261 n.4
    personal relationship with, 97–98,
        100–103, 112–14
    worship-worthiness of, 82–84, 110, 118,
        122
    would act for a reason, 109
God's existence
    biblical perspective on, 7
    neither a proof nor a disproof, 21
    reason to believe in, 8, 152–53
God's hiddenness
    assumed in religious practices, 14
    basis of a case for atheism, 16, 92–104,
        111
    caused by wrong attitudes, 11, 65–72, 115
    cultural dimension, 11, 12, 17, 122
    disadvantages of, 12–14, 109–10
    explanations of, 11, 16–21, 108–15
    main source of nonbelief, 13
    problem for all forms of theism, 14
    two conflicting readings of, 9
    two dimensions, 5
    various construals, 6
Goldstick, Daniel, 269 n.3
goods
    balance of goods, 47, 112–17
    balance of goods assumption, 113, 116
    counterpart, 103–04
    of clarity, 14, 47, 104, 112–16, 262 n.23
    of mystery, 14, 18, 19, 20, 47, 104, 114–17,
        262 n.23
    unknown goods, 87–90, 104, 111, 114
    unknown goods of clarity, 89–90, 113
    unknown goods of mystery, 87–91, 103,
        104, 110, 114, 115, 116, 117,
        262 n.21
Gourley, Frank, xi
Graham, Billy, 134
Gutting, Gary, 155–57, 159, 161–65, 264 n.3,
    266 n.1, 267 n.6, 267 n.11, 267 n.12,
    267 n.13, 269 n.4

handguns, 200
Hanson-Scriven thesis, 92–97

Harman, Gilbert, 156–57, 266 n.2, 269 n.3,
    269 n.5
Hasidism, 28
heaven, 46, 113, 264 n.4
hell, 113
Heston, Charlton, 222
Hick, John, 21, 22, 38, 39–41, 50, 187, 239,
    256 n.20, 256 n.21, 258 n.15,
    258 n.2, 258 n.3, 258 n.20,
    260 n.16
    on choosing wrong actions, 37
    on cognitive freedom, 50
    on the value of being able to act im-
        morally, 40
High Church Anglicanism, 272 n.2,
    272 n.3
Hinduism, 132
Hindu beliefs, 226
Hindu priests, 134
Hindus, 129, 130, 179
hope, 170
Howard, Sir Michael, 267 n.16
Howard-Snyder, Daniel, 263 n.5
human defectiveness theories, 17, 18, 65, 70,
    109
human flourishing, 119–22
Hume, David, 194, 270 n.10
humility, 142–43, 146, 148

Illinois, 219, 232
importance of searching, 81, 110
inhibitors, 66–72
integrity, 129, 184
Ireland, 179
Irish nationalists, 200
Irish unionists, 200
Islam, 113, 132, 134, 163, 198

Jains, 179
James, William, 160, 163, 206, 229, 270 n.1,
    272 n.15, 272 n.18, 272 n.19
Jehovah's Witnesses, 198
Jesus, 23, 73, 124, 130, 157, 183, 191, 217,
    223, 226, 228, 230, 237
Jews, 129, 130, 179, 204
    ultra-Orthodox, 264 n.4
Jewish beliefs, 150
Job, 261 n.8
Jordan, Jeff, xi
Judaism, 113, 132

Kant, Immanuel, 19, 26, 29–34, 84–5, 257 n.4, 257 n.5, 257 n.6, 257 n.8, 257 n.9
   on knowledge of God's existence, 32
   on moral motivation, 33
   on postulating God, 33
   on the summum bonum, 32
Katz, Steven T., 230, 272 n.17
Karma, 22, 23, 157, 219
Keller, James A., 255 n.3, 261 n.6
Kierkegaard, Søren, 18, 104, 144, 256 n.18
King-Farlow, John, 168, 267 n.17, 267–68 n.18
Klein, Roberta Cutler, 268–69 n.1

Lahroodi, Reza, xi
Langerak, Ed, 268 n.24
Lewis, C. S., 151
Liston, Michael, xi
literary criticism, 200
Locke, John, 268–69 n.1
Long, Barry, xi
loss of responsibility problem, 27, 31, 45, 256–57 n.2, 257 n.3
Luther, Martin, 85–87, 262 n.16, 262 n.19, 262 n.20

MacIntyre, Alasdair, 50, 159, 165–66, 258 n.2, 267 n.7, 267 n.15
Mackie, J. L., 24
martyrs, 204
Marx, Karl, 134, 267 n.16
Marxism, 61, 150, 166–67
Mesle, C. Robert, 39–41, 63, 255 n.5, 258 n.18, 258 n.20, 260 n.18, 260 n.19
Methodism, 28
Methodist Hymn Book, 256 n.14
Methodist ministers, 134
Michaelis, Mark, xi
Mitchell, Basil, 266 n.18
moksha, 264 n.4
Mormonism, 198
Mormon elders, 134
Mormons, 195
Morris, Thomas V., 92–97, 255 n.3, 263 n.1
Moses, 183
Muhammad, 130, 134, 157, 161, 162, 223, 225, 226, 228

Muslim beliefs, 124, 134, 150, 151, 161, 162, 225, 226, 228, 272 n.3
Muslim imams, 134
Muslims, 129, 130, 134, 144, 151, 157, 161, 163, 179, 204, 225, 229, 239

natural selection, 157
natural theologians, 202
negative theology, 87
Nevins, Bryan, xi
Niebuhr, H. Richard, 257, n.2
Niebuhr, Reinhold, 142–43, 265 n. 10
Nietzsche, Friedrich, 144
Nirvana, 134, 264 n.4
Nisbet, Richard, 270 n.9
Northern Ireland, 201
Northern Irish Presbyterians, 129

O'Gorman, Paschal, xi
O'Sullivan, Sonia, 121
Otto, Rudolf, 18, 83, 256 n.16, 262 n.13

papacy, 157, 238
Pascal, Blaise, 17, 51, 52, 66, 93, 94, 151, 160, 256 n.6, 256 n.11, 261 n.6, 262 n.24
Penelhum, Terence, 55–58, 60, 159–60, 256 n.20, 259 n.9, 259 n.10, 267 n.9
perseverance, 170
Phillips, D. Z., 15, 256 n.12, 264 n.3
philosophy, 200, 201
Pinnock, Clark H., 10, 256 n.8
Plantinga, Alvin, 116, 146, 182, 255–56 n.6, 266 n.1, 266 n.16
Pojman, Louis, 258 n.1, 259 n.6, 267 n.12
Pope John Paul II, 134
Presbyterian beliefs, 165
privileged person, 149–50
Process Theology, 255 n.1
Protestant beliefs, 150
Protestants, 179, 272 n.2
Putnam, Hilary, 19, 84, 262 n.14

Qu'ran, 139, 157, 161, 162, 223, 225, 226

Radcliffe, Dana, 268 n.21, 268 n.22
reasonable belief and actual existents, 82
reformed epistemology, 139
Reid, Thomas, 235, 264 n.6

relativism, 183
relevant considerations, 21, 110, 262 n.21
religious ambiguity, 21–25, 50, 57, 63, 65, 70, 92, 111, 122, 123, 130, 142, 181–84, 197, 198, 223
religious commitment, 166–77
  cognitive, 167–68, 170
  practical, 167–69
religious experience, 206–53
  Alston on. *See* Alston, William P.
  and background beliefs, 209, 213–14
  conditions in which it occurs, 209, 213–14
  and disagreement about beliefs, 212–15
  diversity of, 215–16
  as evidence for beliefs, 208
  gap between experience and doctrine, 225–29
  indubitable, 221–25
  and justification of religious beliefs, 208–16
  mystical, 219
  numinous, 219
  perceptual, 208
  two sources of, 229–31
  varieties of, 216–20
religious traditions
  adapted to the culture 22
  mesh with experiences, 22
  naturalistic interpretations of, 22
respect for others, 184–85
responsibility for others, 40
Ricoeur, Paul, 83, 262 n.13
Roman Catholicism. *See* Catholicism
Ross, Lee, 270 n.9
Rowe, William, 88, 262 n.22
Runzo, Joseph, 269 n.2
Russell, Bertrand, 134, 151

Saka, Paul, xi
salvation, 264 n.4
Saudi Arabia, 248
Schellenberg, J. L., 41–45, 80–82, 88–89, 92, 97–104, 256 n.10, 257 n.12, 257 n.13, 258 n.19, 258 n.22, 258–59 n.3, 261 n.6, 261 n.9, 261 n.10, 262 n.12, 262 n.22, 262 n.24, 263 n.2, 263 n.3, 263 n.4
  on the desire to be well thought of by God, 44
  on the effects of fear of punishment, 42
  on how a loving God would act, 43, 97–99
  on inscrutable goods, 88
  on personal relationship with God, 97–98
Schoedel, Bill, xi
Schroeder, Bill, xi
Shiism, 28
Sikhs, 179
Sklar, Lawrence, 269 n.3
Soroush, Abdolkarim, 265 n.11
Swinburne, Richard, 24, 26, 29, 34–48, 210–11, 257 n.10, 257 n.11, 258 n.14, 258 n.16, 258 n.23, 260 n.1, 261 n.3, 266 n.19, 268–69 n.1, 270 n.3
  on consequences of intimacy with God, 36
  on limited depravity, 258 n.14, 258 n.16
  on making a genuine choice of destiny, 35
  on situations of temptation, 35
  on the value of being able to act immorally, 40

Teresa of Avila, St., 218–19, 223–24, 271 n.9, 271 n.11
theism, 33
  full, 58–62
  generic, 5
  minimal, 58–62
theology, 200
Tilley, Terrence, 272 n.3
tolerance, 177–80
T-principle, 138, 141, 142, 149, 154, 184, 188, 192, 195, 197–204, 207, 265 n.9, 273 n.8
transubstantiation, 238
Trevor, J., 272 n.18
Trinity, the, 228
Troeltsch, Ernst, 145
trust, 59, 64, 75–80, 261 n.3, 261 n.5
  complete, 75–80
  global, 74, 76, 78
  incomplete, 76–80

United States, 179, 200

Vakili, Valla, 265 n.11
Van Laar, Tim, xi
varieties objection, 60–62
Virgin Mary, 221, 224, 226, 229
Vogel, Jonathan, 269 n.3

volitionalism, 49–55
   direct, 51, 55
   indirect, 51, 53, 55
   strong, 53, 54
   weak, 53, 54

Wainwright, William, 256 n.20
Weir, Alan, 270 n.11
Wesley, John, 81

Winch, Peter, 264 n.3
Wittgenstein, Ludwig, 235
Wittgensteinian fideism, 15
Wolterstorff, Nicholas, 255 n.2, 256 n.8,
   264 n.6, 268–69 n.1
Wykstra, Stephen, 88, 262 n.22

Yeats, W. B., 128
Young, Francis M., 256 n.15